THE PHILOSOPHY OF *THE X-FILES*

The Philosophy of Popular Culture

The books published in the Philosophy of Popular Culture series will illuminate and explore philosophical themes and ideas that occur in popular culture. The goal of this series is to demonstrate how philosophical inquiry has been reinvigorated by increased scholarly interest in the intersection of popular culture and philosophy, as well as to explore through philosophical analysis beloved modes of entertainment, such as movies, TV shows, and music. Philosophical concepts will be made accessible to the general reader through examples in popular culture. This series seeks to publish both established and emerging scholars who will engage a major area of popular culture for philosophical interpretation and examine the philosophical underpinnings of its themes. Eschewing ephemeral trends of philosophical and cultural theory, authors will establish and elaborate on connections between traditional philosophical ideas from important thinkers and the ever-expanding world of popular culture.

SERIES EDITOR

Mark T. Conard, Marymount Manhattan College, NY

BOOKS IN THE SERIES

The Philosophy of Stanley Kubrick, edited by Jerold J. Abrams
Football and Philosophy, edited by Michael W. Austin
The Philosophy of Film Noir, edited by Mark T. Conard
The Philosophy of Martin Scorsese, updated edition, edited by Mark T. Conard
The Philosophy of Neo-Noir, edited by Mark T. Conard
The Philosophy of the Coen Brothers, edited by Mark T. Conard
Steven Spielberg and Philosophy, edited by Dean A. Kowalski
The Philosophy of Science Fiction Film, edited by Steven M. Sanders
The Philosophy of TV Noir, edited by Stephen M. Sanders and Aeon J. Skoble
Basketball and Philosophy, edited by Jerry L. Walls and Gregory Bassham

THE PHILOSOPHY OF
THE X-FILES

UPDATED EDITION

Edited by Dean A. Kowalski

Foreword by William B. Davis

THE UNIVERSITY PRESS OF KENTUCKY

Scholarly publisher for the Commonwealth,
serving Bellarmine University, Berea College, Centre
College of Kentucky, Eastern Kentucky University,
The Filson Historical Society, Georgetown College,
Kentucky Historical Society, Kentucky State University,
Morehead State University, Murray State University,
Northern Kentucky University, Transylvania University,
University of Kentucky, University of Louisville,
and Western Kentucky University.
All rights reserved.

Editorial and Sales Offices: The University Press of Kentucky
663 South Limestone Street, Lexington, Kentucky 40508-4008
www.kentuckypress.com

    13 12 11 10 09   5 4 3 2 1

Library of Congress Cataloging-in-Publication Data

The philosophy of the X-files / edited by Dean A. Kowalski ;
foreword by William B. Davis. — Updated ed.
    p.   cm. — (Philosophy of popular culture)
  Includes bibliographical references and index.
  ISBN 978-0-8131-9227-7 (pbk. : alk. paper)
  1. X-files (Television program) — Miscellanea.   I. Kowalski,
Dean A. II. Davis, William B.
  PN1992.77.X22P45   2009
  791.45'72 — dc22   2008051566

This book is printed on acid-free recycled paper meeting
the requirements of the American National Standard
for Permanence in Paper for Printed Library Materials.

Manufactured in the United States of America.

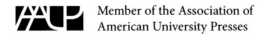

Member of the Association of
American University Presses

Contents

Foreword   vii

Preface   xiii

Acknowledgments   xix

Introduction: Mulder, Scully, Plato, Aristotle, and Dawkins   1
  Dean A. Kowalski

Part I: The Credos

The Truth Is Out There: Abduction, Aliens, and Alienation   17
  Mark C. E. Peterson

Freedom and Worldviews in *The X-Files*   37
  V. Alan White

Postdemocratic Society and the Truth Out There   55
  Richard Flannery and David Louzecky

Some Philosophical Reflections on "Trust No One"   77
  Richard M. Edwards and Dean A. Kowalski

"I Want to Believe": William James and *The X-Files*   93
  Keith Dromm

Part II: The Characters

Ancient X-Files: Mulder and Plato's Sokratic Dialogues   111
  William M. Schneider

Scully as Pragmatist Feminist: "truths" Are Out There   126
  Erin McKenna

Moral Musings on a Cigarette Smoking Man   142
  Timothy Dunn and Joseph J. Foy

Walter Skinner: *The X-Files'* Unsung Hero   159
  S. Evan Kreider

Science and the Mystery of Consciousness:
  A Dialogue between Mulder and Scully   174
  Gordon Barnes

Part III: The Episodes

"Clyde Bruckman's Final Repose" Reprised 2009   189
  Dean A. Kowalski

The Many Tales of "Jose Chung"   209
  Dean A. Kowalski and S. Evan Kreider

Feelings and Fictions: Exploring Emotion and Belief in
  Fight the Future   230
  Christopher R. Trogan

I Want to Believe . . . But Now What?   241
  Dean A. Kowalski and S. Evan Kreider

Appendix A: *The X-Files* Mythology   262

Appendix B: *The X-Files* Debriefed   265

Contributors   283

Index   287

Foreword

This book by its nature raises many questions, not least of which is why an actor would be asked to write the foreword to a book of philosophy. An even better question is, Why would an actor jump at the chance?

Well, this actor, while playing the Cigarette Smoking Man ("CSM" to many) on *The X-Files,* puzzled over many questions raised by the show, such as conspiracy theory, skepticism and credulity, aliens and the paranormal, and the nature of evil itself. And this actor may be unique, given his degree in philosophy and his reading of evolutionary biology and skeptical literature. This actor is also not in the least intimidated by celebrities in his own field but rather stands in awe of the giants of science and philosophy, Richard Dawkins and Daniel Dennett in particular. How embarrassing, then, that this actor starred in a series relentlessly attacked by Dawkins himself.

I was always startled by the assumption of *X-Files* fans that since I was acting in the series, I was obviously not only interested in the subject matter but also a believer in aliens, conspiracies, and the paranormal. I guess viewers understand the life of an actor through interviews with A-list celebrities. Those of us who work in the trenches take on acting roles because we get them. The idea that we sit back and choose from a range of offers is delightful to contemplate, but the reality is that we do the work we get. Trust me, it was a sheer accident that I ended up doing this series for many years. But once in the role, I had to deal with a range of fascinating issues that included explaining to the shocked fan that, no, I don't believe there are aliens among us; I don't believe in high-level government conspiracy; and I certainly don't believe in astrology, past lives, or telepathy.

Probably the most pervasive question I faced was, Why is the series so popular? We were all asked this question, and we all had different answers depending on our angle of view. My response might have been the least expected since I began with a related question: Why was Shakespeare so popular? As a teacher of acting I had often lectured on Shakespeare. I have argued that Shakespeare and his writings were unique because his genius sat on the cusp of two worldviews and he drew inspiration from both. Marshall McLuhan was another early intellectual hero of mine; I was profoundly influenced by his argument that the printing press changed how we see the world, not because of the content of printed works, but because of exposure to the medium itself. In the decades following the invention of the printing press in the late fifteenth century, there were dramatic changes in Western humans' worldview. The medieval world included religiosity, connectedness to the environment, lack of interest in self-identification, anonymous presentation of artistic works, and lack of interest in visual perspective. The beginning of the modern world saw the decline of feudalism, the separation of the individual, the beginnings of modern science and the scientific method, and, soon, the stirrings of the Enlightenment. Shakespeare's brilliance stemmed, in part, from his intimate connection to both worldviews.

What has this to do with *The X-Files*? Is it possible that the show straddled a similar transition of worldview? The 1990s saw the full emergence of computer use and the Internet, following an era of extensive television viewing, and a corresponding decline in use of printed media. If McLuhan's thesis has validity, viewing media in pixels instead of print should have an effect on the perspective and worldview of the user. To this observer at least, it appeared that a major lack of trust in formerly respected authority developed. Books were either not read or, if they were, not trusted. At the same time, there was an explosion of information in the ethereal cyberworld. People no longer knew what or whom to believe. So a television series dealing with those very issues of belief and authority struck a responsive chord.

What do we see moving forward into the twenty-first century? Instead of the rigorous application of science and reason to cope with this world of uncertainty, we see a huge increase in superstition in general and religion in particular, in North America at least. We see a major decline in human rights and a reduction of complex problems to simple—unsuccessful—solutions. In short, we see the end of the Enlightenment. Was *The X-Files* a symptom and a harbinger of a world dangerously veering toward superstition and religion and away from reason and science?

What is the role of narrative in shaping our view of the world? To put an evolutionary spin on the question, Who benefits from narrative and what kind of narrative? Unique in important ways, *The X-Files* is nonetheless typical of popular narrative in our culture because it represents a battle between Good and Evil — the latter being me, in case you were wondering. Why is this the overwhelming narrative in popular culture, and what effect does this narrative have?

Let's imagine two different storytellers in two different hunter-gatherer caves on opposite sides of a valley. One tells the story of the evil tribe on the other side of the valley, of how we must work together to overcome our adversaries and be willing to fight to the death to protect our people. The other tells a story of human complexity, of how some humans are dangerous but most are not, of how we should befriend strangers and open our world to a range of possibilities. The next day the two tribes meet unexpectedly in the valley as they each expand their hunting territory. Guess what? The first tribe wipes out the second while the second is still wondering if the first tribe is friendly or not.

So who benefits? Certainly not the genes of the teller of complex stories and his listeners. Those genes are gone. No, the genes that survive and go on to replicate belong to the storytellers of the conflict of good and evil. In the environment in which humans evolved it may be that narrative in general and this type of narrative in particular had real survival value.

Since we are still essentially the same species that we were as hunter-gatherers, perhaps it is to be expected that we love these stories of good and evil. We were *selected* to love them. But is this a good thing? In our modern environment, does a reduction to good and evil help us? Or does it give us Al-Qaeda and George Bush?

Whether there is really such a thing as Evil is beyond the scope of this foreword. But an actor who tries to portray evil is in serious trouble. What do you do? Grow a long moustache and twirl it a lot? As viewers and fans of the show know, I took a different tack when assigned the role of the antagonist who was referred to by Chris Carter himself as "the Devil." I decided I was the hero and Mulder was the bad guy. Of course as the CSM I was ruthless and unfeeling, but to do what I believed had to be done, how else could I be? Do the so-called evil men of history believe they are the demons others make them out to be? Or are they often doing what they think is right, however horrific that may seem to the rest of us? Put another way, perhaps life is more complicated than a simple division of good and evil.

But what of the other major aspect of the series, its emphasis on the paranormal? What is an actor with a degree in philosophy to make of that? The simple reply to the astonished fan when I confessed my nonbelief in, say, aliens was that the burden of proof was on them, the believers, not on me, the skeptic. Since, naturally, the believers were never satisfied with this reply, I determined to investigate further. Eventually I stumbled on CSICOP—the Committee for the Scientific Investigation of Claims of the Paranormal—and discovered that most paranormal claims had been subjected to rigorous research—and found wanting.

Among the many prominent scientists on the masthead of CSICOP was Richard Dawkins, who had transformed my intellectual life years earlier when I read *The Selfish Gene*. He was also an outspoken critic of *The X-Files*, claiming that it undermined rational thought and promoted pseudoscience. How could I continue to work on a show that so apparently betrayed my own beliefs? Was it enough for me to say, "Well, it's just fiction after all"?

Here is what Dawkins said in the 1996 Dimbleby Lecture:

> A fair defence, you might think. But soap operas, cop series and the like are justly criticised if, week after week, they ram home the same prejudice or bias. Each week *The X-Files* poses a mystery and offers two rival kinds of explanation, the rational theory and the paranormal theory. And, week after week, the rational explanation loses. But it is only fiction, a bit of fun, why get so hot under the collar?
>
> Imagine a crime series in which, every week, there is a white suspect and a black suspect. And every week, lo and behold, the black one turns out to have done it. Unpardonable, of course. And my point is that you could not defend it by saying: "But it's only fiction, only entertainment."

As I have said, I am a great admirer of Dawkins, but is it possible his response to our show has been rather quick and glib? Proponent of science that he is, he has offered no *scientific* evidence that the show actually influences the way people think about the paranormal. Two kinds of studies spring readily to mind. One could survey *X-Files* viewers and a control group to see if paranormal belief is more common among *X-Files* viewers. Or one could do laboratory studies, showing one group episodes of *X-Files* and another group *Animal Planet* and studying the comparative effects on paranormal belief. My own straw polls of college groups when I used to lecture at American universities suggested a level of paranormal belief among fans similar to that in the general population. Not very scientific, I admit, but more than Dawkins has offered.

Furthermore, Dawkins's analogy of the black and white criminals may not hold up under closer scrutiny. After all, for each week's mystery, a solution was proposed by a woman and another by a man. And, "lo and behold," each week the man's solution triumphed. If the show is insidiously presenting a bias under the guise of fiction, why were the feminists not up in arms?

Is my challenge to Dawkins valid? Or, like the Cigarette Smoking Man himself, am I manipulating reason to justify my own actions, in this case, continuing to perform in such a successful series?

Being involved in *The X-Files* was a wild and wonderful journey. To be involved in the publication of this book was yet another unexpected pleasure. The questions raised by the phenomenon of *The X-Files* continue to reverberate.

William B. Davis
Vancouver, Canada

Preface

This volume explores philosophically significant connections to *The X-Files* around three rallying points. Each point is given its own section. The first section is "The Credos." It explores the philosophical significance of the show's three primary slogans: "The truth is out there," "Trust no one," and "I want to believe." The second section is "The Characters." It provides philosophically interesting character studies of Fox Mulder (David Duchovny), Dana Scully (Gillian Anderson), the Cigarette Smoking Man (CSM, played by none other than William B. Davis), and Assistant Director Walter Skinner (Mitch Pileggi). The third section is "The Episodes." In this section, which benefited the most from the new edition, you will find discussions of philosophical issues raised by "Clyde Bruckman's Final Repose," "Jose Chung's *From Outer Space*," *Fight the Future,* and the 2008 motion picture *I Want to Believe,* respectively.

Each section contains chapters written by scholar-teachers who appreciate *The X-Files* almost as much as you do (and, in Professor Foy's case, perhaps more). Within each chapter, you'll find the contributing authors discussing philosophical issues in metaphysics (the study of ultimate reality), epistemology (the study of knowledge), ethics (the study of right living) and axiology (the study of value, of which ethics is one facet), aesthetics (the study of art and beauty), political philosophy, feminism, and existentialism, among others. Because we are teachers as well as scholars, each chapter is written for those new to philosophy; thus, the discussions presuppose very little prior background in philosophy.

The first section contains five chapters. Mark Peterson begins the volume with "The Truth Is Out There: Abduction, Aliens, and Alienation," in which he distinguishes three kinds of inferences: deductive, inductive, and abductive. With the help of Charles Sanders Peirce, Peterson argues that

Mulder's talent for solving "unexplained phenomena" is grounded in his proficiencies in abduction. Scully, an able investigator in her own right, regularly relies on induction. Peterson further argues that Mulder's approach can be beneficial to fledgling and professional philosophers alike. In "Freedom and Worldviews in *The X-Files*," Alan White explores the issue of freedom and determinism. After providing the reader important background on this classic debate, he sets his sights on how Mulder's and Scully's views of things started to merge as the series progressed. There is an important link to the first chapter in this regard: Peterson argued that we should become more like Mulder. As we saw with Scully, this takes some effort. However, White is skeptical of the claim that there is any significant sense in which we are free to change worldviews on the basis of discovered truth, despite what Peterson and *The X-Files* itself seemingly imply. In "Postdemocratic Society and the Truth Out There," Professors Louzecky and Flannery strive to show the contemporary political relevance of *The X-Files*. They begin by articulating the necessary conditions for sound democratic government and argue that the kind of secretive political tactics employed by the Syndicate are necessarily inconsistent with democracy exactly because they undermine publicity and informed decision making. They then go on to use Mulder and Scully as models for how governmental agencies like the Syndicate—be they fictional or real—can be marginalized. "Some Philosophical Reflections on 'Trust No One'" begins exploring the "Trust no one" credo by reminding the reader of the episode that launched it: "The Erlenmeyer Flask." Richard Edwards and I discuss two different philosophical theories that support Deep Throat's charge, albeit in two very different ways. First, if Thomas Kuhn's "paradigm view" of science is correct, then it seems that the scientific community plays a surprisingly large role in shaping which data are accepted and which are rejected. This poses problems for Scully's strict reliance on scientific inquiry to debunk or uphold the veracity of Mulder's work. Can Scully trust herself as a scientist? Second, if psychological egoism is true, then all human persons are naturally selfish; if so, then we cannot trust others to ever act on our behalf (except, perhaps, when our interests coincide). In the final chapter in this section, "'I Want to Believe': William James and *The X-Files*," Keith Dromm uses *The X-Files* to compare and contrast the ideas of William James and W. K. Clifford. Dromm argues that Mulder's approach to belief has much in common with the ideas expressed by William James in his essay "The Will to Believe," while Scully has affinities with the thought of W. K. Clifford as expressed in "The Ethics of Belief." However, Dromm continues,

Walter Skinner more nearly personifies the views in James's later work *Pragmatism*. Dromm then concludes by arguing that, of the three models of belief acquisition, the Skinner model is preferable.

The second section also contains five chapters. William Schneider's chapter, "Ancient X-Files: Mulder and Plato's Sokratic Dialogues," is an innovative attempt at drawing parallels between Mulder and Socrates regarding the latter's charge to "know thyself." In a literary fashion similar to Descartes' *Meditations*, Schneider leads the reader into an introspective soliloquy on Mulder's motivations and convictions regarding his search for the truth. In "Scully as Pragmatic Feminist: 'truths' Are Out There," Erin McKenna focuses on the well-known intellectual shift in the Dana Scully character. At first, Scully is the hardheaded scientist. However, McKenna argues that the season 7 episode "all things" solidifies crucial changes in how Scully sees herself and understands the world around her. This, in turn, facilitates a discussion of contemporary philosophical ideas associated with feminism and pragmatism. Professors Joseph Foy and Timothy Dunn delve deep into the Cigarette Smoking Man character in "Moral Musings on a Cigarette Smoking Man." They utilize core principles and theories of moral philosophy to explore and assess two common interpretations of the one who must "take the elevator up to work" (as Skinner would say). By drawing on many examples from the series, they conclude that both interpretations are inadequate. Undaunted, they boldly argue that the CSM is no ordinary villain but represents a particularly perverse inversion of the moral order and as such fundamentally challenges traditional morality. In this way, through his "transvaluation of power," the CSM character teaches us a deeper lesson about classical images and understandings of evil. "Walter Skinner: *The X-Files'* Unsung Hero" has Evan Kreider present Assistant Director Skinner as a paradigm for understanding Aristotelian and Platonic interpretations of virtue and, in this way, redemonstrates the relevance of ancient Greek virtue ethics for contemporary society. Interestingly, Kreider does not argue that Skinner is the epitome of a virtuous person, due to a recurring character flaw; however, that flaw makes him very human, which might explain why so many can identify with his character. The last chapter of this section is also something of a throwback to ancient Greek philosophy, at least in terms of its presentation. Plato's dialogues are renowned, but very few contemporary philosophers choose to present their material in this form. For our benefit, Gordon Barnes has crafted in "Science and the Mystery of Consciousness" a lively dialogue between Mulder and Scully taking place near the end of season 1, mere hours before the events in "The Erlenmeyer Flask." Our heroes debate the classic philosophical question of whether human persons are nothing over and above their physical bodies. As you might expect, Mulder attempts to argue that, given undeniable facets of human consciousness, persons are not merely the sum total of their physical parts, but Scully is resistant to this idea.

The third and last section contains four chapters. The first two are revised versions of chapters that appeared in the 2007 edition. Each of these highlights Darin Morgan's important role in the evolution of the series. "'Clyde Bruckman's Final Repose' Reprised 2009" provides an analysis of the character played admirably by Peter Boyle. Bruckman possesses the ability to divine the future, raising the classic triad of issues about freedom, fate, and foreknowledge. I argue that philosophical concerns associated with these three issues can be abated so long as we remember that our choices explain what is antecedently true and known about us and not vice versa. I further argue that Darin Morgan's tendency to interpret the Fox Mulder character as dangerously obsessive can be traced back to the Bruckman episode; ironically, it is Morgan who appears prophetic when we see Mulder languishing thirteen years later in the opening scene of *I Want to Believe.* In "The Many Tales of 'Jose Chung,'" Evan Kreider and I team up to bravely offer an interpretation of the wild and wildly popular episode "Jose Chung's *From Outer Space.*" (You know, the one with Alex Trebek.) We argue that Morgan raises classic philosophical concerns about truth and knowledge that ultimately calls into question the idea "the truth" is objectively "out there." This leads us to interpret him as implicitly affirming existentialism. We subsequently enlist the aide of Jean-Paul Sartre to explore the extent to which Mulder and Scully have led existentially authentic lives, especially given who they have become in *I Want to Believe.* This chapter concludes by making it clear exactly why Darin Morgan's episodes were so instrumental in the development of the series. The third chapter of this section is Chris Trogan's "Feelings and Fictions: Emotion and Belief in *Fight the Future.*" Trogan explores the aesthetic content and value of *Fight the Future.* His primary goal is to articulate and assess the paradoxical set of beliefs that it is reasonable to identify and empathize with fictional characters like Mulder and Scully but unreasonable to identify and empathize with your friend's story that his mother recently died when you discover that she is very much alive. Trogan also argues that his preferred resolution to this issue has beneficial ramifications for imaginative moral reasoning and character development. This section concludes with a new chapter written especially for this volume, "*I Want to Believe* . . . But Now What?" Evan Kreider and I again join forces to offer an interpretation of the 2008 motion picture *I Want to Believe*. On one level, the film conveys Mulder and Scully as experiencing what Aristotle calls the highest form of friendship—a genuinely reciprocal relationship, this one fifteen years in the making. On a deeper level, the film serves as a microcosm of the core ideas that drove the series for nine years. This insight leads us to hazard an articulation of what the philosophy of *The X-Files* consists of, which seems like a fitting way to conclude the book.

The book also contains two appendixes. The first, written by Joseph Foy, is a synopsis of the main storyline mythology running through *The X-Files*. Professor Foy reminds us of the intricacies of the Syndicate, the black oil, and pending alien colonization. The second is an episode-by-episode synopsis through *Fight the Future*. (Because of this, only post-season 5 episodes that are directly referred to in the text are listed by season.) In addition to listing story code, episode author and director, and a brief plot summary, I alert the reader to relevant philosophical issues the episode conveys. I also direct the reader to chapters that heavily rely on ideas or plot devices from the episode in question.

The updated edition does a better job of including material from seasons 6 through 9; however, it remains fair to say that seasons 1 through 5 receive more attention. Do not interpret this fact as evidence that I believe the later seasons were somehow deficient (even though I am admittedly a bit partial to the episodes in seasons 3 and 4). Rather, this choice was forced upon me by time and book-length constraints, and the updated edition pushed both limits. There is simply too much quality philosophical content in *The X-Files* to fit into one book. I therefore decided to focus now on seasons 1 through 5 and pray (perhaps with the help of Albert Hosteen [Floyd "Red Crow" Westerman] and the Navajo "holy people") that I'll have a chance in the future to put together a book the emphasizes seasons 6 through 9.

Acknowledgments

I must begin by thanking William B. Davis for kindly agreeing to write the foreword. By the time I gathered enough courage to contact him, it was well into the project, not leaving him a great deal of time to share his perceptive insights and erudition with you. Henceforth, when my students ask me what they can do with a philosophy major, I will tell them that they can become a world-class actor and champion water-skier and make their philosophy professors proud by one day leading the examined life.

I am, of course, indebted to Mark Conard, Steve Wrinn, and (especially) Anne Dean Watkins at the University Press of Kentucky. The latter, along with members of her staff, worked very hard to make the updated edition a reality. Cheryl Hoffman, with her subtle but skilled editorial hand, made the 2007 edition immeasurably more readable. The updated edition likewise benefited from the editorial talents of Erin Holman. I am grateful to the many self-proclaimed X-Philes who offered comments on the hardback edition (especially "WhoToTrust?" and Natalie Floeh), and for those who tirelessly have kept their Web sites active and up to date, but three sites deserve particular mention. First, you can find the script of each episode of *The X-Files* on Clive Banks's site, http://clivebanks.co.uk; this was a proverbial godsend for quoting dialogue. Second, you can find voluminous *X-Files* episode reviews on Sarah Stegall's site, http://www .munchkyn.com; I found her ideas stimulating, especially on "Clyde Bruckman's Final Repose" and "Jose Chung's *From Outer Space*." Finally, you can find summaries of each episode of *The X-Files* at http://xfiles. wearehere.net/xfiles.htm; these were an invaluable resource to me in crafting my own episode summaries. Without their knowing it, their work made my job of editing the book much easier. While I am grateful for the efforts of all my colleagues and contributing authors, I owe tremendous debts of thanks to Professors Evan Kreider and Joe Foy. The former helped me, literally at the last minute, to craft and recraft quality essays for both editions. The latter was a constant source of enthusiastic support; without his efforts (not the least of which was his boyish, ear-to-ear grin, which would come over his face every time we discussed the project), this book might not have made it to print. Finally, I am also very appreciative of my University of Wisconsin–Waukesha students—the "phledgling philosophers"—during the fall semester of 2006. They were incredibly patient and supportive as I finished the manuscript for the hardcover edition.

But each and every good thing that I have achieved in the last ten years I owe to my wife. Despite myself, she remains steadfast, reminding me of what is truly important. In fact, the only actual unexplained phenomenon is why she chose me in the first place. But perhaps it is as "Humbug's" Dr. Blockhead believes: some mysteries are not meant to be explained, merely marveled at and appreciated for what they are. In a very clumsy attempt to show my loving appreciation—and because I don't own a rowboat—I dedicate this book to her:

For Patricia—
"Then We Believe the Same Thing"

Introduction

Mulder, Scully, Plato, Aristotle, and Dawkins

Dean A. Kowalski

That *The X-Files* is such a natural choice for a book like this is not for the reason you might initially think. It's not that it was "metaphysical" in the sense that it was about extraterrestrials and various otherworldly topics that no one could ever really prove true or false. This reminds me of all the times I would find a new bookstore, eagerly throw the doors open, and march straight back to its Metaphysics section, merely to be disappointed — again — at finding only volumes on the healing power of white crystals and how-to books about tarot card reading (once, I swear, with the faces of Stu Charno and Alex Diakun on the cover).

Rather, the very premise of the show incessantly reminded you (and once in Navajo) that "the truth was out there," and then every week beguiled you to find it. Yes, sometimes the truth pursued was about conscious black oil and shape-shifting aliens. But the deeper point remains: we were to search for the truth and were determined to find it, even though we didn't have all the information or all the tools to unearth it that we'd like. This is exactly the mind-set of the philosopher.

Furthermore, the show's two heroes represent two fundamental but disparate search methods. Special Agent Dana Scully (Gillian Anderson), a trained medical doctor who also studied physics in college, is the consummate scientist. The default starting position for her search is to set a naturalistic and empirical course. Her partner, Special Agent Fox Mulder (David Duchovny), also possesses an impressive educational pedigree. He is an Oxford-educated psychologist and an intuitively gifted FBI profiler. In fact, he is considered one of the best analysts ever assigned to the Violent Crimes Division. However, his methods are anything but conventional. Because his interests invariably involve "unexplained phenomena," he often sets methodological courses for "extreme possibilities" that transcend conventional scientific wisdom. Yet, Mulder and Scully invariably engage in respectful, honest dialogue. They regularly insist on substantiating their approaches and hypotheses with evidence (broadly conceived) and logical rigor, all in hopes of locating the truth "out there" that continually eludes them. This, again, is a staple of quality philosophical inquiry.

The School of Athens Analogy

I would like to say—and, dare I say, want to believe—that the divergent approaches embodied in the characters of Dana Scully and Fox Mulder are a bit analogous to those of two giants from the history of philosophy: Plato and Aristotle. I suspect that many of my professionally trained colleagues will scoff at this purported analogy and accuse me of speaking tongue in cheek. But allow me to explain.

There is a famous painting by Raphael called *The School of Athens*. The two focal points are Plato and his star pupil, Aristotle. Curiously, the two philosophers are looking at each other, with Plato pointing to the sky and Aristotle with his arm stretched out horizontally, palm facing down in a cautionary manner. It is widely believed that Raphael was attempting to capture the basic philosophical difference between the two greats: Plato believed that one must reach a nonearthly plane in order to unlock the deepest secrets of truth and knowledge—his "realm of the forms"—but Aristotle believed that truth and knowledge can be obtained through carefully constructed hypotheses grounded in astute observations of our earthly surroundings. Aristotle, then, is cautioning his teacher not to (literally) overlook or underappreciate that which is directly in front of him.

Mulder and Scully are just a bit like that. Mulder is insistent that a complete explanation for what he often experiences must include an unearthly source. If we stay at the conventional level of straightforward empiricism, our account of things will forever remain incomplete. Is Mulder too quick in searching the heavens? Is he irrational in doing so? Perhaps Mulder's methodology has been shaped by nonrational elements; it seems conceivable that his witnessing his sister's alleged alien abduction and his father's involvement in some of the early X-Files somehow help to explain Mulder's psychological penchant for looking skyward. But this doesn't necessarily mean that Mulder is irrational. After all, similar nonrational explanations have also been offered for Plato's proclivities to look toward an unearthly realm, specifically his early involvement with Pythagorean mathematics and the psychological effects of witnessing his teacher's "abduction" by the

Athenian court. These facts might drive Plato to believe that "the truth is out there"; in this way it is beyond the seditious grip of the Sophists, or the untrained Athenian assembly. Scully embodies Aristotle's warning about keeping oneself grounded. Both see the value of empirical study and rigorous scientific testing. The sort of ideal explanations that Plato and Mulder seek are, at best, unwarranted or simply cannot be had, and, at worst, they are merely whims of fancy.

Contemporary philosopher Norman Melchert seems to confirm the developing analogy in this way: "Two quite different intellectual styles are exemplified by Plato and Aristotle. Plato is a man with one big problem, one passion, one concern; everything he touches is transformed by that concern. Aristotle has many smaller problems. These are not unrelated to each other, and there is a pattern in his treatment of them all."[1] I don't know whether series creator Chris Carter had Plato and Aristotle in mind when originally crafting his protagonists — I doubt it — but Melchert seems to be equally describing Mulder and Scully. Melchert continues, "One feels in Plato a profound dissatisfaction with the familiar world of sense . . . Plato is a combination of rationalist and mystic." For Aristotle, however, "truth concerns the sensible world, and our knowledge of it begins with actually seeing, touching, and hearing the things of the world. The senses, although not sufficient in themselves to lead us to knowledge, are the only reasonable avenues along which to pursue knowledge."[2] Everyone is clear that Scully, especially early in the series, is true to Melchert's description of Aristotle; however, some often overlook the fact that Mulder can be understood as a combination of rationalist and mystic.[3] (More on this later.)

Just as there are disagreements in the ivory tower of academia about whether Plato's approach to finding the truth is more effective than Aristotle's, we in the "marketplace" of popular culture can ask the same question about Mulder's and Scully's. Moreover, just as few philosophers anymore are strictly Platonists or strictly Aristotelians, we can also ask how the methods of Mulder and Scully might be beneficially combined. Might doing so give us a better picture of how the world "out there" really is? With a hybrid approach might we be able to answer some questions that we couldn't answer otherwise? If so, which? If not, why not? Questions like these, it seems to me, begin to capture the inherent philosophical significance of *The X-Files* at the most foundational level. And such questions are not idle. Some philosophers believe that, even with all the scientific data we have amassed about human beings, an adequate account of what persons are as conscious beings must go beyond the physical facts about us. Other philosophers reason that if we are free and responsible for our choices and actions, as our experiences seem to indicate, then it cannot be that we are merely the sum total of our physical parts. Therefore, without disparaging or discounting the importance of Scully's trust in quality scientific research, it seems that we might do well to follow Mulder's lead (or something like it) in articulating a complete account of how things are.

Nevertheless, the *School of Athens* analogy cannot be pushed too far. It begins to break down as soon as we remember that Mulder and Scully are television characters and not philosophers. Moreover, Plato offered astute philosophical arguments why his realm of the forms must exist; he was not merely driven by nonrational, psychological factors in seeking the unearthly explanation, as, arguably, Mulder initially was. So, why press the analogy at all? Paradoxically, it's useful because it fails in other, more instructive, ways. When Raphael depicts Plato pointing to the sky, Plato is not literally pointing up to some extraterrestrial plane, even if Mulder might be. The unearthly plane Plato seeks is not some distant planet but an abstraction. While Mulder might countenance the idea that all of his earthly experiences are ultimately explained by ancient visitors from a different solar system, Plato would stress that his realm of the forms exists nowhere in physical space but yet "contains" all the unchanging truths and concepts that literally explain everything we experience (and even some things we don't). Therefore, Plato is the only nonnaturalist in this regard. Moreover, Mulder isn't a straightforward supernaturalist either. He is more suspicious of the dogmatism of organized religion than of Aristotelian attempts to capture the truth. Rather, Mulder's default position (especially once the character is established) seems to be that Scully's naturalism often isn't inclusive enough. If aliens exist and if they somehow account for life on this planet, then Scully's stockpile of current scientific wisdom must be revised and expanded. Thus Mulder isn't antiscience (even if he sometimes comes off that way) so much as he is skeptical of how science rules out some phenomena by fiat merely because they don't accord with what scientists currently know.

The basic point of Mulder's character in this regard is that we should be open to exploring "unexplained phenomena" via "extreme possibilities," especially if no other, more conventional scientific approach seems viable. This doesn't mean that they *always* warrant such treatment. After all, in "Beyond the Sea" Mulder himself tells Scully, "Dana, . . . open yourself up to extreme possibilities only when they're the truth." However, to rule out these possibilities simply by fiat runs the danger of trapping oneself in a myopic view of the world. Of course, Mulder sometimes errs in the other direction. He occasionally eschews sound investigative modes of inquiry, typically by not carefully considering competing hypotheses to his "extreme possibilities" mentality. (Anybody recall the ill-conceived "drowning by ectoplasm" hypothesis?[4]) This tenuous methodology walks a razor's edge. It often causes strife between Mulder and Scully. Recall "Born Again," in which Mulder asks Scully, "Why is it still so hard for you to believe, even when all the evidence suggests extraordinary phenomena?" Scully deliberately answers, "Because sometimes . . . looking for extreme possibilities makes you blind to the probable explanation right in front of you." Also, recall the classic exchange about Robert Modell (Robert Wisden), aka "Pusher," in which Mulder comments, "Modell psyched the guy out. He put the whammy on him." Scully immediately quips, "Please explain to me the scientific nature of the 'whammy.'" A bit perturbed, Mulder asks for Scully's take on the Modell case. Scully admits that she believes Modell is guilty but adds, "I'm just looking for an explanation a little more mundane than 'the whammy.'"[5]

Nevertheless, it cannot be denied that somehow they were successful in blending their two respective approaches to seeking the truth. This is what we would expect from two intelligent truth seekers engaged in honest dialogue. The goal takes precedence over the idiosyncrasies of the individuals engaged in reaching it. Perhaps this is why Mulder's work became more refined once Scully joined him on the X-Files. Perhaps their interactions also explain Scully's slow transformation away from her strict Aristotelianism. They become united without completely giving up their preferred mindsets. A scene from *Fight the Future* (just before the infamous non-kiss) substantiates these claims. Scully arrives at Mulder's apartment to inform him that she is leaving the bureau. He pleads with her not to resign. She reminds him that they were teamed up only because she was to debunk his unconventional work—to ruin him. He confides in her, "But you saved me! As difficult and as frustrating as it's been sometimes, your goddamned strict rationalism and science have saved me a thousand times over! You've kept me honest...you've made me a whole person. I owe you everything."[6]

Professor Dawkins and *The X-Files*

Even after the admission that the analogy to Raphael's *School of Athens* can only be pressed so far, some philosophers will no doubt argue that it is completely misguided, bordering on dangerous. Here I have in mind

Richard Dawkins. In 1996, Dawkins blamed *The X-Files* for making the paranormal fashionable at the expense of careful scientific research:

> Less portentously it [the paranormal vogue in popular media] may be an attempt to cash in on the success of *The X-Files*. This is fiction and therefore defensible as pure entertainment. A fair defense, you might think. But soap operas, cop series and the like are justly criticized if, week after week, they ram home the same prejudice or bias. Each week *The X-Files* poses a mystery and offers two rival kinds of explanation, the rational theory and the paranormal theory. And, week after week, the rational explanation loses. But it is only fiction, a bit of fun, why get so hot under the collar? Imagine a crime series in which, every week, there is a white suspect and a black suspect. And every week, lo and behold, the black one turns out to have done it. Unpardonable, of course. And my point is that you could not defend it by saying: "But it's only fiction, only entertainment."
>
> Let's not go back to a dark age of superstition and unreason, a world in which every time you lose your keys you suspect poltergeists, demons or alien abduction.[7]

Here, Dawkins seems to be offering an argument by analogy. It invites us to imagine a show like *Law and Order*—let's call it *Law and Smorder*. Weekly, on *Law and Smorder*, there are two primary suspects for committing the featured crime; one is African American and the other Caucasian, but, as it turns out, every week the African American is the perpetrator. Dawkins (rightly) believes that such a fictionalized crime drama is socially irresponsible, and perhaps morally objectionable, presumably because it "week after week rams home the same prejudice or bias," and doing so has negative or harmful effects on its audience (or society at large). But, continues Dawkins, *The X-Files* is just like *Law and Smorder* in this regard. A mystery is proposed and then investigated, but week after week, Mulder's paranormal theory wins out over Scully's more rational and conventionally scientific explanation. Therefore, because it, too, weekly rams home the same prejudice or bias that has negative or harmful effects on its audience, it is just as socially irresponsible (and perhaps morally objectionable) as *Law and Smorder* is (or would be, if it were actually on the air).

There are two controversial components to Dawkins's argument. First, some prejudices or biases are morally objectionable, but not all. My bias that the Green Bay Packers are the best NFL football team ever doesn't seem morally objectionable in and of itself. So, we must take care in determining whether the bias in question results in negative or harmful effects. Thus, of course, the bias Dawkins implies about racial stereotypes as they pertain to crime is clearly socially irresponsible, if not morally objectionable; it heightens social tensions and propagates general malaise. But what about Dawkins's contention that *The X-Files* conveys a similar irresponsible or objectionable bias? What negative or otherwise harmful effect might there be in glorifying Mulder's paranormal theories and denigrating Scully's more rational and scientific approach? Perhaps Dawkins is assuming something akin to what W. K. Clifford famously argues in "The Ethics of Belief." Clifford writes:

> Every time we let ourselves believe for unworthy reasons, we weaken our powers of self-control, of doubting, of judicially and fairly weighing the evidence. We all suffer severely enough from the maintenance and support of false beliefs and the fatally wrong actions which they lead to. . . . But a greater and wider evil arises when the credulous character is maintained and supported, when a habit of believing for unworthy reasons is fostered and made permanent. . . . The danger to society is not merely that it should believe wrong things, though this is great enough; but that it should become credulous, and lose the habit of testing things and inquiring into them; for then it must sink back into savagery.[8]

Presumably, then, Dawkins finds *The X-Files* socially irresponsible because it tends to make its millions of viewers, and thus a significant fraction of society, into gullible, simple-minded folk who habitually believe for unworthy reasons (and invariably act on those unjustified beliefs). This would explain his closing comment that we must guard against going back to an age of unreason such that whenever something goes wrong, we blame "the grays" (as Mulder would say). Therefore, the first controversial component of Dawkins's argument is whether *The X-Files* has the kind of mesmerizing grip on society necessary to turn us into the sort of dullards Dawkins and Clifford fear.

Even though *The X-Files* was extremely popular, we must conclude that Dawkins missed the mark on this one. Yes, *The X-Files* spawned a devoted fan following that became incredibly active on the Internet. In fact, fans became so vocal that it was necessary to give them a name for easy reference—the "X-Philes." But I don't know of any X-Phile who bought crates of sunflower seeds, donned a pair of red Speedos, and traveled directly to his local university to upstage its science faculty. Further, I don't know of any X-Phile who avoided vacationing in Cabo because she feared "that Mexican goat-sucking thing" would mortally slime visitors with deadly bacteria. Nor do I know of any X-Phile who traveled far and wide to see Cher concerts in hopes of catching a glimpse of the Great Mutato chomping on a peanut butter sandwich. These suggestions are admittedly tongue-in-cheek, but I suspect that most X-Philes find them well placed.

For all that shameless hyperbole, Richard Dawkins is an incredibly gifted philosopher and scientist. Any second-rate philosopher can critique an argument grounded in empirical predictions about the future that never come to fruition. So, being as charitable as possible to Dawkins's position, perhaps *The X-Files* fueled the paranoia of those prone to adopt governmental conspiracies and in this way may have indirectly spawned various new but unfounded theories about the government's covert involvement in our lives. However, this recent domestic development might also be explained by the (more or less) simultaneous end of the cold war: without the Soviet Union to worry about, who should the paranoid distrust now? Even so, there simply isn't any evidence to the effect that *The X-Files* had (or continues to have) the kind of negative influence on society that Dawkins claims.[9]

The second controversial component of Dawkins's argument is whether he accurately portrays the show. That he doesn't may be even more unpardonable for X-Philes. Consider the following trips down memory lane. In "Beyond the Sea," Mulder questions Scully's appeal to the paranormal in the Boggs case because Boggs is "the greatest of liars." This is evidence of Mulder's discriminatory powers. Furthermore, as early as "Pilot" (the show's very first episode) we see Mulder using empirical methods to substantiate his paranormal claims. When he and Scully are driving down a highway, the radio and clock in their rented car spontaneously malfunction. Mulder recognizes this and suspects extraterrestrial activity. He immediately stops the car, opens the trunk, and (very fittingly) spray paints a large "X" on the highway. His doing so proves crucial to substantiating his "missing time" hypothesis later in the episode. In "E.B.E." Mulder refines this testing procedure by using two stopwatches to demarcate his "missing time" phenomenon.

Three further examples are especially telling against Dawkins's position. First, in the attempt to determine whether Agent Jack Willis (Christopher Allport) or Warren James Dupre (Jason Schombing) survived a gun battle in "Lazarus," Mulder asks Willis to sign a birthday card for Scully. Willis, one of Scully's former lovers, shares the same birthday as Dana. Thus, it is reasonable to assume that Willis would have known that Scully's birthday was still two months away at the time he was approached by Mulder. The man appearing to be Willis immediately signs the card (with his left hand even though Willis is right-handed). Mulder presents this evidence to Scully, implicitly arguing as follows: If the person who signed this card was Jack Willis, he would have known that it wasn't Scully's birthday (and, in any event, would have signed it with his right hand); because the man who signed the card didn't know it wasn't Scully's birthday (and used his left hand to sign the phony card), it follows that the person who signed it wasn't Jack Willis, even if it looks like him. Mulder used this argument to further substantiate his paranormal theory that Willis and Dupre have undergone some sort of psychic transfer such that Dupre now inhabits Willis's body. Second, in "Piper Maru," a season 3 episode, we see Mulder testing his hypothesis that French salvage-ship operators suffer from high levels of radiation due to exposure from an alien craft. Scully offers the competing hypothesis that the sailors could have been affected because the French have resumed nuclear testing. Mulder replies, "I checked. It's [the course of the French salvage ship] thousands of miles away from any test sites." Disconfirming competing hypotheses is the hallmark of good scientific inquiry. Therefore, finally, we shouldn't be too surprised to find Mulder being interested in substantiating his hypotheses with evidence. Recall "Little Green Men," in which Scully tries to comfort a dejected Mulder: "But, Mulder . . . during your time with the X-Files, you've seen so much," to which Mulder candidly replies, "That's just the point. Seeing is not enough, I should have something to hold on to. Some solid evidence. I learned that from you."

While it should now be clearer why Melchert's "rationalist and mystic" moniker seems applicable to Mulder (as well as Plato), Dawkins's complaints against *The X-Files* run into other problems. It simply isn't clear that the paranormal theory always wins out. In "War of the Coprophages," Scully's more conventional explanation is superior. Sometimes, as in "Quagmire," Mulder eventually agrees with Scully that the more naturalistic explanation is epistemically preferable (even though it turns out to be false). There are numerous cases, like "Grotesque," in which we are left to wonder which protagonist offers the preferable theory. This is the real beauty of the show: invariably we are left to decide for ourselves.

In any event, time and time again, Scully's careful empirical methods save the day. Her efforts are significant factors in "Ice," "The Erlenmeyer Flask," "The Host," "Firewalker," and "Død Kalm"—and these examples all come from the first two seasons alone. Furthermore, why would Mulder "encourage" Scully to perform autopsy after autopsy if he weren't at all interested in empirical findings? Mulder is no Gil Grissom, but he's not Scooby Doo either. Thus it is far from clear that the show disparages careful scientific inquiry in the way Dawkins suggests.

If that weren't enough, consider that after Scully has saved Mulder's life in "End Game," we hear her in a voice-over as she sits at Mulder's bedside:

> Transfusions and an aggressive treatment with anti-viral agents have resulted in a steady but gradual improvement in Agent Mulder's condition. Blood tests have confirmed his exposure to the still unidentified retrovirus whose origin remains a mystery. The search team that found Agent Mulder has located neither the missing submarine nor the man he was looking for. Several aspects of this case remain unexplained, suggesting the possibility of paranormal phenomena . . . but I am convinced that to accept such conclusions is to abandon all hope of understanding the scientific events behind them. Many of the things I have seen have challenged my faith and my belief in an ordered universe . . . but this uncertainty has only strengthened my need to know, to understand, to apply reason to those things which seem to defy it. It was science that isolated the retrovirus Agent Mulder was exposed to, and science that allowed us to understand its behavior. And ultimately, it was science that saved Agent Mulder's life.

Three years and dozens of bizarre cases later, Scully never deviates from this mission. In attempting to discover hidden truths about her cancer (in "Redux"), she tells us:

> If my work with Agent Mulder has tested the foundation of my beliefs, science has been and continues to be my guiding light. Now I'm again relying on its familiar and systematic methods to arrive at a truth, a fact that might explain the fate that has befallen me. . . . If science serves me to these ends . . . it is not lost on me that the tool which I've come to depend on absolutely cannot save or protect me . . . but only bring into focus the darkness that lies ahead.

Clearly, careful scientific inquiry has an important role to play in *The X-Files;* thus, it simply isn't clear that the show denigrates science in any obvious way. And if a careful inspection of the show does not support Dawkins's claim that it invariably glorifies irrational paranormal explanations over more-traditional, rational scientific explanations, then Dawkins is not entitled to his conclusion that *The X-Files* is socially irresponsible, let alone morally objectionable, because it fosters credulity in its audience.[10]

Nevertheless, the contributors to this volume owe a debt of gratitude to Professor Dawkins. Ironically, he was among the very first philosophers to publicize the philosophical significance of *The X-Files.* My co-contributors and I wish to follow his lead. We only regret that we couldn't get our act together sooner and realize what Dawkins did a decade ago: *The X-Files* is incredibly rich in philosophical content, as I hope you soon discover.

While I expect you to enjoy reliving your favorite *X-Files* moments, I truly hope that by the time you've studied the pages to come, you'll better understand why I believe that this book will take its rightful place next to similar books about *Seinfeld, The Simpsons,* and *Buffy the Vampire Slayer.* However, I will leave that judgment up to you. If nothing else, like me, you'll never see *The School of Athens* or the Metaphysics section of a bookstore the same way again.

Notes

1. Norman Melchert, *The Great Conversation, Volume 1,* 4th ed. (San Francisco: McGraw-Hill, 2002), 160.

2. Melchert, *The Great Conversation,* 157–58.

3. I don't believe that this description is either anecdotal or anomalous. We can find it in the work of other professional philosophers. Consider W. T. Jones:

> It has been remarked that everyone is born either a Platonist or an Aristotelian. Plato and Aristotle, that is, represent two different attitudes toward the world. . . . Where Plato was otherworldly and idealistic, Aristotle was practical and empirical. . . . Whether one prefers Plato's philosophy or Aristotle's depends in large measure on one's own basic temperamental bias. To some Plato may seem too visionary and impractical; these people will probably prefer Aristotle as a cool, level-headed rationalist. Those who are moved by Plato's "lofty idealism" will probably feel that Aristotle by comparison is pedestrian and uninspiring. (*The Classic Mind,* 2nd ed. [New York: Harcourt Brace Jovanovich, 1970], 217–18)

4. The relevant dialogue from the season 7 episode "all things" is simply too good not to revisit:

SCULLY: (To Mulder, annoyed) I said, I got the lab to rush the results of the Szczesny autopsy, if you're interested.

MULDER: I heard you, Scully.

SCULLY: And Szczesny did indeed drown but not as the result of the inhalation of ectoplasm as you so vehemently suggested.

MULDER: Well, what else could she possibly have drowned in?

SCULLY: Margarita mix, upchucked with about forty ounces of Corcovado Gold tequila which, as it turns out, she and her friends rapidly consumed in the woods while trying to re-enact the Blair Witch Project.

MULDER: Well, I think that demands a little deeper investigation, don't you?

SCULLY: No, I don't.

5. This exchange also deserves to be rehearsed more fully:

MULDER: [In response to Scully's scientific query about "the whammy"] I don't know, maybe, maybe it's some mental aspect of some eastern martial art. You know, the temporary suppression of the brain's chemistry, produced by a specific timbre or cadence in Modell's voice. His voice seems to be the key.

SCULLY: Mulder, Modell's last known employment was as a convenience store clerk. He has never been trained by ninjas. He has never even been out of the U.S. He is just a little man who wishes that he were someone big ... and, and, we're feeding that wish. That, that failed psyche screening ... if, if Modell could actually control people's minds, right now, he'd be an F.B.I. agent, right? He'd be a Green Beret, uh, a Navy Seal.

MULDER: Maybe the ability came to him more recently, like in the last two years.

(Scully looks unsatisfied)

MULDER: Well, o, o, okay. What's your big theory? How do you explain what Agent Collins did? I mean, this was a sane man, a family man with no prior history of psychological problems, sets himself on fire. You witnessed that. How does that happen?

SCULLY: What do you need me to say, Mulder, that I believe that Modell is guilty of murder? I do. I'm just looking for an explanation a little more mundane than "the whammy."

What is so interesting about this exchange is that moments before, Mulder utilizes his training (and incredible intuitive gift) to give an astounding off-the-cuff profile of Modell that impresses Scully. This substantiates the view of Mulder being developed here: he is something of an intuitive mystic (even if mystic isn't quite the right term) and rational (social) scientist.

6. The closing dialogue from the movie further substantiates the idea that their approaches are beneficially blended but still remain distinct. Consider:

MULDER: You were right to want to quit! You were right to want to leave me! You should get as far away from me as you can! I'm not going to watch you die, Scully, because of some hollow personal cause of mine. Go be a doctor. Go be a doctor while you still can.

SCULLY: I can't. I won't. Mulder, I'll be a doctor, but my work is here with you now. That virus that I was exposed to, whatever it is, it has a cure. You held it in your hand. How many other lives can we save? Look . . . (She clasps his hand.) . . . If I quit now, they win. (They walk off together.)

7. The passage is taken from Dawkins's 1996 BBC1 Richard Dimbleby Lecture, "Science, Delusion and the Appetite for Wonder." It can still be found on the Web in its entirety. For the specific quote, see http://www.edge.org/3rd_culture/dawkins/lecture_p12.html. (Accessed Oct. 25, 2006.)

8. Quoted in Michael Peterson, ed., *Philosophy of Religion: Selected Readings* (New York: Oxford University Press, 1996), 69–70.

9. Wouldn't *Star Wars* or *Star Trek* be just as damaging to society? What evidence is there that we will travel faster than the speed of light and meet *friendly* extraterrestrials with something called a "universal translator" pinned to the front of our jumpsuits? Perhaps Dawkins and his scientific skeptical community would reply that these shows are clearly pieces of science fiction, but some shows, like *The X-Files* and now *Medium,* straddle and blur the lines between science fiction, fictional drama, and nonfictional drama. There may be something to this complaint; it would help to explain Darin Morgan's inexplicit statement in "Jose Chung's *From Outer Space*" that the X-Files (and thus *The X-Files*) are somehow responsible for the "non-fiction science fiction" genre. Even with this admission, however, it still remains unclear clear that Dawkins accurately predicted *The X-Files'* grip on society.

10. The counterargument here can be put like this: Even if there is a stereotype against the benefit of good scientific inquiry in Anglo-American culture (something that I'm not willing to automatically grant), only the most serious X-Philes would begin to show the signs of credulity Dawkins fears. However, those who know the show best — the X-Philes — also know that the show doesn't propagate an antiscientific message, as demonstrated with just a few examples above. Therefore, even if there is an antiscientific bias that might be exploited by the media, it is false that *The X-Files* exploits it. Thus, Chris Carter and his production team are not guilty of any social irresponsibility. My thanks go to Evan Kreider, Al White, Tim Dunn, Joe Foy, Mark Peterson, and Greg Ahrenhoerster for a lively debate about Dawkins's position.

For a different potential response to Dawkins's argument, please see chapter 1. In fact, it seems that this book itself is reason to believe that Dawkins has overstated his case.

Part I

THE CREDOS

The Truth Is Out There

Abduction, Aliens, and Alienation

Mark C. E. Peterson

Philosophy and Bad Puns

Each episode of *The X-Files* invariably begins by reminding its viewers that "the truth is out there." This banner, this motto, the show's central epistemic and ontological axiom, conceals a jaw-droppingly awful pun. The pun has two parts. Part one: The truth "out there," the truth from which we are alienated, is that there are aliens. That's bad enough, but the second part is worse and begins like this: Mulder overcomes his alienation by questioning not only the official denial that aliens exist but also the official mind-set that defines which explanations are permitted and which explanations are crazy. Officially speaking, from the FBI's point of view, extraterrestrial aliens are not thinkable at all or, if they are, thinking about them is defined as crazy. Mulder climbs around such doublethink by using a kind of logical inference discussed at length by the father of American pragmatism, Charles Sanders Peirce (1839–1914). And, thus, part two: In contrast to the FBI's privileged standard for explanatory or inferential methods, *deduction* and *induction,* Mulder uses a kind of inference that Peirce called the "inference of hypothesis formation," or *abduction.* Therefore, the epistemic and ontological theme embedded in *The X-Files'* central axiom ("The truth is out there") is that Mulder, alienated from the truth that there are aliens, overcomes his alienation by using "abduction" to infer the existence of aliens.

This is bad enough to bear repeating: The aliens abduct human victims, but Mulder's abductive inference abducts the existence of aliens.[1]

The idea of overcoming your alienation from the truth is familiar territory to philosophy and specifically to *existentialism,* an area of philosophy concerned with the foundations of meaning—but, with a pun this bad, we will need to exercise a bit of caution before jumping in. Horrible puns like this one are a good example of why articles that poke around in popular fiction looking for philosophical themes can seem to be as meaningful or logically rigorous as Madame Zelma's palmistry. On the one hand, it happens that some "analyses" of literature and art are actually built entirely upon the sand of clever jokes rather than on the more time-consuming— and admittedly less hilarious—archaeological excavation of a text required to find buried philosophical treasure.[2] They seem to let amusing verbal coincidences stand in for understanding and are not, therefore, taken seriously by academically respectable philosophers. On the other hand, philosophical analyses of popular art and literature have one advantage. They return philosophy to its roots in the real world, to the marketplace where people barter, lie, tell stories, waste their time, and undertake the most vital activity connected with the advancement of human culture: leisure.[3] To put this a bit more metaphorically, if philosophers define themselves as too good for the Agora (the main market area in ancient Athens, where Socrates blocked traffic), then we exile ourselves to the Acropolis and its lofty, theoretical point of view—high above the marketplace and closer to the gods but disconnected from the concerns of real life.[4]

Testing for Philosophical Depth

So, before launching into a discussion of philosophical themes in *The X-Files,* we must determine whether this pun is simply a joke masquerading as profound philosophical reflection, or something philosophically deep but (thank goodness) funny too. Puns like this can be *suggestive,* but by itself "Mulder abducting aliens" is not enough to assert that *The X-Files* embodies anything philosophically interesting. Something can look philosophically interesting without being philosophically interesting in the same way something can look like a rare seventeenth-century French writing desk without being one. In the same way, any story can be given the look of an existentially rich narrative by dressing it up with a few characteristic features (like darkness, meaninglessness, hopelessness, or people turning into cockroaches). Like a fake antique—a desk made yesterday and shellacked to imitate the surface of the real thing—stories can look like existentialism while only imitating the veneer. Fortunately, we can distinguish superficial attempts from sincere and profound ones in the same way we check to make sure the wood in a two-hundred-year-old desk is really two hundred years old. We turn the thing upside down and check to see if existentialism runs deeper than the surface, whether the themes continue to inform the program underneath the dark and lingering close-ups of Scully wiping her eyes in disbelief. We can test inside its plotlines for less "punny" and more-traditional existential themes.

On the surface, of course, the series looks perfectly existential. It is an homage to Arthur Conan Doyle with Mulder and Scully standing in for Sherlock Holmes and Dr. Watson, and a plotline held together by a glue mixed out of Mary Shelley, Rod Serling, and Emmanuel Levinas.[5] The aesthetic affect of the show, a glossy film noir, carries the full complement of existential motifs usually employed in art and literature when they wish to examine existential ideas—it is chock-a-block with gloom, desperation, surreal characters, and the anxiety of being on the threshold of the terrible secret. The anxiety in this case is not merely that there are aliens, scary enough on its own, but that this urgent "truth" has been intentionally withheld by a conspiracy of dangerous people. So long as the truth is kept from us, so long as *we* do not have it, we must live in service to a truth provided *by someone else,* and thus our lives will be lived, not on our own terms, but on the terms of whoever provides that truth—whether that "truth" is true or not. Existentially speaking, this is precisely what it means to lead an "inauthentic" life, a life we do not author (etymologically speaking, to live authentically literally means to be the author of your own life). "The truth is out there," but we can only get to it if we are willing to creep out to the edge of our comfortable and familiar world to find it. Mulder and Scully wade through their crazy case files, encountering unexplainable disappearances, ghosts, conspiracy nuts (like Mulder's three acolytes from "The Lone Gunmen"), and an occasional humanoid fluke worm from Chernobyl (as in "The Host"). We trail alongside Mulder as he leaves his basement office with Scully and heads out to look for the truth, for a hypothesis that will explain his unsolved cases, cases discarded because they were too crazy, too far outside the accepted realities of the FBI's worldview to be "taken seriously," outliers in the data set too far from the approved linear regression to be considered data at all. Working the frayed edges of an accepted worldview is always the stuff of existential literature and art. It reawakens the meaning in our own lives by evoking the rejected and alien "other" and, in that way, throws into sharp relief the dominant worldview and its effects on what and how we know.[6]

These ornamental curlicues all look like serious existentialism, but we still need to look beneath the surface for traditional existential themes to know whether *The X-Files* truly *is* philosophically interesting or just a knockoff, something crafted to *look* philosophically interesting. Here's how we do that: existential analyses typically identify two underlying causes for alienation from the truth, and we need to see whether we can find one of them running throughout the series. They are (1) that it is impossible to find any truth whatsoever because there is no absolute truth, or (2) that something inherent in how we know things, in knowledge itself, prevents us from gaining an adequate understanding of the truth. Nietzsche's "death of God," which questions the reality of any absolute standard in morality or knowledge, is an example of the first. Once God is no longer believable, scientifically or even logically—in fact, once all absolutes are called into question—the idea of a certain and definite truth, "out there" beyond the windshield of our own psychological preferences, becomes moot. There are no independent truths for us to know or to act as a foundation for our beliefs. The world becomes a hell, the Hieronymus Bosch landscape we find too often in real life or, better, paraphrasing Yeats, with no center, things fall apart.[7]

The second cause produces its own kind of hell, but what does it mean to say that something in our thinking conditions how we can think about things and thus what we can know? Think about it this way: when you think about the world, the thinking you do is like a pair of glasses or lenses stuck on the end of your nose through which you see the world. The glasses are put there by culture and biology. Now, if you forget you have them on, and you will, you might believe that the world *is* exactly the way it *looks.* But sometimes, when the things you look at stray over to the edge of the lens and start to go out of focus, you may suddenly discover (or remember) the lenses stuck there between your understanding of the world and the world you are trying to understand. This is not a problem if you can take the glasses off, but these glasses—which can be called a worldview, a conceptual framework, or a paradigm—are a pair of glasses you cannot remove. Like those lenses, a worldview limits what you can think—what you can focus on—and in this way predetermines what you can know about the truth. By nurture or by choice, each person carries around a model of how he or she believes the world works, a paradigm through which the rest of life's experiences are filtered and reshaped in exactly the way a pair of prescription lenses bends the light entering your eye, and, thus, what you can know about the truth. Orwell's novel *1984* and Huxley's *Brave New World* are probably the best accounts in literature of how this can work, and, in film, *The Matrix* is an obvious example. Philosophically, the effect of worldview on understanding is best described in Plato's "Allegory of the Cave," from *The Republic,* or in Hegel's *Phenomenology of Spirit.*[8]

Fortunately, *The X-Files* tells us explicitly which cause is at work for Mulder and Scully; the series is a perfect case study for cause number 2. The show proclaims that "the truth is out there," that there *is* a truth, and that we are simply kept from it by the FBI's institutional mind-set, the official lenses through which it views the world. These lenses determine what is and is not a reasonable investigation, and what cases should and should not be pursued. From the show's point of view, the FBI's institutional paradigm insists that anything extraterrestrial is crazy. So even if the opening pun seems too clever, *The X-Files* turns out to be saturated with philosophical questions completely familiar to, and well within, the Western intellectual tradition. Peirce's use of the term "abduction" for the logic of hypothesis creation accurately describes Mulder's activity, along with the ontological and epistemological commitments of *The X-Files* series. Mulder's ability to find the right hypothesis, despite institutional and societal blinkers about what counts as real, challenges the conceptual frames of both Scully and the FBI's administrative hierarchy by attending more closely to the data, even the "crazy" data, and by exposing unexamined assumptions that somehow keep everyone else alienated from the truth that there are, gasp, aliens.

Once we scratch the surface, we find that *The X-Files* not only embodies an accessible and contemporary reflection on alienation, and an illustration of the methodological relationship between hypothesis formation and hypothesis testing, but also even suggests how Mulder's use of abduction to overcome his alienation can resolve our own existential alienation and anxiety. We do not have man-eating bacteria to worry about (except, perhaps, in Mexico), but we all occasionally feel a vague and unsettling "alien" something-or-other lurking just beyond what we are able to understand. It could be whether God exists or whether the people we love, love us in return, or whether all the choices we have made about life are wrong. Mulder uses abduction to see through the murky and unsettling *X-I-know-not-what* that keeps him alienated. What works for Mulder might work for us too.[9]

Alienation

In *The X-Files*, the source of alienation and its attendant existential anxiety is that the institutions of power have framed any investigation of the world (and Mulder, remember, works for the Federal Bureau of *Investigation*) in such a way that we will always remain alienated from the truth, the truth that there are aliens. Institutions (like the nefarious Syndicate or the FBI itself) do this in two ways: (1) they mask the data through deliberate obfuscation, and (2) they bend the lenses and twist the explanatory paradigms, the models of "acceptable" explanations, so that any data pointing to an alien truth are ignored, discarded, or ridiculed. Deliberate obfuscation is easy to do and easy to understand. It depends on smoke and mirrors or on crafting "plausible deniability," as the Cigarette Smoking Man (CSM) would say, but it has a weakness. What is hidden, no matter how cleverly, may eventually be discovered; even the Smoking Man might accidentally leave his nicotine-stained fingerprints on something. The second technique is infinitely more subtle and depends on bending the lenses, on constructing an institutional mind-set that makes it impossible to imagine the alien truth in the first place. Any data that point toward the truth are simply defined as "crazy," along with any explanation, or person, crazy enough to take such data seriously. Mulder thus became the youthful, Oxford-educated genius who went crazy and now inhabits the basement along with all those crazy files. Scully is at first ridiculed and then later puts her own career at risk simply by working with "Spooky" Mulder (as in "Squeeze"). We could say, then, that we are kept alienated from at least some of the truth, and from any meaning we might derive from uncovering it, by institutionally accepted models of reality that guarantee that the truth is always excluded. If people cannot "think outside the box," then "outside the box" is the best place to hide the truth. We know this is the case for *The X-Files,* since everyone in the FBI—except the conspirators—thinks that Mulder is crazy, even though Mulder is the only one who knows the truth. Mulder knows the truth (about aliens) because he is the only one able to think outside the institutional box.[10]

In simpler language, everyone is stuck thinking inside the box except Mulder and the conspiracy (in the form of the Syndicate, including, perhaps, Deep Throat [Jerry Hardin] and his successor X [Steven Williams]). Nearly everyone else in the show has been successfully alienated from the truth. But this begs two questions: (1) If the official investigative procedures, the acceptable paradigms of what is and is not allowable, the institutional box, successfully obscure that truth and any data that point to the truth, then how was Mulder able to overcome this alienation, see beyond the deliberate deceptions, and, by treating his officially crazy data seriously, find the truth? And (2) how is it, specifically, that an "institutional paradigm" can keep Scully, perfectly brilliant in her own right, from seeing what Mulder sees?[11]

The short answer is that Mulder can see the truth because he obviously has not been blinkered by the FBI's official version of reality and is therefore free from the institutional filters that would otherwise keep him from using *all the data* to formulate a hypothesis—even the officially crazy data. This begins to address the first part of our pun: *The X-Files'* claim that we are alienated from the truth that there are aliens. We have sketched out the characteristic existential themes we would expect to find in a work of existential fiction, but we now must turn to the second part of our horrible pun, that Mulder uses "abductive inference" to abduct the existence of aliens. For this we need to consider C. S. Peirce's discussion of how abductive inference works and how it is related to its more popular and powerful cousins, deduction and induction, and then see how failing to distinguish abduction from induction answers our second question and explains Scully's predicament: why she is unable to see the truth as Mulder sees it. Once we consider the essential features of abductive inference, we will have both the vocabulary and the technical appreciation to move beyond groaning at the pun and toward understanding the deeper implications of this superficial wordplay.

Peirce and Abduction

Charles Sanders Peirce's discussion of inference sheds light on the question of how data are related to a hypothesis that explains them and what distinguishes the process of hypothesis formation, what he came to call "abduction," from inductive and deductive inferences.[12] The difference among these, and especially between abduction and induction, is critical to understanding how the FBI imposes and maintains its institutional worldview. A quick tour of Peirce should help us make sense of Mulder and Scully and, ahem, how Mulder "Peirces" the veil of smoke surrounding the alien truths out there.[13]

Peirce summarizes the main forms of reasoning in his 1903 Harvard Lectures.

> These three kinds of reasoning are Abduction, Induction, and Deduction. Deduction is the only necessary reasoning. It is the reasoning of mathematics. It starts from a hypothesis, the truth or falsity of which has nothing to do with the reasoning; and of course its conclusions are equally ideal. . . . Induction is the experimental testing of a theory. . . . It sets out with a theory and it measures the

degree of concordance of that theory with fact. It never can originate any idea whatever. No more can deduction. All the ideas of
science come to it by the way of Abduction. Abduction consists in
studying facts and devising a theory to explain them. Its only justification is that if we are ever to understand things at all, it must
be in that way.[14]

Deduction and induction are the familiar forms of logical inference that
allow us to determine, on the one hand, a set of necessary and certain
consequences and, on the other, a probabilistic account of how likely or
unlikely a given hypothesis might be. They are well-established and popu-
larly understood ways of using logic to make sense of the universe. Deductive inferences are most familiar in mathematics. Think about geometry
proofs. You start with a set of axioms or premises from which you then
derive statements that are absolutely certain and that follow with necessity. No additional evidence, for instance, can make the interior angles of
a triangle add up to 180° more than they do already. In a deduction, nothing can make its conclusions more certain because they are necessary and
certain by definition. Science, by contrast, is inductive. Induction works by
collecting data in order to confirm or deny the probability that a hypothesis is true or false. While induction does not provide certainty the way
deduction does, it does provide probability—and with enough data, an
extremely strong and predictive probability. Think about a well-established
scientific hypothesis like gravity. The effects of gravity are not, technically
speaking, deductively certain (in the same way that $1 + 1 = 2$ is certain), and
yet the probability is extremely high that my coffee cup will fall to the floor
when the cat pushes it off the desk. In this case, probability is, "for practical
purposes," nearly as robust as certainty.

If deduction is necessary and certain, and induction is probabilistic,
then where does that leave abduction? Peirce constructed abductive inference in this form:

The surprising fact, C, is observed;
But if A were true, C would be a matter of course,
Hence, there is reason to suspect that A is true.[15]

The process is like trying on explanations, like trying on shoes, until you
find one that fits. Once you find one that seems to fit, you still cannot say it
is a good explanation—not yet. You can only say that it *might be,* and that

is all abduction amounts to; so, compared to deduction and induction, abduction is barely an inference at all. Deduction proves. Induction confirms. Abduction suggests. Where deduction and induction have mountains of justification available for their methodologies, abduction has none at all—but that doesn't matter. "No reason whatsoever can be given for it, as far as I can discover; and it needs no reason, since it merely offers suggestions."[16]

While this seems to give abduction a limited role in explaining the universe and makes it a weakling compared to the deductive certainties or the inductive probability projections of its cousin inferences, abduction turns out to be critical. Deduction, on Peirce's reading, merely derives facts or ideas from a hypothesis and induction only tests a hypothesis: neither of them actually *creates* the hypothesis on which they operate. Therefore, when you want to think something new, something from outside the box, so to speak, you must use abduction. In Peirce's language, "Abduction . . . is the only logical operation which introduces any new idea; for induction does nothing but determine a value, and deduction merely evolves the necessary consequences of a pure hypothesis."[17]

Induction versus Abduction

The subtle issue at work in *The X-Files* is that, sometimes, we confuse induction with abduction: we confuse *testing* a hypothesis we have already presupposed with *creating* a new hypothesis. In fact, nowadays it is customary to think of hypothesis creation as part of the process of working out an induction; that is, working out the likelihood of a particular hypothesis based on the data we have collected. Clearing up this remaining ambiguity gives us a good look at what distinguishes Mulder from Scully. Philosopher Paul Redding describes it this way:

> 'Abduction' was the term Charles Sanders Peirce used in his later writings for a type of inference that he had earlier called 'hypothesis' and that is now commonly called 'inference to the best explanation.' According to Peirce, abduction constituted, alongside induction, a distinct second form of nondemonstrative or probabilistic inference. Especially in his later work, Peirce conceived of abduction methodologically as a distinct step in scientific inquiry. By abduction the investigator postulated some possible nonapparent cause which would explain the existence of otherwise

surprising phenomena. This postulation was then to be empirically tested by procedures drawing on deduction and induction.[18]

Peirce wanted to provide an account for the kind of inference that leaps from a surprising event or collection of data to a new hypothesis that explains them, and his description may as well be referring specifically to Fox Mulder. "The abductive suggestion comes to us like a flash. It is an act of insight, although of extremely fallible insight. It is true that the different elements of the hypothesis were in our minds before; but it is the idea of putting together what we had never before dreamed of putting together which flashes the new suggestion before our contemplation."[19] Even though abduction is often thought to be a *part* of the inductive process in scientific reasoning, it actually precedes the process of testing. It provides the hypothesis we test.

The relation between the hypothesis formulated by an abductive inference and the testing and confirmation performed by an inductive inference can be illustrated a bit more clearly in statistical terms. Imagine a set of data points plotted on a graph. It is possible, statistically, to find a line drawn through those points that describes, or fits, that set of points best. Think about how science typically works. We make observations about the world, map out those observations, and then try to find an explanation that fits them. A linear regression, the line drawn through the cloud of data that fits the data best, is like a hypothesis. Once drawn, that line can be extended along its trajectory to suggest where we might look for more and new data. If the original data suggest a particular line, then, statistically speaking, we can expect to find similar evidence along an extension of the same line. If the original data, to put this another way, suggest a particular line of inquiry, then, if we follow that line, we can expect to find more evidence like the evidence we started with. Of course, in any scientific measurement not all the data—or even most of it—will line up *perfectly*. The data are always somewhat loosely clustered or scattered into a rough shape of some sort, but even a general clumping of data is enough to suggest where you can draw a line that describes most of them. An educated guess at where to draw the line is abductive. Looking for data to confirm the line, after it is drawn, is inductive.

Once a hypothesis has been well established—once we find a lot of data points where an extension of the line predicted they would be, or when we continue to find evidence that maps into our same, original, cluster—we have good reason to become suspicious of new data points that fall too far from the line. In other words, once we have enough evidence to believe our hypothesis is true, new evidence that does not confirm our hypothesis will not be easily accepted. In fact, data points might show up so far off the line that we can reasonably suspect that they are not real data at all but artifacts of the measurement or mistakes in our observations: like a smudge on the lens we mistake for a distant galaxy, or a glowing weather balloon we mistake for a UFO, or even, perhaps, crazy observations that belong to a category we have to label with a variable like "X." Points like this, well off the line of an accepted hypothesis, are called "radical outliers."

Inductive method tells us that when enough radical outliers appear—like a second flock of data points landing adjacent to the flock we used to draw our original line—they stop being radical outliers and begin to suggest that our initial data set was not large enough. A lot of new points suggest that we got it wrong from the start and that our original line needs to be bent or shifted to include them, or that we may have found an entirely separate line of evidence—a second hypothesis we need to look into. Scientists with well-established theories will assert in public that when sufficient amounts of new, nonconfirmatory, data enter the system, the hypothesis will be swapped out for one that accounts for the new data—but this is never what happens. Once accepted, hypotheses have their own inertia. Once we adopt a hypothesis—usually based on a relatively small sample size—we are reluctant to let go of it, regardless of how many radical outliers we find later. A great deal of both data *and* psychological motivation is required to force us to reexamine hypotheses and explanations we have accepted and to which we have grown accustomed. It seemed crazy to fifteenth-century scientists, for instance, to think that Earth orbited the sun. What is interesting is that it was not a preponderance of new data that changed Copernicus's mind about the relation of the sun and Earth. The hypothesis was changed, not by a flood of radical outliers or new data, but by a *reformulation* of Ptolemy's hypothesis into one that would explain *all* the data more economically. Prior to this, data suggesting a different, non-Ptolemaic, orbital arrangement were ignored, ridiculed, or bent into pre-Copernican orbits in increasingly dizzying ways. The power and inertia of a previously accepted hypothesis kept even Einstein clinging to his narrower vision of the universe long after quantum mechanics began to raise serious questions about God and dice.[20]

To plug this back into *The X-Files,* any new data distinct from the established line, no matter how much of it there is, will be seen by those from inside the FBI's institutional point of view as radical outliers: as irrelevant or crazy. Anyone who pursues data points defined as radical outliers, therefore, will appear just as crazy and irrelevant as the radical outliers he or she pursues. This, in part, explains why his colleagues started calling Mulder "Spooky" and began ridiculing and marginalizing his work. An institutionally approved hypothesis, line, or conceptual framework always ensures that nothing alien is ever taken seriously. Alien evidence or any inconvenient data like the alleged existence of aliens can thus be labeled as radical outliers and locked away in the basement with that other radical outlier, Fox "Spooky" Mulder. Here is a bit of relevant conversation from the series itself, at the beginning of the episode "Piper Maru":

> SCULLY: I'm constantly amazed by you, Mulder. You're working down here in the basement, sifting through files and transmissions that any other agent would just throw away in the garbage.
> MULDER: That's why I'm in the basement, Scully.
> SCULLY: You're in the basement because they are afraid of you, of your relentlessness, and because they know that they could drop you in the middle of the desert, tell you that the truth is out there, and then you'd ask them for a shovel—well, maybe not a shovel. Maybe a backhoe.[21]

On Helping Scully Out of the Box

Now we can see that the so-called craziness of the data does not depend only on some quality in the observations—mysterious computer chips implanted at the base of the neck, unexplainable crop circles, and so on. These are red herrings. Craziness is determined by how far those observations fall from the official party line, how far they fall from the expected range of allowable data. That is what defines these data points as crazy. In this way, hypotheses already put in place condition which observations count. Since aliens are excluded from these institutionally acceptable explanatory models, any data that suggest the activity of aliens are also excluded. So, both *what* we can think (the existence of aliens) and *how* we can think (the hypotheses we assume that condition what we look for) are set up to make sure we remain alienated from the truth.

With these ideas in place we can finally answer our earlier question about Mulder and Scully: why can Mulder see through the official mindset when Scully cannot? Peirce's discussion suggests that Mulder is using abduction, while Scully, even though she believes she is using abduction and formulating hypotheses, is not. She merely conducts inductions along already-established and acceptable "lines of inquiry." The proof of this is simply that, for all her effort, her explanations are often wrong while Mulder's are usually (and with regard to aliens, finally) right. When she starts to explain one of the crazy events she and Mulder are sent out to investigate, she selects data that seem reasonable based on what she thinks a reasonable explanation would be. Once she makes the assumption that some explanations are more reasonable than others, try as she might, she automatically filters out any radical outliers (or explains them into sub-mission) that do not confirm her preconceptions about what hypotheses are acceptable: hypotheses that do not, as we know, include fat-sucking mutants who translate medieval Italian texts (as in "2Shy"). This keeps her inside the box, inside the frames of her own expectations about what an explanation should look like, and thus keeps her from finding the truth. To her, of course, Mulder looks crazy because he accepts possibilities that seem crazy to her—and again they seem crazy to her because they do not meet the criteria she has presupposed about what a reasonable hypothesis is. So long as she is stuck in this box (mind-set, institutional paradigm) nothing alien—and for *The X-Files*, remember, that means *the truth*—will ever get in. Her condition precisely illustrates the second of the two under-lying causes of existential alienation mentioned earlier: the alienation from the truth produced by the way our own cognitive processes, our cultural and biological lenses, can limit what we know. She embodies an "unhappy consciousness," the kind of thinking trapped by self-imposed limitations it cannot itself recognize.

Scully's situation is complicated, but Mulder, even though he knows the truth and has managed to free himself from the mind-set that blinkers his partner, is even harder to explain. How did he manage to avoid being absorbed into the institutional paradigm, the corporate mind-set, when nearly every other FBI agent succumbed? The answer to this question is the answer to existentialism's *big* question: how do I get to the truth, the truth from which I am alienated, the truth I need to live an authentic life? The answer looks easy. To escape this alienation, just let go of your conditioning worldview, and then, using all the crazy data, make the leap of abduction.

Finding the Edge of Your Fishbowl

Advice is easy. There is, of course, a catch that sits at the center of all exis-tential thought, like a bad tooth you cannot leave alone. To understand Mulder we must put ourselves in Scully's shoes. Here's the catch: Scully finds herself in a paradoxical situation. Her own explanations often do not satisfy her, and, worse, she begins to suspect that her crazy partner may not be so crazy after all. This edginess is evident from the private reflections she entrusts to her computer diary at the end of the day, after she files her public reports for the FBI hierarchy. In those private entries she confesses to an anxiety not only about all the crazy evidence her official reports explain away but also about her inability to create a satisfying explanation. This uneasiness comes from questioning her own methods, her loyalty to thinking inside the inductive box. Compounding this uneasiness is the fact that, as hard as she tries, she will never be able to question her own methods well enough to see what is wrong with them, until enough radical outliers pile up to force her over the edge. As the series moves along, Scully begins to see what Mulder is seeing and eventually reverses roles when she meets her own earlier skepticism in the person of her new partner, Agent Doggett (Robert Patrick). Agent Doggett plays skeptic to Scully's more evolved point of view just as Scully once played skeptic to Mulder. But this comes later in the series. The task remains impossible for her so long as she attempts to think her way out of the box, so to speak, by using the same kind of thinking that created the box in the first place. Her early anxiety is caused by running up against the rough edges of this box—for the uncertain edge between what we *think* we know and what we *really* know is always rough.[22]

Scully's predicament speaks to the larger existential issue on display in *The X-Files*. It is our own. How do you uncover the presuppositions that condition your thinking by using the same kind of thinking conditioned by the presuppositions you must now try to uncover? It looks unsolvable. "Understanding how our understanding conditions what we understand" looks like an impenetrable, paradoxical tangle. To put it a bit more simply, the goldfish does not know it is in a bowl. We share the goldfish's situation. Locked inside our worldviews we cannot find the sharp edges of our knowledge, of our fishbowls, nor determine how *what* we know conditions what we *can* know. There is, however, some consensus on how to resolve this situation. One approach is to begin by noting that you cannot leap out of your worldview any more than you can leap out of your skin—but you can start to crawl out. Mulder is our example. If Mulder overcomes his alienation by abduction, by using all the data, especially the data society calls crazy, then what about using abduction to overcome the kind of alienation produced by our own existential predicament? We have to start where we are. In *The X-Files,* our alienation from the truth (that there are aliens) is caused by having assumed, in advance of the data, a set of institutionally acceptable explanations for the world that condition the kind of data we accept as reasonable and the kind of data we ignore as mere radical outliers. This process, Peirce suggests, locks us into using induction while at the same time discouraging the formation of new hypotheses that would provide better, if more alarming, explanations. Mulder engages in abduction by beginning with the data themselves and not with the lines drawn by institutional authority or cultural paradigm. He attends to the data, no matter how far out of line they appear, and in that way he veers off the official, culturally reinforced and institutionally acceptable line toward the truth. For us, we must begin by attending to the radical outliers in our experience, by looking for what seems most alien to our worldview. Even if we cannot remove our cultural lenses, we can start to look for the edges, the borders where our understanding and expectations begin to get blurry: where things fall out of focus. Those margins give us the boundary layer for what we think is reasonable and what we think is unreasonable. Once we know that, we can trace the line of our own regression to determine what it avoids and excludes. We cannot see the bowl from the inside, in other words, but only from the suffocating edge where the water meets the air.

Finding the edge of our fishbowl or, better, rooting out the inherent limits of our understanding, is hard work not only because of the nasty logical paradox lurking at the heart of the matter but also for psychological reasons. A terrible and paralyzing anxiety goes along with this kind of self-exploration, and this too appears in *The X-Files*. There the anxiety does not follow from the fear of being swept up into the totalizing, institutional mind-set that hides the truth about aliens, or having your teeth drilled and ovaries supercharged (like Scully in "Ascension").

The anxiety, for Scully as much as for us, comes from stepping off the line of a comfortably satisfying hypothesis, wading into deep and muddy water and into the unnerving suspicion that we may not know everything we think we know. Human beings are profoundly uneasy with the possibility that the truth might not be fixed and eternal, or with the knowledge that what we know is not the whole story. Once you walk up to the edge of your own certainties and stare "out there" into the zone of abduction and mystery — the territory mapped by *The X-Files* — you begin to understand the anxiety existential authors attempt to describe. Letting go of these comfortable certainties and plunging ourselves into the basement with Mulder and Scully is something we instinctively avoid. Existential anxiety, like the

Buddhist notion of *tanha,* is a kind of snarl in the yarn of our desire, a slip-knot tied out of our inherent craving for fixed and unchanging truths or for consistent institutional and conceptual frames that keep us safely apart from the crazy thing we fear most: the rough recognition of our own ignorance that Socrates called wisdom.[23] The alternative, of course, is to live in ignorance of our ignorance. *The X-Files* describes the existential condition of human beings and points toward a solution, an exit. Like Mulder, we have to pick up our flashlights and, filled with expectation and presentiment, explore the darkness in our world, our lives, and ourselves. If we do, what works for Mulder should work for us.

Epilogue

One last thought: in addition to the insights this show offers our everyday lives, there is another, slightly crazier, resonance between Mulder's search for the truth in *The X-Files* and the book you hold in your hands—between Mulder's abduction of aliens and the idea that a philosophy text might look for "the truth" out there, in a popular television show. I say this because a book about finding philosophically meaningful themes in a popular sci-fi TV show is a bit alien to today's academic philosophy.[24] It is the kind of activity that makes serious-minded philosophers wrinkle their noses and use the word "popular" as a pejorative. Like Mulder's abductive inferences, a book like this one includes data points in its linear regression usually excluded from philosophical analysis because they seem "crazy" because they lie outside the academically acceptable boundaries of the academic box. Popular television is out on the fringes of acceptable academic data in exactly the same way Mulder's cases, his X-Files, are on the fringes of forensic responsibility. Perhaps Mulder's example suggests that being open to all the data points, including "crazy" data like popular nonacademic sources in art and literature, might reveal the limitations inherent in contemporary academic philosophy, that is, the edge of our institutional fishbowls. Put another way, perhaps philosophy's adherence to privileged paradigms of reasoning, specifically induction and deduction, exile it *up* to the Acropolis, away from the center of life, rather than help find a way *down* through discarded lines of inquiry and into the basement.[25] If, as Emil Fackenheim used to remind us, paraphrasing Hegel, "philosophy is the Sunday of life," then perhaps in addition to prayerful reflection on the op-ed and business sections of our lives, it is appropriate (and necessary) that we meditate on the Sunday comics, including that televised comic book, *The X-Files*.[26]

What works for Mulder should work not only for us as individuals but also for philosophy.

Notes

1. Maybe turnabout is fair play since the driving psychological motive in Mulder's life was his conviction that his sister had been, noninferentially, abducted by aliens.

2. "Deconstruction" is an example of the kind of analysis that can too often lean on jokes or linguistic coincidence. When done properly, deconstruction produces startling and useful insights, but it is easily abused and, as a result, has earned a rotten reputation. Thus, this now well-worn joke:

> QUESTION: What do you get when you cross a deconstructionist with a Mafia hit man?
> ANSWER: You get an offer you can't understand.

3. Josef Pieper, *Leisure: The Basis of Culture* (South Bend, IN: St. Augustine's Press, 1998).

4. Interestingly enough, and by contrast, just off the Agora Hephaestus and Athena, as gods representing practical and theoretical wisdom, share the temple. In the Acropolis, overlooking Athens, Athena has the main temple to herself.

5. Arthur Conan Doyle authored the Sherlock Holmes series; Mary Shelley is the author of *Frankenstein*; Rod Serling is an author and director of *The Twilight Zone*; and Emmanuel Levinas, one of the twentieth century's greatest philosophers, explored the theme of meaning in the face of totalitarian politics and thinking.

6. Examples of "frayed edges" in existential literature or philosophy include Kafka's use of absurdity to make you rethink what it means for a story or person to be "reasonable." Waking up as a cockroach, for instance, as the main character in *Metamorphosis* does, is the classic example. Something subtler, but even more frightening than six-foot-tall cockroaches, is the frayed edge of religious faith in an age of science: not a faith that blindly runs over rationality but that acknowledges it fully and without looking away. This is the theme of Søren Kierkegaard's *Fear and Trembling*, one of the first texts to embody the kinds of themes we can unearth in *The X-Files*.

7. See W. B. Yeats's (1865–1939) poem "The Second Coming" (1921).

8. This analysis of *The X-Files* points to an interpretation that situates existentialism in what the nineteenth-century German philosopher G. W. F. Hegel called the "unhappy consciousness." At a certain level in its development, consciousness finds itself restrained from advancing further by the very categories it uses to think. Only by

recognizing the way in which its own conceptual categories frame its understanding can consciousness move on to a more adequate point of view and a more adequate comprehension of its relation to what it thinks: in this case, what Hegel called "reason." (See G. W. F. Hegel, *Phenomenology of Spirit,* trans. A. V. Miller [Oxford: Oxford University Press, 1979], 119–38.) While the matter is well beyond the scope of the present discussion, it is important for both philosophical and historical reasons to take note of the issue here. The unhappy consciousness permeates much if not all of the discussion concerning the nature and origin of existential thought. See Jean Wahl, *Le malheur de la conscience dans la philosophie de Hegel* (Paris: Rieder, 1929).

9. John Locke coined the phrase "something I know not what" to describe the underlying substance of primary qualities. Locke believed we do not and cannot have an adequate conception of "substance." John Locke, *Essay Concerning Human Understanding* (London, 1690), Book 2, chap. 23, 2.

10. With regard to the power of wrapping Mulder and his data in the "crazy" label, viewers might remember the Cigarette Smoking Man's comment from "The Blessing Way" to his Syndicate cohorts that "the matter with the FBI will be handled internally, as always."

11. Scully, of course, eventually overcomes her own "paradigm paralysis," a set of institutional lenses strong enough to repress even her own abduction, presumably, at the hands of the aliens. More on this below.

12. Peirce's use of terminology is not consistent across his career. His early work calls this form of inference "hypothesis," but he eventually began referring to it as "abduction" and finally as "retroduction."

13. For a more in-depth discussion of abductive inference, in addition to the citations upcoming, see T. K. Fann, *Peirce's Theory of Abduction* (The Hague: Martinus Nijhoff, 1970); H. G. Frankfurt, "Peirce's Notion of Abduction," *Journal of Philosophy* 55 (1958): 593–97; A. W. Burks, "Peirce's Theory of Abduction," *Philosophy of Science* 13 (1946): 301–6; and F. E. Reilly, *Charles Peirce's Theory of Scientific Method* (New York: Fordham University Press, 1970), 31.

14. C. S. Peirce, *Pragmatism as a Principle and Method of Right Thinking: The 1903 Harvard Lectures on Pragmatism,* ed. P. A. Turrisi (Albany: State University of New York Press, 1997), 217–18.

15. C. S. Peirce, *Philosophical Writings of Peirce,* ed. Justus Buchler (New York: Dover, 1955), 151–52.

16. C. S. Peirce, *Lectures on Pragmatism,* in *The Collected Papers, Vol. V: Pragmatism and Pragmaticism (1931),* lecture 6, §4, para. 171. Online at http://www.textlog.de/peirce_pragmatism.html. Accessed June 24, 2006. Or, put another way, Peirce says, "It is to be remarked that in pure abduction, it can never be justifiable to accept the hypothesis otherwise than as an interrogation. But as long as that condition is observed, no positive falsity is to be feared; and therefore the whole question of what one out of a number of possible hypotheses ought to be entertained becomes purely a matter of economy" (Peirce, *Philosophical Writings,* 154).

17. Peirce, *Collected Papers, Vol. V,* lecture 7, §1, para. 181.

18. Paul Redding, "Hegel and Peircean Abduction," *European Journal of Philosophy* 11, no. 3 (2003): 295.

19. Peirce, *Collected Papers Vol. V,* lecture 6, §4, para. 171.

20. Einstein's famous retort when confronted by the indeterminacy of subatomic physics was that "God does not play dice with the universe."

21. This example, and its episode, illustrates that even while Mulder creates, or abducts, his hypothesis by including all the data, he also goes on to use induction and deduction—testing his hypothesis against new data and working out its consequences to test it for internal contradictions and external contraindications—to rule out competing hypotheses. In this particular case he is interested in why a French salvage team is suffering strange radiation burns. Scully suggests that it is merely because the French have resumed nuclear testing. Mulder replies that he checked and found that the nearest testing site is thousands of miles away from the French sailors.

22. A telling example occurs in the episode "End Game" (season 2). Scully has had Mulder rescued from an ice sheet in the Pacific where he had followed what he claimed to be a shape-shifting alien. Scully narrates: "Many of the things I have seen have challenged my faith and belief in an ordered universe. But this uncertainty has only strengthened my need to know, to understand, to apply reason to those things which seem to defy it." This is a good illustration of her commitment to inductive procedure as the only right way to understand the universe, and of her failure to use abduction to see beyond her line of "reasonable" inquiry to the truth.

23. *Tanha* literally means "thirst," but in Buddhism it refers to the craving to obtain things (or ideas or states of being) that will, one imagines—unhappily and incorrectly—make one happy. In this context, it refers to an inherent hunger humans have for unchanging and fixed truths on which they then expect to hang a meaningful life. This expectation is the origin of sorrow.

For more on the link between existential anxiety and the Socratic idea of wisdom, see Mark C. E. Peterson, s.v. "Wisdom," in *Dictionary of Existentialism,* ed. Haim Gordon (West Port, CT: Greenwood Press, 1999), 494–96.

24. Although this is clearly changing with the recent publication of such books as William Irwin, Mark T. Conard, and Aeon J. Skoble, eds., *The Simpsons and Philosophy: The D'oh! of Homer,* Popular Culture and Philosophy 2 (Chicago: Open Court, 2001); William Irwin, ed., *The Matrix and Philosophy: Welcome to the Desert of the Real,* Popular Culture and Philosophy 3 (Chicago: Open Court, 2002); and even James B. South, ed., *Buffy the Vampire Slayer and Philosophy: Fear and Trembling in Sunnydale,* Popular Culture and Philosophy 4 (Chicago: Open Court, 2003).

25. Consider the observations of Bruce Wilshire and John McCumber. See Bruce Wilshire, *Fashionable Nihilism: A Critique of Analytic Philosophy* (Albany: State University of New York Press, 2002); Bruce Wilshire, *The Moral Collapse of the University: Professionalism, Purity, and Alienation,* SUNY Series in Philosophy of Education (Albany: State University of New York Press, 1990); and esp. John McCumber, *Time in the*

Ditch: American Philosophy and the McCarthy Era (Evanston, IL: Northwestern University Press, 2001); and John McCumber, *Reshaping Reason: Toward a New Philosophy* (Bloomington: Indiana University Press, 2005).

26. G. W. F. Hegel, *Lectures on the History of Philosophy,* trans. E. S. Haldane and Francis H. Simpson (New York: Humanities Press, 1974), 1:92: "Philosophy demands the unity and intermingling of these two points of view; it unites the Sunday of life when man in humility renounces himself, and the working-day when he stands up independently, is master of himself and considers his own interests." In fact, philosophy for Hegel must be the link between Athena and Hephaestus, between the Sunday of profound reflection and the workaday world in which life is lived and finds meaning in its dark and anxiety-producing foundations—down there in the basement.

Freedom and Worldviews in *The X-Files*

V. Alan White

Men can never be free, because they're weak, corrupt, worthless and restless. The people believe in authority; they've grown tired of waiting for miracle or mystery. Science is their religion; no greater explanation exists for them.

—Cigarette Smoking Man, "Talitha Cumi"

Certainly one of the major reasons *The X-Files* garnered such a loyal following is the intricate chemistry that developed over the course of the series between agents Fox Mulder and Dana Scully. In the beginning that chemistry took the form of a radical titration of Mulder's fuming passion to prove that paranormal events exist against the cool skepticism of Scully's devotion to reason and science. In the end the two achieved something more like a covalence of these same elements with a common and complementary vision of a considerably more complex world than either originally conceived. In between, they discovered that they constantly, mutually catalyzed one another to produce various degrees of belief, credulity, and astonishment about what truth might be "out there."

Therefore we can see that one overarching philosophical theme of the series is the question of how it is possible for people to change their fundamental views of the world. Although *The X-Files* poses this question in a sci-fi caricatured way, the question is not much different from more familiar and historical examples of such transformation, such as Augustine's midlife conversion from sinner to (literal) saint, Malcolm X's late-life renunciation of racism, and Lavoisier's rejection of the phlogiston theory of combustion through careful experimentation. The general mystery of this phenomenon of intellectual conversion to an alternative worldview is itself a vexing *X-Files*–like labyrinth of questions about epistemology, psychology, sociology, biology, and the disciplinary subsets intertwining these, and any finally satisfactory account of it would try to answer at least most of these questions in a comprehensive, tight-knit way. To avoid such a necessarily encyclopedic and complete response, perhaps we should limit ourselves to one central and crucial philosophical question nested deeply within all others in such an inquiry: are we truly *free* to choose between worldviews and their various components (or is the Smoking Man on to something in the epigraph about the slavishness of people)? Is there some recognizable component of *free will* in the matter of intellectual conversion to a modified worldview? And specifically in the context of *The X-Files*, were Mulder and Scully *free* to choose what they believed, either as represented at the beginning of the series, during its run, or at the end?[1]

A Crash Course in Free Will

To investigate whether anyone has free will, we must first be clear what we're talking about and looking for—the conceptual nature of freedom and free will. Philosophers have put forward various accounts of what constitutes some conditions of human freedom: lack of constraints, open-future choice, reasons-responsiveness, capability of being held responsible, and so on.[2] However, following J. L. Austin and some others, let's generalize from these more focused suggestions and say that freedom in general always requires two interrelated components of *ability* and *opportunity* (or *opportunities*—more about this in a moment).[3] The idea here is roughly that one can be free if and only if one is *able* to be free in some relevant way, such as being able to think, speak, move, and so on, and one has a course of thought or action open to the exercise of such abilities, so one isn't unduly distracted, one's lips aren't duct-taped, one isn't superglued to the floor, and so on. Note that freedom in general then is a state of affairs where one has some sort of internal capacity or power, and one has as well an external situation so that that capacity or power can complete its function. Only when both these internal and external conditions obtain can one be said to be truly *free* to think, to speak, to move.

Applying this picture of freedom to the specific issue of free *will* requires a bit of explanation. To begin, philosophers are for the most part divided into two mutually exclusive camps that are at odds on the question of how human brains and/or conscious minds function. The question here is whether the basis of consciousness is only an immensely complex system of causes and effects, such as a purely biological account of thought might provide, or whether consciousness might include deviation from the strict rule of cause and effect, for example by appeal to quantum physics or supernaturalism. These two views are respectively termed *determinism* and *indeterminism*. To begin to understand the relevance of these views to the question of the freedom of minds, note that one main difference between them is that by determinism the future of such a mind's function is locally (in the next moment) "closed," and by indeterminism the future of a mind is locally "open." That is, by determinism a given state of mind at one present moment causes one, and only one, state of mind in the next future moment as an effect. All other conceivably different future states of mind relative to the present one are "closed" off by the present causal one. By contrast, the indeterminism of a given present state of mind that is not causal is "open" to at least two alternative local future states of mind. One can see that these two views have one immediate tie-in to opinions about the freedom of such minds. If our minds' futures are always closed by determinism, then those futures based on our "choices" only go one particular way and no other. By indeterminism, on the other hand, our futures are at least sometimes open to this future and that future—as the 1980s Modern English song *Melt with You* goes, "the future's open wide!" So it may seem that determinism robs us of a free will to choose between distinct futures and indeterminism restores it.[4]

Unfortunately, things are more complicated than that in part because, depending on what *exactly* "freedom" means, each of the determinist or indeterminist views of minds can lay claim to free will, and one can be made to exclude it as well. It all depends on what free will *ability* is supposed to be, and what *opportunity* or *opportunities* are additionally needed, and what determinism and indeterminism can provide in terms of these components of freedom.

Say, for example, that a determinist interprets an *ability* to make a free choice as weighing options and coming up with the best one. Sophisticated computers can do this, and they are essentially causal mechanisms (their functional states are such that their futures are always locally closed). So a determinist view of mind can accommodate such an account of ability and thus regard our minds to be a form of mechanistic supercomputer. Say then also that the determinist puts forward an additional account that states, for example, if a mind is *caused* to select the best it can in a situation, and that selection is objectively correct, proper, and satisfactory (by some measure), then it is properly *freely* chosen because no other possible future course of that mind would make sense. Such a view combining deterministic ability with the sufficiency of just one future opportunity is in fact called a *compatibilist* account of freedom, and some like-believing determinists dub themselves thus.[5]

But what if, to the contrary, such a closed future is deemed insufficient for freedom? (That the future, to be freely chosen, *should be* "open wide.") For example, what if the best a mind can select in a situation is a fifty-fifty proposition of heads or tails, without any further preference between the two? A determinist account of this mind says that one actually *is* preferred, for one is finally caused to be selected over the other. But here indeterminists cry foul—how can *that one* be truly *freely* chosen if the other is *equally* preferred?[6] Truly free choices in these circumstances demand that both future alternatives are available for choosing. This means that any such choice requires plural opportunities in the future—and real ones, in a genuinely open future way. And if that is correct, determinism is false, at least for minds that are conceived as free in this way (so they can't be supercomputers). So for philosophers that demand such a plurality of future opportunities for any stated ability of mind to choose freely, freedom is *incompatible* with a determinist account of the locally closed future. Such philosophers of freedom are termed *incompatibilists;* they hold that the necessity of the plurality of opportunities for choice cannot be reconciled with locally closed future determinism. Incompatibilist indeterminists— sometimes called *libertarians*—believe that minds at least sometimes function in indeterminist ways, and when they do, the plurality of future opportunities assures that this free will to choose actually exists.

So there are determinists who believe that compatibilist freedom exists, and indeterminists who believe that incompatibilist freedom exists. But now for a moment think hard (so to speak) on this matter of incompatibilism. Incompatibilism as a belief is only a very abstract conceptual view *about* the philosophical need for locally plural open-future opportunities for freedom of choice *and does not commit to whether such a future exists.* Thus there are some determinists who agree with this view, and since they are also determinists about minds, reject any belief in such freedom of mind and will. For them the truth of determinism rules out such incompatibilist free will. They are called *hard incompatibilists*—determinists who do not believe that the opportunities form of free will exists.[7]

Whew! Our seemingly simple question about whether Mulder and Scully can *freely will* to change their worldviews has at least two different and complicated answers. "Yes, possibly," say compatibilists and libertarians—though their yeses are based on very different ideas about how minds work and what freedom is. "No," says the hard incompatibilist, agreeing with the libertarian about what freedom *ought* to be but then holding that it cannot exist, agreeing also with the compatibilist about the truth of the determinism of mind.

Who's right? The good news is that it appears we would only have to answer two questions in order to find out: how exactly do minds work, especially when they choose or decide things, and does freedom require a plurality of future opportunities or not? The bad news: philosophy has not arrived at a definitive answer to either of these.[8]

So are we stuck? Perhaps not. No matter what the final truth about free will might be, there is still one fact before us. Scully and Mulder (and people in the other historical examples) *did* change their worldviews based on their unusual experiences. Next, let's see what it is to change one's mind in this way, and see if any consequences for freedom pop up.

What Is It to Change Worldviews?

What is a worldview? That also is a complicated question. But our *X-Files* heroes can help us out here. Scully, even to the end of the series, is a true skeptic in the sense that she only believes what the evidence minimally and rationally requires her to believe. Nevertheless, her own extraordinary experiences, including both a near-fatal illness and pregnancy of partial alien origin, convince her that the world in fact involves a secret, systematic alien invasion of Earth orchestrated by government conspiracy in cahoots with the invaders. Mulder of course has something like a belief about the strong possibility of all this from the beginning (remember his cherished "I want to believe" poster?), based on previous (preseries) experiences, though ones dubious in their strength and number. In one sense Scully comes around to Mulder's original worldview, and hers changes more than his—yet we also see that Scully maintains a certain parsimonious attitude about belief that Mulder never shares (except in some episodes in which Mulder actually comes to doubt his beliefs because he is manipulated to do so). Mulder's worldview is always then one fundamentally of *faith* that the world is more than it appears to be, a faith that Scully even to the end never shares (except for her faith in God), committed skeptically to reasons and evidence as the primary basis of forming a view of the world.

A world*view* then is partially a function of *attitude* about what in our experiences counts as evidence of what there is in the world. The spectrum of such attitudes includes not only skepticism and faith but also blind acceptance, obdurate universal disbelief, modest gullibility, and a host of others. Focusing on this more subjective aspect of what a worldview is, the central question here then is which kind of attitude is *best* to obtain truth about the world—which attitude is the most reliable to know what's "out there"?

Despite the Smoking Man's previously quoted quasi defamation of science, and to some extent Mulder's as well, Scully's scientific and skeptical attitude seems the best contender to ferret out truth. In part that is because skepticism includes a tendency for one not to believe, and this hesitancy can compensate for the mind's evolved, natural inclination to work as a confirmation engine, seeking relationships wherever possible.[9] But a scientific attitude also includes another check on rushing to judgment—a conviction that the only reliable evidence is essentially public in character, accessible for verification and falsification by others. As just one example of how we are well served by skeptical science, one just needs to recall the notorious "cold fusion" incident. There some scientists themselves got caught up in exciting experimental data that seemed to indicate that energetic fusion reactions could take place at ordinary temperatures, and consequently they bypassed further trials and peer review to announce this revolutionary discovery directly to the public. But then the shared collective attitude of science took over, and labs around the world found that the data was erroneous and not replicable as a definite fusion reaction. The prospect of such an exciting discovery made the original researchers forgo the checks and balances that thorough scientific process provides—they "wanted to believe" too much that cold fusion was indeed "out there."[10]

Mulder's dedication to his duties, spurred by memory of his sister's abduction by aliens, sometimes likewise disposes him to "cold fusion" moments. In one memorable instance from "Død Kalm," Mulder is convinced that what were apparently rapidly aging sailors on a derelict ship "proved" that time shifts could occur—only for Scully to discover that their condition had a less exotic, if also somewhat unusual, scientific explanation. But the most touted example of this is Mulder's almost flip "drowning by ectoplasm" theory in the season 6 episode "all things." The Ghostbusters would have been proud, but Scully is not at all impressed. The autopsy shows that the young woman drowned in her own margarita mix.

One question we could then pursue is whether worldview-forming attitudes themselves can be freely chosen. Of course, once again that would depend on whether we ever actually have free will, and we now know that the hard incompatibilist would say no here. But if we were to say consistently with a compatibilist or libertarian that we could change our attitudes about the world, what, exactly, would we be claiming to possess? What would be freedom to change the way we view the world?

First, we ought to admit that the idea that we can change our attitudes merely by choosing to do so seems a little odd. People who are dispositionally skeptical, faithful, cynical, loving, hateful, and so on are not usually susceptible to easy change in these attitudes. They are manifestations of individual personality, and personality, once set in us in early life, does not easily change.

Second, though rare, instances of "attitude adjustment" admittedly do occur. Augustine did become faithful to God, and Malcolm X did abandon racist attitudes. Both of these changes, however, occurred within the context of lives in which many past experiences inclined the individuals toward a different way of seeing the world. That is, specific occurrences added up in cognitive significance to make another way of thinking about things reasonable. Lavoisier's experiments likewise convinced him that seeing combustible objects as possessing an internal power to burn—the notorious concept of phlogiston—was less reasonable than seeing them as being able to combine with oxygen in a process of burning.

So it seems that any freedom to adjust our attitudes must fit within this picture of it being a *reasonable* process, where attitudes may change due to the weight of sufficient reasons to do so. (Of course, there must also be *un*reasonable instances of attitude change as well, such as King George III's slip into paranoia due to inadvertent arsenic poisoning, but it is hard to see examples such as these as *free* processes.)[11]

Consider again Mulder and Scully. Both exhibit a persistence of belief attitudes consistently across the course of the series, Mulder's consisting of (not-quite-blind) faith that the paranormal is "out there," whereas Scully is dubious of that claim. But their experiences and the evidence thereof tweaked both of their attitudes. Scully's skepticism has to bend to the facts, and facts about the "black oil," the Syndicate, alien hybrids (including her own child), and so on become, at least past the middle of the series' run, indisputable even to her. On the other hand, the effectiveness of the Syndicate's decades-old cover-up about the pending invasion staves off Scully's assent to these facts for quite some time, and, as mentioned before, actually lead Mulder to question his faith that he is right in "wanting to believe" (for example, Mulder's doubt as orchestrated in "Little Green Men"). Both characters at these points of the series are still responding consistently with their overall attitudes but with respect to the rational weight of evidence as well.

Are Mulder and Scully free to change or adjust their dispositional belief attitudes? If they are, the rational weight of evidence must play an essential part in that phenomenon. And even hard incompatibilists must acknowledge the causal role of evidence in rational changes of attitude, though of course they would not call such changes free. So reasons are either merely causal in rational attitude making, as the hard incompatibilists say (and at least those compatibilists who are determinists), or they are influences compatible with some sense of free rational attitude adjustment.

Thus far we have concentrated only on the subjective side of what constitutes a worldview in studying attitudes that shape it. But any worldview deserving of the name must have an idea of a *world* so shaped. What is meant by the term "world" here?

There appear to be at least two discernible components to an idea of a world (or *universe*, which is the expansive sense we take "world" to mean). One is *metaphysical* or *ontological*. That has to do with what ultimately is real in this world, or what kinds of entities are found in it. When Mulder and Scully first meet, their worldviews are very different in this respect. Mulder believes that the world might well include aliens, spirits, extrasensory perception, and other paranormal phenomena as well as the more mundane material objects of our acquaintance. Scully's world at that time excludes the former exotic stuff in favor of positing only the latter material things that science verifies to exist, such as the elements and forces of chemistry and physics. One overlap between them is that they both ultimately make allowances for theism—that whatever else this world contains, there may well be a God who created it all.[12]

This theistic commitment, which is a commonplace metaphysical feature of most people's worldviews, signals one familiar strategy to integrate the other major component of any worldview. That component is *axiological,* or a sense of the *values* one finds in the universe. All but the most nihilistic worldviews have some sense of what values obtain in the world, from the most basic sense of good and evil in human experience to far-flung accounts of beauty and the meaning of existence itself. Clearly Mulder and Scully share far more axiologically than otherwise in their worldviews, for they have agreeable senses of right and wrong, the nature of good and evil moral character, a high regard for the truth, and both seemed to root these values in some sort of sense of an ultimate ground of being.

The interplay of these two worldview components is a familiar theme in philosophy. *Ethics,* for instance, attempts to see clearly the place of value (if any) in the furniture of the universe. *Philosophy of religion* seeks human value as it relates to the possible existence of God. *Philosophy of science* examines how science studies reality and how value concerns might influence that study. *Metaphysicians* who study free will attempt (as seen above) to see whether that (seemingly) valuable commodity exists, and if so, how.

What philosophy has shown us in these more topical explorations of worldviews is that this interplay of existence and value is one of mutual influence in constructing a picture of the world and its parts. From the philosophy of science, for example, a convincing argument was made by Norwood Hanson that although we tend to sharply distinguish acts of observation from theories we might have about reality more generally, in truth we can't divorce observation from theory, because observation requires interpretation, and theory provides the background for interpretation. One of his examples of this involves the Renaissance figures Johannes Kepler and Tycho Brahe, respectively a Copernican heliocentrist and a Ptolemaic geocentrist, who both might look at the same sunrise. Kepler sees Earth racing east in the direction of the relatively still sun, while Brahe sees an unmoving Earth being overflown by a moving sun. They both in any case see the same thing, which amounts to a new day, yet, what produces that dawn is viewed from very different theories of how the sun and Earth work.[13] Thomas Kuhn (and in a different way, Larry Laudan) argued in addition that one factor influencing which of helio- or geocentrism is held to be correct is itself a function of values the one might hold dear or reject.[14] For example, it seems clear that one reason geocentrism lasted so long was that it was consistent with the traditional value-laden belief that humankind was the center of God's creation, whereas heliocentrism was willing to sacrifice at least a literal interpretation of that belief. Later, an accumulation of other observations from many people (with their own attendant values) swelled into a tsunami of evidence that swamped the anthropocentrism behind geocentrism. That human-laden value could no longer be rationally and literally expressed in terms of the fact of Earth's nonrotation.

Mulder and Scully regularly see the same things going on in the world but the phenomenon often manifests differently for them. For instance, in the episode "Lazarus," Scully is aiding Agent Jack Willis (Christopher Allport), who is also her former lover, in his attempt to catch a modern-day Bonnie-and-Clyde bank-robbing duo, Warren James Dupre (Jason Schombing) and Lula Phillips (Cec Verrell). Both Dupre and Willis are fatally wounded and rushed to the same local hospital. Dupre is presumed dead, but the medical team—and Scully—strives to revive Willis, even

though he's been flatlined for thirteen minutes. At Scully's continued behest, the medical team is finally successful in reestablishing Willis's pulse.
But for the remainder of the episode, Willis acts strangely. In fact, he acts
a lot like Dupre and nothing like Jack Willis. Scully recognizes this. Nevertheless, she resists the conclusion that Willis and Dupre have undergone
some sort of "psychic transference," which is to suggest that Dupre now
inhabits Willis's body. Rather, she concludes that Willis's strange behavior is explained by the fact that he suffers from physical and psychological trauma. After just a bit of investigative work, Mulder soon adopts the
hypothesis that Dupre and not Willis survived the gun battle in the bank.
So, if Scully and Mulder are privy to the same data (and, arguably, Scully
has intimate access to some that Mulder lacks), then why do they interpret
it differently?

Keeping in mind Hanson's position about theory and observation,
recall that Scully's worldview includes placing great value in the explanatory
success of science. From a naturalistic or scientific perspective, it makes
more sense to interpret the data surrounding Willis and Dupre as indicat-
ing that Willis is suffering from trauma and not that Dupre is inhabiting
Willis's body. Interestingly enough, given the title of the episode and Scully's
religious background in the Catholic Church, the viewer might wonder why
Scully isn't more receptive to the idea that the data is supporting a form
of resurrection (especially after her experiences in "Beyond the Sea"). This
might be (and probably is) a case in which the value Scully places on science contravenes the value she places on religion. Mulder, who ironically
isn't all that religious (at least in any conventional sense), is pretty quick to
interpret the data as supporting a resurrection-type hypothesis. Mulder's
interpretation is probably better accounted for by his value-laden belief
that seeking the truth out there sometimes involves an appeal to extreme
possibilities, especially for unexplained phenomena.

What's interesting here is that what is taken to be a fact is a function of
what one values, and one's values are in turn influenced by what one takes
to be the facts. The additional factors of influence are indisputably what
is taken to be "out there"—what our experiences directly show us as we
interpret them and how we take into account the reported experiences of
others. As we tend to see our experiences and these reports as commensu-
rate with our values, our worldview is stable and verified, and as making
sense, rational. But as our experiences conflict with our values, something
has to go, or we risk sliding into incoherence and irrationality. Either we
must adjust the facts as we take them to be within the system of values we

hold (e.g., we surrender geocentrism for heliocentrism), and/or we reorder or jettison parts of the system of values itself (e.g., we abandon belief in God as the basis for anthropocentric values, or, more likely, we retain belief in God and dismantle our strong appeal to anthropocentrism).

Consider Mulder and Scully's worldviews as the series progresses. Both apparently started from a nominally theistic worldview (e.g., as Scully signals in "Revelations" and "All Souls," and yes, apparently even Mulder, who holds his views to his vest throughout the series like unplayed cards, as disclosed in the final episode [see note 13]) with a strong respect for truth and morality. Beyond this intersection of their values, however, they split attitudinally as to how these basic values should be implemented in establishing facts. Mulder often intuitively trusts experience for what it seems to be on its face. If an experience is colored with tinges of supernaturalism, then so be it—there may be more in heaven and earth than in Scully's (naturalistic) philosophy. Scully on the other hand initially distrusts her personal experiences that have that same occult character, on the basis of a more scientific approach that places greater value on collective and interpersonal experiences than potentially deviant personal ones (she recognizes, so to speak, the folly of cold-fusion wishful thinking, even if it is spawned in a lab). What enables them to continue this entangled disagreement is of course the nature of what they are actually dealing with. It involves a massive conspiracy orchestrated from the highest levels of international authority to cover up an ongoing plot by extraterrestrials to dominate the planet. The intricacy of the cover-up, involving deception layered on deception that intrudes into the personal histories of Mulder and Scully, often give both of them ample reason to question the veracity of particular experiences and even their respective root values of belief and skepticism.

Still, as the events and experiences mount through the seasons of the series, it becomes indisputable to both Mulder and Scully that things in the world are not as they have always assumed them to be. Mulder comes to see that even his deep-seated personal beliefs about his own family are erroneous (e.g., his mother's "involvement" with the CSM), and that the government he works for is partly corrupt and manipulating him for secret nefarious purposes. Scully on the other hand comes to see that ordinary and familiar scientific explanations do not work for some phenomena, and that what she took to be the scientific nature of reality had to be vastly expanded to include extremely unusual occurrences and unanticipated realities (as in "The Erlenmeyer Flask," "Redux I and II," and, of course, *Fight the Future*). Both their worldviews change, and both merge more tightly together, especially in their common grasp of a startling and grim truth about the possible course of humanity's fate. And though their adventures and the revelations thereof are not exactly what is termed "normal" or "natural," within the sphere of *The X-Files* universe, it only makes sense that they relent to the evidence, in however tortured a manner it is presented to them, and see the world for what it really and terribly is. Their worldviews change, but within the context of the series, they change rationally.

Mulder and Scully: Free or Unfree?

Does either or both of *The X-Files* protagonists *freely* change worldviews? To formulate a good, conservative answer let's examine one other case of (relatively minor) worldview revision. This one involves an intriguing argument about free will itself and was put forward by the distinguished philosopher Peter van Inwagen.

Van Inwagen has long argued for the truth of libertarianism, by his own admission as an essential feature of a theistic worldview requiring that view of free will. One of his most familiar defenses for the incompatibilism that libertarianism posits is known as "the consequence argument." Though the particulars of this argument need not concern us here, suffice it to say that van Inwagen concludes that closed-future determinism of mind cannot be compatible with what we need for an adequate concept of free will. In other work van Inwagen held that only indeterminism of mind, along with its essential commitment to the need for plural future opportunities of choice, could provide for free will.[15]

That is, until recently, when van Inwagen stirred up the philosophical world by declaring that it appears that indeterminism of mind is *incompatible* with free will as well. His argument essentially shows that given that a mind can choose between at least two different alternatives, there can be no possible way to guarantee that that mind fully *controls* its final selection.[16]

Van Inwagen argues roughly as follows. Assume that indeterminism is true. Then stipulate that someone makes a choice among some group of alternatives, and furthermore allow that the final choice actually made is the most rational one among those alternatives. Can the chooser have good reason to assure anyone (including herself) before (or after) the actual choice that the choice is genuinely *hers* in the sense that she was able to prevent any other possible decision? If the choice process was indeterministic, and thus had to be undertaken with the real possibility that some other choice could be (or could have been) made, this additional fact would force a "no" answer to this question. The open future for an indeterministic choice *means* that any choice alternative, reasonable or not, is genuinely available to the mind making that choice, and thus assurance that the choice somehow *absolutely* rules (or ruled) out the others that are (were) possible cannot be sustained. Another way of saying this is that indeterminism *by definition* appears to block a mind's final ability to control its decisions.

To understand the force of this a bit more, let's go back to one of the strongest responses for the libertarian-indeterminist against the determinist. That response depended on the case that one was faced with two distinct possibilities of choice, but two that were fifty-fifty in the sense that neither was reasonably favored above the other. If the selection of one (heads, say) was realized by mental determinism so that the other really could not occur, then the other (tails) would not be available to that mind. So the unavailable possibility, which would otherwise be as reasonable a choice as the one caused to occur, cannot be one *free* for a reasonable mind to choose. This claim is based on the insight that since what is reasonable seems intuitively an accessible option for choice, if freedom is to be maximally consistent with reasonable possibilities, determinism cannot say that a causal resolution of such a situation is free.

In this ideal situation of different alternatives that are perfectly rationally balanced ones, van Inwagen's complaint about indeterminism is at least diminished a little. For a mind that makes a fifty-fifty toss-up decision can say that its control of what is finally decided is in fact as rational as it can be, for *any* decision it makes is equally rational, and any further control placed upon one alternative against another is thus not justifiable as being a *rational* one. Just as the opportunities are maximal for a rational choice in this case, so is the ability to control such a choice (because this case requires a *minimum* of control for a rational outcome). However, shift to any other case of choice where the alternatives are not perfectly balanced as rational choices. Then van Inwagen's complaint about an indeterministic process of choosing returns with a vengeance.

But here's where the van Inwagen account steers back in the direction of our inquiry about Mulder and Scully. After offering his double-edged incompatibilism of free will with both determinism and indeterminism, van Inwagen declares a curious form of "mysterianism" about free will. That is, he stubbornly believes that people have this freedom (at least sometimes), but he cannot rationally sort out how! This trenchant belief in the face of insufficient reasons can be fairly easily explained from the overall perspective of van Inwagen's worldview. His core belief in God, which for him unites what is ultimately real with what is of ultimate value, cannot let free will slip from the picture of how everything in the universe works. If there were no free will, then people would be either the unwitting pawns of God or some senseless, valueless creatures of God self-deceived into believing that they really have worth and choice. And van Inwagen cannot countenance either option and retain an idea of God as having created us as truly valuable beings. So free will stays in his worldview—even if it can't be understood as part of it.

Is this irrational of van Inwagen? It is too easy just to respond flatly, "Of course." For him, detailed questions about free will are lower-order ones with respect to his worldview, and if his worldview is overall a correct one, then the large-scale need for *some* account of freedom to reconcile God's providence with human value supersedes the specific need for answers to those detailed questions. From the perspective of his worldview, van Inwagen's mysterianism about free will translates into a rational, open-ended question, in which his posited belief in the ultimate meaningfulness of free will is anchored in the rationality of the entire worldview (and therefore kicks the whole question of whether van Inwagen is rational in his mysterianism back to the question of whether his worldview is rational).

Mulder and Scully both exhibit similar mysterian tendencies to believe in something despite not being able to make sense about it throughout the series, and often because such beliefs are required in the context of their worldviews (and specific episodes). Scully's religious belief in God, of course, is basic to her worldview, though she recognizes that it is not always clear even to her that her belief in God makes sense (as in the season 7 episode "Orison").[17] Mulder's belief in the authenticity of his memory of his sister's abduction likewise at some points becomes suspect to him as well (recall "Little Green Men"). Some of these beliefs, as it turns out, are justified, others not, and still others remain open. And, as for van Inwagen, the attitude of faith that carries these beliefs forward only makes sense within the larger sense-making of their worldviews. Their "choices" to continue or to jettison these dicey beliefs are functions of what they take to be sufficient worldview reasons to do so.

However, one real lesson about the nature of these arguably free "choices" can be skimmed off this. If free-will decisions are to be anything really worthwhile, they must be made in the context of reason. For if reasons for making a decision cannot be said to be part of the causes that compatibilists rely on to explain their version of free will, then that form of free will does not yield a rational picture of the mechanisms of mind as they "choose." And equally, if reasons for a decision cannot be aligned with how indeterministic minds arrive at their one alternative from an open future smorgasbord of them, then that account of working minds is not rational. In short, to be valuable, any freedom, compatibilist or incompatibilist, ironically must be slave to reason.

So do Mulder and Scully alter their worldviews of their own free will? We really don't know, and in part because we don't have those final answers to how minds work and what freedom really is. But we do know that in the context of the series, their experiences, and those of others around them, do grow into a force of reason to rationally require them to reshape their worldviews, freely or not. In that respect the Smoking Man as quoted above did have a point: if one actually has good reasons for believing things that any current science cannot embrace, then one might be better off expanding one's worldview beyond that limited perspective. However, unless we throw in with something like a worldview such as van Inwagen's, perhaps we should also say about our *X-Files* heroes that we should be a little more like Scully, and a little less like Mulder, when it comes to strongly believing that free will *must* have played a genuine part in their adventures.

Notes

I thank Dean Kowalski for many suggestions for improvements, though of course any lackluster content is wholly mine; I'm especially grateful for the many opportunities he afforded me to bask in his masterful knowledge of *The X-Files*, which (I would say) abetted my freedom to spout off on this topic.

1. For details of the historical accounts of shifting worldviews, see Saint Augustine, *The Confessions*, bk. 8, http://www.gutenberg.org/etext/3296 (accessed August 20, 2006); Alex Haley, *The Autobiography of Malcolm X* (New York: Grove Press, 1965); for Antoine Lavoisier, http://historyofscience.free.fr/Lavoisier-Friends/a_chap2_lavoisier.html#Phlogiston (accessed August 20, 2006).

2. For examples of philosophers who have held these different respective visions of freedom, see David Hume, *An Enquiry Concerning Human Understanding* (Indianapolis: Hackett, 1977); William James, *The Dilemma of Determinism* (Billings, MT: Kessinger, 2005); John Martin Fischer, *My Way* (New York: Oxford University Press, 2006); Philip Pettit, *A Theory of Freedom* (New York: Oxford University Press, 2001).

3. J. L. Austin, "Ifs and Cans," in *Philosophical Papers* (Oxford: Oxford University Press, 1961).

4. A good contemporary defense of the deterministic view of human nature is Ted Honderich, *A Theory of Determinism* (Oxford: Oxford University Press, 1988). A classic representative of the need for an "open future" for human freedom to exist is Richard Taylor, *Metaphysics,* 4th ed. (New York: Prentice Hall, 1991). It should be noted that Taylor's argument is based on his belief that determinism entails the fatalism of the future. While I am skeptical of the truth of that claim, it nevertheless shows that Taylor believed that a determinist-like closed future is incompatible with freedom.

5. A prominent philosopher who champions combining mind-mechanism with compatibilist freedom is Daniel Dennett, *Elbow Room* (Cambridge, MA: Bradford Books, 1984), and *Consciousness Explained* (New York: Little, Brown, 1991).

6. The astute reader will question whether my various uses of cognates of "prefer" in these two sentences aren't equivocal about the role of control in preference, where the former determinist use means "control by cause" and the latter indeterminist use means "control of all real possibilities." This potential difference between what the disputants mean by "preference" respectively reflects what John Fischer has termed the difference between "reasons control," which is consistent with determinism, and "guidance control," which is not. See Fischer, *My Way.* My ambiguous use of "prefer" is meant to convey a sense of this difference without getting into technicalities. Later, in the section "Mulder and Scully: Free or Unfree?" I submit a more detailed version of this argument put in terms of reasons and control.

7. A good contemporary representative is Derk Pereboom, *Living without Free Will* (Cambridge: Cambridge University Press, 2001).

8. Dean Kowalski quite rightly challenges my apparently unqualified claim that resolving factual, empirical issues about how the mind works might resolve the problem of free will. If my claim is taken to mean that knowing how minds work is a necessary condition for resolving the free will problem, then that would be obviously false, for at least some (if not all) compatibilist concepts of freedom are consistent with both determinism and indeterminism. But any demonstration that the mind works deterministically (or not) would be sufficient to eliminate some views on free will, and to that extent any prospect of discovering the empirical truth about the mind is quite relevant.

9. For an explanation of what I mean by saying the mind is a "confirmation engine," see Karl Popper, *Conjectures and Refutations* (New York: Routledge, 2002). Ultimately I agree with Popper's view that evolution has tended to favor the psychological tendency of minds to see connections in experience, since many such connections about dangers, predators, resources, and the like would promote survival and reproduction. The downside of this, as is part of Popper's point, is that minds are skewed by nature to see connections where there are none.

10. See http://partners.nytimes.com/library/national/science/050399sci-cold-fusion .html (accessed August 20, 2006).

11. For an account of George III's condition, see http://www.dfci.harvard.edu/abo/ news/press/attacks-of-king-george-3rd-madness-linked-to-metabolism-molecule.asp (accessed August 20, 2006).

12. Some readers will be jolted by this claim, since in many episodes Mulder's only open skepticism about anything—and then often in the form of near mockery—concerned Scully's Catholic faith. But this exchange in the final episode undermines Mulder's seeming persistent scorn of traditional theism:

MULDER: "Mm. I've been chasing after monsters with a butterfly net. You heard the man—the date's set [for the alien invasion]. I can't change that."

SCULLY: You wouldn't tell me. Not because you were afraid or broken . . . but because you didn't want to accept defeat.

MULDER: Well, I was afraid of what knowing would do to you. I was afraid that it would crush . . . your spirit.

SCULLY: Why would I accept defeat? Why would I accept it, if you won't? Mulder, you say that you've failed, but you only fail if you give up. And I know you—you can't give up. It's what I saw in you when we first met. It's what made me follow you . . . why I'd do it all over again.

MULDER: And look what it's gotten you.

SCULLY: And what has it gotten you? Not your sister. Nothing that you've set out for. But you won't give up, even now. You've always said that you want to believe. But believe in what, Mulder? If this is the truth that you've been looking for, then what is left to believe in?

MULDER: I want to believe that . . . the dead are not lost to us. That they speak to us . . . as part of something greater than us—greater than any alien force. And if you and I are powerless now, I want to believe that if we listen to what's speaking, it can give us the power to save ourselves.

SCULLY: Then we believe the same thing.

MULDER: Maybe there's hope. ("The Truth," season 9, episode 20)

If we are to take Mulder at his word here, then he always quietly held much the same theistic convictions as Scully—and perhaps only needled her as a form of ironic reversal of her skepticism about the paranormal.

[The fact that Mulder grasps the gold cross Scully wears around her neck in this scene is telling. However, because Mulder often thought that theologians can be just as dogmatic as scientists when it comes to unexplained phenomena, we might alternatively interpret Mulder's scorn for organized religion in "Revelations" and "All Souls" at face value. Mulder's spirituality, as seen in "The Blessing Way" and "The Field Where I Died," might then be the key to understanding Mulder's relevant dialogue to Scully in "The Truth." On this alternative, however, we must conclude that Mulder and Scully don't quite believe in the same thing (Mulder doesn't share her Roman Catholic theism), but they might share a belief in some form of minimalist (yet redemptive) theism.–ed.]

13. Norwood Hanson, *Patterns of Discovery* (New York: Cambridge University Press, 1958), 4–19.

14. Thomas Kuhn, *The Structure of Scientific Revolutions* (Chicago: University of Chicago Press, 1970); Larry Laudan, "Dissecting the Holistic Picture of Science," in

Philosophy of Science: The Central Issues, ed. Martin Curd and J. A. Cover (New York: W. W. Norton, 1998), 159–69. Crudely put, the main difference between these accounts on the issue of value is that Kuhn holds that values guiding scientific worldviews and their parts ("paradigms") are completely relative to those worldviews, while Laudan argues that values can carry over from one worldview to another.

15. Peter van Inwagen, *An Essay on Free Will* (New York: Oxford University Press, 1986).

16. Peter van Inwagen, *"Free Will Remains a Mystery,"* in *The Oxford Handbook of Free Will,* ed. Robert Kane (New York: Oxford University Press, 2002), 158–77.

17. This exchange at the end of the episode (season 7, episode 7) is relevant here, after Scully has killed a murderous psychopath:

MULDER: You can't judge yourself.

SCULLY: Maybe I don't have to.

MULDER: The Bible allows for vengeance.

SCULLY: But the law doesn't.

MULDER: The way I see it . . . he didn't give you a choice. And my report will reflect that . . . in case you're worried. Donnie Pfaster would've surely killed again if given the chance.

SCULLY: He was evil, Mulder. I'm sure about that, without a doubt. But there's one thing that I'm not sure of.

MULDER: What's that?

SCULLY: Who was at work in me? Or what . . . what made me . . . what made me pull the trigger?

MULDER: You mean if it was God?

SCULLY: I mean . . . what if it wasn't?

If it wasn't—was it the Devil, as Scully seems to suggest? Or does she mean to question the very existence of free will?

Postdemocratic Society and the Truth Out There

Richard Flannery and David Louzecky

It's not a war, it's a pageant.
—Robert De Niro to Dustin Hoffman in *Wag the Dog*

A people who mean to be their own governors must arm themselves with the power knowledge gives. A popular government without popular information or the means of acquiring it is but a prologue to a farce or a tragedy or perhaps both.
—James Madison

Do we live in a "postdemocratic" society, a society of illusions where only the gullible believe in anything except their own interests and where the powerful make policy decisions in secret? *The X-Files* raises that possibility in almost every episode. It is our contention that Fox Mulder and Dana Scully both passionately reject this idea. "The truth is out there," and we need it. The problem is finding it, and finding the evidence that will be convincing. Our two detectives illustrate different approaches to solving the truth problem, Scully the orthodox and Mulder the knight-errant, but the search unites them, and they are not content with the search itself, the process. They want answers, and they are willing to take all sorts of chances with their careers, their lives, and their sanity to overcome the obstacles, many of which are the interests of powerful people and organizations in maintaining ignorance and secrecy. Scully and Mulder use their official credentials and positions to be warriors for democracy, truth-out-in-the-open democracy. They provide the sharpest possible contrast with the behavior of so many of our real bureaucrats covering their behinds and obfuscating the truth as a way of life. Do our heroes suggest an agenda and a method of reviving democracy through individual actions instead of institutional reform? We think so.

The X-Files is about one of the most important philosophical problems of our everyday political lives: publicity. The secrecy of contemporary governments is destroying democracy by undermining one of the preconditions without which democracy is not possible. Democracy requires that citizens make informed decisions about public policy; that cannot be done without publicity. If political leaders are making decisions in secret, those decisions are outside the scope of public discussion and argument. They are undemocratic. *The X-Files* is a particularly powerful exploration of this problem. Certainly an invasion by aliens constitutes conditions for secrecy if anything does, and a consortium of political and corporate leaders constitutes the best and the brightest experts to make decisions about how to handle this invasion. Mulder and Scully, however, make heroic efforts to discover the truth and inform all of us. By trying to provide us with what we need to engage in the democratic political process, they demonstrate their own democratic citizenship.

The Show

We should always remember that *The X-Files* is a network television show created in hopes of reaching the mass TV audience for the then fledgling Fox network in the early 1990s. Chris Carter tells us that the series was specifically inspired by one of his own TV favorites, *Kolchak: The Night Stalker*. Darren McGavin, the original Kolchak, even appears in *The X-Files* as Mulder's predecessor at the FBI. *The Night Stalker* was a TV tribute to the famous noir films of the 1940s. These are low-budget, black-and-white movies, mostly thrillers and mysteries. The films are called "noir" because they are very dark, shot at night with a heavy use of light and shadow. They are also dark in terms of what's happening, the motives of the characters, the incomplete explanations, the interference in the plot by powerful outside forces, and the violence, which in these films is likely to be directed at the lead characters as well as the victims. Sound like *The X-Files*? Notice that Scully and Mulder are repeatedly beaten, abducted, and abused. Unlike Arnold Schwarzenegger or Bruce Willis, however, they rarely hurt anyone, and Mulder and Scully are often running *away*. *The X-Files* isn't really noir; the stars of those movies were at best antiheroes. Their main motives were likely to be survival or revenge. Mulder and Scully are heroes. They could save themselves by just walking away from the X-Files and getting on with promising FBI careers. That's exactly what their enemies and their FBI bosses want them to do. But not these two. Flashlights in hand, they persist. They want truth and justice, and they want *us* to find out what's going on. We're rooting for them because they're on our side. It's television.

Television shows originate in Hollywood even when they're filmed in Vancouver. Hollywood guys like Carter are not trying to impress us with their erudition and sophistication. They're trying to get us to watch again next week. They use things they think the audience already knows or feels. Carter is trying to scare the pants off us because he knows we like scary movies. He has decided to make extraterrestrials an important part of the series, but he doesn't invent a new story about aliens. He relies on the most well-known myths, Roswell and alien abduction, to construct his plot. Many of the visual images in *The X-Files* come directly from Steven Spielberg's blockbuster *Close Encounters of the Third Kind*. See the dancing lights? See the totally massive alien ships that fill the screen?

If *The X-Files* has political content, as we're arguing here, what does Carter figure the TV audience knows and feels about politics? Remember, this is the early 1990s, long before Fox News decided to grab audience share by becoming a Republican version of *Pravda*. (*Pravda* [Truth] was the old official Communist Party newspaper in the Soviet Union). Carter figures, just like most social scientists, that the mass audience neither knows nor cares much about politics, and conventional political talk irritates and bores them. So he doesn't bother with it; politics will turn people (and their TV sets) off. Social scientists call this "depoliticization," and few would contest that the American TV audience of the early 1990s was depoliticized. It became quite fashionable to think that politics was just plain irrelevant in face of the "new" technology and the "new" economy. A new "global" society was emerging, and the old structures and ideas were just obsolete. See *New York Times* columnist Thomas Friedman's famous 1990s book *The Lexus and the Olive Tree* for a characteristic presentation of these themes; better still, check out the cover stories of the country's newsmagazines of that era.[1]

Notice how little all this matters in *The X-Files;* it's not discussed and it's rarely mentioned. Does that mean we're making all this up and seeing things in the show that just aren't there? No, because *The X-Files* offers a counterview to all this conventional wisdom week after week. People are oblivious because they're living in a dream world—not a "real" dream world like *The Matrix*, but a decadent and uninformed dream world like

The Titanic. They don't know because the truth—which *is* out there—is being kept from them by powerful forces inside and outside their government and the other governments and this has been going on for a long time. The television audience doesn't have to feel stupid; people and institutions have betrayed them. Mulder and Scully are trying to save the day by bringing the truth to the light of day. Once the folks find out, they will presumably do the right thing because democracy will go to work. (Would the folks really do the right thing if democracy *could* work? More on that below.) *But* democracy can't start without truthful public information; it will be a sham—our point exactly.

For many years a staple of political science texts about U.S. politics has been a discussion of the "trust and confidence" question. This is a question asked by pollsters: Can you trust the government all of the time, most of the time, some of the time, or almost never? Back in the olden days of Truman and Ike and JFK, Americans used to respond "all the time" and "most of the time," most often in the range of 60 to 70 percent. Then in the days of Vietnam and Watergate public confidence fell off the cliff. Everyone figured it was understandable: people found out the government had been lying. But Watergate and Vietnam faded into history books and public confidence remained low. Why? There were contending explanations. It was the media, which were always debunking everything. It was the economy—the median income remained about the same from the early 1970s to the late 1990s after thirty years of rising fairly steadily—and people were blaming the government, following the view of politicians like President Ronald Reagan, who told them government was the problem. Some said that both the people and the media lived in a new age in which pessimism was replacing traditional USA optimism. As Chris Carter started *The X-Files* in September 1993, he had every reason to think the mass audience would *not* be put off by a story that depended on a basic premise that the government was engaged in a massive cover-up. Just to make sure his audience remembers, Carter calls Mulder's first inside source Deep Throat, a nickname Watergate reporters Bob Woodward and Carl Bernstein used for their inside source. Most of America knows about that. We even had a big movie about it: *All the President's Men,* starring Robert Redford and Dustin Hoffman.[2]

In the world of *The X-Files* how has the cover-up been maintained? Partly, the forces protecting the secrets have used their government and corporate powers to hide things. They intimidate people into silence by threatening their livelihoods and families. They have also been enormously successful at discrediting the truth-tellers. Why don't Mulder and Scully just go to the newspapers? The newspapers won't touch their story without the same kind of evidence that Scully keeps telling Mulder he hasn't got, the kind of proof that could be presented in a courtroom. Mulder knows a lot of the truth, but he's desperate to get the "proof" that will convince others, beginning with Scully. There is a free press in the United States, but it is caught up with being respectable and conventional. It trusts conventional sources and conventional evidence *not* renegade FBI agents with axes to grind. Very few reporters show up in *The X-Files* as intrepid truth-seekers. Instead, Chris Carter has the Lone Gunmen, unofficial and unrespectable hackers. He anticipates the bloggers and Web sites of today with these often comic but indispensable allies. So the free press is there, but its business-as-usual approach is an impediment to getting at the deeper secrets.

In the episode "The Blessing Way" Albert Hosteen (Floyd Westerman), who saves Mulder, does a little soliloquy explaining that Native Americans have come to trust memory rather than history because history can be, and has been, controlled by dangerous men with their own agendas. History is about documents and official reports, the kind of thing the Cigarette Smoking Man and the Well-Manicured Man and their associates can and do manipulate every week. We've recently learned (once again) how skeptical we need to be about government-sponsored reports after the revelations about the falsity and exaggeration of the "intelligence" reported concerning Saddam Hussein's famous weapons of mass destruction. Important writers for the country's two flagship newspapers, the *New York Times* and the *Washington Post*, were in collusion with government advocates of an attack on Iraq. The writers of the eighteenth and nineteenth centuries such as Immanuel Kant and Jeremy Bentham and Thomas Jefferson and even John Stuart Mill assumed that a constitutionally free press guaranteed that the truth would come out. In our own time we have discovered that a comfortable establishment mass media monopolizing most of the normal ways people get their information can have problems truth-telling and truth-seeking.[3]

Noble Lies

Alfred North Whitehead, one of the greatest philosophers of the twentieth century, said, "The safest general characterization of the European philosophical tradition is that it consists of a series of footnotes to Plato."[4] That's an exaggeration, of course, but only a slight one, and only slightly less of one than saying that politics is also a series of footnotes to Plato. In the interest of social stability and absolute loyalty Plato thought it was not just permissible but necessary for rulers to lie to their subjects.[5] These lies are noble because instead of trying to advance their personal wealth or status, the rulers are trying to advance the interests of the citizens. In our recent political history Watergate is the most widely discussed example of the noble lie. President Nixon, as well as the other members of his administration, was engaging in deception on several levels, but while he was drowning, Nixon claimed that no one intended to profit from the deceptions; they had the interests of the citizens in mind. Nixon thought that the president needed to do what had to be done to defeat our communist adversaries in the cold war. He also believed that his Democratic opponent, George McGovern, was soft on communism and would betray the country. Many agreed with Nixon, later regretting that he had "gone too far," "crossed the line," but not that he was wrong in principle.

Similarly in *The X-Files,* the leaders who are lying and secretive are not trying to enrich themselves. Like Plato they think the citizens must be deceived for their own good. They are engaged in a noble lie. Not only does calling a character Deep Throat recall Watergate, but also the Cigarette Smoking Man keeps filing evidence that Mulder and Scully gather from their investigations and provides some protection for them at crucial junctures because they provide him with the best data about the matters that the noble lie is designed to hide—and perhaps because, like Vietnam-era secretary of defense Robert McNamara, he thinks the truth should eventually be made known in a democratic society. He must take great care, however, to prevent Mulder or Scully from turning into a Daniel Ellsberg, who was working on and archiving "the Pentagon Papers" as a secret study for the Pentagon civilian and military brass when he decided to take his "x-file" to the media.[6]

We were engaged in the Vietnam War, and Ellsberg thought that citizens in a democratic society should know how and why we got into that war. Making that material public was essential to inform us; otherwise, we couldn't make good decisions about whether and how to continue or end the war. Our leaders thought that if we were informed, we would make decisions so bad that society would be destabilized. Even McNamara thought that the truth should be told only eventually, after our having the information could not interfere with the decisions of the leaders. The Pentagon Papers would provide the material for an interesting historical narrative, but in order to learn from history, we have to be able to apply it—and that requires being *fully* informed about the current situation.[7]

For all of that, in the episode "Conduit" the mother asks Mulder why it's always so important that the truth be known. That's a hard question that reminds us that when the philosopher Baruch Spinoza was asked by the charwoman who cleaned the building where he lived whether he believed in God, he answered, "Yes, of course." His lie was comforting and perhaps justifiable. Nevertheless, we don't have the greatest respect for people who need comforting lies. Suppose we discovered that tens of thousands of our fellow citizens and millions of the citizens of other countries were killed in Vietnam and Iraq for unjustifiable reasons. It would hurt deeply and irrevocably. Nevertheless, the truth must be known if we are to make responsible policy decisions. The condescending sympathy that just might pass in personal relationships has no place in political life.

The X-Files is an interesting, exciting, and compelling dramatic discussion of one of the most pressing political problems of the modern age: publicity or secrecy? Will we demand that our leaders provide the information we need to make rational decisions about how we are governed, or will we tolerate noble lies when our leaders think we are incapable of handling the truth? No one will tolerate lies concocted to enrich the rulers and their cronies. The question is whether we will tolerate the noble lies told in our interest, to promote social stability and loyalty. This chapter argues that we should not. Publicity is a fundamental and necessary condition of democracy because democracy assumes that citizens are making informed decisions about public policies.[8] Insofar as we tolerate noble lies, we undermine democracy.[9]

It is difficult to determine whether the deceptions involved in our invasion of Iraq were intended to enrich some large organizations or protect us from terrorism, because the information we need to make that determination has not been made public. The beauty of *The X-Files* as dramatic political philosophy is that the element of personal and organizational enrichment has been effectively eliminated, leaving us with the uncluttered question about the connections among noble lies, publicity, and democracy. In *The X-Files* we are being visited (invaded) by aliens, and the corporate-government consortium, the Syndicate, is engaged in a series of programs to deal with the situation. Should we be informed, have a public discussion, and decide on policies—or are we incapable? Would being informed lead to panic and chaos—instability and disloyalty?

Plato thought that the people of his ideal society needed to be told they were put in their various (mostly subordinate) social roles because of their genetic profiles. This was his infamous "myth of the metals" (414b–415d). Believing that their subordination was inevitable and "natural," he thought, would keep the people in line. The most fundamental argument against democracy is that people are too stupid to make important decisions about the way society should function. They will make huge mistakes (Plato thought democracy meant that people would decide to do what their "passions" told them to do) and there will be chaos and disaster. Nowadays, most everyone believes in democracy in general because nobody has much confidence that there is any special ruling elite produced by lineage or schooling that is a better judge of things than the citizens are. Nevertheless, Plato's undemocratic argument lives on in the view that there are some decisions that need to be made in secret and sometimes kept secret because the decisions are just too technical for people to understand, or else (as in the case of *The X-Files*) letting the big news out would cause panic and chaos that would hurt everybody. Think what would happen to the stock markets!

What about this idea that democracy is dangerous because the seething, panicky masses will run amok when they find out? First of all, people who believe in democracy believe that it's the only kind of politics that can possibly justify people obeying the laws and observing the rules. John Rawls made this argument in great detail in his book *A Theory of Justice,* and there's hardly a political philosopher anywhere outside of the Islamic fundamentalists who disagrees with his "first principle," the first statement of which is: "Each person is to have an equal right to the most extensive basic liberty compatible with a similar liberty for others."[10] Beyond this ethical reason for democracy there are some good practical reasons for it. Democracy generates consent: people make the rules, and they have ways to change the rules using their political institutions. You don't have to have a bloodbath to get rid of a bad ruler like Claudius in *Hamlet.* Leak it to the newspapers, haul him into court, have an election. There's less drama, but there's much more order because people can go about their business. They are "represented" by the whole design of democracy. (Sure, plenty of people are overrepresented and underrepresented in the real democracies we all know, including the United States, but the solution isn't less democracy, but more.)

What would happen if the big secret of the alien invasion got out? It would be a big media event, no doubt, and some people would panic. We can be pretty sure that most people would demand that the government "do something" about it as with AIDS or the September 11 attacks. Furthermore, the people would want to know what their government was doing, but most people wouldn't want to know too much about the details—that's what Congress and the papers and all those interest groups are for. And they might not mind if the government kept some stuff it was doing secret *if* the secrecy was necessary to fool the aliens, for example, in order to develop the antidote to the "black oil." Did America fall apart on 9/11? No; most people thought the country became more united and resolved and public-minded. So the big chaos the Cigarette Smoking Man and his coconspirators seem to expect is a myth of their own imagination not supported by what we know about how big democratic societies work.

Would the decisions made by the government democratically be better or worse than those made by the Syndicate Mulder is trying to expose? There is no way of knowing for sure, but the decisions would have to consider the broad interests of the public or at least appear to take those into account. It's dubious that a democratic government could possibly agree to a scheme that would make most people slaves of the aliens, for instance. Please notice, however, that a democratic government would have a far better chance of organizing vast resources to foil the alien invasion *and* it would be in a much better position to make and keep some deal with the aliens if that's what it decided to do, because it would have public support. Our point is that elitism arguments about the necessity of nondemocracy in some special cases usually don't turn out to be very convincing on either philosophical or pragmatic grounds.

Bentham and Kant on Publicity and Democracy

We all tend to focus on the benefits of democracy and slight the underlying conditions that make democracy possible. We enjoy being able to worship freely and speak our minds. We are irritated by technological, governmental, and corporate invasions of our privacy. We like to think we are equal to all of our fellow citizens and will be treated justly by the system. The benefits of democracy are seen and experienced daily, but the underlying conditions, being less visible, are easier to miss. Freedom and privacy, equality and justice are fundamental values and *benefits* of democracy, whereas publicity and rationality, also fundamental values, are *necessary conditions* of democracy. We cannot have a democratic society without publicity and rationality.

In *Spheres of Justice,* Michael Walzer characterizes democracy this way:

> The citizens must govern themselves. "Democracy" is the name
> of this government, but the word doesn't describe anything like a
> simple system; nor is democracy the same thing as simple equal-
> ity. Indeed, government can never be simply egalitarian, for at any
> given moment, someone or some group must decide this or that
> issue and then enforce the decision, and someone else or some
> other group must accept the decision and endure the enforce-
> ment. Democracy is a way of allocating power and legitimating its
> use. . . . What counts is argument among the citizens.[11]

Argument among the citizens is essential to democracy, and that argument cannot be legitimate unless it is informed. By its nature argument is
rational, and the citizens cannot be informed without publicity enabling
public scrutiny. Leaders must make public the information that citizens
need to make rational policy decisions.

Since those in power are conspiring to deceive, there is ample room for
conspiracy theories in discussing *The X-Files*. "Suspicion always attaches to
mystery. It thinks it sees a crime where it beholds an affectation of secrecy;
and it is rarely deceived," says Jeremy Bentham. A bit later he points out
that "secrecy is an instrument of conspiracy; it ought not therefore, to be
the system of a regular government." Conspiracies are great fun to discuss
at cocktail parties, but they are distracting, for the aim here is noble—saving us from panic, chaos, and disastrous actions. Remember, in *The X-Files*
we are not engaged in invading a foreign country for empire or profit; we
are being invaded by foreign powers—but not by an identifiable country,
by aliens. That's even scarier than terrorists.[12]

We shouldn't be flip, for many think that the danger of terrorists justi-
fies secrecy. In *The Lesser Evil*, Michael Ignatieff argues that "while open
proceedings are fallible, they at least create the possibility for correcting
error." Later he says, "The war waged against terror since September 11 puts
a strain on democracy itself, because it is mostly waged in secret, using
means that are at the edge of both law and morality. . . . Openness in any
process where human liberty is at stake is simply definitional of what a
democracy is." Nevertheless, "we are faced with evil people, and stopping
them may require us to reply in kind. If so, how do we keep lesser evils
from slipping into greater ones?" Although Ignatieff doesn't recommend
a noble lie, he does sanction secrecy. We avoid destroying democracy, he
thinks, by not being secret about the secrecy—and not making it permanent: "Electorates and legislators are invariably told by their leaders, 'If you

only knew what we know. . . .' But this is not good enough. It is the very nature of democracy that we *should* know what they know. It may not always be possible to know immediately: a government can be justified in withholding information on a sensitive operation if disclosure would actually jeopardize lives. But the justification for secrecy can be only temporary, not permanent." *The X-Files* is about this perennial and fundamental philosophical problem, publicity in a democratic society—a problem that is particularly urgent right now.[13]

The term "publicity" is part of a long democratic tradition and is defended by the most prominent members of both the teleological and deontological camps. That is, to decide political policies in a principled way, we consider two different sorts of things: the consequences of the policies and the rights of the participants. If we let the consequences override the rights, we are deciding teleologically; if we let the rights override the consequences, we are deciding deontologically. When teleologists and deontologists disagree, matters get really tough. However, both Jeremy Bentham (teleologist) and Immanuel Kant (deontologist) are clearly in agreement about the fundamental necessity for publicity (albeit for different reasons). In his essay "On Publicity" Bentham has this to say: "The greater the number of temptations to which the exercise of political power is exposed, the more necessary is it to give to those who possess it, the most powerful reasons for resisting them. But there is no reason more constant and more universal than the superintendence of the public. . . . [If] it be impossible that any thing should be done which is unknown to the nation . . . you take away all the weapons of discontent." The suggestion to "take away all the weapons of discontent" contrasts sharply with the views of Plato, who recommends the noble lie as necessary for political stability. Bentham continues: "That a secret policy saves itself from some inconveniences I will not deny; but I believe that in the long run it creates more than it avoids; and that of two governments, one of which should be conducted secretly and the other openly, the latter would possess a strength, a hardihood, and a reputation which would render it superior to all the dissimulations of the other." It is worth remembering that democratic countries have in fact done much better than their adversaries in the wars of recent history even though they haven't been as effective at keeping secrets.[14]

In dealing with some objections to publicity Bentham points out that the main one is that "the public is an incompetent judge. . . . This then is the reasoning of the partisans of mystery:—you are incapable of judging, because you are ignorant; and you shall remain ignorant, that you may be incapable of judging." There are of course exceptions to publicity, and one of the important philosophical problems is to specify with some clarity what they are. Here are Bentham's suggestions: (1) when it favors the projects of enemies, (2) when it unnecessarily injures innocent persons, and (3) when it inflicts too severe a punishment on the guilty. And that's the rub: if the aliens know that we are working on a vaccine for their virus, then publicity may be counterproductive. But the double rub is that the Syndicate has already decided for us exactly how we will respond to the alien invasion. And that is unacceptable in a democratic society.[15]

In *To Perpetual Peace* Kant sets out six conditions for perpetual peace among peoples and nations. As the translator and commentator Ted Humphrey says about Kant's view, "Publicity is the context and goal of political life, to seek and preserve peace. . . . In this way, citizens exercise their free rationality openly. . . . Publicity provides the only context for true civic life." Since Kant grounds his metaphysics of morals on rationality itself, aliens are clearly included if they possess rationality, and the ones in *The X-Files* do possess rationality. Anyone familiar with Kant's categorical imperative would expect exactly the formulation that Kant gives this underlying condition of democracy: "All actions that affect the rights of other men are wrong if their maxim [description] is not consistent with publicity."[16]

Modern and Postmodern

Much of the discussion of *The X-Files* among philosophers has been about epistemology and metaphysics. Epistemology is about knowledge, belief, truth, and reasons—what they are and how we get them. To disagree about whether "the truth is out there" is to disagree about what's real. That's metaphysics. Mulder and Scully seem to be using different epistemological methods to find the truth, and they frequently come to different conclusions about what's real. Scully is scientific and gets everything wrong. Mulder is wild and crazy, postmodern, and gets things right. Wrong. They are both modern and scientific. They both pay attention to empirical evidence and hypotheses. They are both careful. They both think "the truth is out there." And Scully gradually comes round to alien hypotheses. "Gradually" is the operative term: she's responsible—she comes around only after her more conventional and conservative hypotheses fail to fit the evidence. When, in the film *Fight the Future,* she tells Mulder that she plans to quit because she's been hindering him, he points out, only a bit romantically, that she's been not just helpful but necessary: "Your strict rationalism has kept me honest." As far as we can tell, there is no postmodern epistemology or metaphysics here.

Modernism, sometimes called the Enlightenment, begins with the scientific revolution. People always gathered evidence and reasoned, but in the seventeenth century, or a little before, they began organizing the practice and paying more attention to it. Some think that modernism, the enlightenment project, has failed and want to replace it with what they call "postmodernism," one tenet of which is that "the truth is *not* out there." For us moderns, the truth is out there, and our task is to figure out what it is. The postmodernists make up the truth to serve their interests and impose it on what is out there.

Every couple of years there is a spate of media articles about the differences in textbooks from country to country: The Japanese story (interpretation) of the Second World War is different from the Chinese story. We usually judge the quality of *their* stories by comparing them with *ours*. This is not postmodernism; it's jingoistic educational propaganda. To be modern is to think that an accurate and complete description of the Second World War is possible. The problem is that we don't have all the evidence and never will. That means we either honestly admit our ignorance—or fill in the gaps with a story, called a historical narrative. Since multiple narratives are consistent with the evidence, we have to choose among them, if we want one. How? Postmodernists would never be so sleazy as to choose a narrative for a government to use for indoctrination. Their narrative choice will be dictated by some grand value, like equality, justice, or democracy.[17] The postmodernists add one more metaphysical point: there is no truth out there beyond their morally laudable narrative. This claim is backed with an epistemological point: not only don't we have all the evidence, not only can't we get all the evidence, but talking about even the possibility of getting all the evidence is incoherent because our understanding is confined to some narrative or other.[18]

There is a great deal more to postmodernism than this, but it is perfectly clear that *The X-Files* is not a gripping epistemological conflict between a modern Scully and a postmodern Mulder. They are both moderns: they both think the truth is out there, gather evidence, and reason from that evidence. Mulder begins with wilder hypotheses. As Scully is exposed to evidence that doesn't fit her conventional hypotheses, she too begins to move toward wilder alternatives. This is standard, modern scientific practice. Just think about wormholes and superstrings with thirteen (or is it eleven?) dimensions. In addition, Scully especially is thinking about what will hold up in court. Nevertheless, she fills her reports with data and speculations that don't meet the courtroom criteria. As a result she must face the exasperation and derision of her colleagues and superiors (as in "Squeeze," "Gethsemane," and "Redux I and II"). The real problems faced by Scully and Mulder are not epistemological; they are political.[19]

Questions about postmodern politics are still more complicated and controversial than those about epistemology and metaphysics. If the truth is not out there to be discovered, then the alternative is to adopt a narrative that satisfies our interests—whether that model be scientific or political. Well, not exactly *our* interests but the interests of the powerful, for while high-minded academics may be devoted to democracy, the narratives (e.g., those of war, and energy and environment) in terms of which policy is conducted are the narratives of those in power. In a case of art imitating life, the wise Navajo Albert Hosteen (Floyd Westerman) in "Blessing Way" tells us:

> There is an ancient Indian saying that something lives only as long as the last person who remembers it. My people have come to trust memory over history. Memory, like fire, is radiant and immutable while history serves only those who seek to control it, those who douse the flame of memory in order to put out the dangerous fire of truth. Beware these men for they are dangerous themselves and unwise. Their false history is written in the blood of those who might remember and of those who seek the truth.

We have the same narrative problem with Iraq that we've had with Vietnam. When Osama Bin Laden was fighting the Soviets (with our help), he was a freedom fighter; now he's a terrorist. Since the narrative that governs policy is the narrative that furthers the interests of those in power, postmodernism is postdemocratic . . .

Postmodernism, like Plato's views, is a matter of academic discussion, but *The X-Files* is about one of the most important political problems of our everyday lives: publicity. The secrecy of contemporary governments and corporations is destroying democracy, not in the sense of replacing modern democracy with something called postmodern democracy, but in the more mundane sense of violating one of the conditions without which democracy is not possible. Without rationality and publicity we don't have democracy; we have rule by the powerful. Most leaders think that they know better than the citizens. And in Plato's *Republic*, a founding document of Western politics, we find the justification for the noble lie that they use to lead undemocratically. Thus, through Plato and postmodernism some might lead us to postdemocratic political society. We can either "resist or serve," as the infamous tag line of "The Red and the Black" says.

The focus on epistemology among philosophers is not surprising. After Descartes, almost everything else in philosophy became peripheral to epistemology. Nevertheless, it is still a bit surprising because in 1971, John Rawls brought philosophers back to taking an interest in politics and ethics, and he is perfectly clear, again and again, in both *A Theory of Justice* and *Political Liberalism,* that publicity is essential for a good society, which is one in which free and equal citizens cooperate fairly. Public reason characterizes persons in public roles, is about public goods, and is based on public ideas. Freedom and justice depend on public reason and public justifiability. In addition, contrary to Plato, public reason is necessary for social stability.[20]

Safety and Information

"Safety from external danger is the most powerful director of national conduct. Even the ardent love of liberty will after a time, give way to its dictates.... To be more safe ... [nations] at length become willing to run the risk of being less free," says Alexander Hamilton in *Federalist Paper 8.* "The vast secrecy system shows no signs of receding," wrote Senator Daniel Patrick Moynihan three years before 9/11, and we suspect there has been a great increase since then in secrecy, including the secret monitoring of citizens. When information of the greatest importance for the conduct of our public lives is kept secret, we can always blame the media. They should do a better job. But the primary fault lies elsewhere: with a system of information management and with all of us as democratic citizens.[21]

The X-Files focuses on the problem of secrecy, but it also dramatizes another problem of information in democratic society. Much public information in our country is generated by government agencies and news organizations. The process these organizations use to create and manage information from the facts they gather is not simple. There seem to be several steps:

1. Which stories deserve investigation? Should the X-Files Unit of the FBI remain open? Which cases can Mulder investigate, and which must he leave alone?

2. How should the investigations be managed? Is the proper focus on physical evidence or eyewitnesses? Whose testimony counts? Who is credible? Scully and Mulder are forever wrangling about these issues.

3. What parts of the total amount of information should be included in the report? One of Scully's jobs is to report the results of the investigation to the bosses back at the bureau.

4. How should the evidence be interpreted? Mulder "wants to believe," but Scully is skeptical. Beyond our two heroes, what is the FBI position? The bosses frequently meet in little panels to roast the latest report from the X-Files Unit.

5. What should be done with the information and analysis? Mulder and Scully's investigations are usually buried, but what if they were released and democratic institutions had to deal with the alien threat? Would there be a "war on aliens"? Is that the reason the conspirators don't want the secrets to get out? We have tried to deal with this hypothetical question above.

Each of these steps offers the possibility for confusion, conflict, and the distortion of information. In *The X-Files* the major problem is that the conspiracy (the Syndicate) is actively sabotaging the investigation, but even if there were no sabotage at all, there would be serious problems in generating accurate information from such a process.

If you'd like confirmation that all this conflict about information procedure portrayed in *The X-Files* is real and significant, there's no better place to look than *The 9/11 Commission Report.* The FBI and other government agencies produced information that could have, and probably should have, foiled "the planes operation" of Al-Qaeda, but it wasn't processed or managed well enough.[22]

Philosophers have probably not analyzed this aspect of public information nearly as much as it deserves. It's not just observers and facts; it's the political process by which "information" is created that bears on the truth and accuracy of the information. How is it that Hollywood guys like Chris Carter can be sensitive to this aspect of our political life? We suspect the reason is that movies and TV shows are created by a similar collaborative process in which many individuals and many agendas are involved. It is part of their own daily routine, so they're alive to it when they see it in other places.

Democratic Behavior

The character of Walter Skinner may be the closest to real life of all *The X-Files* personae. He's a recognizable character, the sincere bureaucrat who wants to do the right thing. Skinner has many scenes with the Cigarette Smoking Man. It is always obvious that Skinner's skin is crawling. How dare this interloper use and manipulate *his* agency? He'd like to throttle the Smoking Man, but he has to deal with him. Skinner protects our heroes more than anyone else, but there are limits and conditions to his assistance. Mulder and Scully need to do things the FBI way or he can't help them. Mulder especially chafes at Skinner's caution and priorities and rules.

Mulder and Scully provide us with models of democratic political behavior. Democracy has always depended on the willingness, indeed eagerness, of persons to act as responsible individuals in the face of large organizations. In dramatic cases from Nuremberg to My Lai we recognize that "I was just following orders" does not cut it as a response from citizens. They must be willing to get informed, to reason, and to act in the face of opposition. Few of us will find ourselves at Nuremberg or My Lai, but we are all members of large organizations that function much better when we "follow the procedures," as Scully is forever being told and reminding Mulder. But our responsibility as citizens and especially as members of large organizations is not to simply follow procedures and file reports. The responsibility of the agents of the FBI is to investigate and ferret out the truth. This is one message of *The 9/11 Commission Report,* and it was corroborated by the trial of the executives at Enron. Officials of public and corporate institutions need to be loyal to the larger democratic mission of their organizations if our society is going to work well. In another case of art imitating life, in "Deep Throat" Deep Throat tells Mulder that sometimes the truth needs to be kept from the public, at least for a while. It's both a claim and a warning, but Mulder, democratic hero that he is, investigates anyway.

Real or pretended dangers prompt secrecy and restrictions on publicity. If we intend to keep our democracy safe from consortiums of corporate and government leaders who undermine it to suit their convenience and their power, then we all need to model our behavior after Skinner, Scully, and Mulder both as citizens and as members of large organizations. They are the heroes of our time. The truth is out there. Our task as democratic citizens is to find it and make it public. In this way, we can resist becoming a postdemocratic society.

Notes

We would like to thank Jon and Ruth Jordan, editors of *Crimespree Magazine,* and Lynn Gordon, Tamara McNulty, and Tom Zillner for their help in preparing this chapter.

1. Thomas L. Friedman, *The Lexus and the Olive Tree: Understanding Globalization* (New York: Farrar, Straus & Giroux, 1999).

2. Do watch the movie *All the President's Men;* it's great fun and an important part of our political history; so is the book by the same title. President Richard Nixon, a Republican, was running for reelection and, fearing that he might not win, authorized the break-in at the headquarters of the Democratic opposition in the Watergate, a hotel/office building in Washington, D.C. The burglary was bungled, and the local police considered it just a burglary. But two fledgling reporters, Woodward and Bernstein, on the Washington crime beat, witnessed the arraignment of the burglars, men in suits with past FBI and CIA connections, and suspected something bigger was afoot. So, with the support of Ben Bradlee, editor of the *Washington Post,* they pursued the investigation that eventually implicated the president of the United States. Facing the likelihood of impeachment, Nixon resigned. Interestingly, there was no need for the burglary, for Nixon was far ahead of his rival, George McGovern. This episode does not speak well of the caliber of our political leaders and provides a forceful example in favor of a policy of publicity.

3. See, e.g., W. Lance Bennett, *News: The Politics of Illusion,* 7th ed. (New York: Longmans, 2006); and Robert W. McChesney, *The Problem of the Media: U.S. Communication Politics in the Twenty-First Century* (New York: Monthly Review Press, 2004).

4. Alfred North Whitehead, *Process and Reality* (1929; New York: Harper & Row, 1960), 63.

5. Plato, *The Republic of Plato,* trans. Francis MacDonald Cornford (London: Oxford University Press, 1941), 105–7. Since there are almost as many editions of Plato's dialogues as there are of the Bible, the easiest way to find passages is by using Stephanus numbers, from the complete Renaissance edition of Plato's works by a man named Stephanus; they are like chapters and verses in the Bible. The "noble lie" passage is found at 414b–515d.

6. The Pentagon Papers really are akin to an x-file. They were a secret history of our entrance into, and conduct of, the Vietnam War and recorded all of our deceptions about the reasons for entering the war, the body counts of people killed, and the failure of our relocation programs. As in Iraq, we talked about it as a war to win the hearts and minds of the people. There are of course many differences; however, both sets of documents, Mulder's and Ellsberg's, are about government and corporate secrecy that prevents people from being informed and participating in democratic decision making. See Daniel Ellsberg, *Secrets: A Memoir of Vietnam and the Pentagon Papers* (New York: Viking, 2002).

In the episode "Red Museum" the government is using a vegetarian religious sect as a control group to conduct experiments with exotic chemicals on the rest of the residents and then destroys (almost) all the evidence when the experiment begins to go badly. As usual Mulder is left suspecting, but unable to prove, what was going on. Did this plot come to Carter in a dream? Probably not. If you think *The Manchurian Candidate* is just a cool movie, you should read John D. Marks, *The Search for the Manchurian Candidate: The CIA and Mind Control* (New York: W. W. Norton, 1991); and Martin A. Lee and Bruce Shlain, *Acid Dreams: The Complete Social History of LSD—The CIA, the Sixties, and Beyond* (New York: Grove, 1986). Interestingly, much of the evidence was destroyed here too. Someone must have suspected that it wasn't right.

7. Regarding our involvement in Vietnam, recall that President Dwight Eisenhower began supplying various sorts of noncombat support to the South Vietnamese in their war with the North Vietnamese, and President John Kennedy increased that support. During the Johnson administration one of our ships, which was supplying the South Vietnamese with intelligence, was fired on in the Gulf of Tonkin. President Lyndon Johnson went on TV and misled the American people. Secretary of Defense Robert McNamara went before Congress and misled the legislators, twice: first, he said that we had not been supplying intelligence support for the South Vietnamese, and second, he said that our ships were attacked a second time. Largely on the basis of his deceitful testimony and the president's televised address, Congress virtually unanimously passed the Gulf of Tonkin resolution, which gave President Johnson permission to bomb North Vietnam and commit American ground troops to the war. Just change "Vietnam" to "Iraq" and "Gulf of Tonkin" to "weapons of mass destruction," and we move right into the second Bush administration. In both cases the major media had good reason to suspect that the administrations were engaged in deception, yet they wholeheartedly supported the administrations' interest in going to war. If we don't have responsible media, we can't be informed, and if we can't be informed, we can't have democracy. If, instead of hiding behind the cloak of national security, presidents were required to conduct this sort of business in public, we would never stand for it. Publicity would go a long way toward improving our lives politically and every other way. See Tom Wells, *The War Within: America's Battle over Vietnam* (New York: Backinprint.com, 2005); and Daniel C. Hallin, *The "Uncensored War": The Media and Vietnam* (Berkeley: University of California Press, 1989).

8. Perhaps the most vivid example of this from the show is "The Pine Bluff Variant." A faction deep within the CIA works covertly through the FBI, without the bureau's knowledge, to test a biological weapon on unsuspecting Americans at a movie theater in Ohio so as to ensure it would work effectively on our enemies at some undetermined and unspecified future date. This episode is such a vivid illustration of why publicity is required for democracy that we quote the dialogue at length:

SCULLY: Mulder, before you go any further you should know that the bio-
    toxin they used may have come from government labs. Our government.
MULDER: You're saying I was set up?

SKINNER (Mitch Pileggi): We have no definitive information to justify that position.

MULDER: I was being used? This whole operation? The people who died in that theatre?

CIA AGENT (Michael St. John Smith): (Walking over) Agent Mulder. Our government is not in the business of killing innocent civilians.

MULDER: The hell they aren't. Those were tests on us to be used on someone else.

CIA AGENT: Those bills have been analyzed. The money in the vault gave no readings. There's absolutely no evidence of any bio-toxins. So, before you climb on any bandwagon . . .

SCULLY: You knew about this all along. You knew about this the whole time!

MULDER: I want that money rechecked.

CIA AGENT: That money has been cleared. It's being used as evidence in a federal crime.

MULDER: That money's as dirty as you are, isn't it. Isn't it?

CIA AGENT: Say that were true. Then what do you hope to accomplish, Agent Mulder, as a whistle-blower? To mobilize a civil rights action? To bring down the federal government? To do the very work that group you were a part of is so bent on doing? What do you want? Laws against those men, or laws protecting them?

MULDER: I want people to know the truth.

CIA AGENT: Well sometimes our job is to protect those people from knowing it. Excuse me.

This piece of poignant fiction reminds us of the infamous Tuskegee incident. It has been proven in a court of law that doctors, with the approval of the government, didn't inform a group of black inmates in a prison in Tuskegee, Alabama, that they had syphilis; the doctors wanted to follow the progress and spread of the disease. Not only are there better ways to study this, they could have simply read other studies in a book. As with the fictive case "The Pine Bluff Variant," we like to think that if citizens were informed prior to the Tuskegee study, they would not have allowed it. No doubt that's the reason for the secrecy. Is the government still conducting biochemical experiments without "real" voluntary consent? This is one of the questions that "The Pine Bluff Variant" raises, again supporting our contention that *The X-Files* is an effective pedagogical medium. An investigative reporter might get enough evidence to have good reasons to think it is true without having the solid evidence necessary to go into court. Yet it might well be enough evidence to institute protective policies and actions.

9. "Intelligence 'is not a matter on which public discussion is useful.'" President John F. Kennedy, message to Congress, May 25, 1961. Quoted in Harry Howe Ransom, *Can American Democracy Survive Cold War?* (Garden City, NY: Doubleday, 1963), 174.

10. John Rawls, *A Theory of Justice* (Cambridge, MA: Harvard University Press, 1971), 60.

11. Michael Walzer, *Spheres of Justice: A Defense of Pluralism and Equality* (New York: Basic Books, 1983), 304.

12. See Jeremy Bentham, "On Publicity," in *The Works of Jeremy Bentham*, ed. John Bowring (1838–1843; New York: Russell & Russell, 1962), 2: 310, 315.

13. For these quotes, see Michael Ignatieff, *The Lesser Evil: Political Ethics in an Age of Terror* (Princeton, NJ: Princeton University Press, 2004), 11–12, 51. For similar ideas, see also Dennis F. Thompson, "Democratic Society," *Political Science Quarterly* 114, no. 2 (1999): 181–93.

14. Bentham, "On Publicity," 310–11.

15. Bentham, "On Publicity," 312–15. Alasdair Roberts provides a recent formulation of Bentham's criteria: "Central to this global 'right to information' movement is the presumption that information held by government should be publicly available, unless government officials can make a good case that legitimate interests—perhaps the public interest in preserving national security, or the need to protect another citizen's privacy—would be harmed by releasing information." *Blacked Out: Government Secrecy in the Information Age* (Cambridge: Cambridge University Press, 2006), 9.

16. Immanuel Kant, *To Perpetual Peace: A Philosophical Sketch*, trans. Ted Humphrey (1795; Indianapolis: Hackett, 2003), ix—xii, 37.

17. For a powerful defense of postmodernism using democracy as the grand value, see Richard Rorty, *Philosophy and Social Hope* (London: Penguin, 1999).

18. The Syndicate, the FBI, Scully, and Mulder—even the alien colonists—all have different narratives, but Mulder is not after a satisfying narrative; he wants to find the truth: What happened to his sister? Was she abducted? Was she sacrificed for experimental purposes? The personal force that drives him beyond what most consider a rational curiosity is an interest in the truth. Although we are offered a plethora of narratives of Iraq and Vietnam, many of us are also interested in the truth, satisfying or not, because people died, and because "there are people under fire," as Jackson Browne sang.

19. This conflict between investigating to discover the truth and gathering evidence to support a court case may have contributed to the inadequate performance of the FBI in protecting us from the events of 9/11. Before 9/11 FBI agents saw themselves as primarily law enforcement—as gathering evidence about violations that had occurred in order to charge and prosecute people in court. However, some of what was learned could have been used to prevent the attacks. Intercepts may suggest avenues of further investigation or even preventive actions. A reasonable suspicion that someone is likely making liquid explosives to blow up airplanes may be enough, given the horrendous consequences, to disallow liquid carry-ons even without enough evidence to indict particular persons. Many people are frustrated by courtroom rules of evidence because they incorrectly believe that a courtroom is designed to discover the truth.

The courtroom is a place to render a just verdict; consequently, much that pertains to the truth is inadmissible because it is unfair.

20. John Rawls, *Political Liberalism* (New York: Columbia University Press, 1993), 66–71, 143–44. See also *A Theory of Justice*. Modern political scientists have continued to try to provide useful definitions of democracy based on the experience of many actual democracies, not just theory; see Philippe C. Schmitter and Terry Lynn Karl, "What Democracy Is . . . and Is Not," *Journal of Democracy* 2, no. 3 (1991): 75–88.

21. Alexander Hamilton, James Madison, and John Jay, *The Federalist Papers*, ed. Clinton Rossiter (1787–1788; New York: New American Library, 1961), 35. Daniel Patrick Moynihan, *Secrecy: The American Experience* (New Haven, CT: Yale University Press, 1998), 214.

22. *The 9/11 Commission Report: Final Report of the National Commission on Terrorist Attacks upon the United States*, authorized ed. (New York: W. W. Norton, 2004). See chap. 8, "The System Was Blinking Red," for the dramatic climax of this well-written report. The report is available in its entirety online free of charge at http://www.9–11commission.gov/ (frozen 9/20/04). For still more recent discussions of the difficulties of information management in large organizations, see Ron Suskind, *The One Percent Doctrine* (New York: Simon & Schuster, 2006); and Thomas E. Ricks, *Fiasco: The American Military Adventure in Iraq* (New York: Penguin, 2006).

Some Philosophical Reflections on "Trust No One"

Richard M. Edwards and Dean A. Kowalski

The credo "Trust no one" was firmly established in both the mythos and the ethos of *The X-Files* television series in episode 23, "The Erlenmeyer Flask," which aired on May 13, 1994, as part of the first season of *The X-Files*. Mulder and a skeptical Scully are advised by the government insider and Mulder's secretive guide, Deep Throat (DT, played by Jerry Hardin), to "trust no one." All of the previous episodes contained the tag line "The Truth Is Out There" in the opening credits. "The Erlenmeyer Flask" introduced a new tag line, "Trust No One." While this piece of advice seems well placed, especially given what we know about the government and those working behind (or above) it in *The X-Files* and in American history, the assertion, if pushed far enough, seems rationally flawed. After all, if Mulder literally cannot trust anyone, it follows that he cannot trust DT's advice. Furthermore, Mulder does not always follow the dictum. He seems to trust the Lone Gunmen implicitly, and he comes to trust Scully and later Skinner (Mitch Pileggi). Why does Mulder almost always trust these characters even though he almost never trusts the Cigarette Smoking Man (CSM, played by William B. Davis) or the various governmental agencies? This chapter explores how two theories from the history of philosophy—the Kuhnian conceptual relativist or constructivist view of scientific truth and Hobbesian "psychological egoism"—weigh in on *The X-Files* imperative to "trust no one."

More carefully, this chapter has three goals. First, it will explore Scully's initial "scientism," or unquestioning acceptance of scientific theories, and how it might prevent her from locating the truth "out there." Second, it will show how the behavior of various characters (although the CSM predominantly) seems illustrative of psychological egoism—a theory of human nature to the effect that all human behavior is motivated by self-interest.

If psychological egoism is true, then trusting others seems like a dangerous business. Third, examples taken from various episodes of the show, but "The Erlenmeyer Flask" in particular, will be used to demonstrate the philosophical weaknesses of the two theories in question.

"The Erlenmeyer Flask"

"The Erlenmeyer Flask" begins with Mulder being awakened by a telephone call from DT. Mulder is instructed to watch a video clip about to appear on a local news broadcast, but even with Scully's help he is unable to glean the importance of a car chase ending with a man jumping from a pier. Mulder and Scully decide to investigate the incident site and there learn that three other law enforcement agencies are already investigating the circumstances of the man's supposed death, as no body has yet been recovered.

Seeking additional clues to the man's identity, Mulder and Scully examine the impounded automobile. Mulder notices that the caduceus sticker—two snakes intertwining around a staff, the emblem of the American Medical Association—that was visible on the vehicle in the video is absent from the car that he and Scully are examining. Mulder enhances the video and traces the license plate to a Dr. Berube (Ken Kramer), a physician ostensibly working on the Human Genome Project for the Emgen Corporation in Gaithersburg, Maryland. When he is questioned, Berube claims to know nothing of the events. Mulder and Scully do not understand DT's interest in the incident, and their disillusionment with DT's cryptic parceling out of information emerges in a confrontation between Mulder and his guide when Mulder returns home. DT encourages Mulder to stay the course, asserting that Mulder has "never been closer." Mulder's and Scully's interest is again piqued when the supposed dead man emerges alive from the waters off the pier and Dr. Berube is found dead.

Mulder discovers an Erlenmeyer flask with a label reading "Purity Control" while going through the debris of Berube's ransacked laboratory. Scully has the contents of the flask analyzed at Georgetown University (GU) while Mulder goes to Berube's home. There he intercepts a phone call to Berube from the man who had jumped from the pier. Mulder drives to the injured man's location but does not find the caller. Scully learns that the flask contained bacteria with plant-cell components called chloroplasts and viruses used in animal somatic gene therapy. The importance of this discovery is clear when Scully calls Mulder in scene 16 with the preliminary analysis of contents of the flask: "Now, I may be understating the strangeness of this, Mulder. Bacteria like this ... it may have existed, but not for millions of years, not since before our ancestors first crawled out of the sea." Mulder traces a number frequently called from Berube's residence to a company called Zeus Storage. At the company, he finds what appear to be living humans suspended in fluid-filled tanks. The next morning Scully learns from a DNA specialist that the bacteria in the flask are extraterrestrial. Mulder takes Scully to Zeus Storage and finds the facility emptied of the bodies and all equipment.

Mulder comes to believe that Berube had been experimenting on humans using extraterrestrial viruses. DT confirms Mulder's hypothesis and informs Scully and Mulder that the injured man, Dr. Secare (Simon Webb), was part of the experiment and that the governmental group overseeing the program is in the process of sanitizing and hiding what remains of it. Scully learns that the DNA specialist has died in an automobile accident, and Mulder succeeds in finding Secare in the attic of Berube's home just before a man in a gas mask shoots Secare, exposing Mulder to a deadly gas that seeps from Secare's wound. Secare's body is removed and a stunned Mulder is taken into custody.

Scully finds DT at Mulder's apartment the next morning and is told that evidence of the program in the form of alien tissue is still housed in the High Containment Facility at Fort Marlene, Maryland. Scully retrieves what appears to be an alien fetus, and DT arranges to exchange the tissue for Mulder on a bridge outside Washington, D.C. Mulder is released, but during the exchange DT is mortally wounded. DT's dying words to Scully are "Trust no one." The X-Files section of the Federal Bureau of Investigation is closed, Scully and Mulder reassigned, and the alien fetus safely deposited by the CSM in the basement of the Pentagon.

Though the dictum "Trust no one" is an explicit directive to be skeptical of all people and their motives, it also tacitly includes being skeptical of the process or processes that one uses to glean objective truth(s). In other words, the dictum applies not only to people and aliens, if the latter exist, but also to the different methods trusted by Scully (and Mulder) to determine the "truth."

Scully's Worldview

Scully believes that the truth "out there" is discoverable and wholly explainable by naturalistic science and that that which is true corresponds to the facts correctly understood (apart from her religious convictions, perhaps).

She asserts an objective reality that is knowable and understandable as "it is." Scully's "realism" is based on the belief that the world and its operative laws can be known by the knower via careful scientific inquiry as it is and that the knower's worldview does not affect or diminish knowing the world as it is even though different people having different senses may experience the world differently. Truth can be known and it can be known objectively for truth does not depend on the knower, it exists independent of the knower. For Scully, the truth "out there" is hidden only by a lack of naturalistic knowledge (even if the Syndicate sometimes makes finding it doubly difficult).[1]

For example, Scully's reliance on science and scientific knowledge is well expressed by a scientist (or perhaps an actor playing a scientist on Mulder's television) in scene 2 of "The Erlenmeyer Flask": "Science does not jump to conclusions. Science is not a guessing game." Later, in scene 20, Scully tells Mulder, "I've always put my trust in the accepted facts," in other words, an objective, external truth. Furthermore, Section Chief Blevins (Charles Cioffi)—probably at the behest of CSM—wouldn't have assigned Scully to the X-Files if she weren't the consummate scientist. Remember that she was to debunk Mulder's work.[2]

Thus Scully represents a distinctive worldview, one associated with some form of scientific naturalism (and probably methodological naturalism—the idea that science proceeds as if there are no supernatural explanations without explicitly discounting the existence of the supernatural). A *worldview* is a paradigm or comprehensive framework of belief through which an individual, people, or society experiences, interprets, or understands the world. This framework encompasses the breadth of human experience and perception, including of course science, but also such things as religion, culture, ethics, money, art, politics, and all that constitutes the world known to the individual or society at large.

All humans interact with the world from and through their worldviews. One's worldview is an interpretive matrix or paradigm through which one perceives the world, much like viewing the heavens through the lens of a telescope or the visible world through eyeglasses or a microscope. A worldview or paradigm is like an array of pigeonholes in a post office or the file structure of a computer: incoming information is organized and contextualized within a known and accepted structure. Incoming data are sorted and made understandable by the pigeonholes or file structure. Mail is not dumped onto the floor of a post office nor e-mails sent into cyberspace without an address. There is an organizing structure that makes these data understandable. The organizing structure of our mind is our worldview, and as our worldview receives and understands new information, it is reshaped by the additional information. A worldview is a living and evolving organic unity

As our worldviews or paradigms morph to accommodate any new information, anomalies—information that is not easily contextualized into the paradigm—continually arise. When the volume of anomalies overwhelms our morphing worldview's ability to accommodate new information, a "paradigm shift" occurs. This shift signals that a worldview is discarded and a new one that more adequately contextualizes or explains the totality of the available information is adopted. In science this is called a "scientific revolution."

Kuhn on the Importance of Paradigms

University of Chicago physicist Thomas Samuel Kuhn (1922–1996) believed that scientific worldviews or paradigms play a surprising role in shaping what we know about the natural world.[3] Kuhn's theory of the progression of scientific knowledge seems to assert that the "truths" of science are relative to the currently accepted concepts of the scientific community. "Truths" are those theories and data that correspond to the accepted set of scientific theories. Kuhn's theory of the progression of scientific knowledge may be outlined (very) roughly as follows:

The process begins with "normal science." Normal science is conducted within the parameters of an accepted set of scientific theories that cohere into a transcending paradigm or worldview. New data are processed or made understandable by correlating them to the existing paradigm. Anomalies, repeatable data that do not correlate to the paradigm, are disregarded until the number of anomalies becomes so great as to bring into question the validity of the paradigm. The questioning of paradigmatic validity is called a "crisis," and the scientific community responds by changing, massaging, or "resolving" the paradigm in such a way that it accounts for a sufficient number of the anomalies, relieving the pressure on the accepted system. The resolution of a sufficient number of these anomalies ushers in a new period of normal science, which continues until the theory can no longer resolve the anomalies without destroying the theory. This destruction and creation of a new paradigm is what Kuhn calls a "scientific revolution." Science then enters into a "pre-paradigmatic" phase in which various paradigms compete to account for the available data in the most efficient and coherent manner. This competition ultimately reconstructs a new accepted transcending paradigm. "Truth" then becomes that which correlates with the new paradigm, and the process begins anew.

Paradigms are ultimately a set of received beliefs accepted by a scientific community. Paradigms provide the framework of accepted knowledge that a student learns, and in many cases—medicine, for example—the accepted paradigm provides the objective basis of the licensing of practitioners. Scully is a physician trained in and accepting of a particular paradigm as true. Kuhn's theories assert that Scully's truth is relative to the truth of the currently accepted paradigm and that as it changes—via being resolved or a revolution—what Scully thought to be true may not be true in the new set of received beliefs. Thus her knowledge base changes when one paradigm is replaced with another.

Kuhn's historical analysis of how science progresses seemingly questioned the acceptance of scientific truth as objectively and immutably descriptive of reality. Kuhn showed that science does not discover or establish objective truth, nor does it gradually evolve toward objective truth as the knowledge base expands. Kuhn demonstrated that science and scientific knowledge undergo radical changes or revolutions that reinterpret supposedly established objective truths. When these paradigm shifts occur, the whole interpretive matrix (science or a subset thereof) formed by the knowledge base changes to accommodate new knowledge and old unexplained data (anomalies) in new ways that alter, reconfigure, or completely reject established "truths." Scientific truth is therefore relative to an ever-changing knowledge base that makes universal or absolute truth impossible.

Kuhn seemingly holds that although new scientists are indoctrinated with the dominant methods and concepts of a discipline, scientific truth, though grounded in the external world, is only representative of the external world within the confines of the shared interpretive matrix of that scientific discipline and the more transcending concepts of science in general. If this is so, Scully cannot trust herself to be an effective guide and partner in investigating the X-Files with Mulder because she will reject data, events, people, or actions that do not correlate to dominant methods and concepts. Scully's original assignment was to debunk Mulder's work, and if Kuhn is correct, she tries to do so, not because Mulder's work is inaccurate or does not represent the external world, but only because her (then) current paradigm determines any data inconsistent with it to be inconclusive (at best) or, more likely, illusory or misinterpreted.

Therefore, it seems to follow on Kuhn's view that because the scientific community determines what data is real, it—and not the external world—determines scientific truth. This explains why Kuhn's view of science is often called the conceptual relativist or constructivist theory of science: scientific truth is relative to current scientists' conceptual schemes and is, thus, constructed by them. On this interpretation, Kuhn's view runs counter to the credo that "the truth is out there." In fact, it's tempting to claim that, according to Kuhn, the so-called truth "out there" is actually contained in the scientific community.

The X-Files is replete with examples of the tension between Scully's current scientific paradigm and her new findings (data) from working with Mulder. A vivid early example is from scene 18 of the "The Erlenmeyer Flask." This scene continues the analysis of the contents of the flask Scully took to Georgetown's microbiology department in scene 16. At 11:45 P.M. Dr. Carpenter (Anne DeSalvo) hands Scully the completed analysis of the bacteria and reveals a startling conclusion concerning some anomalous data: "A fifth and sixth DNA nucleotide. A new base pair. Agent Scully, what you are looking at . . . exists nowhere in nature. It would have to be, by definition . . . extraterrestrial." This new finding leads Scully to confide in Mulder: "You know, I've always held science as sacred. I've, I've always put my trust in the accepted facts. And what I saw last night . . . for the first time in my life, I don't know what to believe." Thus, in an admittedly simplistic way, we see the very beginning of a pending scientific revolution for Scully (at least if she cannot resolve the data, which seems unlikely given that, as shown in "Pilot," her current paradigm excludes extraterrestrials). This tension is only heightened when she later retrieves the alien fetus from Fort Marlene.

Scully's (fictive) example here seems problematic for Kuhn's conceptual relativist theory of science, at least as typically conceived. If the scientific community determines which data are true (kept) and which are false (rejected), then we might wonder why revolutions occur at all. Where would obvious and significant anomalous data then come from if not from the external world? But if such data comes from the external world, then the scientific community doesn't determine scientific truth in the way Kuhn (seemingly) believes.

However, it must be stressed that the basic methodology of Scully's scientific paradigm—the scientific method broadly conceived—cannot simply reject the DNA analysis as an anomaly. Though the analysis does challenge Scully's paradigm, it does not challenge the underlying methodology that gives rise to that paradigm. The methodology that gave rise to that paradigm is the same methodology that gives rise to the new data. The scientific method is not wrong. New (unexpected) data has been entered into the knowledge base, and the scientific method and Scully's received paradigm evaluate it appropriately. The anomaly is too great to be shunted aside, and Scully is forced to alter her received paradigm to account for the data. "The truth is out there" and is discoverable, but the process of discovery and finding that truth ends only when the external world is completely understood. Though the knowledge base and understanding of that knowledge may alter, the scientific method works to resolve the changes. The truth of Scully's received paradigm may not be totally and objectively descriptive of the external world; however, her truth is resolving itself in accord with her objective methodology. This is part of Scully's personal "scientific revolution," which continues throughout the series as her knowledge base expands and her scientific paradigm changes to account for the infusion of new knowledge (not to mention the growing or recurring prominence of her Roman Catholicism).

Therefore, in response to the objection leveled at Kuhn's view of science, it seems to be a misunderstanding of Kuhn to assert that his resolutions, reconstructions, and revolutions mean that scientific truth does not accurately represent the external world or that the external world will never be known as "it is" with no future resolutions, reconstructions, and revolutions necessary. Kuhn is actually asserting that all available data is revelatory of the external word and that a transcending or overriding truth is possible when all of the data is available from which to construct a transcending theory of the external world. Kuhn's intent is not to assert that all truth is relative; rather he is asserting that there is an orderly process that moves in spurts, or revolutions, that holds the potential of understanding the external, physical world as "it is." Scully's personal scientific revolution is what Kuhn would expect, an orderly evaluation of the available data that adjusts the received theory allowing for the acceptance of the new data. Yes, the new theory may be different or expanded, it may even change in great leaps or revolutions at times, but the process or methodology through which it is developed remains valid and the same. Thus perhaps Kuhn's views don't present a problem for Scully after all, despite initial appearances (which were probably due to an overinterpretation of Kuhn's views).[4]

This is Scully's personal evolution throughout the series. For Scully, "The truth is out there" means that anomalies may be effectively resolved by the application of the scientific method and that the application of the scientific method accurately describes the external, physical world as "it is" in light of the available knowledge base that is expanding, with the eschatological potential of creating an immutable transcending theory.

Scully's dilemma is that she cannot fulfill her assignment of debunking Mulder's work if she does not hold to a rigid set of scientific theories that disregard anomalies on the basis that they do not fit the received interpretation of the extant knowledge base, yet she is repeatedly faced with such anomalies. Scully is thus forced as the series progresses to rely less on the received interpretation of the extant knowledge base and more on the scientific method to merge the new knowledge with the old knowledge, trusting that the method will allow her to progressively comprehend and then ultimately understand the external, physical world. If she is careful enough, then perhaps she can trust herself and her methods as Mulder's partner on the X-Files.

Deep Throat, the Cigarette Smoking Man, and Psychological Egoism

In describing the theory of human nature known as "psychological egoism," the seventeenth-century British philosopher Thomas Hobbes asserted that selfishness is the fundamental driving force of human actions. He writes: "During the time men live without a common Power to keep them all in awe they are in that condition called War; and such a war, as is of every man against every other man."[5] Thus, according to Hobbes, our natural inclination is to act in ways that gain us advantage over our associates. Even such apparently selfless acts as charitable acts or good deeds done for no reward are motivated by the selfish desire to be recognized, to feel superior to, or more powerful than, the person for whom the good deed was done or the charity given.[6] James Rachels describes "psychological egoism" in his book *The Elements of Moral Philosophy* in this manner: "We may believe ourselves to be noble and self-sacrificing, but that is an illusion. In reality, we care only for ourselves."[7]

The X-Files provides many memorable examples that seem illustrative of psychological egoism. Recall DT's comment to Mulder at the end of the "Deep Throat" episode, "As I said, I can provide you with information, but only so long as it's in my best interest to do so."[8] DT's successor, the mysterious X (Steven Williams), reminds Mulder (in "One Breath") of their precarious arrangement, "You got him killed! You got her killed. That's not going to happen to me. You're my tool, you understand? I come to you when I need you." The CSM, however, may be the best example of a character who illustrates psychological egoism; he regularly acts from selfish motives. Season 5 has at least three episodes that demonstrate the driving force behind the CSM's actions. In "The End" the CSM advises FBI Special Agent Jeffrey Spender (Chris Owens), who will later in the episode be revealed as the CSM's son: "Don't become part of someone else's cause or crusade. Pursue your own self-interest. Always."[9] In "Redux II," the CSM offers to help Mulder find the cure for Scully's cancer, but that offer itself is driven by the CSM's own self-interests. This episode also reveals that the Syndicate (perhaps at the behest of the CSM) has helped Mulder for its own self-interest. Here the CSM is challenged by another member of the Syndicate after the CSM allowed Mulder to escape: "We're too vulnerable. Our man in the FBI is exposed, what Mulder may have seen could expose our plans." The CSM's response demonstrates the motivation for the freeing of Mulder: "What Mulder's seen only serves us. Serves to ensure our plans."

Even our heroes can serve as examples of psychological egoism. Recall the "Leonard Betts" episode. Leonard Betts survives and rejuvenates by consuming human cancers. His job as emergency medical technician in Pittsburgh allows him access to the necessary cancer biologicals that are "waste" to others but the essential nutrient for him. He grows his head back when he is decapitated in an ambulance accident and then grows a second body, which is sacrificed in a later fiery crash in an attempt to convince Mulder and Scully that he is dead. Ultimately the original Betts corners Scully in an ambulance and tries to extract a cancer that he perceives is growing inside her. Scully kills Betts by discharging an ambulance defibrillator to his head. After Betts's fiery death, Scully says, "Well, whatever he was doing, he's taking the secret to his grave." To which Mulder replies, "Yeah, for the second time."

Scully does not tell Mulder why she was attacked. Perhaps this is due to the challenge that the attack poses to her evolving scientific paradigm. Perhaps it is due to a desire for privacy and certainty before sharing. Perhaps it is due to her unwillingness to worry Mulder needlessly. Perhaps it is due to a myriad of other possibilities that are never divulged. All speculation aside, regardless of the specific reason, Scully presumably withholds the information because she feels that it is in her best interest to do so. The episode closes with Scully realizing that a drop of blood on her pillow may indicate that Betts's perception that she has cancer is correct.

Her actions in ensuing episodes, particularly "Redux I and II" of the next season, demonstrate that Scully's withholding of the information is based both in her desire to determine that a cancer exists and in her concern for Mulder. The first reason demonstrates Scully's scientific propensity not to jump to conclusions. However, the second (as we'll soon see) challenges the idea that Scully always acts in her own best self-interest, which presents a pressing problem for psychological egoism.

In fact, it is undeniable that throughout the series both Mulder and Scully frequently choose the other's best interest over their own. Again, one might assert, for example, that Scully was acting not in her best interest but in Mulder's when she did not inform Mulder of Betts's perception. In "Redux I" Scully helps Mulder fake his own death so that he can more easily investigate the supposed Department of Defense cover-up of the proof for extraterrestrial life, even though initially she did not want to participate in the charade. Most vividly, perhaps, Mulder risks his life to save Scully's in *Fight the Future*. Recall that the rescue mission was occasioned by the Syndicate's desire to finally be rid of Mulder "without turning his quest into a crusade." One of the leading Syndicate members, Conrad Stughold (Armin Mueller-Stahl), decides, "Then you must take away what he holds most valuable. That which he can't live without"—Scully. However, one might also interpret such examples of Scully's and Mulder's actions as self-motivated; indeed, the psychological egoist must hold this. Mulder and Scully would then be caught in games of self-deception if either believes that one sometimes acts merely on the behalf of the other.

Before moving forward with the critique of psychological egoism, consider one last telling example. In "Redux II," the CSM asks Mulder to resign from the FBI and join him in the Syndicate, where Mulder will have power, respect, and perhaps even the truths about the pending colonization conspiracy and, more important, his sister. The potential selfish motivations of both the CSM and Mulder are reflected in the following dialogue:

> MULDER: What do you want from me?
> CSM: Want from you?
> MULDER: You give me these things, the only things I ever wanted and I can't think of any reason for you to do so.
> CSM: *Well that's true, no act is completely selfless.* But I've come today not to . . . not to ask, but to offer. To offer you the truth that you've so desperately sought. About the project, about the men who've conspired to protect it.[10]

Mulder quickly rejects the offer. We again see the CSM (clearly) supporting psychological egoism. But if psychological egoism is true, then *all* human action is selfish. What about Mulder's behavior here and elsewhere? What about Mulder and Scully's interactions generally? The preponderance of apparently nonegoistic actions in the Mulder-Scully relationship seems to indicate that not all people are exclusively driven by selfishness. However, unless the psychological egoist is prepared to reinterpret all the data in such a way that any purported counterinstance of egoistic behavior actually results from self-deception, there seems to be much evidence to falsify this theory of human nature.

But even if the psychological egoist attempts this reinterpretation, a new problem then presents itself. Rachels explains the problem of ascribing egoistic motives to all actions in this manner:

> Once it becomes the controlling assumption that all behavior is self-interested, everything that happens can be interpreted to fit this assumption. But so what? If there is no conceivable pattern of action or motivation that would count against the theory—if we cannot even imagine what an unselfish act would be like—then the theory is empty. . . . People act from greed, anger, lust, love and hate. They do things because they are frightened, jealous, curious, happy, worried and inspired. They are sometimes selfish and sometimes generous. Sometimes . . . they are even heroic. In the face of all of this, the thought that there is but a single motive cannot be sustained.[11]

In some circles, the objection that Rachels describes is called a self-sealer fallacy. If it becomes impossible to falsify a theory grounded in empirical findings, then the theory is no longer persuasive. Rather, it becomes a prejudice. Rachels is arguing just that: in cooking up all the data to fit a preconceived quasi theory of human nature, psychological egoism remains unsubstantiated.

So, how should we explain why Mulder trusts Scully (in addition to the Lone Gunmen and Skinner)? It simply might be the regularity with which these associates put his interests on a par with his. This also explains why Scully comes to trust Mulder: he regularly is willing to place Scully's interests either above or on a par with his own. In this way, mutual trust develops and a meaningful relationship (to some degree or another) blooms. This is also why Mulder almost never trusts the Syndicate and the CSM: They almost never put Mulder's interests on an equal footing with their own. Put another way, even if psychological egoism is false, people still have the option to act on selfish desires. Those acquaintances who regularly choose not to act selfishly become trusted allies (the Lone Gunmen and Skinner) or friends, and sometimes something more. Indeed, they become that which we cannot live without (Scully).

Societal Trust

Though Rachels rightly rejects psychological egoism as the sole driving force in individual or societal actions, he argues that something like it is at least the primary force for creating societal trust in the social contract theory of morality: "the idea that morality consists in the set of rules governing how people are to treat one another that rational people agree to accept, for their mutual benefit, on the condition that others follow those rules as well."[12] What Rachels is asserting is that members of a society cede their individual self-interests for mutual or societal self-interests.

"Trust" is neither earned nor innate within humanity; rather trust is negotiated much along the lines of the cold war concept of "mutually assured destruction" (MAD). The USSR did not attack the United States and the United States did not attack the USSR because an attack by either side would have resulted in the destruction of both. It was to the mutual benefit of the United States and the USSR to act according to their tacit contract. This idea of trust asserts that humans will act in a trustworthy manner because it is to their benefit to do so, not because trust is inherently good or right or because being "trustworthy" is a virtue. Rachels asserts that "we follow the rules because it is to our own advantage to live in a society in which the rules are accepted."[13] The rationale is as egoistic as the rationale of the CSM and his cabal. They act in the manner that protects and promotes their power and privilege. Surely, then, DT was correct in directing Scully and Mulder to "trust no one," for they and we never know who might have an advantage or who is seeking an advantage that is consistent with their perceived best self-interests and not our perceived best self-interests or a society's perceived best self-interests.

Rachels recognizes this weakness and asserts that the social contract must have penalties for those who break the rules, for "only then can we feel safe."[14] Yet for the CSM and his cohorts there seem to be few rules and penalties, only power and privilege, at least until the alien conspiracy to produce human-alien hybrids fails and the Syndicate, save the CSM, is incinerated by alien rebels fighting the alien colonists with whom the Syndicate was in league (season 6, episode 12, "One Son"). Perhaps the Syndicate's trust in the alien colonists was misplaced, or perhaps the alien colonists acted in their own perceived best self-interest in not protecting the Syndicate from, or giving them more information about, the alien rebels. In retrospect, the Syndicate should have recognized the long-established patterns of untrustworthy behavior of both the alien colonists and the alien rebels. Neither could be trusted because of an established pattern of acting in their own perceived best interests.

The members of the Syndicate maintained their conspiracies, power, and privilege by being above the law; or, rather, as guardians of the social contract, they were like the pigs in George Orwell's *Animal Farm,* "more equal" than the other animals on the collective. These guardians used the social contract to their benefit and rarely suffered for it, for they had little fear that they could be harmed, because they eliminated those who might harm them. This was why Scully and Mulder were reassigned after the Erlenmeyer flask incident: their investigations endangered the privilege and power that that these guardians enjoyed by living outside or above the social contract.

Why then should we trust other people in society? Rachels answers that it is because it is mutually beneficial to all members of the society to do so. The CSM and his associates are the exceptions because they have the power and privilege to live outside or above the social contract. They can do as they please to achieve whatever they wish, and therefore they are not to be trusted within the context of the social contract because there they have little or no fear of retribution. In effect, the CSM and the rest of the Syndicate are not part of the social contract. If this analysis is true, then it is irrational for anyone to trust anyone who is outside of one's social contract. Why then did the U.S. government trust the Russians? One answer is that the relationship between the United States and the USSR, at least relative to nuclear weapons, was a social contract among equals. One could also assert that both the United States and the USSR had established behavioral patterns that made a nuclear strike anomalous—though possible, given the worldwide political climate of the cold war—to the global political paradigm as well as not coincident with either country's perceived best self-interest.

Mulder and Scully were to "trust no one" because those who had the power and privilege to abrogate the social contract could and would abrogate it if they deemed it to be in their best interest to do so. Trust may be fostered by a social contract among equals, but those who are "more equal" cannot be trusted. And, as with Mulder and Scully, trust seems to grow among equals who regularly treat each other accordingly. Certainly there is risk in personal relationships if people act egoistically even some of the time, but those risks are mitigated as Scully and Mulder's relationship blossoms and their knowledge of each other's behavioral patterns deepens.

Notes

1. Of course, Mulder also seeks objective truth, whether it concerns the abduction of his sister, the existence of aliens and human-alien hybrids, or any other phenomena. For Mulder, the truth is invariably hidden by a lack of naturalistic, supernaturalistic, paranormal, and extraterrestrial knowledge that, when blended, gives a clearer (even if not perfect) understanding reality.

2. Perhaps "End Game" is the best early example of Scully's reliance on science as a tool to understand the world. The relevant dialogue is quoted in the introduction to this book.

3. Thomas S. Kuhn, *The Structure of Scientific Revolutions*, 3rd ed. (Chicago: University of Chicago Press, 1976).

4. Whether this rejoinder can be sustained will probably depend on whether Kuhn's view can be infused with these elements of scientific realism and still be consistent with the overall tenor of his view. For example, Kuhn writes:

> Examining the record of past research from the vantage of contemporary historiography, the historian of science may be tempted to exclaim that when paradigms change, the world itself changes with them. Led by a new paradigm, scientists adopt new instruments and look in new places. Even more important, during revolutions scientists see new and different things when looking with familiar instruments in places they have looked before. It is rather as if the professional community has been suddenly transported to another planet where familiar objects are seen in a different light and are joined by unfamiliar ones as well. Of course, nothing of quite that sort does occur: there is no geographical transplantation; outside the laboratory everyday affairs usually continue as before. Nevertheless, paradigm changes do cause scientists to see the world of their research engagement differently. In so far as their only recourse to that world is through what they see and do, we may want to say that after a revolution scientists are responding to a different world. (*Scientific Revolution*, 111)

It might be that Kuhn can be understood as more of a scientific realist here, but, admittedly, whether this interpretation holds up to scrutiny will require further exploration. For an apt discussion of the different ways Kuhn has been interpreted, see Del Ratzsch, *Science and Its Limits*, 2nd ed. (Downers Grove, IL: InterVarsity Press, 2000).

5. Thomas Hobbes, *Leviathan* (London, 1651), chap. 13.

6. James Rachels, *The Elements of Moral Philosophy*, 4th ed. (NY: McGraw-Hill Higher Education, 2003), 65–67.

7. Rachels, *Moral Philosophy*, 64.

8. Interestingly enough, Mulder immediately asks his guide, "What is your interest?" to which DT answers, "The truth." It's not immediately clear that DT's further motive here is illustrative of psychological egoism, but more on this sort of insight later.

9. This might also be interpreted as illustrating ethical egoism because the CSM seems to be giving his son an imperative. However, as is well known, the most plausible reason for asserting ethical egoism is a prior conviction of the truth of psychological egoism. Thus, this bit of dialogue might be illustrative of both theories.

10. Emphasis added.

11. Rachels, *Moral Philosophy*, 74–75.

12. Rachels, *Moral Philosophy*, 150.

13. Rachels, *Moral Philosophy*, 150.

14. Rachels, *Moral Philosophy*, 150.

"I Want to Believe"

William James and *The X-Files*

Keith Dromm

In philosophy, there is likely no more important difference than that between believing in something with justification and believing in something for no or insufficient reasons. According to many philosophers, even though a belief is true, if the believer doesn't have good reasons for holding it, then not only does the belief not count as knowledge, it should never have been adopted.[1] In his classic essay "The Ethics of Belief," the nineteenth-century mathematician and philosopher of science W. K. Clifford (1845–1879) argued for such an attitude toward unjustified belief. He wrote there that "it is wrong always, everywhere, and for anyone, to believe anything upon insufficient evidence."[2] However, in response to Clifford's essay, the American philosopher and psychologist William James (1842–1910) composed an equally famous essay, "The Will to Believe," in which he argued that we have a *right* to hold certain beliefs even when justification is wanting. James argued that this was true, for example, of religious beliefs. Beliefs like these have such a far-reaching and profound influence on our lives that to forgo holding them because the evidence is not available can do more harm than adopting what might turn out to be a false belief. Whenever that is the case, it would be an "irrational rule" that prohibited us from adopting a belief of this sort because we lack the justification for it.[3]

The James essay resembles the caption and sentiment of one of the most recognizable images from *The X-Files*: the "I Want to Believe" poster that hangs on the wall of Fox Mulder's office in the basement of the FBI building. In addition to that poster, there is much else in *The X-Files* that shows Mulder and James to have a similar attitude toward belief. There is another interesting similarity between James and Mulder. James also had an interest in the paranormal. For much of his life, he pursued research in this area alongside his more typical scientific and philosophical investigations. While Clifford also had an interest in the paranormal, he was mainly concerned with debunking reports of paranormal phenomena. Dana Scully, in her skepticism about the paranormal and her adoration of science, bears a resemblance to Clifford.

This chapter will explore the parallels between the two central characters of *The X-Files* and these important philosophers. Each pair represents a different model for how we should form our beliefs. While the respective virtues and vices of each model will be considered, neither will be recommended. There is another character on *The X-Files* who represents a better model for how we should go about acquiring beliefs: Assistant Director Skinner. His constant efforts to balance the obligations of his job with his desire to take seriously the work of Mulder and Scully resemble the approach to belief acquisition that James articulated after he wrote "The Will to Believe." He offered this model in his writings on the philosophical view known as *pragmatism*, for which he was the most prominent advocate. In the first section of this chapter I will describe the relevant similarities between Clifford and Scully. In the second section I will do the same for the early James and Mulder. In the final section I will argue that Skinner's pragmatic approach is both more just and more efficacious than either of the other models.

Scully and Clifford

Dana Scully had been assigned to the X-Files in order to "debunk" Mulder's investigations or, as it was more diplomatically explained to her in the pilot episode, to submit them to the "proper scientific analysis." In her first conversation with Mulder, Scully reveals that she shares with her superiors some of their skepticism about his work. When Mulder asks her whether she believes in the existence of extraterrestrials, Scully replies: "Logically, I would have to say 'no.' Given the distances needed to travel from the far reaches of space, the energy requirements would exceed a spacecraft's capabilities."[4] Mulder dismisses this as "conventional wisdom." He has already warned her that in his work the "laws of physics rarely seem to apply." Scully, on the other hand, finds "fantastic" "any notion that there are answers beyond the realm of science."

W. K. Clifford was also a debunker of reports of the paranormal, though probably a more enthusiastic one than Scully.[5] He believed that it was not only intellectually but also morally irresponsible to believe in things that go beyond science or, as he might also put it, since he seemed to believe the two equivalent, to believe on insufficient evidence.

He begins his essay "The Ethics of Belief" with a sort of parable. He asks us to imagine a shipowner who has let sail an unseaworthy ship of emigrants. The ship sinks, taking all on board with it. The shipowner, however, *believed* that the ship was seaworthy. He initially had doubts about this. The ship was old and had often needed repairs. Others had communicated to him their concerns about the ship's seaworthiness. But he managed to rid himself of his doubts. He reminded himself that the ship had sailed successfully many times before. He also "put his trust in Providence," who he believed would certainly protect the passengers, who were innocent of anything but the desire for better lives. The shipowner came to believe sincerely and strongly that the ship would complete its voyage. His belief turned out to be wrong, but is he responsible for the consequences? He let the ship sail only after he came to believe it was safe. Clifford argues that the shipowner is "verily guilty" of the death of the passengers.

For Clifford, the strength and sincerity of the shipowner's belief is irrelevant. What is more important is how he arrived at the belief: "The sincerity of his conviction can in no wise help him, because *he had no right to believe on such evidence as was before him.*"[6] He lacks that right because he did not arrive at his belief through, as Clifford puts it, "patient investigation" but only by "stifling his doubts." Instead of assuring himself of the ship's seaworthiness by inspecting it and then, if needed, repairing it, he performed a mental exercise that allowed him to forget his doubts. He should have taken his doubts seriously and dispensed with them only if he could *prove* them to be unfounded. He merely pushed those doubts out of his mind by allowing himself to think of only the positive, but weak, reasons for believing the ship to be seaworthy. Such positive thinking might be effective in improving one's self-esteem, but it cannot save a ship from sinking.

Now, not all our false beliefs will have such dramatic consequences. But, Clifford argues, while the pernicious effects of a wrongly held belief might be neither immediate nor by themselves great, over time and through the accumulation of such bad beliefs, the consequences can be severe. For example, Clifford argues that "no one man's belief is in any case a private matter which concerns himself alone."[7] We typically do not keep our beliefs to ourselves. We share them with others. They are sometimes adopted by our neighbors and friends and inherited by our children. Many of the beliefs we acquired in school once had humble beginnings in the mind of a single person. No one, whatever his or her position in society, escapes the responsibility to adopt only justified beliefs, because each one of us has some influence on the beliefs our fellows adopt. Scully discusses one kind of such influence in "Fresh Bones." Despite Mulder's research into the "zombification phenomenon," Scully dismisses voodoo as a superstition that "only works by instilling fear in its believers," as do all superstitions. So, even though "it's as irrational as avoiding a crack in the sidewalk," beliefs like voodoo will spread among people because of the fear of disbelieving them but not because of any evidence in their favor.

Clifford also describes the effects a wrongly held belief can have on the believer. Every time we allow ourselves to accept a belief on insufficient evidence, "we weaken our powers of self-control, of doubting, of judicially and fairly weighing the evidence."[8] It takes practice and discipline to be a good thinker. In the same way that an athlete will lose some of her ability, or at least slow her progress, if she relaxes her regimen or strays from her diet, our thinking ability will be degraded every time we use it improperly. And even if the belief I wrongly acquire turns out to be true, while I might escape some immediate harm to myself or others, I will become increasingly credulous the more beliefs I adopt without good reason, and I might eventually "lose the habit of testing things and inquiring into them."[9]

Scully never seems to give up this habit, even though she eventually comes to adopt many of Mulder's beliefs about alien abduction around which the central story arc of the series revolves. Her acceptance of those beliefs is gradual and based on the accumulation of evidence and her own direct experience. In contrast, Fox Mulder's beliefs about the paranormal, while in some cases strongly supported, are based more on such things as *hope*. He admits as much in the episode "Quagmire," in which Scully and Mulder are investigating a series of killings attributed to Big Blue, a supposedly mythical sea serpent that has made a tourist attraction out of a lakeside community. After Mulder and Scully conclude—incorrectly, as it is revealed only to the audience—that the murderer was merely a voracious alligator, Mulder expresses some disappointment: "I guess I just wanted Big Blue to be real. I guess I see hope in such a possibility." Scully understands; "People want to believe," she replies. But Clifford warns that the comfort a belief gives one—for example, the hope it might fulfill—does not provide a legitimate reason for its adoption: "The fact that believers have found joy and peace in believing gives us the right to say that the doctrine is a comfortable doctrine, and pleasant to the soul; but it does not give us the right to say that it is true."[10] While Clifford might be correct that simply wanting a belief to be true is no indication that it is actually true, James reveals in his essay "The Will to Believe" that Clifford himself is not entirely innocent of allowing his emotions to influence what he believes.

Mulder and James

James's first published writings were mostly on psychology. He is, in fact, considered the founder of American psychology. He believed that psychology would allow for the scientific study of the mind, replacing philosophy as the principal discipline for its study. His two-volume textbook *The Principles of Psychology* remains influential. Mulder would likely have read it or other works by James while he was studying psychology at Oxford. But James's interests were various and far ranging, though all in some way related.[11] These other interests included the paranormal. He devoted a good amount of time to investigating reports of ghost sightings, mediums, mesmerism, telepathy, thought transference, and extrasensory perception. He was a member and cofounder of the American Society for Psychical Research, and he wrote and lectured on this research.

However, James discovered that most of the reports of the paranormal that he investigated were frauds or hoaxes. He nevertheless continued with his investigations. He wrote to a friend: "If I go on investigating, I shall make *anyhow* an important discovery: either that there exists a force of some sort not dreamed of in our philosophy, (whether it be spirits or not)—*or,* that human testimony, voluminous in quantity, and from the most respectable sources, is but a revelation of human imbecility."[12] He continues and says that "I hate to settle down into this last conviction." Mulder would also at times express doubts about his own investigations. In "Little Green Men," he wonders whether he has only been chasing such figments of his imagination and laments that his merely having seen things that point to the existence of extraterrestrials is insufficient proof: "Seeing is not enough; I should have something to hold on to." But despite this lack of evidence, he perseveres. The evidence, in any case, seems mostly for convincing others, not himself. While he occasionally expresses these doubts about his beliefs, they seem to rest on something stronger than evidence. In the episode "E. B. E.," Scully suggests what this might be in a warning she gives to Mulder: "I have never met anyone so passionate and dedicated to a belief as you. It's so intense that sometimes it's blinding. But there are others who are watching you, who know what I know and whereas I can respect and admire your *passion,* they will use it against you. Mulder, the truth is out there but so are lies."[13]

In his essay "The Will to Believe," James observes that it is often our *passions* that determine what we believe. For example, he argues that the disagreement between himself and those like Clifford is not over whether and when we should use our intellectual faculties; rather, it is a conflict of passions: "It is not intellect against all passions ... it is only intellect with one passion laying down its law."[14] In his elevation of scientific explanation over any other way of making sense of reality, Clifford is submitting to his passions no less than Mulder, and the passion he has chosen to follow comes with risks like any other.

James identifies two sometimes conflicting views about our responsibilities when it comes to acquiring beliefs. We can take our primary duty to be respecting the principle "*We must know the truth.*" Alternatively, we can favor the principle "*We must avoid error.*" The two are not equivalent. While believing in a truth will typically save us from error, it does not necessarily follow that by refusing to believe a falsehood, we end up believing in the truth. For example, Scully might refuse to believe one of the wilder conspiracy theories of the Lone Gunmen, but that refusal won't entail her belief in the true explanation of the event their theory was intended to explain. She might simply not believe in any explanation of the event.

According to James, Clifford has chosen "We must avoid error" as his guiding principle. What determined that choice? It is not intellect according to James. "We must avoid error" is a principle that instructs us how to use our intellect properly, so without circularity our intellect cannot be the arbitrator of the two conflicting principles. Only our "passional nature," as James would put it, can make such a choice. He explains, "We must remember that these feelings of our duty about either truth or error are in any case only expressions of our passional nature."[15] One person might be more worried about falling into error or making mistakes than she is concerned with learning the truth. Her greatest fear might be of becoming a dupe or someone's fool. Another person might feel that truth is of the greatest importance and be more willing to risk error as long as she increases her chances of discovering truth. Each view comes with risks. While the first person, in respecting above all the principle "Avoid error," will be less likely to become anyone's fool, she decreases her chances of discovering the truth. The person who takes "Know the truth" as her guiding principle will increase her chances of discovering the truth, but she pays for that with a greater tendency toward error. Although our passions will typically incline us toward one principle over the other, we can still manage to resist or surrender to our passions, and being made aware of the risks associated with each choice can lessen or strengthen our commitment to a passion.

James does not believe that we should obey one principle to the exclusion of the other. He argues against dogmatic obedience to either. In certain cases, but not all, we are warranted in elevating the search for truth above the risk of error. These are cases in which the evidence is not sufficient for making a choice as to what to believe, but a choice must be made nevertheless. As they did with our choice between the two principles, our passions will here have a role to play. In such cases, it is permissible to allow our passions to incline us toward a particular belief. As James explains, "Our passional nature not only lawfully may, but must, decide between propositions, whenever it is a genuine option that cannot by its nature be decided on intellectual grounds; for to say, under such circumstances, 'Do not decide, but leave the question open,' is itself a passional decision—just like deciding yes or no—and is attended with the same risk of losing the truth."[16] He believes that religious beliefs are an example of such a choice. It is the nature of most central religious beliefs that the absolute proof of their truth is available to no one but the omniscient. But it also true that beliefs of this sort typically promise a reward for those who simply hold them. For beliefs such as these, it cannot be true "that to yield to our fear of its being in error is wiser and better than to yield to our hope that it may be true."[17] We certainly assume a greater risk of being in error by holding such beliefs, but the possible reward of their truth outweighs the risks associated with holding a false belief. So, for James, only an "irrational rule" would proscribe our assuming these risks.

The beliefs of James and Mulder in the paranormal seem similarly based on hope and other elements of their "passional nature." Mulder admits in "Colony" that he lacks proof for the beliefs that motivate his investigations and acknowledges the risks of holding such beliefs:

> I have lived with a fragile faith built on the ether of vague memories from an experience that I can neither prove nor explain. When I was twelve, my sister was taken from me, taken from our home by a force that I came to believe was extraterrestrial. This belief sustained me, fueling a quest for truths that were as elusive as the memory itself. To believe as passionately as I did was not without sacrifice, but I always accepted the risks to my career, my reputation, my relationships, to life itself.

James's essay "The Will to Believe" is a defense of our right to assume such risks for beliefs like these.

James does not believe that our passions should be the final arbiter of all our beliefs. In science and law, for example, "the need of acting is seldom so urgent that a false belief to act on is better than no belief at all." In such cases, it is better to wait on objective evidence before adopting a belief. He would also not endorse the shipowner's belief in his ship's seaworthiness. The shipowner was presented with a choice that certainly could have been decided on "intellectual grounds." And our *willing* cannot bring about any sort of belief. This will only work and be appropriate for those choices between beliefs that meet certain criteria; those options that James calls forced, momentous, and living.[18] The choice has to be unavoidable, of great importance, and relevant to us given our background. Mulder's search for his sister and the truth about her disappearance is an example of such a choice. As his narration in "Colony" reveals, Mulder was aware of the risks of believing so "passionately" in the existence of extraterrestrials, but his belief "sustained" him, as he puts it, suggesting that without it he would be assuming even greater risks to his well-being.

Skinner

In *Fight the Future,* Mulder asks Scully rhetorically, "Five years together Scully, how many times have I been wrong?" Although Mulder did turn out to be right most of the time, that not only adds nothing to the justification for his beliefs, it also fails to demonstrate that he was acting responsibly in holding them. How to act responsibly in forming beliefs is an important issue. Not only *what* but also *how* we believe can have profound effects on our own lives and the lives of others. Mulder and Scully provide different models of how we should go about forming beliefs. Choosing between them determines the kinds and amounts of risks that we are willing to assume for ourselves and others.

But while Clifford recommends one model over the other, James—as it was explained in the previous section—actually argues for adopting both and using each where it is most appropriate. Mulder also seems to recognize that neither model works well to the exclusion of the other. He admits to Scully in *Fight the Future:* "Your strict rationalism and science has saved me a thousand times over. You kept me honest." However, there is something missing from both models that should cause us to pause before settling on this approach. It is something that James emphasizes in his later writings: a respect for "older truths."

In addition to his developments in psychology, James is at least equally well known as the chief proponent of the philosophical view called *pragmatism*. Over the course of his career, James's research and writings became increasingly concerned with philosophical topics as his interest in experimental psychology waned. Pragmatism, however, was not a later view of James. There is evidence of pragmatic views in his earlier writings on psychology. But it was not until later in his life, most notably with the lectures that were published under the title *Pragmatism*, that he presented his fullest and most developed articulation of these views.

Pragmatism is, according to James, primarily a *method,* but it is also associated with a famous theory of truth. The pragmatic method holds that the practical consequences of a concept exhaust its meaning.[19] Borrowing ideas from another American philosopher, Charles Sanders Peirce (1839–1914), James argues that concepts can only be distinguished by their practical effects, their *cash-value,* as he calls it. What a concept means can be no different from the practical consequences its truth can have. So, if for any two concepts we can imagine the same effects, the concepts are the same; as he puts it, "There can *be* no difference which doesn't *make* a difference."[20] And if for any concept we cannot imagine *any* practical difference its truth can have, then it is meaningless. This method is used by James to resolve seemingly interminable disputes in philosophy, such as the one about the nature of truth.

Pragmatism tries to rid the concept of truth of its metaphysical mysteriousness. A popular view in philosophy to this day takes the truth of a belief to consist in its *agreement* or *correspondence* with reality. However, what it is for a belief to agree or correspond with reality, according to James, had never been clearly articulated; it had become a "meaningless abstraction."[21] The pragmatic method explains all that agreement with reality could possibly mean: it refers to those beliefs that "we can assimilate, validate, corroborate and verify"; they are the beliefs that "pay" in this way.[22] This is "truth's cash-value." If a belief gets us lost more often than it helps us find our way about, if it doesn't allow us to anticipate correctly the future, or if it isn't conducive to the success of any of our other projects, only a peculiarly strong form of dogmatism would allow one to accept that belief as true. A belief that does manage without fail to do those things would unhesitatingly be taken as true. The instrumental value or usefulness of a belief is all that we can mean by designating it as true. As James explains, "That is the practical difference it makes to us to have true ideas; that, therefore, is the meaning of truth."[23]

Questions about the truth of a belief arise most often with respect to novel experiences. When we encounter a fact that we have never experienced before, various explanations might offer themselves as candidates for belief. These might be suggested to us; they might occur to us spontaneously. It is up to us to decide which explanation best accounts for the novel fact. Most of *The X-Files* episodes revolve around such encounters; an ostensive definition of the FBI's X-Files would point at examples of them. As we have seen, *The X-Files* presents us with two different models for dealing with new experiences. Mulder is often willing to accept the most fantastic explanation for a novel fact, whereas the skeptical Scully is hesitant to accept any explanation that she cannot comfortably describe as "scientific," leaving her at risk of not adopting any new belief about the fact.[24] The pragmatist will accept the belief that has the most instrumental value. And, as James shows, a belief that has that quality will have to be one that can be accommodated by one's prior beliefs with the least amount of adjustment.

James says that any new truth must be one that "marries old opinion to new fact so as ever to show a minimum of jolt, a maximum of continuity."[25] A new belief that fails to fit with the older ones will have little instrumental value. It will either float free of the other things we believe, being either superfluous or an encumbrance, or it will upset too many of our older beliefs by contradicting them. This threatens to leave us bereft of the very means for adjudicating its truth, which can only come from the stock of our already-held beliefs. To avoid this, James explains, we must act conservatively when adopting new beliefs by showing a proper degree of respect for older truths.

All older truths were once new ones. When new truths become old, "their influence is absolutely controlling."[26] James is anticipating some ideas of the twentieth-century Austrian philosopher Ludwig Wittgenstein (1889–1951). Wittgenstein uses the analogy of a riverbed to describe how new truths become old ones and the function served by the latter:

> It might be imagined that some propositions, of the form of empirical propositions, were hardened and functioned as channels for such empirical propositions as were not hardened but fluid; and that this relation altered with time, in that fluid propositions

hardened, and hard ones became fluid. . . . And the bank of that river consists partly of hard rock, subject to no alteration or only to an imperceptible one, partly of sand, which now in one place now in another gets washed away or deposited.[27]

Like James, Wittgenstein believes that there is nothing irrevocable about this process. The old truths can eventually be washed away, again becoming part of the "fluid" that gets carried along the river. But no new belief can be adopted without taking into account the hardened beliefs of the riverbed.

Neither James in the "The Will to Believe" nor Clifford in "The Ethics of Belief" pays enough attention to the role played by older truths. Clifford imagines that they all could and should be tested, that this is "not only possible and right, but our bounden duty."[28] But this attitude is not simply too ambitious, it also fails to recognize that any testing must take place against the background of such "older truths" or "riverbed" beliefs. As Wittgenstein puts it, "All testing, all confirmation and disconfirmation of a hypothesis takes place already within a system"; this system is "the inherited background against which I distinguish between true and false."[29] This system provides the prior beliefs that we must use in assessing the truth of any new candidate for belief, for example, Scully's beliefs about science or Mulder's beliefs about paranormal phenomena. James in "The Will to Believe" is too intent on redeeming the role that passions play in our acquisition of beliefs and does not give enough attention to the role played by older truths in this process. Their counterparts in *The X-Files* suffer from similar faults. Mulder, in typically preferring the more novel or peculiar explanation for a phenomenon, shows little concern with reconciling those explanations with "older truths."[30] Scully fails to appreciate that the beliefs that make up her "conventional wisdom," as Mulder once characterized it, were once all novel facts and, while "hardened," will never lose their susceptibility to being displaced from their current position. A better model for belief acquisition in *The X-Files*, the pragmatic approach, is Assistant Director Skinner.

The X-Files series begins with Skinner playing the role of Mulder and Scully's nemesis, as a possible collaborator or minion of the Smoking Man. It is eventually revealed that his allegiances are, like Mulder's and Scully's, to the *truth*, and he becomes their ally. But in honoring this allegiance he has to respect other commitments as well. He complains to Scully in "The Blessing Way," "I think you underestimate the duties and responsibilities of my position as Assistant Director." These responsibilities include balancing the respect he is obligated by his job to show to his superiors with his desire to take seriously the novel facts uncovered by the investigations of Mulder and Scully. This is a responsibility for which Mulder and Scully, and possibly *The X-Files* audience, never had enough appreciation.

Taking those authorities to be analogous to the "older truths," and Mulder and Scully's investigations as a supply of "novel facts," Skinner manages them like a pragmatist. He works within the "system" to achieve the goal he shares with Mulder and Scully, the *truth,* but his strategy for achieving it is both more just and more efficacious. Mulder's tendency to accept a belief simply because of its novelty is unreliable, and Scully's resistance to novel explanations sometimes amounts to an unreflective obedience to authority.[31] In contrast to both, Skinner acts so as to balance the new with the old, or to "play the middle," as he puts it in his narration in the season 6 episode "S.R. 819": "Every minute of every day we choose. Who we are. Who we forgive. Who we defend and protect. To choose a side or to walk the line. To play the middle. To straddle the fence between what is and what should be. This was the course I chose." His allegiances might seem ambiguous at times, unless we take them to be ultimately to the truth and not to either the new or the old exclusively. Scully suffers from the same blindness she attributes to Mulder. Both of their respective "passions" sometimes distract them from the truth, causing each to make a fetish of the old or the new. Skinner's allegiances are arguably more firmly attached to the truth, despite the tensions that frequently erupt in his relations with Mulder and Scully and the lack of sympathy he might sometimes receive from the audience.

Skinner is a model of pragmatism in another way. He is sometimes a mediator between the impatient passion of Mulder and the incredulity of Scully. As the one to whom they report, the person who makes the final decision on the disposition of their reports, he must often decide between their respective "passions." This is analogous to the role that James assigns pragmatism. It is intended to mediate between what he calls the "tender-minded" idealist and the "tough-minded" skeptic. James describes pragmatism as a "mediating way of thinking."[32] Whether or not he decides correctly in every case, this is Skinner's burden, another one of his "responsibilities." It is quite easy to come up with the most fantastic explanation for a phenomenon or to refuse to accept any explanation that does not fit with one's settled view of the universe. Skinner doesn't enjoy these liberties. His job requires him to make a decision that will in the end have some pragmatic value. In "The Blessing Way," Scully is suspended for "misconduct." After the meeting in which this decision is handed down, she confronts Skinner in the hallway and asks, referring to the officials who made the decision, "Who are these people?" "These people are doing their job," Skinner replies. "These people have a protocol to follow, which is something you and Agent Mulder did not do." Skinner knows very well that for his beliefs to have any influence, to be at all *useful,* he must respect certain protocols. These include a respect for "older truths," which his deference to "these people" can be taken to represent. And while Mulder and Scully are sometimes suspended or reassigned because of their lack of deference, Skinner maintains his power (apart from one well-designed plot from the CSM in "Avatar"), limited though it is, and thereby often manages to be more effective in the propagation of the truth.

James reveals in "The Will to Believe" how an apparent commitment to rationality might actually keep us from the truth. In his writings on pragmatism he more fully recognizes the responsibilities we must honor in our efforts to know the truth. While he never repudiated the role he assigns to our will in "The Will to Believe," he came to recognize further constraints on how we should go about acquiring beliefs. In particular, our beliefs must be *useful.* They cannot be so if we do not respect "older truths" in adopting them. This respect is missing from both the Clifford/Scully and the early James/Mulder models of belief acquisition. This leaves them in danger, in the former case, of believing too little, and in the latter, of believing too much.

While the pragmatic approach is modeled by Skinner, James's personality remained throughout his life more closely aligned with Mulder. He persisted in his belief that—to use a slogan for which James would likely have had great affinity—"the truth is out there." He believed that there was more to reality than what was presented of it through our ordinary senses. He suggested that "our ordinary human experience, on its material as well as on its mental side, would appear to be only an extract from the larger psycho-physical world,"[33] and he believed it was possible to get "a sense of present reality more diffused and general than that which our special senses yield."[34] For James, the paranormal, as well as such things as mystical experiences, was potentially evidence of this greater reality. His status as a prominent academic and intellectual likely afforded him the liberty to hold these beliefs and to persist as he did with his search for this greater reality. He never had the same responsibilities as a person like Skinner. Even though he was the chief proponent of pragmatism, there were very few pragmatic constraints on what beliefs he espoused. Such liberty is not merely enviable; it is likely to the benefit of us all that thinkers like James—and perhaps fellow investigators of the paranormal like Mulder—are allowed to enjoy it. Their views, like any others, are equally candidates for the truth, and the more such candidates there are, the more likely we are to arrive at the truth, even pragmatically conceived.

Notes

I want to thank Heather Salter and Dean Kowalski for their comments.

1. *Knowledge* has traditionally been defined, though not without controversy, as true, justified belief.

2. W. K. Clifford, "The Ethics of Belief," in *The Ethics of Belief and Other Essays* (New York: Prometheus Books, 1999), 77.

3. William James, "The Will to Believe," in *William James: Writings, 1878–1899,* ed. Gerald E. Myers (New York: Library of America, 1992), 477.

4. Philosophers would correct her use of "logically" here. There is nothing illogical about our being visited by extraterrestrials. The very fact that it has been imagined demonstrates this. What she offers is a reason for thinking that such visitations are scientifically or physically impossible, or perhaps just extremely unlikely. That is, they would break certain scientific or natural laws as we understand them, but they would not break any laws of logic. We are unable even to imagine what such a violation would be like.

5. Timothy J. Madigan, introduction to *Ethics of Belief,* by W. K. Clifford, xv.

6. Clifford, "Ethics of Belief," 70.

7. Clifford, "Ethics of Belief," 73.

8. Clifford, "Ethics of Belief," 76.

9. Clifford, "Ethics of Belief," 76.

10. Clifford, "Ethics of Belief," 83.

11. James is also the author of an important and widely read work on religion, *The Varieties of Religious Experience* (1902). It combines his interests in psychology and philosophy, and it is not entirely unrelated to his interest in the paranormal.

12. Quoted in Linda Simon, *Genuine Reality: A Life of William James* (New York: Harcourt Brace, 1998), 141.

13. Italics mine.

14. James, "The Will to Believe," 475.

15. James, "The Will to Believe," 469.

16. James, "The Will to Believe," 464.

17. James, "The Will to Believe," 475.

18. James, "The Will to Believe," 458.

19. Following James, who also uses the terms "notion" and "idea," "concept" is being used here very broadly to include things such as propositions, beliefs, and theories, as well as definitions; anything, that is, that is capable of being true or false.

20. William James, "Philosophical Conceptions and Practical Results," in *William James: Writings, 1878–1899,* 1,081.

21. William James, *Pragmatism* (1907), in *William James: Writings, 1902–1910,* ed. Bruce Kuklick (New York: Library of America, 1987), 590.

22. James, *Pragmatism,* 573 and 581.

23. James, *Pragmatism,* 573. There is a serious, perhaps unavoidable, problem with his theory, but one that seems endemic to all efforts to define meaning, e.g., logical positivism, the early Wittgenstein of the *Tractatus,* etc. That is, the definition proffered for *meaning* does not itself seem meaningful according to the definition. Some have tried to show how these theories escape this apparent dilemma. These efforts will not be reviewed here.

24. Mulder's preference for the more fantastic explanation is satirized at the beginning of the season 7 episode "all things": Scully arrives at the office to share the results of an autopsy she performed for their investigation of a possible drowning. Scully informs Mulder that the victim did drown but not from inhaling ectoplasm, as he had suggested, but rather something much more commonplace: margarita mix.

25. James, *Pragmatism,* 513.

26. James, *Pragmatism,* 513.

27. Ludwig Wittgenstein, *On Certainty* (New York: Harper & Row, 1969), §§96 and 99. These ideas might have come from James, whom Wittgenstein read and greatly respected. James's views also anticipate those of the twentieth-century American philosopher W. V. O. Quine and his notion of a "web of belief."

28. Clifford, "The Ethics of Belief," 87.

29. Wittgenstein, *On Certainty,* §§105, 94,

30. Mulder is actually a little more discriminating in how he goes about acquiring beliefs than might have been suggested so far. For example, in "Clyde Bruckman's Final Repose," he is the first to recognize that Yappi the psychic is a fraud. Also, throughout the series we see that Mulder's investigations rely upon methods and tools (for example, in the pilot he uses two stopwatches to detect the presence of paranormal phenomena), authoritative sources like "Deep Throat," and his encyclopedic knowledge of paranormal events and research.

31. See, e.g., "Fallen Angel," in which Scully appears too willing to accept the government's explanation that a Libyan jet has crashed instead of Mulder's hypothesis, which turns out to be correct, that it was an alien craft.

32. James, *Pragmatism,* 504.

33. William James, "The Confidences of a 'Psychical Researcher,'" in *William James: Writings, 1902–1910,* 1,264.

34. William James, *Varieties of Religious Experience,* in *William James: Writings, 1902–1910,* 63. James did believe that there was pragmatic evidence for this view. As he writes in the lecture "Pragmatism and Religion" in *Pragmatism:* "On pragmatic principles we can not reject any hypothesis if consequences useful to life flow from it. Universal conceptions, as things to take account of, may be as real for pragmatism as particular sensations are"; and as to the usefulness of belief in a reality greater than that of sense-experience: for James this has been "proved by the whole course of men's religious history" (606).

Part II

THE CHARACTERS

Ancient X-Files

Mulder and Plato's Sokratic Dialogues

William M. Schneider

It is November 12, 1997, and FBI Special Agent Fox Mulder has just returned to his apartment from Trinity Hospital after receiving news that his partner of four years, Special Agent Dana Scully, is a living miracle. Literally overnight, her terminal cancer has gone into remission. But a shadow of guilt still haunts Mulder. He has difficulty accepting, or even fathoming, the fact that his quest for the truth has put Scully's life in such jeopardy. As he sits at his desk, his mind wanders from Scully to the other woman bound up with his life of searching, his sister, Samantha. He is still confused about his meeting with her—or a young woman claiming to be Samantha—two nights ago. Mulder gazes once more at the blood- and tear-soaked picture of him and Samantha taken so many years ago. While the tears are his, the blood is allegedly that of the nefarious Cigarette Smoking Man. Assistant Director Skinner informed Mulder that there is reason to believe that the Smoking Man was assassinated, shot from outside the window of his apartment.

Mulder leans back in his desk chair, staring at but hardly noticing the desk's more than typically chaotic appearance, in the wake of the recent police and FBI crime-scene searches. His mind is now nearly as disordered as his desk. He reconsiders all that Michael Kritschgau has told him and also the Cigarette Smoking Man's claim that Kritschgau's information wasn't entirely to be trusted, that it was only a now familiar mix of fact and fiction designed to further the ends of . . . of whom? Too vexed to follow that train of thought any further, his mind shifts to recall the uncomfortable and accusatory discussion with his partner's brother, Bill Scully, outside Dana's hospital room. This leads him to think again about Scully's suffering and how much blame he might bear for it, his thoughts circling back to where they began.

Mulder sighs and shifts his eyes from the desk to take in the wreckage surrounding him; the disordered contents of his life lie littered around his apartment. Still too numb to clean Scott Ostelhoff's blood from his rug, Mulder lets his eyes wander past it to the closest bookshelf. His eyes come to rest on an 1865 first-edition copy of George Grote's *Plato and the Other Companions of Sokrates*, and he immediately thinks back to his studies at Oxford. His philosophy professor, like Grote, preferred "Sokrates," with the Greek kappa, to the now more familiar "Socrates." (After all, that's how Socrates would have spelled it, he'd remark.) Beginning to stir from this brown study, Mulder reaches over and pulls the book from the shelf. He recognizes the well-worn sections of the text, sections through which he now remembers searching for clues to the contents of Plato's dialogues, especially those early dialogues — the so-called Socratic dialogues — that feature most prominently Sokrates the searcher, the teacher, the willing guide to the good life.

Almost without thinking, Mulder now finds himself grasping his copy of *Plato's Complete Works* as well as R. E. Allen's translations and commentaries on some of Plato's early dialogues. But he's really grasping for something he can't quite remember, or perhaps for something that has always just eluded him, like the answer to one more X-File, one whose outline was vaguely visible to him years ago, in his student days, and which hovers near, promising helpful connections to his present conundrum.

Mulder begins to reexamine the notes he placed in the margins of Plato's early dialogues. He is again taken in by Plato's writing, as he was so many years before. Although he is alone, we can hear Mulder's thoughts . . .

In his speech of defense during his trial for being a public menace, the Greek philosopher Sokrates puts his audience in mind of a bit of wisdom attributed to the so-called Seven Sages and inscribed at the temple at Delphi: Know thyself. Reflecting this wisdom, Sokrates cautions his listeners, "The unexamined life is not worth living for men."[1] Moreover, he reminds those in attendance at his trial that he has spent virtually his entire adult life questioning the citizens of Athens about who they thought they were, often revealing to them the self-deceptions that obscured their understanding of themselves and their place in society. If there is anything remembered by the typical reader of Plato's *Apology*, it is Sokrates' emphasis on the fundamental importance of seeking self-knowledge and finding the truth. But what *more* do I need to know about the beliefs and recommendations of the historical Sokrates before I can safely conclude that this single-minded pursuit of self-knowledge and truth is the path to Sokratic excellence and the good life *for me*? And what are its dangers?

It was three citizens of Athens — Meletus, joined by Anytus and Lycon — who brought Sokrates to trial in 399 BCE. These three purported to be working for the best interests of the state, according to the protocol for the Athenian system of legal justice. The Athenians had no public official corresponding to the role of district attorney, as we have, to bring state charges against an individual. Instead, it was left to concerned citizens to provide a check on potentially dangerous activities of others in the state. If someone acted in a manner contrary to the state's best interests, the citizens were expected to bring the matter before the magistrates for legal action, if the magistrates determined such action was warranted by the questionable activity. In Sokrates' case, the magistrates were moved by the appeal of Meletus and his confederates to issue formal charges against Sokrates. Diogenes Laertius, the ancient chronicler, on the authority of Favorinus, a first-century historian who claims to have searched out this information in the Athenian state archives, reports the indictment in this way: "This indictment and affidavit is sworn by Meletus of Pithus, against Socrates, the son of Sophroniscus of Alopece: Socrates is guilty of refusing to recognize the gods recognized by the state, and of introducing other new divinities. He is also guilty of corrupting the youth. The penalty demanded is death."[2]

But weren't the three formal charges a convenient fiction, a screen to conceal the real intentions of those powerful Athenians with vested interests in the status quo who wanted Sokrates discredited or, ideally, out of the way entirely so their work could continue, uninterrupted by the searching questions of one who made it his life's work—his "divine mission," he calls it in his speech of defense—to uncover the truth? What are the real facts in this case?[3]

The date of Sokrates' trial was fewer than five years removed from Athens's humiliating defeat at the hands of her archrival, Sparta. What followed that defeat was a period of near-tyrannical rule by a cadre of thirty, installed by Spartan command in place of the Athenian democratic institutions. But the democratic tradition, with roots running back over a hundred years to the reforms of Cleisthenes in the late sixth century BCE, would not be so easily swept aside. Staunch democrats—among them Anytus, one of Sokrates' eventual accusers—outlasted the "tyranny of the Thirty" and had reestablished a fragile democracy by the century's turning.

But what about Sokrates? Why would the influential among the Athenian democrats fear him enough to want him "disappeared"? And if Sokrates was a *genuine* threat to the state, why the facade of religious charges? Why not just expose him as an enemy of the state? If there are answers to these questions, they're likely to be found in Plato's dialogues, but they certainly won't be obvious.

If I remember anything from my Oxford days, it's that these dialogues always work on multiple levels; like X-Files, nothing in them is *exactly* as it seems. Not recognizing the fact until now, it seems I've been reading X-Files long before I lobbied to reopen that FBI unit in 1991. Sokrates' trial might have been the very first X-File, millennia before J. Edgar Hoover's Native American werewolf in 1946. And just as is the case with my FBI X-Files, I've never been entirely satisfied that I've solved the case of Sokrates.

In Plato's *Apology*, Sokrates reminds the jurors of his day-to-day activities, tracing back to the time the oracle at Delphi proclaimed Sokrates wisest among men. Confused by the oracle's statement, Sokrates begins a search for its possible meaning. He explains:

> I went to see one of those reputed to be wise. . . . Then, when I examined this man—there is no need for me to tell you his name, he was one of our public men—my experience was something like this: I thought that he appeared wise to many people and especially to himself, but that he was not. . . . After this I approached another man, one of those thought to be wiser than he, and I thought the same thing. . . . After that I proceeded systematically. . . . I found that those who had the highest reputation were nearly the most deficient. . . . After the politicians, I went to the poets, the writers of tragedies and dithyrambs and the others. . . . Finally I went to the craftsmen. . . . So even now I continue this investigation as the god bade me—and I go around seeking out anyone, citizen or stranger, whom I think wise. Then if I do not think he is, I come to the assistance of the god and show him that he is not wise.[4]

What result would these Sokratic inquiries have had on the mind-set of the average Athenians who daily witnessed them in the public places of Athens? They would see that these generally respected men are not experts, are not fit to guide their city. Worse, the thoughtful citizen must also begin to recognize that the *demos*—the '*people*' in '*demo*cracy'—have thus shown themselves unable to function properly in their role as the ultimate source of power in the state, the force that places power in the hands of those who will propose and implement policies on behalf of Athens and her citizens. These Athenian citizens, after all, were responsible for appointing those figures whose incompetence to govern Sokrates' questioning reveals. If there are no wise men among the electorate, there will be none among the elected; and none will be the wiser regarding their sorry state. Wisdom is required for effective democracy, and Sokrates' daily activities bring into clear focus the weaknesses of both the democratic process and those who make it run.

In a fragile democracy, there is no place for Sokrates.

Is there a place for me in this democracy? What would those early defenders of democracy think of me? Would they act to discredit or remove me, too? And Scully? Since I opened my first X-File six years ago, but especially now, as more and more details fall into place, the picture that has come into focus for me is of a government incapable of protecting its own citizens, of looking out for their best interests, along with a kind of shadow government whose work is, at best, ambiguous, but which seems, above all, bent on obscuring its true aims. To what end? The best interests of the citizens? But a shadow government can have only shadow citizens, and these are not *us*.

That the Athenian democrats would have acted to stop me is no sure measure that this work of mine ought to be abandoned. Like Sokrates' efforts in Athens, my work must be judged on its own merits. Can it be favorably compared with the work of Sokrates, twenty-four hundred years ago in that nascent democracy at Athens?

What good came of Sokrates' unceasing investigations? Plato's dialogue *Euthyphro,* set chronologically shortly before Sokrates' speech of defense in the *Apology,* provides a potentially frightening suggestion. In this dialogue, Sokrates and the priest Euthyphro bump into each other just outside the law courts in Athens. Sokrates is on his way into the court to hear a reading of the charges contained in Meletus's formal indictment, so that he may begin to prepare his speech of defense for the trial. Euthyphro, though, is there with the intention of seeking an indictment for murder against his own father for having captured, bound, and abandoned one of his own slaves who had, in a drunken rage, killed another of his servants. Euthyphro's father had taken no thought of what might happen to this drunken, murdering slave while he sent to the temple priests at Athens to discover what should be done with him. Before the messenger returned with instructions from the temple, the murdering slave had died of neglect.

Euthyphro's friends, relatives, and family members are outraged that Euthyphro dares to bring this case to the attention of the magistrates, pleading that the gods will surely be offended by this affront to his own father. Euthyphro is not deterred—is perhaps, in fact, spurred by this general resistance to his plan—and assures Sokrates that it is the right and pious thing to do. Euthyphro boldly remarks, in an affected third-person voice, "Euthyphro would not be superior to the majority of men if I did not have accurate knowledge of all such things."[5] The priest Euthyphro has thus set himself up as an expert on the subject of pious behavior, and Sokrates is eager to test the knowledge Euthyphro claims to possess.

Characteristically, it doesn't take long before Euthyphro is confounded by Sokrates' questions, offering conflicting accounts to Sokrates in his effort to make clear his ideas. Initially so confident in his wisdom, Euthyphro soon admits to being unable to tell Sokrates what he means concerning the nature of piety, justice, and right action. At the close of this short dialogue, Euthyphro abruptly flees the scene in confusion, pleading other important business to which he must now attend.

It is interesting to note that the defense Euthyphro presents for bringing this criminal complaint against his father is one that we find familiar; in fact, the justification Euthyphro offers is strikingly akin to our own *ideal* of justice: our personification of Justice holds a balance scale to weigh the evidence while wearing a blindfold over her eyes so as not to be biased by mere appearances. One ought not to pay attention to *who* stands before the bench—friend or stranger, wealthy or poor, black or white—but only to the *facts* that bear on that person's guilt or innocence. As Euthyphro points out to Sokrates: "One should only watch whether the killer acted justly or not; if he acted justly, let him go, but if not, one should prosecute, [even] if . . . the killer shares your hearth and table."[6] While it is not included in this dialogue, Sokrates articulates the same view in another of Plato's dialogues, the *Gorgias,* when he urges his interlocutors that a person "should accuse himself first and foremost, and then too his family and anyone else dear to him who happens to behave unjustly at any time," so that the wrongdoer might be properly punished and so become a just person once again, recovering the health of his soul.[7]

What is it, then, that prompts me to revisit this dialogue now, as I search for an answer to whether my search for the truth parallels Sokrates' own "divine mission"? What does Sokrates' questioning of Euthyphro accomplish? In this case, Sokrates seems to move Euthyphro from what even Sokrates seems to believe is the correct course of action—bringing his father's actions to the attention of the court magistrates to determine whether a crime has been committed, so that the action, if criminal, may be properly punished—to paralyzing Euthyphro with doubt about his actions. Sokrates seems to have taken away Euthyphro's confidence in his action and replaced it with nothing positive but only perplexity. Euthyphro departs, seemingly at a loss, perhaps unsure about what he ought to do now. One more respected "expert" has been publicly knocked from a pedestal. How many such can Sokrates knock down before society becomes unmoored?

If I succeed in learning the facts about myself, of finding those truths for which I've been searching past all obstacles, and along the way uncover what seems an almost unimaginable conspiracy, will *I*, like Sokrates, take from people their beliefs about a well-founded, democratically run society, leaving citizens with an awful truth and nothing to install in its place? Should I, in my searching for my past—my *self*—and the larger truth that increasingly seems to be bound up with it, properly be seen, as those staunch democrats perhaps saw Sokrates, as an enemy of the people, a threat to be quieted or removed?

Mulder catches himself contemplating taping an X on the window in front of him, hoping that someone will appear with answers to these difficult questions. But Deep Throat is dead, as is the mysterious X—two more apparent casualties for Mulder's cause, his quest for the truth. After bouncing his basketball a few dozen times, Mulder sits back down to revisit the second of his ancient X-File cases involving Sokrates . . .

Am I a threat? If so, to whom, or what? Who am I? What am I becoming? . . .

The unexamined life is not worth living. Know thyself. These sayings rattle in my head like a taunt, telling me *what* I should do without telling me *how* to succeed. I think I've tried as hard as anyone—harder than most ever do—to piece together my life, to fill in the gaps, to make sense of everything that has happened to me. My father, his work, his shadowy connections; what my mother knew of all this, and only later came to understand. And my sister, Samantha, now brought before my eyes, finally, after all these years, then taken away just as quickly, trailing even more questions, as she drove off with one who seemed to be my very nemesis, suddenly turned potential benefactor. What happened? What's happening? If I can't fill in these blanks, or am given too many false leads and phony answers, will it be impossible for me to fulfill the Sokratic dictum? Will "they" have gotten rid of *me* as surely as if they had put a bullet through my chest, as they did with Cancer Man the other night?

Still, now in the midst of these ruminations on Sokrates and the dialogues of Plato, I can't shake the feeling I'm overlooking another possibility in my search. There's more here to be learned.

Plato's dialogue *Meno* is set in Athens, chronologically just a few years prior to the events described in the *Euthyphro* and the *Apology*. Most likely,

Sokrates' conversation with Meno takes place about 403 BCE, shortly after the overthrow of the short-lived tyranny of the Thirty, in the early days of the recovered democracy. It needn't be a factual account of an actual meeting between Meno and Sokrates—and, later in the dialogue, Anytus, staunch defender of democratic Athens—but it may have been. Meno is certainly a historical figure, as we find reference to him in accounts other than Plato's dialogues. It is perhaps in this dialogue that Plato most forcefully drives home what it is to know oneself—to *have* a self to know, or to *be* a self that can be known—by showing us a frightening example of a non-self: Meno.

The *Meno* starts almost like the other Sokratic dialogues begin, with Sokrates quickly shifting his interlocutor's attention to the importance of discovering the definition of a moral concept, in this instance, virtue. But unlike Plato's other early dialogues, Sokrates' main interlocutor, Meno, is not interested in developing his own proposals for a definition of virtue. By comparison, for example, in the *Euthyphro* the priest tenaciously defends his favored conception of piety by repeatedly making revisions to his initial definition that address potential difficulties raised during the course of Sokrates' questioning. Indeed, Euthyphro is so enamored of his favored candidate for a definition of "piety" that he finally and happily returns to it, without immediately recognizing that fact, just prior to the close of the dialogue; he is so convinced that something like his original general definition is correct that, through a number of revisions that had seemed to leave that definition behind, he eventually wends his way back to it in response to Sokrates' questions. Yet Meno, by comparison, after three times offering *different* popular definitions of virtue, will do nothing either to explain or defend any of them. He simply drops each proposed definition at the first hint of trouble.

As eventually becomes clear over the course of this dialogue, Meno is really only interested in having others tell him things, things that sound impressive and that will make him appear intelligent when he repeats them in public; he even boasts to Sokrates, at one point, that he has made a thousand fine speeches on virtue. But the unfortunate result of Meno's practice of memorizing others' beliefs is that he no more understands these ideas than a parrot knows the meaning of what it has been trained to recite. Lacking understanding, Meno is unable to edit the beliefs he picks up; he becomes a walking set of conflicting beliefs, without the skill to recognize that embarrassing fact. More important, though, it is not obvious that there is anyone we can honestly call "Meno." For this figure in Plato's dialogue who answers to that name is really no more than a collection of *others'* beliefs and ideas (others who are themselves, perhaps, no more than that, as well). Meno cannot fulfill Sokrates' request, cannot come to know himself; there is no self to know. Certainly there is a physical human being here, called Meno. It occupies space and time. It even has a history. Some collection of past and present events can be ascribed to this physical entity. But there is just as certainly nothing about it to make it more than accidentally unique, to stamp it with the mark of *a self*. Perhaps the best indication of this is that it is Sokrates who excuses himself and abandons the conversation, thus bringing this dialogue to a close.

If Meno cannot come to know himself because he is no more than a collection of others' ideas and convictions, how could any of us who have been raised and taught by others, who are the beneficiaries of long traditions of belief and practice—or who have been fed a steady diet of lies and half-truths—ever hope to accomplish this task? Unless Sokrates is a charlatan—a popular suspicion to which Sokrates refers in his speech of defense, and against which he believes he must defend himself in the court of popular opinion—there must be an answer in these dialogues, buried in details and implications, waiting to be uncovered.

Sokrates works tirelessly in the *Meno* to get Meno to do his own work on the problem of defining virtue, expressly telling Meno to set aside the ideas of his teacher, Gorgias, and to explain his own beliefs, so that these can be investigated in their conversation. At least this much is clear to me: Sokrates sees this inquiry into one's beliefs as the key to coming to know oneself. This activity constitutes the self-examination Sokrates stresses as essential to any human life worth living. Why is that? Because it is only in this process of stating, clarifying, comparing, revising (or perhaps rejecting) beliefs that one begins to understand the content of those beliefs and, as a result, the content of one's self. For it is just these beliefs that make us who we are. These are the beliefs and ideals that motivate us to act as we do, and so define our character. The beliefs and ideals we choose, as a result of rational inquiry—and not those features that we come to possess by mere historical or biological accident—are what mark a person as who he or she is.

Yet it is just these beliefs that Meno refuses to examine. He never makes any belief his own by working to understand it, fitting it into a consistent network of beliefs, and consciously affirming it as his own. No search. No self. No wonder Sokrates leaves at the close of this dialogue. He leaves no one behind; he has been talking to a ghost all along.

Nowhere in Sokrates' troubling exchange with Meno does Sokrates show the slightest interest in any historical facts about Meno. His emphasis is wholly on beliefs—especially beliefs related to the key moral concepts under discussion—and the process of investigating those beliefs. I can now see that we're meant to conclude that the self is not a collection of mere historical accidents but the product of informed and deliberate choices, the products of careful Sokratic investigation. The activity of examining one's life is, in fact, the activity of constructing the self. The self emerges through this activity; it is not discovered as some artifact might be.

If Sokrates is correct about Meno, they couldn't kill me by keeping my past from me. Still, . . . that may be small comfort if I don't yet know *who* I am in this deeper Sokratic sense.

But perhaps the most important lesson here is that who I am is always under *my* control, because the choices I make in these inquiries are always mine. And it is up to me to be willing to do all the difficult work—the work that Meno shuns—to *craft* an answer to Sokrates' question: Who are you?

Mulder reaches into his desk drawer for a stashed bag of sunflower seeds. However, he happens upon an old family photo album. He flips through the pages, now wondering more than ever why he believes knowing the past will help him to know who he is now. Perhaps Sokrates is of more help. He sets the album aside and again begins paging through Plato's *Apology,* studying the details of Sokrates' trial, to begin the day's third philosophical investigation of the unexplained . . .

I returned to Plato's Sokratic dialogues after all these years removed from them, prompted by something I only half remembered about them, like a familiar tune running on a loop through my head but whose lyrics I couldn't quite pin down. I was looking for something to guide me through the latest, most vexing developments in my own search for the truth. But what have I found? Nothing but more X-Files, this time from ancient Greece. I stare at the words on the pages, follow the details of each conversation, examine each argument Sokrates advances, and am all too keenly aware that these are just the pieces of a bigger puzzle Plato requires us to assemble, if we wish to understand. To understand the dialogues? More: to understand ourselves.

After my latest reflection on the *Meno,* I'm also sure it's necessary that it is *I* who assemble this picture. Plato can't do that for me, or hand me the answer. He even says that much, in his *own* voice for a change, in a public letter he wrote, now referred to as Plato's "Seventh Letter": "This knowledge is not something that can be put into words like other sciences; but after long continued intercourse between teacher and pupil, in joint pursuit of the subject, suddenly, like light flashing when a fire is kindled, it is born in the soul and straight away nourishes itself."[8] Even if Plato *could* hand us answers, he wouldn't. Through these dialogues, Plato has Sokrates show us why it is so crucial that we do this work on our own, why there is no other way to arrive at the lessons, the wisdom, the knowledge of self he wants us to gain, on our way to living well.

Who am I? *Am* I an enemy of the people? Or am I one of those concerned citizens, like Meletus, Anytus, and Lycon, who act on behalf of the state when it can't—or *won't*—act on its own? Then, am I, perhaps like Meletus and his cohorts, mistaken in my beliefs about my cause, or misguided in my intentions or motives? Am I so sure my reasons aren't petty, or merely personal, as perhaps were the motives of Sokrates' accusers? Perhaps another hard look at the *Apology*—an examination of Sokrates' motivations—will help me with my own case, if I can only sort through the relevant details of that ancient X-File.

The speech of defense Sokrates offers the Athenian jury is presented as a defense against the formal charges brought by Meletus and his colleagues, and it is that. But it is also more than that. A careful reading of the speech reveals Sokrates' larger defense of his life as a philosopher, Sokrates' own *Apologia pro Vita Sua.* In recalling this speech to us, Plato is asking us to judge Sokrates on yet another level: can Sokrates be acquitted for choosing to live his life as a philosopher, for questioning any Athenian he encounters, and for going "around doing nothing but persuading both young and old ... not to care for [the] body or ... wealth in preference to, or as strongly as for the best possible state of [the] soul"?[9]

Sokrates, repeatedly in his speech of defense and in others of Plato's Sokratic dialogues, states his interest in the well-being of the people of Athens and his role as a genuine benefactor of the state. He goes so far as to call himself the "true statesman," the only one living who practices the true political craft.[10] It seems absurd to think of Sokrates on the campaign trail, making political speeches to the electorate with the hope of moving them to vote for him. In fact, parts of his speech of defense, and nearly the whole of the *Gorgias,* seem to cast him as the *anti*politician. He makes it a point to distance himself from the ordinary practices of the orator, telling the jurors he will not resort to mere rhetorical tricks or shameless spectacle in order to be acquitted of the charges in Meletus's formal indictment. What, then, can he mean when he says he is the only true politician? There must be an answer in the texts; these lines don't flow idly from Plato's hand, then survive for twenty-four hundred years.

The beginning of an answer to this question comes by way of a variation on the typical Sokratic question: What is the *role* of the politician in the state? What is Sokrates' conception of the true political craft, and how does he see it connected to his life as a philosopher? In the Athenian democracy—far more direct than our own representative democracy—the politician was charged with representing the best interests of the citizens by trying to make the best possible community in which they could live. One way to accomplish this goal is through establishing laws and policies to regulate the behavior of citizens in a way most conducive to the good of all citizens. However, with the establishment of any law come the lawbreakers, those who feel themselves above the law and so not bound by its dictates. With each illegal act of these lawbreakers, the good of the community is undermined a bit more. The typical politician's response, certainly in our day, is to enact ever-harsher penalties with the hope that these will finally curb the criminal interests of the lawbreakers. But this seems to be a vain hope. Nor does this description seem apt for the figure of Sokrates Plato describes to us in these dialogues. Sokrates is no lawmaker, and certainly no enforcer of public codes.

So what am I overlooking in this speech of defense? What details are here, in this text in front of my eyes, but still eluding my grasp? What other way could there be to practice the craft of the politician, to work for the best interests of the citizens, without falling into our stereotypical mold of the politician?

Why didn't I go out and rob someone this morning? Why didn't I murder anyone today? Certainly not because I was afraid of the law and its corresponding punishments. I simply have no desire to do those things, because I believe they're wrong, and I think it's important for me to avoid doing things that are wrong. Perhaps I shouldn't be thinking of laws that are imposed on people, external forces capable of shaping the behavior of citizens of the state, but laws of another sort altogether. I've given these laws to myself and, in so doing, stamp them as ones that I *want* to obey, not break, regardless of what punishments might be associated with them. I'm governing myself.

What does this perspective on law have to do with Sokrates? Everything. The daily activity Sokrates describes in the *Apology* is activity designed to get each individual citizen of Athens to think about these sorts of laws, to test and refine their understanding of these important principles, so that they may be used to help guide them in their choices day to day in order to live a better life, in order for *all* to benefit from that life well lived. The person who could bring an entire community of individuals to the level of self-reflection necessary to govern themselves justly would certainly deserve the title "true statesman." Such a person would be a genuine benefactor of the state, as Sokrates proclaims himself in his speech of defense.

I'm confident Sokrates' motives in questioning the Athenians are as he explains them in his speech of defense; Sokrates takes himself to be on a divine mission to improve the citizens of Athens and so to make the state a better place for them all. His tireless search for the truth, as well as his acting as a guide to each citizen he interrogates, is just the work of the true statesman. If he has fallen short of his goal, it isn't through any fault of his own. How else could he educate in a way that would produce the understanding necessary for knowledge in a setting where so many already believed they knew the answers to these important questions of his? If anyone thinks he's in possession of something, he isn't going to look for it; it's only when a person recognizes that something is lacking that he will start his search. The confusion that arrives in the Sokratic inquiry is a necessary first step in prompting understanding, and so in gaining knowledge. If one of Sokrates' interlocutors fails to pursue the inquiry past that intermediate state of perplexity, that is the risk and price of true education, the kind necessary to establish a firm foundation for the democracy Athens cherished. While a state *could* run well on mere true belief, it would only do so by luck; no true statesman would settle for *chance* as a dictator.

How many of us, though, could ever be statesmen of this sort? Plato's Sokrates is often said to be a model, yet inimitable—himself a character as puzzling as the content of any FBI X-File Scully and I ever encountered.

I'm struck, suddenly, by another line from Plato's *Meno*, spoken by Anytus in response to Sokrates' question concerning who teaches virtue: any Athenian gentleman could teach a willing student about virtue; we've all learned it—had it handed down to us—from those who have come before us.[11] When Anytus utters this, in the context of the dialogue, it is obvious that he is colossally mistaken, and we are meant to recognize the enormity of his error. As I step back from the *Meno*, back into my world, though, this exchange suddenly seems more hopeful. Perhaps it doesn't take a city full of Sokrateses but only one Sokrates who can make a city full of virtuous citizens, citizens who know themselves and, hence, govern themselves with moral principles that have survived Sokratic scrutiny.

I don't need to imitate Sokrates the statesman. I need to imitate Sokrates the person. I need to recognize that *I* don't know many things—and now I'm not talking about mere historical facts—and that it is important for me to be actively searching for that knowledge; for it's only by actively searching that I'll come to understand, to know, and so to live well. In one sense perhaps, and surprisingly, Plato is asking me to become more like Anytus or Meletus—just a plain citizen concerned and willing to act for the state's well-being—but with this important difference: I must be a citizen whose judgment isn't obscured, one who, unlike Meno, never tires of doing the hard work necessary to understanding and so who *knows* what is best, and so does what is best, but not merely accidentally, as Euthyphro seemingly acts against his father.

Perhaps, then, in this regard I'm not too far different from Sokrates the person. After all, aren't we both seeking the truth with a single-minded determination, truth that will serve the best interests of the state, that is, the citizens whose lives are bound up with one another's? But if rereading these dialogues has taught me anything, it's that surface comparisons are always only an invitation to inquiry. It's certainly possible for two people to be doing the same thing yet to be poles apart with respect to the moral worth of their actions and their corresponding characters. Maybe I'm more like the *vengeful* Meletus—driven by the memory of my sister's abduction—or the *shortsighted* Anytus—blindly rushing forward with the best intentions, only to harm those close to me, like Scully—than the virtuous and virtue-seeking Sokrates.

I think I must, now more than ever, take to heart the very advice Sokrates gives to himself: "*I* have long been surprised at my own wisdom—and doubtful of it, too. That's why I think it's necessary to keep reinvestigating whatever I say, since self-deception is the worst thing of all. How could it not be terrible, indeed, when the deceiver never deserts you even for an instant but is always right there with you? Therefore, I think we have to turn back frequently to what we've already said, in order to test it by looking at it 'backwards and forwards' as the . . . poet puts it."[12]

Notes

1. Plato, *Apology,* trans. G. M. A. Grube, in *Plato: Complete Works,* ed. John M. Cooper (Indianapolis: Hackett, 1997), 38a. All quotes from Plato, other than those from R. E. Allen, are from this anthology.

2. Plato, *The Dialogues of Plato*, ed. R. E. Allen (New Haven: Yale University Press, 1984), 1:61.

3. Plato, *Apology*, 30a.

4. Plato, *Apology*, 21c–23b.

5. Plato, *Euthyphro*, trans. G. M. A. Grube, 5a.

6. Plato, *Euthyphro*, 5b.

7. Plato, *Gorgias*, trans. Donald J. Zeyl, 480c.

8. Plato, "Letter VII," trans. Glenn R. Morrow, 341c–d.

9. Plato, *Apology*, 30a.

10. See Plato, *Gorgias*, 521d; and Plato, *Meno*, trans. G. M. A. Grube, 100a.

11. Plato, *Meno*, 92e–93a.

12. Plato, *Cratylus*, trans. C. D. C. Reeve, 428d.

Scully as Pragmatist Feminist

"truths" Are Out There

Erin McKenna

At the start of *The X-Files* Scully is the obvious opposite of Mulder. The traditional dualisms of reason/emotion, objective/subjective, and scientific (hard) knowledge / felt (soft) knowledge (among others) are clear. The typical male/female dualism, however, is interestingly reversed between the two characters. Throughout the series the writers play with the tensions within Scully, and Mulder as well. They also begin to challenge the dualistic structure itself. It seems as if we were supposed to come to see that the strength is in the complementary nature of the opposites (a kind of Rousseau-style marriage without the radical inequality).[1] However, over time we see a change in Scully (and Mulder as well). I will not try to analyze the whole series here but rather use a single episode to ground a discussion of Scully's approach to knowledge and truth and how it develops over the years.[2]

The Importance of "all things"

In season 7, an episode entitled "all things" (written and directed by Gillian Anderson) represents an important shift in Scully's scientific approach to knowledge and truth. In this episode Scully encounters a former lover and, with Mulder out of the country, embarks on a series of encounters that open her to other ways of knowing—auras, chakras, visions, the importance of coincidence. While there were hints of a growing openness to such ways of knowing before, this episode goes further.

I will argue that in the transformation we see a shift in views of metaphysics and epistemology that mirrors the shift that occurs with the emergence of American pragmatism and is strengthened by certain elements of feminist philosophy. In this shift reality is changing rather than static, knowledge becomes a working hypothesis rather than something certain, truth becomes plural rather than singular. Further, philosophy becomes an experiential enterprise that finds meaning in practical consequences rather than the logical relations of concepts. On the move away from more classic philosophical methods, Charlene Haddock Seigfried writes:

> Pragmatism and feminism reject philosophizing as an intellectual game that takes purely logical analysis as its special task. For both, philosophical techniques are means, not ends. The specific, practical ends are set by various communities of interest, the members of which are best situated to name, resist, and overcome the oppressions of class, sex, race, and gender. The problem with philosophy's enchantment with 'the logic of general notions' is that it forces specific situations into predetermined, abstract categories. Pragmatism's fundamental criticism of traditional philosophy is that it 'substitutes discussion of the meaning of concepts and their dialectical relationship to one another' for knowledge of the specific groups of individuals, concrete human beings, and special institutions or social arrangements.[3]

While the pragmatist feminist shift seems to threaten the more rational, objective, conceptual, scientific approach often held up as the ideal, it need not. That remains a way of knowing, and an important and often reliable or workable way. Pragmatism is itself grounded in the scientific method. However, pragmatism and feminism make room for other ways of knowing. They may even require them in order to fill out the possibilities of reality.

Episode Summary

In "all things" we find Scully as her usual skeptical self, not paying attention as Mulder explains the increasing complexity of crop circles. She refuses to join Mulder as he heads off to England to wait for the appearance of an expected crop circle. Mulder asks Scully to go see a woman at the American Taoist Healing Center to pick up some information he needs on the crop circles. She does not make this a priority, and when she finally does go, she is rude and dismissive, even though she does not know what the center does. However, through a series of coincidences, she finds her former lover (and former teacher), Dr. Daniel Waterston (Nicholas Surovy), in the hospital. He has been living in Washington, D.C., for ten years, and she did not know it. He has heart problems and may be dying.

We find out he was married and had a family when he and Scully were previously involved. Scully had left to end the affair and left medicine to join the FBI. Subsequently Daniel's marriage had dissolved, and his daughter blames Scully for what has happened to her family. This pushes Scully further in her questioning of life paths not taken, of the choices we make along the way—an overarching theme of this episode.

When Scully finally visits the American Taoist Healing Center, the material she picks up for Mulder drops from her hand and reveals information on the heart chakra. Later, when she returns to the center, she says, "I'm a medical doctor and a scientist and you're right, I don't know what it is that you do." She had been intrigued, though, when the woman had previously told her she needed to keep her mind open and slow down. She is back to find out what the woman meant and to sort out what all the coincidences, near accidents, and visions might mean. She encounters an entirely different perspective on disease and life. Accidents and disease may be ways of getting our attention so that we focus on our choices (our life paths) more clearly. The woman at the center, who was a physicist herself, makes the judgment that Scully is more open than she may realize; it is a matter of what she does with the openness. More coincidences and some visions finally push Scully to try a different approach. With Daniel now in a coma, she has someone come to the hospital to run energy through his chakras. His physician gets very upset, but Scully argues that if it is not harming Daniel, they should be open to it. The daughter agrees, and it seems to work. Scully believes it may be what saved his life. Daniel belittles this belief as he seeks to get her to go back both to medicine and to him.

At the end of the episode, the vision of a woman in a ball cap and hooded jacket, which has repeatedly led Scully to critical junctures, appears one more time. This time when Scully chases her, she catches the woman, and it turns out to be Mulder. He is back early because no crop circles appeared. Scully and Mulder end up in a late-night conversation about how we find our path in life and what might happen if we miss important signs along the way. They apparently spend the night together.

Some Basics of a Pragmatist Approach to Knowledge and Truth

To understand pragmatism, one needs to place it in the larger context of the history and development of philosophy. I apologize if the brevity of this treatment results in a caricature of any position. I cannot hope to present a full picture of pragmatism here, but I will focus on William James's *Pragmatism* to pull in the concepts most central to my present analysis.

Pragmatism takes Darwin's theory of evolution seriously. This view required some radical rethinking of metaphysics. Reality was no longer static but changing—in process. Nor could knowledge and truth any longer be singular, universal, and unchanging. Knowledge and truth became working hypotheses rather than something fixed and final. Pragmatism is at its core a melioristic philosophy; it sees the world as malleable and seeks growth and improvement. However, it recognizes that humans are fallible, that our perspectives are always partial and limited. This, combined with a changing world, calls for an experimental method as the most reliable way to gain knowledge and a theory of truth that embraces pluralism. Knowledge and truths are partial (not complete), perspectival (not neutral, universal, or objective), and provisional (not final or finished).

As James says, "The widest field of knowledge that ever was or will be still contains some ignorance, . . . Some bits of information always escape."[4] Further, individuals cannot ever know it all. We all have our biases, and we always approach things from a certain perspective. This perspective colors what we see and limits what we pay attention to. The fact that as humans we make mistakes, that we miss things, that we see things through specific lenses, results in a view of knowledge that cannot (and does not seek to) make claims to objectivity and certainty. More-traditional views of science and philosophy seek to find ways to neutralize such "bias" and through logic and controlled experiments to find *the* objective truth. For pragmatism, our knowledge grows through experience and the experimental method, but it is never finished. This impacts the pragmatist view of truth as well. Truth is seen as both partial and in process, and so a pluralistic view is embraced.

The pragmatists, too, believe that "the truth is out there." As James says, for pragmatism, "*true ideas are those that we can assimilate, validate, corroborate and verify. False ideas are those that we can not. That is the practical difference it makes to us to have true ideas; that, therefore, is the meaning of truth, for it is all that truth is known-as.*"[5] Truth, on this view, is a process; it requires verification. This sounds very much in line with the hard, empirical, scientific approach to knowledge and truth that is tied to Scully early in the series. But then James says, "You can say of it then either that 'it is useful because it is true' or that 'it is true because it is useful.'" According to James, both of these phrases mean exactly the same thing, namely that here is an idea that gets fulfilled and can be verified. "True is the name for whatever idea starts the verification-process, useful is the name for its completed function in experience. . . . Primarily, and on the common-sense level, the truth of a state of mind means this function of *a leading that is worth while.*"[6] This view seems to make room for Mulder's softer, more subjective approach to knowledge and truth. His hypotheses, proven or not, do lead inquiry in some productive directions. In "all things" Scully clearly begins to meld these two approaches (though she is still obviously uncomfortable with the new ways of seeing) and so can be seen to represent the pragmatist approach to knowledge and truth.

Over time Scully moves from being a scientific empiricist who seeks materialist explanations that confirm *a* truth of the matter to being a pluralist and radical empiricist who seeks materialist explanations but is open to other input. She becomes more comfortable with uncertainty and develops an openness to multiple perspectives. James's notion of radical empiricism states that only "things definable in terms drawn from experience" shall be debated, that relations between things are matters of experience, so there is no need of "trans-empirical connective support" to explain the universe.[7] That is, we can have purely empirical explanations of all debatable phenomena. However, because we are fallible and need to embrace a pluralist stance, this does not rule out the hypothesis of God or something "beyond." It does rule out dogmatic beliefs, but "if the hypothesis of God works satisfactorily in the widest sense of the word, it is true. Now whatever its residual difficulties may be, experience shows that it certainly does work, and that the problem is to build it out and determine it so that it will combine satisfactorily with all the working truths."[8] With a scientific approach one does not *need* God or the supernatural, but the pragmatist approach does not rule out such perspectives.

This matches very well with Scully's blending of science with her personal religious beliefs, her scientific certainty with her growing willingness to question and doubt. It also matches the blending of Scully and Mulder themselves. In "Beyond the Sea" we have a nice twist in which Scully takes on Mulder's openness and Mulder takes on Scully's scientific rigor and skepticism. In this episode, when Scully's father dies, she has a vision of him. (She has such visions of the dead in multiple episodes.) She starts to look in the X-Files at a folder labeled "Visions of the Dead," but she slams the drawer shut. She and Mulder then begin to investigate a case in which a psychopathic prisoner claims to have psychic abilities that can aid the agents in rescuing kidnap victims. Mulder is sure he is faking. Scully begins to believe. He knows things about her and her father. She follows his clues and finds evidence that helps to break the kidnapping case. Afraid to be publicly tied to such unconventional ways of thinking, she lies to the police about how she came to find the evidence but admits to Mulder that she found it on the basis of what the "psychic" said. Mulder tells her not to trust him, but Scully responds by saying she thought Mulder would be proud of her. She says, "I never thought I'd say this, but what if there is another explanation?"; "I've opened myself to extreme possibilities." Mulder responds by saying that one should only open oneself to "extreme possibilities" when they are true. With Mulder in the hospital with a gun-shot wound (predicted by the psychic), Scully successfully concludes the investigation, finding further confirmation along the way that the prisoner is indeed psychic. Then at the end of the episode, as Scully and Mulder switch back to their more usual roles, Scully begins to explain to Mulder how the prisoner could have known all the things he did without any supernatural abilities. Mulder asks why, with all that she has seen, she can't believe. She says, "I'm afraid to believe." The tension Scully faces in this episode, and her struggle with competing belief structures, is very much in line with the pragmatist view of how knowledge and truths change and grow with experience.

James cautions that our "truths" must agree with the world we experience and the ideas we live by. Scully would generally agree. Any new truth must "derange common sense and previous belief as little as possible, and it must lead to some sensible terminus or other that can be verified exactly. To 'work' means both these things; and the squeeze is so tight that there is little loose play for any hypothesis. Our theories are wedged and controlled as nothing else is."[9] It is this squeeze that Scully feels throughout the series. Mulder's hypotheses usually "derange common sense and previous belief" too much. Many episodes match their competing explanations for events; Scully is usually able to find one that does not "derange common sense and previous belief."

My favorite example of this is "War of the Coprophages." Mulder is in a town where people are apparently dying from cockroach attacks. He has gone there to investigate strange lights, which he thinks might be connected to UFOs. With each death, Mulder calls Scully to ask her to come help him; he makes it clear that these attacks need to be taken seriously because they have been witnessed by scientists not yahoos. Each time, she is able to explain the death in a scientific, rational way. One is an allergic reaction, one is the result of psychotic disorder connected to drug use, another is due to a brain aneurysm. By the time there is a fourth death, Scully is on her way to join Mulder because she finds the growing number of deaths improbable and strange. She suspects a new species of cockroach has been imported in the manure being sent to an alternative-fuel research facility. The sheriff in the town posits killer cockroaches from some government research gone awry. Mulder, on the other hand, begins to form a theory that the cockroaches are alien robots sent out into the universe as scouts and that the lights he came to investigate are "insect swarms." He reaches this conclusion with the help of two other scientists, who in the end go off together. The lights disappear and the cockroach attacks end. Scully sarcastically notes that by the time there is another "invasion of artificially intelligent dung eating robotic probes from outer space," the children of the two scientists will know what to do.

Scully, believes the existence of intelligent life on other planets is highly improbable given the random working of evolution (she declares herself a Darwinian at the beginning of the episode). She sees no real need to revise her final hypothesis here, though she had been moved to agree with Mulder that something strange was happening in the town. Her rational, scientific explanations of each individual death do not add up to a satisfying explanation for all of them. Further, in the end, there is room for another view that may lead us forward productively. Mulder, typing on his computer at the end of this episode, points out that through evolution we share the insect's brain as a basic reactive mechanism. If probes are sent to study us, what will extraterrestrials think of us? he wonders—as he smashes an insect that appears on his plate. Here Scully's way of seeing sits side by side with Mulder's. However, in other episodes such as "Beyond the Sea," Scully is pushed to assimilate new ways of seeing (even as she tries to back away) when old ways do not yield satisfying answers. The new "makes itself true, gets itself classed as true, by the way it works; grafting itself then upon the ancient body of truth, which thus grows much as a tree grows by the activity of a new layer of cambium."[10] This is where the pluralism of pragmatism comes into play. We have truths, rather than Truth; truths are out there.[11]

William James borrows a helpful metaphor to explain the pluralist stance of pragmatism. He describes a hotel corridor with many rooms off it. Pragmatism is the corridor. It is open to a variety of beliefs and approaches.[12] What holds pragmatism together is its approach or method. As James says, pragmatism seeks to understand events, beliefs, and theories in terms of their practical consequences. "What difference would it practically make to any one if this notion rather than that notion were true?"[13] The effects equal the conception. "The whole function of philosophy ought to be to find out what definite difference it will make to you and me, at definite instants in our life, if this world-formula or that world-formula be the true one." It is important to note here that pragmatism is more a method than a particular view. It is open to the new and stands "against dogma, artificiality, and the pretence of finality in truth."[14] Pragmatism draws on various schools of thought and life views.

James's radical empiricism calls for careful analysis of "facts" but encourages us to be open to all types of knowledge. Pragmatism "'unstiffens' our theories. She has in fact no prejudices whatever, no obstructive dogmas, no rigid canons of what shall count as proof. . . . She will entertain any hypothesis, she will consider any evidence."[15] Pragmatism is open but not overly permissive. Pragmatism, like Scully, retains a skeptical side but without a dogmatic refusal to consider other ideas. This is the philosophy most suited to the X-Files, which by definition present open, live questions that push our thinking in new directions. Though Scully may have been an unwilling participant in these explorations at first, experience brings her to a new place. The dualisms of reason/emotion, objective/subjective, and scientific (hard) knowledge / felt (soft) knowledge (among others) are blended.

Some Basics of a Feminist View of Knowledge and Truth

As with pragmatism, feminism also rejects dualistic ways of thinking. One result of this is that a pragmatist feminist perspective calls for a concept of the individual as a social self. The classical liberal notion of the self (the conception that most informs current Western thinking) is based on a false dualistic caricature. The classical liberal, rational, impartial, objective, scientific way of knowing is built on a picture of the individual as rational, competitive, autonomous, and atomistic (radically separate from others). This notion of the self underlies most social contract theory and theories of democracy. Here rational, competitive, autonomous, and atomistic individuals follow their enlightened self-interest and agree to form a contract to come together and live under a sovereign in order to gain increased peace and security. This notion of the self underlies the notion of the invisible hand and laissez-faire capitalism. This is the idea that things work out for the whole of society if rational, atomistic, autonomous individuals look out for their own self-interest without the undue interference of the government.

Both pragmatists and feminists have critiqued this view of the self as inaccurate and inadequate. They believe persons are not only rational but also emotional. Neither pragmatists nor feminists find compelling evidence that individuals are completely self-interested. In contrast to the neatly linear explanations of the origins and development of persons and society found in social contract theory, pragmatists and feminists see the development of individuals and societies as continuously ongoing and cooperative enterprises. Individuals are born into the middle of things, societies develop and change. Individuals are interconnected and interdependent from the start.

Lorraine Code offers an interesting critique of the liberal individual and traditional views of autonomy by arguing (using Annette Baier's work) that we are all "second persons." That is, we gain our sense of self and individuality through our relationships with others. The picture of the atomistic and competitive self just does not make sense for a biological creature that procreates sexually, gestates for nine months, is born helpless, and has one of the longest and most dependent childhoods of any animal we know. Starting from this, "a person perhaps is best seen as one who was long enough dependent upon other persons to acquire the essential arts of personhood. Persons essentially are second persons. Implications of this claim . . . add up to a repudiation of individualism in its ethical and epistemological manifestations, which is less an explicit critique than a demonstration of the communal basis of moral and mental activity. It is possible to endorse Baier's 'second persons' claim without renouncing individuality, if 'individuality' is not equated with 'individualism.'"[16] While this view of the self can also be found in the work of the pragmatists, feminist analysis has done much to deepen both the critique of the classical liberal individual and the development of alternative models. Most specifically for this chapter, feminist analysis has drawn attention to how our thinking about gender affects our view of the self, and so of knowledge and truth. If the self is not atomistic but rather is social, does not present itself as fully grown and autonomous but rather as dependent and developing, our notions of knowledge and truth are challenged as well.

As with pragmatism, a paper like this cannot begin to do justice to the rich history and variety found within feminist theory. So here I will continue to rely on Lorraine Code's *What Can She Know?* to make the points most central to my analysis.

First, feminist analysis reveals the ways in which women have been discredited as knowers. Through most of the history of philosophy women have been connected more to emotion than reason, more to the body than the mind, more to the particular than the universal, more to the concrete than the abstract, more to the subjective than the objective. Agent Scully must defy this picture of the feminine to gain credibility as a doctor and as an FBI agent. As a man, Mulder is granted credibility, which is then undermined by his unorthodox beliefs. Understanding that women start off with a lack of credibility is important for understanding why pragmatist and feminist views of knowledge and truth are often seen as suspect. Traditionally in philosophy "theoretical knowledge ranks as the highest achievement of reason. It is abstract, universal, timeless, and True. To attain this status it must transcend the particularity of practice (praxis) with its preoccupation with the contingent, the concrete, the here and now."[17] Women like Scully work hard to transcend as well, so they will be taken seriously. Both pragmatism and feminism challenge this idea and embrace a view of knowledge and truth that begins and ends with practice and is seen as partial and perspectival—that is, subjective. As Code says, "There is no good reason to believe that taking subjectivity into account *entails* abandoning objectivity."[18] But many who embrace the more traditional view see it this way. Both pragmatists and feminists see knowledge and truth as a slow, communicative *process.* Knowledge and truth are never fixed or complete but always tentative. Embracing the sociality and uncertainty of knowledge and truth claims is seen by pragmatists and feminists as a "safeguard against dogmatism and rigidity."[19] More-traditional views dismiss it as relativism.

In the realm of philosophy, relativism is usually seen as an "anything goes" approach to knowledge that lacks rigor and objectivity. Relativism is seen as synonymous with a lack of critical thinking and judgment. There is, however, a critical or mitigated relativism that is open to the uncertainty of knowledge, and so is able to embrace multiple perspectives, while still enabling a critical perspective capable of making informed judgments. One example of this can be seen in feminist approaches to knowledge, perhaps most clearly embodied in feminist approaches to science.

This kind of approach calls for respect for what is being studied rather than a cool distance, an ability to listen to others rather than an attempt to reduce and control others, an understanding of positionality that allows one to understand differences rather than a purported universal stance, and a willingness to be held accountable for one's actions rather than a position of neutrality.[20] One begins to wonder if this is not just good science, rather than a particularly feminist approach. Science is a project of testing hypotheses. It requires a community of inquirers to replicate and challenge results and theories. It requires control in an experiment but also an ability to see and hear the unexpected. It requires that we take the approach Lorraine Code calls mitigated or critical relativism: "Hence I have argued for a mitigated relativism, constrained by objectivity and a commitment to realism, but capable of taking subjectivity, accountability, and a range of perspectives seriously into account by refusing the tyranny of ideal objectivity, universality, and gender-neutrality."[21] Feminist approaches to knowledge and truth, then, see that the perspective of the knower is always at play and that this subjectivity must be acknowledged in order to attain anything like objectivity. Denial of subjectivity results in the misguided attempt to make a particular perspective or experience into a universal perspective or experience. Feminists understand the consequences of such a move all too well, as that is what the history of knowledge and truth claims has been — male perspectives and experiences universalized as human perspectives and experiences.

This insight supports and deepens the pragmatist approach to knowledge and truth. Pragmatism, feminism, and good science all require a processive approach to knowledge and an understanding of truth as partial, perspectival, and tentative. This calls for a pluralistic approach that is open to alternatives. The episode "all things" pushes just this point as Scully shifts her approach.

Scully's Pragmatist Feminist Approach: "all things" Considered

Throughout the series, as she seeks to explain the cases she and Mulder work, we see Scully embodying the process of developing knowledge and belief that James describes (ascribed to Schiller and Dewey). She encounters a problem that is an open question and she deliberately seeks to resolve the problem and explain the unexplained. She hits a roadblock and is pushed to consider other explanations. As James says:

> The individual has a stock of old opinions already, but he meets a new experience that puts them to a strain. Somebody contradicts them; or in a reflective moment he discovers that they contradict

each other; or he hears of facts with which they are incompatible; or desires arise in him which they cease to satisfy. The result is an inward trouble to which his mind till then had been a stranger, and from which he seeks to escape by modifying his previous mass of opinions. He saves as much of it as he can, for in this matter of belief we are all extreme conservatives. So he tries to change first this opinion, and then that (for they resist change very variously), until at last some new idea comes up which he can graft upon the ancient stock with a minimum of disturbance of the latter, some idea that mediates between the stock and the new experience and runs them into one another most felicitously and expediently.[22]

We see this in episode after episode. Scully offers her empiricist scientific explanation at the start of each case. She pursues her investigation along these lines until something she cannot explain clearly persists or something new arises. Then we are usually left to consider Mulder's more eccentric theory, with Scully's doubts ringing in our ears. She does not, however, usually rule out his ideas completely.

In "all things" we see Scully encounter a "state of perplexity, hesitation, doubt."[23] When she dismisses Mulder's trip to look for crop circles, saying she is not interested in "sneaky farmers who happened to ace geometry in high school," she is sure of her more rational scientific view and approach. When she goes to the hospital to pick up the autopsy results that confirm her view of a case as drowning, not from "inhalation of ectoplasm" as Mulder contested, but from rapidly consumed margarita mix, she is even more sure of herself. But when she opens the envelope, instead of autopsy results she finds an X-ray with her former lover's name on it. She goes back to the nurse's station to clear up the problem and confirms that the patient is indeed her former lover. She would never have known he was in D.C., much less that he was sick, if she had not worked the case with Mulder that led her to go get these autopsy results and if those results had not gotten mixed up with his file. She tries to ignore this coincidence and get on with her business, but she almost gets into an automobile accident. Being distracted by what becomes a repeated vision of a woman in a baseball cap and hooded jacket is the only thing that saves her. At the American Taoist Healing Center she first encounters the idea that the coincidences and accidents might be something more and that she should pay attention.

When Daniel's heart stops, she takes appropriate medical action, but he ends up in a coma. We then see Scully engage in an "act of search or investigation directed toward bringing to light further facts which serve to corroborate or to nullify the suggested belief."[24] When she returns to the Taoist healing center to get more information, she is engaged in investigation. When she follows the vision of the woman in the baseball cap into a Buddhist temple, she is engaged in investigation. When she brings in the man to run energy through Daniel's chakras, she is engaged in further investigation that might serve to corroborate or nullify the new beliefs she is encountering. In the end she tells Daniel it was no accident that he got sick, signaling an embrace of this knew way of thinking and knowing.

John Dewey says, "To maintain the state of doubt and to carry on systematic and protracted inquiry—these are the essentials of thinking."[25] Scully had done this throughout the series. In this episode it results in a more radical shift of perspective. In the end, when she and Mulder are talking over everything that has happened since he left town, he says, "I leave town for two days and your whole life changes?" "I didn't say my whole life changed." When Mulder notes, "You spoke to god in a Buddhist temple and god spoke back," she says, "I didn't say god spoke back." We see that Scully begins to qualify this new view of things and subject the whole experience to her more accustomed methods. These are to be seen, not as competing systems, but as complementary, as are Scully and Mulder themselves. That they apparently sleep together that night can be seen as a metaphor for the integration of the two approaches Scully and Mulder represent. That pluralism is the pragmatist feminist approach to knowledge and truths.

Conclusion

Both pragmatism and feminism are seen by some as fringe elements of philosophy. Their approach to knowledge and truth are often singled out as the grounds for dismissing them as not "real" philosophy. They are accused of being relativistic and subjective—sins from the perspective of the more traditional view of knowledge and truth, which seeks a single, universal, and objective perspective. However, careful reading of the wide variety of views explored in these traditions (again, something beyond the scope of this chapter) reveals that their relativism is a critical relativism, not an "anything goes" approach to knowledge and truth. Their subjectivity actually results in a more informed and objective stance.

Perhaps pragmatists and feminists who have worked hard to gain credibility for these schools of thought will cringe at the idea of connecting them to some of the more radical beliefs found in *The X-Files* series, and in this episode in particular. However, it is important to remember that both these schools of thought, in all their diversity, are grounded in both a radical empiricism and a radical pluralism. Knowledge and truth are always partial and incomplete, which means dogmatism and close-mindedness are not viable options. Their brand of relativism, while not overly permissive, does require remaining open. Scully remains skeptical and careful and moves her beliefs a little at a time, like James's grease spots.

> Our minds thus grow in spots; and like grease-spots, the spots spread. But we let them spread as little as possible: we keep unaltered as much of our old knowledge, as many of our old prejudices and beliefs, as we can. We patch and tinker more than we renew. The novelty soaks in; it stains the ancient mass; but it is also tinged by what absorbs it. Our past apperceives and co-operates; and in the new equilibrium in which each step forward in the process of learning terminates, it happens relatively seldom that the new fact is added *raw*. More usually it is embedded cooked, as one might say, or stewed down in the sauce of the old.[26]

Scully allows her experiences, strange as they may be, to become part of the experiences she brings to the inquiry—an inquiry based on long-held beliefs and practices. She uses intelligence, purpose, and foresight to achieve the critical engagement with the world that John Dewey calls lived experience—the most complete and satisfying kind of experience.[27] I think pragmatists and feminists alike should embrace Agent Scully as a great example of the kind of inquiry they seek to promote.

Notes

1. Rousseau's ideal marriage between Emile and Sophie is described as a complementary union of opposites. Emile's education prepares him to be rational and to evidence proper empathy so he can be a public citizen and participate in the formation of the general will. Sophie's education prepares her to be pretty, charming, and malleable. Her duties remain in the private realm, she takes on his religion and political views, and she is dependent on Emile. Rousseau argues that Emile and Sophie need to remain opposites so they can complement each other when they unite in marriage—a stronger state for each than when they are on their own. We find, however, that Sophie cannot be on her own. She is necessarily dependent on a male figure, while Emile can exist productively in his own right (just missing the refinements Sophie provides).

Thus, the complementary divide between Sophie and Emile leaves Sophie incomplete and very vulnerable.

2. This chapter can only scratch the surface of pragmatism, feminism, and *The X-Files*. There are many additional episodes to analyze and angles to be taken. For instance, a paper on Mulder and William James's essay "The Will to Believe" is just crying out to be written. Here James argues that when an issue is unsettled, with evidence and arguments on both sides, one is free to believe what works best, as long as the belief does not violate common experiences and beliefs. Would James support Mulder's will to believe? [On this topic, please see chapter 5—ed.]

3. Charlene Haddock Seigfried, *Pragmatism and Feminism: Reweaving the Social Fabric* (Chicago: University of Chicago Press, 1996), 37–38.

4. William James, *Pragmatism and Four Essays from "The Meaning of Truth"* (New York: Meridian Books, 1955), 112.

5. James, *Pragmatism*, 133.

6. James, *Pragmatism*, 135.

7. James, *Pragmatism*, 199.

8. James, *Pragmatism*, 193.

9. James, *Pragmatism*, 142.

10. James, *Pragmatism*, 52.

11. Another good example of an episode in which Scully is pushed to look beyond her current beliefs is "The Erlenmeyer Flask." Here she and another scientist discover two new base pairs of nucleotides in the "alien virus," and she is forced to admit the possibility of something extraterrestrial. She says, "I've always held science as sacred. I've always put my trust in the accepted facts. And what I saw last night—for the first time in my life, I don't know what to believe." This episode, though, ends up challenging the content of her beliefs more than her way of knowing. She is still trusting in science.

12. James, *Pragmatism*, 47.

13. James, *Pragmatism*, 42.

14. James, *Pragmatism*, 45.

15. James, *Pragmatism*, 61.

16. Lorraine Code, *What Can She Know? Feminist Theory and the Construction of Knowledge* (Ithaca, NY: Cornell University Press, 1991), 82.

17. Code, *What Can She Know?* 242.

18. Code, *What Can She Know?* 41.

19. Code, *What Can She Know?* 38.

20. Code, *What Can She Know?* 150–51.

21. Code, *What Can She Know?* 251.

22. James, *Pragmatism*, 50.

23. John Dewey, *How We Think* (Boston: D. C. Heath, 1910), 9.

24. Dewey, *How We Think*, 9.

25. Dewey, *How We Think*, 13.

26. James, *Pragmatism,* 113.

27. Another very interesting paper could explore how Scully, unlike Mulder, represents Dewey's highest level of experience, in which one is fully engaged with the environment in a satisfying and fulfilling way. I believe Mulder tends to live at the level of received experience more than Scully, who embraces lived experience (this may not apply equally to their social lives, however).

Moral Musings on
a Cigarette Smoking Man

Timothy Dunn and Joseph J. Foy

> CIGARETTE SMOKING MAN: "It's a scary story. You want to come
>   sit on my lap?"
> AGENT SCULLY: "You don't scare me."
> CIGARETTE SMOKING MAN: "My story's scared every president
>   since Truman in '47."
>
> — "The Truth"

In a series filled with intriguing and enigmatic characters, the Cigarette Smoking Man (CSM) is surely one of the most fascinating. From his initial appearance in "Pilot," in which he is first seen lurking in the background as Dana Scully is assigned to work on the X-Files, to his almost mythical demise in the series finale "The Truth," the CSM is shrouded in mystery. He is a man of many nicknames (Smoking Man, CIA Man, Captain, Old Smokey) and aliases (C. G. B. Spender, Mr. Hunt, Mr. Bloodworth). He is allegedly responsible for numerous historical events, from the assassinations of John F. Kennedy and Martin Luther King Jr. to the United States' "Miracle on Ice" Olympic hockey victory over the Soviet Union in 1980. While much is revealed about him, his identity remains largely inscrutable.

But while there is no consensus regarding his identity, most X-Philes agree about his character. Dressed in a dark suit, always smoking, rarely smiling, he is the quintessential villain and the principal enemy of Mulder and Scully, the heroes of the series. Full of lies and deceit, he will stop at nothing to accomplish his mission, even if it means sacrificing his wife for secret genetic testing or attempting to kill his son. He is as ruthless as he is clever, and his contempt for humanity is perhaps the only thing he does not bother to disguise. The conventional wisdom regarding the CSM is supported by series creator Chris Carter, who once referred to him simply as "the devil."[1]

Yet a minority of X-Philes—including William B. Davis, the actor who plays the CSM—argue that the conventional wisdom is mistaken. In their view, the CSM is not a sinister villain but rather a hero compelled by extraordinary circumstances to lie, deceive, and even kill, all for the sake of protecting humanity. He is one of the few people with the courage and the steely resolve to do what is necessary, even if it means ignoring traditional moral norms. He should be honored, not condemned, for what he does.

What are we to make of such disparate interpretations? Is his character, like his identity, ultimately inscrutable? Is there anything to be learned from an ethical analysis of his character? In this chapter, we will attempt to answer these questions. In our view, the conventional wisdom is partially correct, but it does not explain *why* he is evil. Our goal is to sketch an interpretation of his character that sheds some light not only on the CSM but also on the nature of evil more generally. Our conclusion is that the CSM is no ordinary villain but represents a particularly perverse inversion of the moral order and, as such, challenges traditional morality in a far more fundamental way.

The CSM as Immoral Villain

In "Musings of a Cigarette Smoking Man," Melvin Frohike (Tom Braidwood) claims, "If you find the right starting point and follow it, not even the secrets of the darkest men are safe." Our own starting point will be the conventional account of the CSM's moral character. Before discussing the conventional wisdom, however, a few words about our methodology are in order. There are at least two ways in which we might morally evaluate a person's character and actions. First, we can rely on widely accepted, prereflective, commonsense moral judgments and principles. Taking these as given, we can then use them to evaluate a person's character or the moral quality of his actions. For example, almost everyone agrees that lying and killing innocent people are wrong, and anyone who routinely commits these acts is normally considered to be an immoral person. Such a method is sometimes called a "bottom-up" approach: generalizations regarding a person's character are drawn from specific examples of clearly immoral conduct. Alternatively, we might opt for a more theoretical, "top-down" approach, arguing from general, abstract ethical principles and sophisticated moral philosophical frameworks to a conclusion about a specific person or action. Such an approach begins by assuming the truth of a given ethical theory and ends with a judgment about a specific case. These two methods are complementary; we can use widely held moral intuitions to form generalizations, and in turn use these generalizations to reach conclusions about specific cases.

Using either approach, a prima facie case can be made in support of the conventional wisdom. Consider, first, the bottom-up method. Lying and killing innocent persons are, as we said earlier, widely considered immoral. And this is precisely what the CSM does over and over again. His obfuscation of the truth ranges from artfully manipulating Mulder into drawing conclusions that the CSM wants him to reach (he is quite adept at carrying out his own order to Marita Covarrubias [Laurie Holden] in "Zero Sum" to tell Mulder "what he wants to hear"), to directly lying to Deep Throat in "Musings of a Cigarette Smoking Man" when he says that he has "never killed anyone."[2]

The conventional analysis of his character becomes clearer when we consider the broader X-Files mythology. As a member of the shadow organization known as the Syndicate—which some X-Philes refer to as the Consortium—the CSM is involved in an ongoing secret collaboration with aliens who are plotting to colonize Earth. As part of this Vichy-style alliance, he attempts to perpetually deceive humankind in order to divert attention from the covert operations of the Syndicate and the alien colonists. The CSM's con of humanity, therefore, places him in an antagonistic position in relation to Mulder and Scully and their pursuit of the truth and makes him, in a sense, a traitor to humankind. That he smokes, is always dressed in a dark suit, oversees events from the shadows, and so on, only makes the conventional wisdom seem obvious: if the series has a clear and unambiguous villain, surely it is he.[3]

The harsh judgment of moral common sense seems to be further supported by standard ethical principles and theories. We will limit our discussion to two of the most important ones, beginning with Kantianism. For Immanuel Kant, our moral duties are derived from a principle known as the Categorical Imperative. Kant held that all moral obligations arise from this one principle, though he believed that it could be expressed in more than one way. According to one version of this principle, known as the Universal Law Formula, we must "act only according to that maxim by which . . . [we] can at the same time will that it should become a universal law." Exactly what this means and how this principle is supposed to be applied are complicated matters; however, Kant himself clearly intended it to preclude lying and murder. The core idea behind the Universal Law Formula is that, in order for an action to be ethical, we must be able to will that everyone in similar circumstances act in a similar fashion; otherwise, we are merely making exceptions for ourselves.[4]

Consider, for example, lying. Why is it wrong to lie? Although a detailed explanation is quite complicated, for Kant the simple answer is that it is ethically unacceptable because if lying were a universal law, then lying itself would become impossible. In a world in which everyone lied, no one would be believed. Thus, lying, which requires that one succeed in getting another to adopt a false belief, would become impossible. (Perhaps this is why the CSM has the phrase "Trust no one" engraved on his lighter. He himself is not to be believed, thus he does not believe anyone else.) The liar, therefore, contradicts himself, and no contradictory principle can be morally correct. Since the CSM routinely lies, and presumably is motivated by a desire to lie, his behavior, and indeed his character, is clearly vicious.

Our assessment of the CSM's actions would fare no better if we adopted the second version of the categorical imperative, sometimes called the Respect for Persons Formula. In this version, we must always treat persons as ends in themselves, never merely as a means. What, exactly, does this mean? According to Onora O'Neill, to treat persons merely as a means is "to involve them in a scheme of action *to which they could not in principle consent.*" Since lying involves misrepresenting the facts, and such misrepresentation is inconsistent with genuine consent, lying violates the second formula of the categorical imperative as well.[5]

If the CSM were simply a pathological liar, he would not be the personification of evil many X-Philes consider him to be. But of course he is far more than that, as the list of his iniquities ranges from having an affair with Teena (Rebecca Toolan), the wife of his friend Bill Mulder (Peter Donat), to the merciless execution of those who get in his way. Consider, for example, his willingness to murder his son in order to keep his secrets—and those of the Syndicate and alien colonists—hidden. In the season 6 episode "One Son," the CSM watches his son, Jeffrey Spender (Chris Owens), turn from furthering his father's interests to helping Mulder and Scully in their pursuit of the truth. In the end, the CSM confronts his son, and realizing that young Spender will not aid him in hiding the truth, he shoots his son in cold blood. The attempted murder of one's own son crosses the line between the prosaic immorality of lying and manipulation and irredeemable villainy, demonstrating the depths to which the Cigarette Smoking Man will sink to conceal the truth from the world. Such an act is widely assumed to be inconsistent with both versions of the categorical imperative.[6]

The judgment of Kantian ethics is further supported by utilitarianism. Utilitarians believe that actions are right insofar as they tend to promote happiness, and wrong insofar as they tend to promote unhappiness. For the classical utilitarians, happiness is equivalent to pleasure, and unhappiness is equivalent to pain. Thus, for utilitarians, an action is right if it produces more overall happiness than any alternative. Unlike Kant, utilitarians do believe that lying and even murder are sometimes morally permissible. However, such actions are permissible only if they produce more good than harm.

Similar to Kantianism, therefore, utilitarian ethics seems to provide ample reason to condemn the CSM. His actions, after all, frequently cause harm, suffering, and even death to others. For example, he orders his subordinate, Alex Krycek (Nicholas Lea), to carry out a number of assaults and assassinations—including a raid of Dana Scully's apartment that leads to the murder of her sister Melissa (Melinda McGraw) in "The Blessing Way"—and then in turn orders the failed attempt to eliminate Krycek with a car bomb in the season 3 episode "Paper Clip." Likewise, the CSM is thought to be tied to the abduction of innocent people for a variety of genetic tests, including the abduction tests performed on Agent Scully as indicated in the episodes "Ascension" and "One Breath." The CSM also uses people's weaknesses in an effort to control them. For example, he toys with Agent Mulder, capitalizing on his obsession with finding his sister to manipulate Mulder by allowing him to meet Samantha (Megan Leitch) in "Redux II." However, it was later revealed to Mulder that this Samantha was a clone, just like the clones of his sister that he found working the Syndicate's bee colony in "Herrenvolk." Finally, the sheer delight he takes in inflicting this pain is indicative of a sadistic character. In the season 6 premier, "The Beginning," the Cigarette Smoking Man says of his actions regarding Mulder: "You can kill a man, but you can't kill what he stands for. Not unless you first break his spirit. That's a beautiful thing to see."

In sum, from the perspective of both moral common sense and two prominent ethical theories, the Cigarette Smoking Man's actions are highly immoral. Unless a justification can be found for his behavior, it seems that the conventional wisdom is correct.

The CSM as Moral Hero?

Despite the above arguments, there are those who are unhappy with the conventional wisdom and are unlikely to be convinced by our arguments in support of it. William B. Davis himself offered a spirited defense of the CSM in an online interview conducted on March 11, 1999. Davis essentially argued that the CSM's actions, though at times ruthless, were necessary to prevent a far greater evil. If humanity ever discovered the truth about the impending alien invasion, the world would erupt in chaos and panic. And though not all X-Philes would go as far as Davis does, many of them argue that the CSM cannot be summarily dismissed as purely evil.[7]

Davis's defense of the CSM is more plausible when we recall the elaborate mythology of the series. Alien colonists are looking, not to subjugate humanity to slavery, but to use their bodies as a host for the black oil, a virus that gestates and feeds off the human body while it comes to term as a full alien life form. Thus, the success of the colonists would necessarily mean a new form of holocaust in which all of humanity is eliminated. The aliens have solicited help from the Syndicate in order to implement their plans to more efficiently and effectively create a slave class of genetically engineered, human-alien hybrids. They are fully capable, however, of using brute force to completely destroy humanity should they deem it necessary, and there is no evidence that there is anything anyone can do to stop them. Yet we learn in the 1998 feature film *Fight the Future* that the CSM is a part of a secret plot to refine and produce a vaccine that would prevent the alien virus from infesting humans and using their bodies as hosts for incubation. Such a plot is enormously risky. If the truth ever got out that a vaccine was being developed, the alien colonists would step up the timetable for colonization, resulting in the inevitable extinction of humanity. On the other hand, if the members of the Syndicate were to succeed in deceiving both the aliens and humanity, then the development of the vaccine might defeat the plans of the alien colonists.[8]

In such extraordinary circumstances, many of the CSM's actions seem morally defensible. Recall that, for utilitarians, even lying and murder are morally permissible if the good to be gained (or the harm to be prevented) thereby is sufficiently great. In the circumstances described above, the development of a vaccine is humanity's only realistic hope for survival. On the plausible assumption that the vaccine's development depends on absolute secrecy, preserving that secret using any means necessary is at least arguably justified. Moreover, what are the alternatives? If he does nothing, the CSM essentially consigns himself and all of humanity to near certain doom. In all likelihood, anyone he kills will die anyway. It is of course uncertain whether killing his son is, for example, necessary to protect the secret plan, but it is a reasonable calculation. In some cases, his single-minded devotion to protecting humanity actually saves lives. In "Ascension," for example, the CSM actually persuades fellow Syndicate members not to kill Mulder, on the grounds that killing him would turn "one man's religion into a crusade," thereby increasing chances of exposure.

Ironically, given this perspective, it is the series's putative heroes, Mulder and Scully, who pose the greatest threat to humanity. Their relentless search for the truth, while generally a noble endeavor, is in this case a grave threat. Not knowing the truth, of course, they should not be blamed. But that is precisely the point. The CSM does know the truth, and he knows what he must do, no matter the cost. Thus, the conventional wisdom that the CSM is a despicable villain fails to acknowledge the circumstances in which he is forced to act.

In real-life cases, of course, the morally correct course of action will often be much more difficult to determine. Ruthless actions such as torture and murder, even when done for the sake of society or humanity, will in practice almost invariably involve troubling moral trade-offs, ethical ambiguities, and potentially disastrous side-effects. Our argument above, therefore, is not to be interpreted as a blank check for public officials to do whatever they deem necessary for the public good. Nevertheless, utilitarians would argue that, even in real life, if the potential gains were sufficiently great, ruthless actions such as those done by the CSM would be justified.

Interestingly, the Cigarette Smoking Man himself tries in "Talitha Cumi" to defend his actions. Borrowing from the infamous Inquisitor character from Fyodor Dostoyevsky's novel *The Brothers Karamazov,* he claims that "men can never be free, because they're weak, corrupt, worthless and restless." He then offers renegade alien Jeremiah Smith (Roy Thinnes) the justification alluded to above: if humanity were ever to learn the truth, anarchy and chaos would erupt. Humankind, therefore, needs someone like the CSM who has the mettle and fortitude to do what must be done. He summarizes this position in "One Breath" when he tells Mulder, "If people were to know the things I know, it would all fall apart." From a utilitarian perspective, therefore, his actions seem defensible.

One might think that, even if utilitarians would, in light of further examination, approve of his actions, Kantians would clearly not. Recall Kant's argument that lying is wrong because no rational being could will that the maxim of his action should become a universal law. Kant thought that lying was wrong in all circumstances, regardless of the consequences. Even lying to save an innocent person's life would be wrong, as Kant explicitly argues in his essay *On the Supposed Right to Lie for Philanthropic Reasons.* Needless to say, many people find Kant's insistence on the absolute wrongness of lying highly implausible. Some philosophers summarily reject Kant's theory on the grounds that it leads to such absurd conclusions, but Kant's defenders have argued that the problem is not with Kant's theory itself but rather with Kant's own application of it. Again, the argument here is rather complicated, but the basic idea is that while lying in general is not universalizable, lying to save an innocent person's life is universalizable and one could consistently will that exceptions be made in such cases. This is consistent with the spirit of Kantianism because as long as one is willing to say that it would be morally permissible for anyone to lie in similar circumstances, one's actions pass the universal-law test. In defense of the CSM, we could likewise argue that his actions are universalizable and hence permissible from a Kantian perspective.

The above arguments represent a mere fraction of the sophisticated philosophical resources available. The Kantian and utilitarian arguments alone barely scratch the surface. It is important to keep in mind, therefore, that the above is intended only as a sample of the kind of argument one could offer in defense of the CSM. At this point some might conclude that enough has been said to vindicate him from the charge of moral turpitude. Unfortunately, the above defense, while persuasive as far as it goes, overlooks certain important facts. While some of the CSM's actions might be justified by virtue of his role in the dual cover-up, there are too many examples of behavior that cannot be so justified. For example, in "Talitha Cumi," when Jeremiah Smith informs him he is dying of cancer, the CSM threatens the plans of the alien colonists—as well as jeopardizing everything the Syndicate is attempting with the development of a vaccine—by releasing Smith. His reason, however, was not for mercy or charity but for a tit-for-tat exchange: if he releases this renegade, Smith will cure his cancer. This shows that, although he likes to present himself as someone who will sacrifice anything for the sake of humanity's survival, the CSM is a hypocrite. Likewise, a true hero would likely seek to cause no more harm than is absolutely necessary for the sake of his mission. But much of the evil the CSM causes has no bearing whatsoever on his mission but is completely gratuitous. In fact, the CSM performs so many nefarious deeds that he amusedly asks Mulder in the season 7 episode "The Sixth Extinction II: Amor Fati": "How does anything I do surprise you now? Aren't you expecting me to sprout vampire fangs?" Concomitantly, unlike a morally justified but reluctant hero, the CSM seems to perform moral actions only when he can get something in return. He admits to Scully in the seventh-season episode "En Ami" that he believes that "no sacrifice is purely altruistic. We give expecting to receive." In overlooking the essentially gratuitous nature of much of the harm he causes, the CSM's defenders paint a distorted picture of his character.

In sum, while both ethical theory and commonsense morality offer a potential justification for some of the CSM's actions, much of his behavior remains unjustifiable by any plausible moral standard. All too often, he displays a reckless disregard and contempt for humanity. This leads us to suspect that he is not primarily motivated by moral concerns but rather by something altogether different. What follows is a reevaluation of the CSM that goes beyond the traditional arguments about his character, and an examination of the true motivation driving his behavior.

The CSM and the "Transvaluation of Power"

Both the conventional wisdom about the CSM and the challenge raised by his defenders capture part of the truth but ultimately miss the mark. While he is not uniformly evil, at least not in any ordinary sense, he nevertheless is no moral hero. Of the two positions, the conventional wisdom is perhaps closer to the truth. However, it does not really adequately explain why he is evil, and for that reason it fails to come to terms with the distinct nature of the CSM. Moral theories such as utilitarianism and Kantianism help to explain why his actions are wrong, but they do not explain why he does them. What does the CSM ultimately stand for?

To answer this question, we must employ some basic philosophical terminology. Philosophers distinguish between *intrinsic* and *extrinsic* goods. Intrinsic goods are things that are good in themselves, or good for their own sake. Extrinsic goods (also known as instrumental goods), on the other hand, are things whose value depends on their usefulness in promoting other values or goods. They are good, not for their own sake, but rather for the sake of other things. Utilitarianism, for example, holds that the only thing intrinsically good is happiness. All other goods—health, wealth, knowledge, and so on—are valuable only insofar as they promote happiness.[9]

One of the defining characteristics of the CSM is his lust for power. According to most moral theories, power has extrinsic, but not intrinsic, value. That it has extrinsic value, both good and bad, is easy to see. Power can be used for numerous purposes, from the magnificent to the mundane. It can be used to move mountains, build bridges, irrigate drought-stricken lands, and liberate oppressed peoples. It can also be used to destroy mountains and bridges, flood cities, and oppress liberated peoples. This standard view of power is that it is simply a tool: by itself morally neutral, but capable of producing good or bad results depending on how it is used.

Perhaps the most interesting and disturbing thing about the CSM is that he appears to perform what we call a transvaluation of power. By this we mean that he elevates power to the level of intrinsic goods. For him, power becomes not merely a means to an end but an end in itself. All other values, including friendship, virtue, and even his own happiness, become subordinate. The CSM regards power as singularly valuable in itself, and everything else is valuable only insofar as it enables him to maintain or increase that power. Rather than viewing power as a means to some type of end—even an immoral end, as, say, the classic examples of Hitler and Stalin would do—the CSM regards power itself as the rightful object of human affairs. His closest parallel is neither Stalin nor Hitler but rather the character O'Brien in George Orwell's *1984*. O'Brien's vision of the future is one in which the party reigns supreme and humanity is ultimately vanquished. Nothing escapes the clutches of the party, not even objective truth. If the party says that $2 + 3 = 7$, then it is so. If the party says someone never existed, then he did not. To what end does the party seek such power? Certainly it is not for such vulgar purposes as the abolition of capitalism or bolshevism. No, the party seeks power for the sake of acquiring more power, which in turn will enable it to acquire still more power.

There is ample evidence from the series to support our assessment of the CSM's character. Consider, for example, the way in which his obfuscation of the truth increases his authority over others. In "One Breath," Mulder threatens an unarmed CSM with a gun. The CSM, however, is only too delighted to reveal to Mulder that, although he is unarmed, he is still the one with the power. "You can kill me now, but you will never know the truth," he explains. "And that's why I'll win." Likewise, he is able to control his subordinates, such as Alex Krycek, by withholding information from them while they act on his behalf. In "Ascension," for example, when Krycek insists that he has the right to know the CSM's plans for Scully, he solidifies his power over Krycek by continuing to withhold the information. "You have no rights," he told Krycek, "only orders to be followed." Here he is clearly demonstrating that Krycek is not an equal partner, not someone who gets to be in on the plan. Having complete access to the truth that he denies to others gives him power to control situations, people, and outcomes.

Critics of our view might point out that while these examples show that the CSM values power, they do not yet show that he values power for its own sake. For all we have shown so far, the CSM may well value power as a means to some "higher" end. He might still be criticized as a villain for his actions, but he would be a much more ordinary villain than we imagine him. We have two responses to such a challenge.

First, there are just too many examples in which the CSM seems to take pleasure in the mere possession of power over others. For example, at the end of "Musings of a Cigarette Smoking Man," he sits alone, staring through the sight of a sniper rifle targeted on Frohike. Rather than shooting him, the CSM quotes from one of his supposed Jack Colquitt novels: "I can kill you whenever I please—but not today." Only he would ever know that at that moment he held the power of life and death over another human being, but he seems to bask in the sadistic joy that such power brings him. It is the same twisted pleasure that he seems to derive when, in "Paper Clip," he venomously describes to Assistant Director Skinner (Mitch Pileggi) all the ways he could kill Skinner and make it look like an accident should he so choose (arrange for a plane to crash, cause him to get botulism or have a heart attack). One might still try to argue, of course, that such behavior is really motivated by a desire to promote some other end, but the simpler explanation seems to be that he desires power for its own sake. This point is further supported by considering examples in which he appears to have used his power for completely trivial purposes (e.g., preventing the Buffalo Bills from winning the Super Bowl). It is hard to imagine what end would be served thereby, other than delighting in one's own power.

Additionally, if he did desire power merely as a means to an end, what end would this be? Two plausible candidates (each corresponding roughly to one of the competing interpretations of his character that were discussed earlier) are his own self-interest or happiness, or the altruistic end of protecting humanity from the alien plot. Neither of these possibilities, however, holds up under scrutiny. Consider, first, the idea that he really desires power in order to promote his self-interest or as a means of achieving happiness. The main problem with this interpretation is that his pursuit of power does not in fact serve his interests, nor does it make him happy. The power he possesses enables him to survive, but he lives only to acquire more power. Seeking such power robs him of whatever happiness he might hope to achieve, as symbolized in his isolated existence. He lives alone. When he is shown celebrating holidays, it is by himself. He is despised by every member of his family and is alienated from the rest of humanity. Insofar as happiness is a necessary part of a person's well-being, his pursuit of power seems to run counter to his self-interest. Thus, the acquisition of power, if unchecked, does not even benefit its possessor, while its possessor threatens all others. This inversion of the moral order, in which pleasure and happiness (not to mention Kantian or Aristotelian virtue) are sacrificed for the sake of more power, is indeed a potent challenge to traditional morality.

It is also implausible to say that his desire for power is motivated primarily by altruistic concerns. For one thing, as we have already argued, there are too many examples in which the CSM causes gratuitous harm. If he desired power only as a tool for protecting humanity from harm, he would not take such delight in causing harm, even if such harm were necessary. Furthermore, the CSM's pursuit of power contrasts with that of fellow Syndicate members such as Bill Mulder, Deep Throat (Jerry Hardin), and the Well-Manicured Man (John Neville). Although less is known about them, each of these characters eventually forsakes his pursuit of power because such power interferes with other values that he cares about. In *Fight the Future* the Well-Manicured Man, for example, is assassinated for defecting from the Syndicate in an attempt to bring about a better future for his children and grandchildren. Likewise, although deeply involved with the Syndicate's activities for many years, men like Bill Mulder, Deep Throat, and Alvin Kurtzweil (Martin Landau) also reach a point where the power struggles and deception become too much for them. They indicate that their involvement with the Syndicate's shadow conspiracies were for their families and humanity and to hold on to a hope for the future. With the CSM, however, his involvement in developing a vaccine for the alien virus — or developing the tools to cure cancer, as in the season 7 episode "En Ami" — could be easily seen as being done, not for his own good or humanity's, but simply because having such cures offers him substantial power over life and death.

Perhaps the most telling example of his transvaluation of power is revealed even as he draws what were to be his final smoky breaths. In the series finale, "The Truth," after detailing the plan for a full alien colonization by 2012, he wickedly delights in telling Mulder: "My power comes from telling you. Seeing your powerlessness, hearing it. They wanted to kill you, Fox. I protected you all these years; waiting for this moment. To see you broken, afraid. Now you can die." His last appearance on the show offers us a reminder that his only joy is not in the success of saving the planet from the alien colonists, or subjugating humanity as one of their collaborators, but simply in having power over others. That is his raison d'être.

If our analysis is correct, then the defining moral characteristic of the CSM is his monomaniacal pursuit of power for its own sake, no matter what the cost. His willingness to sacrifice all other values for the sake of something that, in itself, seems morally neutral is a particularly insidious perversion of the moral order. This is in part what makes the CSM such a fascinating villain. But the question remains whether such a character teaches us anything interesting about the nature of good and evil.

Insights into Good and Evil

One conclusion seems fairly certain: the CSM's moral pathology is highly unusual, but it is not without literary or pop cultural precedent. A similar transvaluation of power can be seen not only in Orwell's O'Brien but also in such popular science fiction characters as Sméagol/Gollum (*Lord of the Rings*) and Palpatine / Darth Sidious (*Star Wars*). Likewise, this brand of moral pathology is not limited to power. Dickens's Ebenezer Scrooge is like the CSM except that it is not power that he desires above all but money. Scrooge's desire for pecuniary gain comes to dominate and pervert his system of values in an analogous fashion. The CSM is of interest in part because of his similarity to these and other fictional characters.

But he is also of interest because his peculiar pathology is not limited to fictional characters. Examples of an analogous transvaluation of money can be found in real life as well. Consider the argument made by Robert E. Lane concerning the transvaluation of prosperity in many of the world's advanced economies. While he does not use the language of transvaluation, Lane empirically demonstrates that although wealth that allows people to meet their basic needs greatly increases their overall happiness, beyond that it has a diminishing marginal return. In fact, at a certain point, the pursuit of more wealth actually generates greater relative *un*happiness. Yet, in many advanced economies in the world, people work over seventy hours a week to make more and more money. The cost is often their families, health, psychological well-being, and overall happiness, but the pursuit of more and more wealth supersedes all that. Of course, if asked, we would never admit that our values are as distorted as all that. Yet our behavior suggests otherwise. Real-life examples of a transvaluation of power, such as this example provided by Lane, abound in everything from politics to interpersonal relationships to sports, and indicate the propensity of humans to invert the traditional moral order by valuing power as an end rather than a means to an end.[10]

The CSM's moral pathology is of interest, then, because it is not utterly foreign to us. In fact, it is all too familiar, though not to such an extreme. The CSM represents the logical conclusion of the inversion of moral value. Note that this does not mean that the CSM will always be evil in the ordinary, mundane sense. To make power an end in itself does not necessarily result in bad behavior. As we have seen, some of the CSM's actions are at least partially justifiable, and his pursuit of power is not altogether lacking in salutary effects. Indeed, our analysis helps explain why there is no consensus regarding his character. His detractors point to the harmful consequences of his lust for power, while his defenders point out its good effects (or at least a context in which such a pursuit is morally imperative). However, neither side sees that the problem lies with the CSM's distorted sense of the value of power itself.

This point can be most clearly seen when we contrast the CSM with Bill Mulder. Bill Mulder is involved in the same type of Syndicate activities as the CSM, but he never sees power as anything other than a tool for use in protecting humanity. Eventually realizing that the CSM and other members of the Syndicate are no longer seeking power for benevolent ends, Bill Mulder defects from the Syndicate. While one may object morally to his exercise of power in pursuit even of noble ends, one cannot deny Bill Mulder's ultimately instrumental understanding of the value of power. It is Bill Mulder, in fact, who more closely resembles the tragic hero the CSM's defenders imagine him to be. Bill Mulder is the man the CSM could have been.

We have argued that the CSM is no ordinary villain, but a particularly disturbing one. In so arguing, we might have left the impression that he is morally worse than ordinary villains—that his perversion of the moral order is more pernicious than mere garden-variety immorality. One might wonder whether this implication really follows. After all, if, as utilitarians insist, consequences are what ultimately matter, then to view power as an end in itself but not to exercise it may be a moral perversion but is far less morally disturbing than the instrumental exercise of power in the service of deeply immoral ends. In other words, what difference does it make if the CSM values power for its own sake, as long as he does not exercise it? If it is only because he uses power to harm others that we care about his lust for power, then he is no worse (and in some respects is significantly better) than a Hitler or a Stalin, for whom power was merely a tool that caused enormous suffering.

This is a difficult question, and a full response to the above line of reasoning is well beyond the scope of this chapter. But there are at least two reasons to think that the matter is not that simple. First, insofar as he regards power as intrinsically good, worth pursuing at whatever cost, the CSM necessarily degrades the value of other things. He has no room for happiness, virtue, or the promotion of human welfare precisely because of his single-minded and wrongheaded pursuit of power. Those who pursue immoral ends need not be as single-minded, nor need they necessarily degrade other values. To that extent, the CSM is arguably worse. Moreover, the transvaluation of power creates a moral vacuum in which, all too often, immoral ends rush in. Those who seek power for its own sake are unlikely to be satisfied with its mere possession: eventually, the temptation to use it will become overwhelming. Consider, for example, the argument that the mere possession of nuclear weapons creates a temptation to use them. Once one has decided that power alone is valuable for its own sake, it no longer matters to what ends one uses power. Given plausible assumptions about human nature, the person who values power for its own sake is, in practice, more likely to use it for immoral ends.

The second, and arguably more important, reason the CSM is a more disturbing type of villain has to do with the possibility of moral persuasion. The ordinary villain sees power as a means of promoting immoral ends. Even if he is unwilling to abandon his ends or otherwise subject them to moral or rational criticism, we can at least engage him in rational dialogue. We can attempt to persuade him that the possession or exercise of power is not the best means to achieve his ends. For example, even if we disagree with Al-Qaeda's ends, we might succeed in persuading its leaders that the use of terrorist tactics is unlikely to achieve its objectives. The ordinary villain typically allows some room for rational discussion and is in a limited sense committed to the pursuit of an objective moral truth—he simply disagrees with us regarding its content. The CSM, however, will brook no rational or moral criticism. Not only does he regard the alleged intrinsic value of power as self-evident, he also will not allow anyone to criticize its use, precisely because its use-value and end-value have become one. When power becomes an end in itself, there is nothing left for it to serve but itself. The CSM thus disengages from rational and moral criticism altogether, making it nearly impossible for him to alter his behavior or his viewpoint. To that extent, we think, he is worse.

Notes

1. Gabriel Smith, "'X-Files' Cancer Man Lands at EMU," *Michigan Daily Online,* October 21, 1997.

2. "Musings of a Cigarette Smoking Man" reveals a number of inconsistencies among the Cigarette Smoking Man's claims. One interesting "lie" is that the CSM claims in 1963 to "never touch" cigarettes when offered one by General Francis, and he indicates his dislike for cigarettes when he tries to convince Lee Harvey Oswald to give up smoking just before the assassination of JFK. However, in a flashback to 1953 in "Apocrypha," which aired the season before "Musings," the CSM is seen lighting up after listening to a sick and injured navy crewman. Although some might consider this a mere inconsistency with the writing and a goof on the time line of the show, it seems to speak more directly to the fact that the CSM, as Assistant Director Skinner puts it, "deals only in lies" ("Memento Mori").

3. See Randy Dotinga, "Onscreen, Evil Needs a Cigarette," *Health on the Net Foundation,* August 18, 2005; http://www.hon.ch/News/HSN/527414.html; Jonathan McDonald, "TV's Most Beloved Bad Guy," *Vancouver Province,* February 7, 1999; Smith, "'X-Files' Cancer Man Lands at EMU"; Lisa Crovo, "His Career Is Going Up in Smoke," interview with William B. Davis, *Salon.Com,* page 2 of "X-Istential Crisis" series, June 22 and 23, 1996, http://www.salon.com/weekly/xfiles2960729.html.

4. Immanuel Kant, *Groundwork of the Metaphysics of Morals* (1785), Cambridge Texts in the History of Philosophy, ed. Mary J. Gregor (Cambridge: Cambridge University Press, 1998).

5. "Kant and Utilitarianism Contrasted," in *John Arthur, Morality and Moral Controversies,* 6th ed. (Englewood Cliffs, NJ: Prentice Hall: 2002), 41. Italics in original.

Philosophers and lawyers alike hold that consent is nullified when fraud or deception occurs. For example, if I alter my car's odometer, your willingness to pay me $10,000 for the car depends on your falsely believing that you are buying a relatively new car. Such "consent" is not regarded as genuine.

6. The qualifier "attempted" is used here because, as X-Philes know, Jeffrey Spender was not killed but instead lived to return to the show in the season 9 episode "William." However, since the CSM intended to kill his son, he is morally just as guilty as he would be had he succeeded.

7. See Smith, "'X-Files' Cancer Man Lands at EMU"; *SciFi.Com,* "William B. Davis, the Cigarette Smoking Man from the X-Files," transcript of online interview conducted on March 11, 1999, reprinted online at http://www.scifi.com/transcripts/1999/

WilliamBDavis.html; Allison Cossitt, "X-Files 'Smoking Man' a Skeptic!" CSICOP Announcement Mailing List, *SI Digest,* November 12, 1997; and Erik Arneson, "The X-Files: The Truth Is Out There," *MysteryNet.Com* (1996, 2005), http://www.mysterynet.com/tv/profiles/xfiles/.

8. We learn in seasons 4 and 5 that a shadow Russian organization had developed an initial vaccine for the black oil alien virus, which was later stolen and delivered to the Syndicate by Alex Krycek. (See "Tunguska," "Terma," "Patient X," and "The Red and the Black.")

9. Different moral theories have different conceptions of intrinsic goods. Hedonistic utilitarianism, for example, holds that pleasure is the only intrinsic good; all other goods are good only insofar as they tend to promote pleasure. Some philosophers have argued that it is not pleasure, but rather something else, that is intrinsically good. For example, Aristotle held that the only thing intrinsically good is *eudaimonia,* which is usually translated as "happiness" or "human flourishing." Kant thought that the only thing good in and of itself is a good will. All of the above have been criticized for having too simple a conception of the good. Surely other things are valuable as well: knowledge, beauty, friendship, the development of one's character, and so on. For our purposes, the important point to note is that many (although not all) moral theories hold that some thing or things are intrinsically good, and everything else that is valuable derives its value from its usefulness in promoting that intrinsic value.

10. Robert E. Lane, *The Loss of Happiness in Market Democracies* (New Haven: Yale University Press, 2001).

Walter Skinner

The X-Files' Unsung Hero

S. Evan Kreider

Fellow *X-Files* fans sometimes ask me, "Who's your favorite character: Mulder or Scully?" To this, I cheekily reply, "Neither." To be perfectly frank, I've never felt that either one of them exhibits much personal character. Mulder strikes me as self-centered, obsessive, and immature, while Scully seems cold, passive, and inconsistent in her beliefs (though I'm quite sure I'll be hearing from fans of Mulder and Scully about why I am so very wrong about this). I would argue that if anyone on the show is truly worthy of admiration, it is their boss, Assistant Director Walter Skinner. In particular, Skinner is especially admirable in terms of classical philosophical ideals of virtues such as courage, good temper, and temperance. In the following pages, I will discuss these virtues and then demonstrate how Skinner embodies each of them. Finally, I will raise the question of whether Skinner's virtue guarantees him "the good life"; that is, is Skinner happy for being virtuous?

Theories of Virtue: Classical Sources

In the minds of many contemporary philosophers, Aristotle offers the best classical theory of virtue. Whether or not one agrees with this judgment, Aristotle certainly does provide us with a clear and systematic account of the character virtues, so if nothing else, this gives us a good starting point for our discussion. According to Aristotle, each of the character virtues is a mean between extremes. For example, the virtue of generosity (the mean of giving—giving an appropriate amount of one's resources) lies between the vice of extravagance (the extreme of excessive giving—giving too much) and the vice of stinginess (the extreme of deficient giving—giving too little); the virtue of pride (the mean of self-worth—feeling an appropriate amount of self-worth) lies between the vice of vanity (an excessive feeling of self-worth—thinking more highly of oneself than is merited) and the vice of undue humility (a deficient feeling of self-worth—thinking less of oneself than is merited); and so on. In some cases, the virtues and vices seem to be related to behavior or actions of some sort (e.g., generosity, extravagance, and stinginess are related to the action of giving); in other cases, the virtues and vices seem to have to do with an emotion or desire of some kind (e.g., pride, vanity, and undue humility are related to the feeling of self-worth). In either case, the basic idea is captured by the age-old cliché "All things in moderation." Virtue manifests itself in a person's feeling or behaving in the appropriate amounts, in the appropriate ways, at the appropriate times, toward the appropriate people, rather than feeling or behaving too much or too little, in the wrong ways, at the wrong times, toward the wrong people. It's also important to note that the mean is not always exactly in the middle; sometimes it is closer to one extreme rather than the other (e.g., pride is closer to undue humility than to vanity; generosity is closer to extravagance than to stinginess).[1]

Plato does not provide us with the same kind of systematic theory of virtue that Aristotle does, at least not in any particularly obvious way. Because of this, it's tempting in discussions such as this simply to leave Plato out, if only for the sake of expediency. This is unfortunate, since Plato has a great deal to say about virtue. Some of his ideas are similar to Aristotle's—not surprising, since Plato was Aristotle's teacher—and in those cases, simply sticking with Aristotle makes a certain amount of sense, if only to add to the clarity and conciseness of the discussion. However, on other occasions Plato's ideas about virtue are significantly different from (and in some cases, possibly superior to) Aristotle's. For this reason, I believe it is a serious error to ignore Plato entirely; thus, I will incorporate Plato at several points in the following discussion, either to supplement Aristotle or to provide an alternative to Aristotle, especially since I believe certain aspects of Skinner's virtues are better characterized by Plato's account of virtue than by Aristotle's.[2]

The Virtue of Courage

Courage is an excellent virtue to discuss first, given the large role that it plays in so many dramatic works, *The X-Files* included. According to Aristotle, courage is the mean concerning fear and confidence. The courageous person feels neither too much nor too little fear or confidence, but rather the appropriate amounts of fear and confidence, in the appropriate situations, toward the appropriate objects. One vice is cowardice, which involves feeling too much fear and too little confidence. The other vice is recklessness, which involves feeling too little fear and too much confidence. While the viciousness of cowardice is rather obvious, the viciousness of recklessness is less so. Is it really bad to feel no fear? Isn't that the ideal? Not according to Aristotle. All natural emotions, including fear, play some legitimate role in human motivation, as long as they do so in moderation. For example, a soldier with no fear whatsoever might be tempted to fight an unwinnable battle or to ignore an order for a strategic retreat. Also, an appropriate amount of fear helps a soldier to keep his or her guard up and to be aware of the very real dangers of the battlefield. Furthermore, according to Aristotle, only the mean of fear and confidence of death in battle is properly called courage; thus, only the soldier has the opportunity to exercise the true virtue of courage. A mean of fear and confidence toward other objects such as dishonor, poverty, and so on, bears some resemblance to courage but is not true courage.[3]

Obviously, Aristotle's concept of courage is extremely narrow by contemporary standards. We tend to think that courage is a virtue that anyone can possess, whether or not he or she is a soldier; for example, it seems obvious that a teacher, a parent, and a prospective job candidate all need courage. We also tend to think that courage is a virtue that anyone may need to draw upon in a variety of situations, not just on the battlefield; for example, it seems obvious that public speaking, giving birth, and interviewing for a job all require courage. However, this does not make Aristotle's account irrelevant, especially in the context of our discussion. Skinner, as a law enforcement officer, is a soldier of sorts and sees his share of violent conflict. As a result, Aristotle would have no problem with our discussing Skinner's courage. However, Skinner also demonstrates courage in other contexts, so we need a broader account of courage to supplement the account given to us by Aristotle. For such an account, Plato is an excellent source to investigate.

Plato discusses the virtue of courage in a number of works, but for our purposes here, we will examine the account given in his most famous work, *The Republic*. In this dialogue, Plato discusses everything under the sun (pun intended for those who may have read *The Republic*), but one subject in particular is that of "the just person"—that is, a person who embodies the virtue of justice, which in turn requires the virtues of wisdom, courage, and temperance. Each of these three virtues corresponds to one of the three parts of a person's soul: wisdom is the virtue of reason, courage is the virtue of the spirit, and temperance is the virtue of the appetites. At the moment, we're concerned only with courage, but we will examine temperance later on and briefly discuss wisdom in the last section of this chapter.[4]

Plato gives us a much broader (and, as a result, superior, I think) account of courage than Aristotle. According to Plato, courage is a virtue not just for soldiers but for everyone. Courage is not defined as a virtue dealing only with feelings of fear and confidence, nor is it concerned only with death in battle. Plato's idea of courage is nicely captured by the phrase "having the courage of one's convictions." According to Plato, courage is holding fast to one's beliefs, especially one's beliefs about right and wrong, especially in the face of emotions such as fear, greed, and various temptations that might lead one astray. According to Plato, a person with a courageous spirit is someone who does what reason says is the right thing to do, even if there is some other part of that person (especially that person's emotions or desires) that doesn't particularly want to do the right thing. The superiority of Plato's version of courage to Aristotle's seems to me rather obvious: courage is something that all of us need, not just the soldier, and it is something which is relevant to all walks of life, not just the battlefield.

Finally, it's worth noting that the Greek word for courage that both Aristotle and Plato use is *andreia,* which is cognate with *aner,* which means "man," in the specific sense of a male person. Thus, *andreia* could also be translated as "manliness." Historically and culturally, it's understandable that the ancient Greeks might see courage as a distinctly male virtue, given that it is the sort of virtue easily associated with and ascribed to soldiers, and given that ancient Greek soldiers were typically male and that war was a more central part of ancient Greek life than it is (arguably) with modern life. In Aristotle's case, I suspect the connection is intentional, given that he believes that only men are capable of total virtue. In Plato's case, I suspect the connection is not intended, given that he believes that courage is not just for soldiers and that virtue more generally is not just for men. Though I personally find Plato's conception of courage far superior, I shall not ignore Aristotle's narrower—and probably sexist—conception of courage, since both can help us shed some light on Skinner's character, given that in addition to being human, he is also more specifically a man and does on occasion fulfill a soldier-like role in his work for the FBI.[5]

When we first meet Skinner in the episode "Tooms," he doesn't exactly strike us as courageous, warrior-like, or manly. In fact, he comes off as a caricature of the stereotypical bureaucrat, almost asexual or even entirely inhuman. He is a balding man, sitting behind a desk, wearing glasses. He speaks and acts in a strictly professional manner. He gives no indication of having any real independence but appears to take his direction from the Cigarette Smoking Man. He criticizes Mulder and Scully for their failure to abide by conventional investigation techniques and demands that they operate according to procedure, "by the book," from here on out.

However, we soon learn that first impressions are seriously misleading and that Skinner is in fact very much the modern-day warrior. For example, as explained in "One Breath," Skinner is a Vietnam veteran who saw serious combat. Also, he takes an active role in field operations throughout the series, especially in a capacity much like a military leader. For example, in "The Field Where I Died" he heads up the team that shuts down a potentially dangerous religious cult that has been hoarding weapons. However, he is not merely a giver of orders but is also capable of direct combat when necessary. Late in the series we discover that Skinner trains as a boxer. This discovery would not have come as a surprise to regular viewers, since Skinner had repeatedly demonstrated his competence in hand-to-hand combat. For example, in "End Game," Skinner engages in fisticuffs—not to mention a couple of well-placed head-butts—with X (one of Mulder's Deep Throat–like contacts) to get information about Mulder's mysterious disappearance. Eventually, X gets the upper hand and draws his gun, but Skinner does not back down. Even with a gun in his face, Skinner looks X in the eye and demands to know Mulder's whereabouts: "You pull that trigger, you'll be killing two men. Now I want to know where Mulder is."

Skinner demonstrates not only the Aristotelian courage of a warrior but also the Platonic courage of acting upon the courage of his convictions. He does this consistently, even at great risk to himself, whether the risk of physical harm or the more mundane risk of professional suicide. Specifically, we see Skinner standing up to the Cigarette Smoking Man on several occasions, even though the CSM clearly has great power over Skinner's position in the FBI. In particular, Skinner sticks up for Scully and Mulder when he feels that they are pursuing the right goals. One particularly notable example of this is Skinner's reopening of the X-Files in "Ascension" contrary to the wishes of his superiors. Another important example, from "Paper Clip," is Skinner's essentially blackmailing the Cigarette Smoking

Man for Scully's and Mulder's safety by suggesting that he might reveal the location of a data tape containing sensitive Defense Department files. That particular scene is especially notable for the obvious look of fear on the Cigarette Smoking Man's face—possibly the first real fear we've seen from him—in contrast to Skinner's confident and controlled demeanor.

Clearly, then, Skinner embodies the virtue of courage and does so in the whole variety of ways in which Aristotle and Plato characterize the courageous person. The above examples demonstrate that he possesses not only the courage appropriate to a soldier but also the courage needed to act according to his beliefs. Moreover, it's interesting—if also a little amusing—to note that the show's creators made a special point of showing Skinner shirtless on more than one occasion (as in "Avatar" and "Tunguska"). It's rather surprising to see how muscular he is, especially in contrast to the initial impression of the assistant director of the FBI as an asexual bureaucrat. Beyond possibly trying to add some sex appeal to the show for a segment of the audience, these scenes also reinforce Skinner's "manliness," once again making him a good example of the ancient Greek virtue of courage.

The Virtue of Good Temper

Anger is an emotion that gets a bad rap in many ethical systems, including some other ancient Greek ones, but Aristotle has an appreciation for the legitimate role that anger in moderation can play. He points out that neither the mean nor the extremes of anger have particularly obvious and convenient names—something true of both ancient Greek and modern English. Thus, he has to settle for "good temper" for the mean and "irascibility" for the extreme of excess. The extreme of deficiency he leaves nameless, which perhaps is just as well, given that the awkward "inirascibility" seems the only option. Anger has many sources and objects but seems particularly appropriate as a response to oneself or one's family or friends being harmed or wronged in some way. Thus, anger serves as a legitimate motivation for morally justified retaliation against those who have wronged us. However, the mean of good temper is probably closer to the deficiency than it is to the excess; we probably ought to feel moderately less anger rather than more, else we risk becoming vengeful.[6]

Plato doesn't explicitly characterize good temper as its own virtue, but there are some occasions in which he discusses the kinds of emotions and behavior that Aristotle addresses. According to Plato, the spirit is the source of anger; in fact, the Greek word that Plato uses that we translate as "spirit" (*thumoeides*) is related to the Greek word for anger (*thumos*). Since the spirit is also the source of courage, it might be argued that Plato's conception of the virtue of courage contains within it good temper as a sort of auxiliary virtue. Extrapolating, we might say that Plato conceived of the courageous/good-tempered person as one who is able to call upon the emotion of anger for motivation in times of danger and conflict. These dangers could include both the dangers that a soldier faces in battle—for example, a soldier might use his anger toward his enemies to help him overcome his fear of death or injury—and the more subtle dangers that each of us faces in trying to live a moral life—for example, a spouse who has been propositioned for an extramarital affair might be able to overcome the temptation by becoming angry with herself for even considering it.[7]

Skinner routinely shows just the right amount of anger in his capacity as assistant director of the FBI. On numerous occasions (e.g., in "Little Green Men") Skinner chews out Mulder and Scully for their failure to follow proper procedure, a precedent he sets early on and in no uncertain terms. On every one of these occasions, his level of anger is appropriate: he raises his voice but does not scream and shout, he shows his anger on his face but does not lose his composure, and so on. Displaying his anger in these ways is always just enough to get across to Mulder and Scully the gravity of the situation. If Skinner were to display too little anger, he would fail to establish the seriousness of their breaches of conduct. If he were to display too much anger, he would shift the attention away from the issue at hand and toward himself instead. Thus, the appropriate use of anger helps to establish Skinner as a competent superior officer.

Skinner also displays appropriate anger after he has begun to identify more strongly with Mulder and Scully and their goals and has started to engage more directly in off-the-books activities to support them. For example, in "Terma," Skinner becomes appropriately angry at Mulder and Scully for not being kept in the loop regarding the contents of a mysterious diplomatic pouch. His anger is completely justified because they are putting him in a potentially difficult situation, in terms of both personal safety and professional well-being, especially given that he may soon be called to testify before a special committee regarding the X-Files and the whereabouts of Mulder. His anger is an appropriate response to being wronged.

Skinner also understands that there are situations in which anger is not appropriate at all. This nicely demonstrates Aristotle's idea that a "moderate" amount of anger (or of any emotion, for that matter) means feeling anger only in the appropriate situations, toward the appropriate people, and so on. In "Apocrypha," for example, Scully visits Skinner in the hospital after he has been shot, apparently for looking into Scully's sister's murder even after the case has been closed. Scully takes the shooting as a sign of conspiracy and indicates that she will pursue the matter. Skinner wisely cautions her: "Listen to me, anger is a luxury that you cannot afford right now. If you're angry you're going to make a mistake, and these people will take advantage of that." Here Skinner shows us that sometimes the appropriate amount of anger is none at all.

Skinner also demonstrates good temper in his dealings with the Cigarette Smoking Man. For example, in "Tunguska," when the Cigarette Smoking Man approaches Skinner about the aforementioned pouch, Skinner all but tells him to take a hike. However, he does so in an extremely controlled manner and as a result is able to prevent himself from tipping his hand and revealing any information to the Cigarette Smoking Man, including whether he knows anything at all about the pouch. A more dramatic example can be seen in "Zero Sum" when Skinner attempts to cut off all ties with the Cigarette Smoking Man, despite previously having figuratively sold his soul to him in return for Scully's life. Skinner contemplates killing the Cigarette Smoking Man but instead merely fires a few rounds into the wall next to the CSM's head. This display of anger is exactly appropriate to the situation: Skinner uses his anger to get the Cigarette Smoking Man to back off, without getting carried away and doing something that he would regret.

Finally, my favorite example of Skinner displaying an appropriate amount of anger is the scene in "Tunguska" in which Skinner greets Krycek, whom he is placing under protective custody. "He'll be safe here," Skinner says, opening the door to his apartment. Once Krycek is inside, Skinner punches him hard in the stomach. "Relatively safe," he explains. Some might interpret this as excessive anger, but it seems to me just right, given Krycek's status as one of the most despicable characters in The X-Files.

The Virtue of Temperance

Both Aristotle and Plato identify temperance as an important virtue. According to Aristotle, temperance is the mean of the desire for pleasures of touch, which in Aristotle's biology includes the sense of taste as well. Thus, temperance is the virtue concerned with pleasures such as food, drink, and sex. The extreme of excess is called "self-indulgence," though in English "overindulgence" is perhaps more precise. Specific kinds of overindulgence have additional names, such as "gluttony" for an overindulgence in food and "licentiousness" for an overindulgence in sex. Aristotle claims that the extreme of deficiency is so rarely seen as to lack an obvious name—once again as true for the ancient Greeks as it is for us now—and so the awkward "insensitive" has to do. As with anger, the mean desire for pleasure is probably closer to the deficiency than it is to the excess—in general, we are probably better off with moderately less food and sex than we are with more. However, a complete lack of such desires seems inhuman, not to mention potentially harmful. For example, an individual's health would be severely compromised if he or she failed to eat enough, and humanity as a whole might risk extinction without some interest in sex.[8]

Plato talks about temperance in terms similar to Aristotle's, but he broadens the relevant desire to include other, less strictly biological pleasures such as desires for wealth and material possessions. Like Aristotle, Plato believes that we are better off with moderately less of such things than we are with more, and so a good life is a fairly simple one, not a life of luxury. Plato also discusses an additional dimension of temperance not mentioned by Aristotle, a kind of knowing of one's place in the scheme of things. According to Plato, in an ideal republic each member of society would stick to his or her class and contribute to society in the ways appropriate to that class. For example, the producers (that is, those who produce the goods that fulfill the basic needs of society, such as food, clothing, and shelter) wouldn't try to rule the republic, the rulers wouldn't try to fight battles, and so on. The idea of "knowing one's place" probably rubs many of us in the twenty-first century the wrong way, connoting as it does imperialism and oppression. Still, we might agree that there is something at least practical about each of us finding a place in the scheme of things and playing a positive role in society.[9]

Temperance may not seem like the most interesting of virtues from a dramatic point of view. After all, the courage of a hero can be demonstrated by having him dodge bullets, but temperance tends to manifest itself by not doing anything too terribly interesting. However, it does play an essential dramatic role, albeit a more subtle one, in the respect that it is easier for an audience to identify with temperate characters than with overindulgent or insensitive ones. For example, a drunken, gluttonous womanizer isn't an easily likable sort of character (though I'm told some people actually like the James Bond character). On the other extreme, a character with no appetites whatsoever seems inhuman and is difficult to identify with.

During the first several of Skinner's appearances on *The X-Files,* he gives the impression of suffering from the vice of insensitivity. As previously noted, he initially seems almost inhuman in his devotion to the bureaucratic trappings of his role as assistant director. Furthermore, he appears to have no personal life at all—no relationships, no hobbies, no interests, no personal desires or appetites—at least as far as anyone working with him can tell. "Truth is, we don't know very much about him. We don't know what he does off duty, who he really is," says Scully of Skinner in "Avatar," already well into season 3. By all impressions up to that point, Skinner seems more like an extra than a main character and certainly not the sort of character of whom one might say, "He's my favorite."

We soon learn that there is more to Skinner than meets the eye and that he is not one to completely forgo human pleasures. In particular, the episode "Avatar" is devoted to exploring Skinner's personal side for the first time. In this episode, we discovered that Skinner is married, though separated and on the verge of getting a divorce. We see him drinking alcohol, though without becoming drunk, a sign of moderation. He even becomes sexually involved with an attractive stranger he meets at a bar. She later turns up dead, and Scully, performing the autopsy, notes that "there was some irritation, probably an allergic reaction to latex." Mulder remarks, "At least they were having safe sex." This is a rather dark joke considering the outcome, but it is also another sign of Skinner's temperance: he's not the sort of man to let his desires prompt him to do anything foolish, such as having unprotected sex with a total stranger. Toward the end of the episode, Skinner admits to Mulder that he had partaken of various indulgences as a young soldier in Vietnam: "I was no choir boy. I inhaled." All of these examples are essential to establishing Skinner as a temperate person rather than an overindulgent or insensitive one. This in turn establishes him as person with whom we can empathize and makes him into a dramatic character we can support throughout the series.

The other dimension of Plato's account of temperance—"knowing one's place"—provides much of the dramatic tension for Skinner's character. As the assistant director, Skinner is basically the FBI equivalent of upper-middle management. He must constantly balance his obligations to his superiors and subordinates while also taking into consideration his beliefs about the right thing to do in any particular situation. Given that his subordinates include the likes of Mulder and Scully, this is clearly not an easy task. As Skinner himself puts it in "F. Emasculata," "I stand right on the line that you keep crossing." He must constantly search for ways to play by the book as far as his superiors are concerned (or at least aware), while occasionally operating more independently off the clock, sometimes through less-than-orthodox channels.

Sometimes Skinner can achieve this balance while still playing by the book—for example, in "Piper Maru" when he has to tell Scully that the official investigation into her sister's murder has been put into inactive status. Despite this, he tells her he will do everything he can, including filing appeals and rechecking the investigation personally. This shows Skinner acting within the appropriate bounds of his role in the FBI, respecting the wishes of his superiors and the feelings of his subordinates, and at the same time trying to do the right thing.

However, playing by the book isn't always possible, and when it is necessary, Skinner shows himself capable of bending and stretching the rules, without ever quite lapsing into outright insubordination or abuse of his office. For example, during one of Mulder's disappearances, Skinner initially refuses to help Scully pursue the matter. He rejects her request to investigate through unofficial channels, citing his duties to the FBI. However, we later see Skinner (in "End Game") pursue this information off the clock, without abusing his position or resources in the FBI, when he confronts X (as we saw in the section on courage).

Finally, we see a perfect example of Skinner's "standing on the line" in his reopening of the X-Files. When the X-Files were closed a few episodes earlier, the order had come down from Skinner's superiors. However, this is not exactly an order in the obligatory sense, since Skinner does technically have the authority to keep the X-Files open. Thus, when he exercises that authority (in "Ascension"), he is not guilty of insubordination and is well within the boundaries of his role in the FBI. However, it is also clearly a decision he makes to the dissatisfaction of his superiors, and it demonstrates his willingness to stand directly on the edge of the line of keeping his place if he believes it is the right thing to do.

Virtue and the Good Life: Is Skinner Happy?

I've made the case that Skinner embodies the virtues of courage, good temper, and temperance. To conclude our discussion, I want to consider the question of whether, for all his virtue, Skinner has achieved "the good life." Put another way, we might ask, Does the fact that Skinner is a virtuous person make him happy? Unfortunately, the answer seems to be no. As we see throughout the series (and especially in "Avatar"), Skinner does not have a particularly happy life. His marriage is on the brink of collapsing, and he spends his time off alone or sitting alone in bars (not usually an activity of someone with a fulfilling personal life). In addition, his desire to do the right thing, especially to protect Scully and Mulder, often gets him into professional trouble.

Can Skinner's unhappiness be explained within the context of classical theories of virtue? Perhaps. According to Aristotle, the character virtues are just one part of the good life; in addition, the development and exercise of the intellectual virtues is required. On Aristotle's account, the intellectual virtues include theoretical wisdom and practical wisdom. Theoretical wisdom is the kind of wisdom and knowledge gained from engaging in fairly abstract, highly theoretical intellectual disciplines such as math, physics, certain kinds of philosophy, and so forth. Practical wisdom is roughly what we might call prudence, in the older sense of the word: a kind of moral understanding and wisdom. For reasons we needn't get into here, Aristotle claims that exercise of theoretical reasoning and the development of theoretical wisdom are superior to exercise and development of practical reasoning and wisdom; thus, Aristotle says that the happiest person is the philosopher—in the term's older, broader sense, which includes scientists, mathematicians, and other people professionally engaged in high-level theoretical intellectual enterprises, including (I hope) some contemporary academic philosophers.[10]

So the Aristotelian answer to the question of why Skinner isn't happy might simply be that he isn't a professional egghead. However, this isn't a particularly satisfying answer from our perspective; it's quaint at best, elitist at worst. Moreover, even Aristotle himself thought that a life of practical reasoning and wisdom, especially as demonstrated through a life of public service, made for a fairly close second-best happiness. This being the case, Skinner certainly ought to be happier than he is, even from Aristotle's perspective: he lives a life of public service in his work for the FBI and certainly seems to be a moral person.

Thus, if the problem isn't particularly with Skinner's choice of profession or any lack of relevant wisdom, perhaps the problem lies back where we started: in the character virtues. I've made the case that Skinner has some virtues—courage, good temper, and temperance—but this short list hardly exhausts all the character virtues. Is there any virtue that Skinner lacks, or at least fails to exercise consistently? Does Skinner have a character flaw? I believe so. Like many heroes in classical literature, Skinner suffers from a "tragic flaw." In fact, Skinner has the most common of such flaws: what the Greeks called *hubris,* roughly translated as "excessive pride."[11]

Skinner's particular brand of hubris manifests itself in his routinely holding himself to a higher moral standard than others. When we hold ourselves to a higher standard than someone else, it suggests that we believe that we are morally and rationally superior to them. For example, we don't hold children to the same moral standards as adults, precisely because we know that adults are more morally and rationally developed than children. Neither do we ascribe the kinds of moral obligations to animals that we do to humans, precisely because there is a sense in which we think of humans as superior to animals with regard to our moral and rational capacities. Thus, by holding himself to a higher moral standard than he does others, Skinner shows us that he believes that he is in some sense superior to those around him.

Two key examples, one from his personal life and one from his professional life, clearly demonstrate Skinner's hubris and its serious consequences. In his personal life, Skinner's hubris manifests itself in an unwillingness to open up to his wife. She herself (in "Avatar") testifies to this fact during her first meeting with Mulder and Scully: "He lives under this misguided notion that silence is strength. He's built a wall to keep everyone out." Skinner's belief that he has to be strong for both of them shows that he does not believe that his wife is capable of being similarly strong—not because he necessarily thinks she is weak, but because he believes that he is stronger. Needless to say, such an attitude has disastrous consequences on a relationship that is supposed to be based on trust, respect, and—most important—equality.

In his professional life, Skinner's hubris manifests itself in his taking on greater moral obligations than those he assigns to others with whom he works. Of course, there are times when this is justified. Skinner should take on greater obligations than those he assigns to Mulder or Scully when such obligations are directly related to his role as their superior officer. However, Skinner's hubris causes him to ask more from himself than from those around him even when his professional status does not demand it. A key example of this occurs after Scully has been diagnosed with a terminal illness. In "Memento Mori," Mulder asks Skinner to set up a meeting with the Cigarette Smoking Man, intending to sell his soul in return for a cure for Scully. Skinner refuses to let Mulder sell himself out, even for Scully: "Find another way . . . there's always another way." However, as we soon learn,

Skinner has simply made the deal himself and as a result turns himself into one of the Cigarette Smoking Man's puppets, at least for a while. Faustian deals are not part of Skinner's job description and are no more required of him than of Mulder, and yet Skinner makes this deal contrary to his own professed judgment about the wisdom of such a course of action. In doing so, Skinner shows us that he believes that he has moral obligations that Mulder does not, which suggests that he thinks of himself as morally superior to Mulder—a sign of hubris.

The X-Files' Tragic Hero

Skinner remains a hero despite this flaw, and possibly even because of it to some extent. As Aristotle argues in *The Poetics,* the dramatic hero must be a good person but not perfect, or else the audience will not be able to identify with him or sympathize with him when he meets misfortune. Skinner's virtues and his tragic flaw make him a person we can admire, support, cheer for when he succeeds, and pity when he suffers. Thus, Skinner is not only *The X-Files'* unsung hero but also its tragic hero—and so much the better for us, his admiring viewers.[12]

Notes

1. The main source for Aristotle's theory of virtue is *Nicomachean Ethics (NE);* in particular, his general theory of the character virtues can be found in book 2. References in this chapter are to the standardized line numbers, so that interested readers may look them up in any edition or translation. My preferred translation is still the one by David Ross (Oxford: Oxford University Press, 1998), though Terence Irwin's (Indianapolis: Hackett, 2000) is perhaps more popular these days; either would serve any casual reader well. As far as translation issues are involved, I usually follow Ross's choices, though I occasionally substitute Irwin's or my own when it seems best suited to the modern English-speaking reader.

2. As with Aristotle, my references to Plato will be to the standardized line numbers, so that interested readers may refer to any edition. A particularly good collection of excellent translations is *Plato: Complete Works,* edited by John Cooper (Indianapolis: Hackett, 1997).

3. Aristotle, *NE,* bk. 3, 1115a7–1117b21. Though Aristotle says that true courage is concerned with death in battle, I suspect he would be amenable to broadening it slightly to include a concern with injury in battle.

4. Plato, *Republic,* bk. 4, 435b ff. There are some translational issues that are confusing for the speaker of modern English. For example, "soul" is a typical translation

of the Greek *psuche*, which did not necessarily have religious connotations, and in the context of this section of *The Republic* might just as well be translated "psyche" or "mind." "Spirit" is a potentially misleading translation of the Greek word *thumoeides*, which means "spirit" somewhat in the sense of the English word as we find it in expressions such as "keeping one's spirits up" or "having school spirit," not in the sense of the word as we find it in discussions of mythical evil spirits or religious concepts of the soul.

5. Aristotle argues that complete virtue requires the development and exercise of our highest rational faculties. He does not believe that women possess these faculties. Thus, on Aristotle's account, women are not capable of total virtue. In contrast, Plato says on at least one occasion that both men and women have the same "souls," and so both possess the same faculties, including reason and the capacity for virtue. Thus, according to Plato, both men and women are capable of attaining virtue, at least in a society that would allow them to do so.

6. Aristotle, *NE*, bk. 4, 1125b27–1126b11.

7. Plato, *Republic*, bk. 4, 439e ff.; bk. 5, 465a ff.

8. Aristotle, *NE*, bk. 3, 1117b23–1119b20.

9. Plato, *Republic*, bk.4, 430d ff.

10. Aristotle, *NE*, bk. 6; bk. 10, 1176a30–1179a33.

11. Aristotle, *Poetics*, bk. 13, 1453a6 ff. "Tragic flaw" is a traditional translation of the Greek *hamartia*. There is some disagreement about whether this refers to a flaw of character or simply a mistaken course of action based on an error in judgment. Though strictly speaking I tend to sympathize with the latter view, I think the idea of the tragic flaw as a character flaw has become ingrained solidly enough in our common consciousness—not to mention standard literary analysis—that I'm happy to treat it that way. Furthermore, there is some debate about whether the tragic flaw, if it is a character flaw, is a full-fledged vice or merely an occasional lapse of virtue. A solution to this debate requires more time and attention than can be offered here. However, in Skinner's case, his flaw seems more like the occasional lapse than an enduring state, as evidenced by the few (though serious) occasions on which it manifests itself.

12. See Aristotle, *Poetics*, bks. 13 and 15 for a discussion of character in tragedy.

Science and the Mystery of Consciousness

A Dialogue between Mulder and Scully

Gordon Barnes

It is May 9, 1994. Special Agent Dana Scully telephones Special Agent Fox Mulder at his apartment. Mulder's telephone is bugged, and somewhere in the silent darkness, a man smoking a cigarette is listening. He subtly but smugly smiles as he lights up another Morley. Mulder and Scully begin discussing their philosophical differences, and the man smoking the cigarette is both amused and intrigued.

MULDER: That's the difference between you and me, Scully. I think there are limits to what science can explain. Not everything can be reduced to the physical, chemical, and biological dimensions of reality. Not everything can be modeled in the current paradigms of the natural sciences, which exist solely for the purpose of predicting and controlling a universe that is much larger and more complex than our limited human minds will ever comprehend. That's my view. But not you. You think that science can explain everything.

SCULLY: The scientific method is predicated on the assumption that all natural phenomena are governed by laws of nature, and that these laws can be discovered by formulating hypotheses and testing them with experiments. As a scientist, I accept this view. I believe that the universe is governed by physical, chemical, and biological laws, and that the scientific method is the best way to discover these laws. Of course, we have not yet discovered every law of nature, nor can we explain every natural phenomenon. However, it is possible, at least in principle, that everything will be explained by the methods of science. Nothing is beyond the power of science to explain.

MULDER: Why do you think that? Why think that science can explain everything?

SCULLY: My commitment to the scientific method is based on the success of science in explaining natural phenomena. No other method of investigation has increased our understanding of the world as much as science. You've seen it for yourself, Mulder. Last November, when we visited the Arctic Ice Core Project in Alaska, we discovered tapeworms that produced violent behavior in their hosts. Do you remember that?

MULDER: Yes, I remember.

SCULLY: We eventually figured out that the tapeworms were affecting the hypothalamus. Medical science has taught us that the hypothalamus secretes a hormone called acetylcholine, and this hormone in large quantities causes violent behavior. So the scientific method enabled us to explain why the tapeworms were causing their hosts to be violent. Science explained what was happening to those people, and that's just one example out of many. When it comes to explaining natural phenomena, the scientific method has proven to be the most reliable method.

MULDER: But since you've joined the X-Files, Scully, you've also seen things that science cannot explain. Remember Luther Boggs?

SCULLY: Yes, of course I do. I will never forget him.

MULDER: When Luther first claimed to be a psychic, even I was skeptical. I thought that there must be some natural explanation of what Luther knew. My suspicion was that Luther was cooperating with the killer, and that's how he knew what he knew. But then Luther said things about your father that he couldn't possibly know unless he was psychic. You told me that he called you "Starbuck," which is a nickname that only your father ever used. Isn't that right?

SCULLY: Yes, Mulder, that's true, and I am as puzzled as you are about Luther Boggs. I don't know what to make of it. But even if Luther is actually psychic, that does not mean that science will never explain his ability. Maybe science will one day explain how psychic powers are possible. After all, science has a long history of explaining mysterious phenomena. The ancient Vikings could not explain where lightning came from, and so they invented the myth that the god Thor made the lightning. However, science now tells us that lightning is an electrical discharge. Many ancient tribes believed that evil spirits caused our diseases, but then science discovered bacteria and viruses. So science has a long history of explaining mysterious phenomena. I think that is likely to continue in the future.

MULDER: Well I don't doubt the historical success of science, Scully, but I think there are some mysteries that science will never explain.

SCULLY: It sounds like you have a specific example in mind, Mulder. What is it? What will science never explain?

MULDER: Albert Einstein once said that science cannot explain "the taste of soup." You might think that he was just joking, but I don't think so. I think he was talking about consciousness. That's what science will never explain, Scully, consciousness.

SCULLY: I've read that remark by Einstein, back when I was researching my thesis on his "twin paradox." But I want a clear definition of what you mean by consciousness. People use the word "consciousness" to refer to lots of different human capacities. Sometimes they mean our capacity for self-awareness, and sometimes they mean our ability to reason, and sometimes they mean something else altogether. So tell me what you mean by consciousness.

MULDER: Well, by consciousness I mean a certain feature of our experiences. To say that an experience is conscious is to say that there is something that it feels like to have that experience. For example, when I nibble on the shell of a sunflower seed, I have an experience that feels a certain way; it has the feeling of a salty taste. Every experience feels a certain way. The smell of a rose feels one way, and the sound of a violin feels another way, but all experiences feel some way or other. So when I talk about consciousness, I'm talking about the fact that our experiences feel a certain way.

SCULLY: Philosophers actually have a term for this, Mulder. They call these feelings "qualia." Qualia are the ways that our experiences feel to us—the way that salt tastes, the way a rose smells. Those are qualia.

MULDER: Yes, that's exactly what I'm talking about. I don't think that science will ever explain qualia. Why does a rose smell the way it does? Why does salt taste the way it does? In fact, why do any of these things cause us to have any feeling at all?

SCULLY: Science has a lot to say about this, actually. Take the taste of salt, for example. Salt activates the receptors of certain sensory cells in the taste buds of the tongue. This activation then causes a series of signals in the nervous system, which leads up to a pattern of electrical activity in the taste center of the brain. Whenever you have this pattern of electrical activity in the taste center of the brain, then you have an experience that feels like a salty taste. That is the scientific explanation of why salt causes you to have an experience that feels the way it does. So I think that science does explain why salt tastes the way it does.

MULDER: But does that really explain it? Notice what all that science does not explain. When you get to the end of your scientific explanation, you say that a certain pattern of electrical activity in the brain causes me to experience a salty taste. But this is where my question starts. Why does that pattern of electrical activity in the brain cause an experience that feels like a salty taste? Why doesn't it cause me to experience the smell of a rose, or the sound of a violin?

SCULLY: It is because this pattern of electrical activity wasn't caused by a rose or a violin. It was caused by salt.

MULDER: But that doesn't really answer the question. I asked you why salt causes an experience that feels exactly the way it does, rather than feeling some other way, or no way at all. You said that science could explain that, and you told me that salt causes a chemical reaction that leads up to a certain brain state, and then that brain state causes me to have an experience that feels like a salty taste. So then I asked you why that particular brain state causes me to feel a salty taste, and you answer that this brain state causes a salty taste because it was caused by salt. But that doesn't answer the question, because it still doesn't tell us why salt causes an experience that feels exactly the way it does, rather than some other way, or no way at all. Do you see?

SCULLY: Yes, I think so, but go on.

MULDER: I started out asking you why salt causes an experience that feels exactly the way it does, and you've come back to saying that it's because the experience was caused by salt. But that's exactly what I want explained: why does salt cause me to have an experience that feels exactly this way, rather than feeling some other way, or no way at all? I think that you were right to describe the physical process that leads from salt to a particular state of my brain, but then that's where the real problem of consciousness begins. Why does that particular brain state cause that particular feeling, rather than some other feeling, or no feeling at all?

SCULLY: I wonder if you're expecting too much out of a good explanation here. Science often explains things by identifying their causes, and once we have identified the cause of something, then we consider it explained. So if we can identify the cause of a conscious experience as being a particular state of the brain, then why isn't that enough to explain that conscious experience?

MULDER: It's not enough because it leaves a perfectly intelligible question unanswered. Why does this electrical activity in the brain cause me to feel the taste of salt, rather than feeling some other way, or no way at all? That is a legitimate question, and it hasn't been answered.

SCULLY: But even if science has not yet answered this question, why think that it never will? Maybe this question has not been answered because scientific research is not finished yet. I've already admitted that there are many phenomena that science cannot explain just yet. But you want to say that science never will explain this. What evidence do you have for that?

MULDER: That's a fair question, but I think I have an answer. As you demonstrated just a minute ago, we already know an awful lot about the mechanisms that cause taste experiences. We know about the receptors in the sensory cells of the taste buds, and about the series of signals in the nervous system. And when it comes to the brain, we know that the brain is made up of neurons, and that these neurons give off electrical discharges across synapses, and so on. None of this science is likely to be refuted in the future. We're only likely to add to it. So whatever new scientific information we get, it will almost certainly be more information of the same kind. What we are likely to discover in the future is just more detailed information about neurons and their electrical discharges. Now here is the important point. No matter how much more of that kind of information we get, it will still be just as puzzling why certain electrical activity causes an experience that feels a certain way. More details about the electrical activity won't dispel the mystery. So I don't think that science is likely to discover anything that will solve this problem.

SCULLY: Well, I'm not certain that future science will be "just more of the same," but for the sake of the argument I will concede that for now. It occurs to me that there is a theory of consciousness that I've been overlooking, and it's very relevant here. Some philosophers think that consciousness itself is really just a state of the brain and nothing more. This is sometimes called the *identity theory,* because it says that every state of consciousness is identical with some physical state of the brain. According to the identity theory, it is misleading to say that our brain states cause our consciousness, because that suggests that we are talking about two different states, one of which is a physical state of the brain and one of which is a state of consciousness. However, the truth is that every state of consciousness is really just a physical state of the brain and nothing more. So it is misleading to say that a pattern of electrical activity in the brain causes an experience of the taste of salt. In reality, the pattern of electrical activity in the brain is the very same thing as my experience of the taste of salt. There is just one event happening here, not two. It's just that we have two different ways of talking about this one event. We can describe it as a conscious experience, or we can describe it as a brain state, but either way we are talking about the very same thing. Now suppose that the identity theory is true, and that my experience of the taste of salt is really just a physical state of my brain and nothing more. Then when you ask why this pattern of electrical activity causes me to experience the taste of salt, you are failing to realize that the experience of the taste of salt is really nothing more than this pattern of electrical activity. So there is really nothing left to explain here.

MULDER: So you're going to solve the problem by denying that consciousness is real? Only brain states are real?

SCULLY: No, Mulder, I'm not denying that consciousness is real. What I'm saying is that consciousness really is a physical state of the brain. I'm not denying that it's real; I'm just putting forward a theory of what it is. Here's an analogy. I pointed out earlier that lightning is really an electrical discharge from clouds to the earth. In saying that, I wasn't denying that lightning is real. I was just telling you what lightning really is. In the same way, when I say that consciousness is a physical state of the brain, I'm not denying that consciousness is real. I'm just saying what consciousness really is.

MULDER: Well I don't think that consciousness is just a physical state of the brain. In fact, there is an argument that refutes that idea. An Australian philosopher named Frank Jackson first stated the argument, which goes like this.[1] Imagine a time in the distant future when science has discovered all the physical and chemical facts that there are to know about the universe. Now imagine a scientist in this distant future. We'll call her Mary. Suppose that Mary spends her entire life studying the physics and chemistry of taste. By the end of her life, Mary knows all the physical and chemical facts there are to know about the human sense of taste. Take, for example, the taste of salt. Mary knows the exact molecular structure of salt, and she knows exactly which chemical reactions these molecules cause in the taste buds of the tongue. Mary also knows everything there is to know about the physics and chemistry of the process that leads up to the brain state that causes the taste of salt. Finally, Mary knows everything physical and chemical that there is to know about the final brain state that occurs when we experience the taste of salt. Mary knows all that. Okay, but now here is the twist. Mary has never tasted anything salty. Mary has a medical condition that requires that she be fed intravenously. So Mary has never tasted much of anything at all. Now, here is the important point in all of this. Even though Mary knows all the physical and chemical facts that there are to know about the taste of salt, there is still something that she does not know: she does not know what it feels like to experience the taste of salt, because she has never tasted it. For all the physical and chemical facts that she knows, Mary still does not know what it feels like to experience the taste of salt. Now, what does this prove? Well, if the experience of the taste of salt were really just a physical or chemical state of the brain, then once Mary knew all the physics and chemistry of this state of the brain, she would know everything there is to know about this experience. But as we've just seen, Mary doesn't know everything there is to know about this experience, because she doesn't know what it feels like to have this experience. I think this example shows that the experience of the taste of salt is not just a physical or chemical state of the brain. And of course this generalizes to other experiences as well. If a conscious experience were really just a physical or chemical state of the brain, then if you knew all the physical and chemical facts about that state of the brain, you would know everything there is to know about that conscious experience. But the example of Mary shows that you wouldn't necessarily know everything there is to know about the experience, because you wouldn't necessarily know what it feels like to have the experience. So conscious experiences are not just physical states of the brain. That's the argument.

SCULLY: I have several questions. Let me start with this. Are you sure that someone could really know all the facts that you say Mary knows? Could one person really know all that physics and chemistry?

MULDER: Well, that's why I've limited Mary's knowledge to the human sense of taste. I only say that she knows all the physical and chemical facts about the human sense of taste. If you want, we could even limit her knowledge to the specific taste of salt. I could use that modified story to prove my point just as well.

SCULLY: Well, even when it comes to a specific experience, like the taste of salt, I think all the physics and chemistry of that experience would be a huge amount of information, and I'm not sure that one person could really know all that. But I'm willing concede that for now. I think there is a much more serious problem with your argument. First of all, it is important to understand that there can be more than one way of thinking about the same thing. Here is an example to illustrate the point. Think about Eugene Victor Tooms. Dr. Aaron Monte knew Tooms as "Eugene," the shy, mild-mannered person who worked for the city's animal control unit. By contrast, you and Detective Frank Briggs knew Eugene as "Tooms," the one-hundred-year-old genetic mutant who needs five human livers every thirty years to sustain his hibernations. Now, when Dr. Monte thought about Eugene, and when Detective Briggs thought about Tooms, they were both thinking about the same person. They were just thinking about this person in two different ways. Moreover, since Eugene and Tooms were the same person, any fact about Eugene was also a fact about Tooms. Suppose that both Dr. Monte and Detective Briggs followed Tooms after work one day. As Dr. Monte followed him, he might think to himself, "There goes Eugene, past the pharmacy," and Detective Briggs might think to himself, "There goes Tooms, past the pharmacy." When Dr. Monte and Detective Briggs think these thoughts, they are really both thinking about the same fact. It's just that they are thinking about that fact in two different ways, because they are thinking about the same person in two different ways.

MULDER: What does any of this have to do with my story about Mary?

SCULLY: I'm getting to that, Mulder. Be patient. Here is how this is relevant to the case of Mary. I think that the experience of the taste of salt is really just a brain state, but there are two different ways of thinking about this brain state: we can think of this brain state as a physical state of your brain, or we can think of it as an experience of the taste of salt. These are just two different ways of thinking about the same thing. So I think that when Mary knows all the physical facts about your brain when you taste salt, she really does know what it feels like to taste salt. She just doesn't know it in the same way that you and I know it. She knows this feeling as a physical state of the brain, which is what it is, whereas you and I know this feeling as the feeling of the taste of salt. On my view, Mary and I know the very same things and the very same facts, but we know them in two different ways. Just as Dr. Aaron Monte and Detective Frank Briggs know the same person in two different ways, so Mary and I know the same state of the brain, but in two different ways. So I don't think that Mary lacks any knowledge of any real facts. All that she lacks is one way of knowing those facts.

MULDER: Okay, I think I understand the idea. According to you, Mary does not really lack any knowledge of any real fact, but only one way of thinking about a fact. I get the idea, but I don't think it's going to solve the problem. In order to explain why, I need to clarify how I'm going to use a certain term. Let's use the term "property" for any real feature or characteristic of something. For example, the shape of an object is a property of that object, and the size of an object is also a property of that object. If we were to list every property that I have, the list would include properties like being a man, being an FBI agent, and believing that consciousness is not physical. These are all properties of me, which is just to say that they are real features or characteristics of me.

SCULLY: I understand. Scientists often use the term "property" in the same way. For instance, they say that the mass of a particle is a property of that particle, which is just another way of saying that the mass of a particle is a feature or characteristic of the particle. Other physical properties include charge and spin. To say that these are properties is just to say that they are features or characteristics of things.

MULDER: Exactly. Now let's go back to the example of Tooms. We can think of this person in two different ways: we can think of him either as Eugene or as Tooms. But now notice something. The reason that we can think of this person in two different ways is that this person has two sets of properties. We could call these two sets of properties the Eugene properties and the Tooms properties. The Eugene properties include properties like being mild mannered and working at the city's animal control unit. The Tooms properties include properties like being a genetic mutant, being able to stretch and contort in fantastic ways, and needing five human livers every thirty years. Now, the reason that we can think of this person in two different ways is that he has these two different sets of properties, and we can think of him either as the person who has the Eugene properties, or as the person who has the Tooms properties. So it is because he has these two really different sets of properties that we can think about him in these two different ways. If he didn't have both sets of properties, then we couldn't think of him in both of these ways. For example, if Eugene didn't have the properties that make him Tooms the killer, then we couldn't think of him as Tooms the killer. The moral of the story is that whenever there are two ways of thinking about the same thing, that is because that thing has two truly different properties. Finally, then, let's come back to the case of consciousness and brain states. You say that thinking about a conscious state, like the taste of salt, and thinking about a physical state of the brain are two different ways of thinking about the same thing. Is that right?

SCULLY: Yes, that's right.

MULDER: Well, as the Tooms example shows, whenever there are two different ways of thinking about something, it is because that thing has two different properties. So if we can think of a brain state in two different ways, either as a brain state or as a state of consciousness, then it must be because this brain state has two different properties. And I think it's clear what these two different properties must be. Obviously a brain state has physical properties, like mass and charge, and if this brain state is also a state of consciousness, then there is some way of feeling such that it also has the property of feeling this way. And that is why we can think of this brain state in two different ways. It is because this brain state has two different properties, one being a physical property (or set of physical properties), and the other being the property of feeling the way it feels to be in that brain state. But then, at the end of all this, it seems to me that your response to the story of Mary—that she only lacks one way of thinking about brain states—implies that brain states have properties that are not physical properties. Think of it this way. If brain states had only physical properties, then there would only be one way of thinking about those brain states—the physical way. If Eugene only had the Eugene properties, and not any of the Tooms properties, then there would only be one way to think about Eugene, namely, as Eugene. The reason that we can think about him in another way is that he has more properties—the Tooms properties. Likewise, if you admit that the physical way of thinking about brain states is not the only way of thinking about them, because we can also think about them as states that feel a certain way, then you are committed to the conclusion that these brain states have more properties than just their physical properties. So your defense of the identity theory leads straight to what is called *property dualism*. Property dualism is the view that our brains have two really different kinds of properties. They have physical properties, like mass and charge, but they also have mental properties, like the property of feeling a certain way, and the mental properties are not just more physical properties. They are nonphysical properties.

SCULLY: That's a very interesting argument, Mulder, but I can tell you exactly where I disagree. You say that whenever there are two different ways of thinking about something, there must be two different properties. What you are assuming is that the only way to think about something is to think about it in terms of one of its properties. Is that your view?

MULDER: Yes, that's my view.

SCULLY: Well, then, that's where I disagree. I think it's possible to think about something directly, without thinking about any of its properties at all. For example, suppose that I come home one day to find a strange-looking object on my desk, and suppose that I ask myself, "What is that?" Now, I have just had a thought about this object. After all, I asked a question about the object, and in that very act I have succeeded in thinking about it. But I have not thought about any of its properties yet. I simply asked, "What is that?" So it is possible to think about something without thinking about any of its properties. How is this possible? It is possible to think about this object directly because I am in direct contact with it. I can literally point to it, and thus I can think about it directly, without thinking about any of its properties at all. Whenever a person is in direct contact with something, I will say that they are acquainted with it. Being acquainted with something is a different way of thinking about it than knowing any of its properties. For that reason, the English philosopher Bertrand Russell distinguished between two kinds of knowledge: knowledge by acquaintance and knowledge by description. I will start with knowledge by description. Knowing something by description is knowing true descriptions of it. For example, I know lots of true descriptions of Tooms: that he is a genetic mutant, and that he can stretch and contort in fantastic ways, and that he needs five livers every thirty years. When I know these true descriptions of Tooms, then I have knowledge by description of Tooms. But when I meet Tooms, I acquire something new: I become acquainted with Tooms, and my acquaintance with Tooms is a new way of knowing him. Now here is the important point. The Tooms that I know by description and the Tooms that I know by acquaintance are the very same person. This illustrates how it is possible to know the same person in these two different ways, first by description, and then by acquaintance.

MULDER: Okay, so how does all of this apply to the case of Mary?

SCULLY: When Mary is locked in her environment devoid of taste, learning brain science, I think she is acquiring knowledge by description of conscious experiences, since conscious experiences are really brain states. When Mary learns the brain science of tasting salt, for example, I think she is learning exactly which physical and chemical descriptions are true of that experience. In fact, I think that Mary could learn every true description of the experience in this way. However, I agree that until Mary tastes salt for herself, she is lacking something. So what does Mary lack at this point, before she has tasted salt? What Mary lacks is simply an acquaintance with the taste of salt. Mary knows lots of things about the taste of salt, but her knowledge is all knowledge by description. Until she actually tastes salt for herself, she does not yet have any direct acquaintance with that experience. But now remember, knowledge by description and knowledge by acquaintance can be knowledge of the very same thing. I can know Tooms by description, and then I can know Tooms by acquaintance, and I am just knowing the same person in two different ways. Likewise, in the case of Mary, I think that when Mary knew all of the physical facts about the brain when a person tastes salt, she actually knew all the facts about the taste of salt. So when she tasted salt for the first time, she didn't learn any new facts about the taste of salt. Rather, she just came to know the taste of salt in a new way: by acquaintance.

MULDER: I agree that when Mary tastes salt for the first time, she becomes directly acquainted with that taste for the first time. However, it seems to me that this new acquaintance also gives Mary knowledge of something new, namely, what it feels like to experience the taste of salt. I don't deny that there is such a thing as direct acquaintance, but I do deny that this is all that Mary acquires when she tastes salt for the first time. It just seems clear to me that through her new acquaintance, Mary learns a new fact about the experience of the taste of salt, and since Mary already knew all the physical facts about the brain, this fact cannot be a physical fact about the brain.

SCULLY: Well, I'm just not convinced, Mulder. I think it's possible that Mary has simply become acquainted with something that she already knew by description. Say, Mulder, I hate to interrupt you, but all this talk about sunflower seeds has made me really hungry. Could we continue this discussion over dinner?

MULDER: Sure, Scully, but before we get a bite to eat, I'd like to show you a video I made last night from a local news broadcast at the suggestion of our inside contact. I'd tell you about the contents of the tape over the phone, but I'm suspicious. Although we found the bug not so inconspicuously disguised as a pen and the bug wrapped around the electrical outlet, you never know when they'll be listening next and from where. Anyway, safe to say, I think we'll be soon traveling to Ardis, Maryland.

SCULLY: Okay, Mulder. Let's meet in the office.

Notes

Thanks to Marnie Barnes and Dean Kowalski for helpful suggestions on previous drafts of this paper.

1. For a good discussion of Frank Jackson's famous argument, together with objections and replies, see Frank Jackson and David Braddon-Mitchell, *The Philosophy of Mind and Cognition: An Introduction* (Maldon, MA: Blackwell, 1996), 127–35. For some of the best recent articles in this debate, including the so-called acquaintance view, see Peter Ludlow, Yujin Nagasawa, and Daniel Stoljar, eds., *There's Something*

about Mary: Essays on Phenomenal Consciousness and Frank Jackson's Knowledge Argument (Cambridge, MA: MIT Press, 2004).

[This dialogue is limited to natural phenomena; thus, we are to believe that Scully's religious beliefs are not relevant. We might imagine her position here to be similar to that in "Gethsemane," when she tells Mulder that God's existence can't be proven. — ed.]

Part III

THE EPISODES

"Clyde Bruckman's Final Repose" Reprised 2009

Dean A. Kowalski

Darin Morgan's *X-Files* episodes are wickedly clever. "Clyde Bruckman's Final Repose" is no exception. Clyde Bruckman (Peter Boyle) has captured what Mulder so elusively seeks—the truth out there—at least a part of it. The St. Paul, Minnesota, resident cannot foretell next week's winning lottery ticket numbers, but he can foresee how people will die. In telling his tale through Bruckman, Morgan may be poking fun at those who take soothsayers too seriously. After all, recall Scully's reaction to seeing "the Stupendous Yappi" (Jaap Broeker) on a late-night commercial and, more important, the various fortunetellers' inabilities to discern that Puppet (Stu Charno) is about to kill each of them. Nevertheless, it's clear that we are supposed to take Bruckman seriously. He lives alone, sees his gift as a curse, and tries to deal with his unique perspective on the future by becoming a life insurance salesman. His attempt doesn't succeed, however; he becomes dour and resigned and eventually commits suicide—a death that he apparently foresaw and one that no insurance policy would cover.

Morgan's writing is as thoughtful as it is clever (and more on this later). Among other interesting topics, his Clyde Bruckman story also reminds us of the classic philosophical "freedom and foreknowledge" problem.[1] At the intuitive heart of the alleged problem is the following: In order for one to know what *will* happen in the future, there must *now* be truths about it to be known. But if there are now such truths, then the future is already determined. If the future is already determined, it cannot be altered, and if the future cannot be altered, then we cannot act any differently in it than we do. Therefore, insofar as foreknowledge requires that descriptions of the future are true now, foreknowledge of our choices is inconsistent with our freely making them. In this chapter, however, I hope to show two things.

First, once it is clearer how Bruckman is able to see the future at all, it will be argued that contrary to popular opinion—including Aristotle's—the reasoning at the heart of the problem is faulty. The so-called freedom and foreknowledge problem generated by the antecedent truth of statements about the future ("future contingents") rests on arguments that tend to confuse "determinate truths" with "determined truths." But only the latter truths are problematic for human freedom. Second, upon conducting a careful philosophical investigation into the antecedent truth of future contingents, we will better see why the sort of fatalistic resignation Bruckman adopts about the future can be avoided, even if one foreknows the future.

Determinism and Human Freedom

Before tackling the so-called freedom and foreknowledge problem, it may be worthwhile to briefly explore a different, but related, philosophical problem between human freedom and determinism. The beliefs that we are genuinely free and that determinism is true are commonly held. Both beliefs attempt to describe basic features of the world around us, but when conjoined, they unfortunately seem to be logically inconsistent. We can begin to better understand both beliefs and how they seem incompatible by turning to the episode at hand.

Recall that once Mulder begins to believe that Bruckman has psychic abilities, the two men and Scully visit a crime scene under investigation. Mulder asks Bruckman "why the killer is murdering people in the way that he is," including the doll collector (who was also an amateur tasseographer). Bruckman replies, "Why does anyone do the things they do? Why do I sell insurance? I wish I knew. Why did this woman collect dolls? What was it about her life? Was it one specific moment where she suddenly said, 'I know . . . dolls!' Or, was it a whole series of things? Starting when her parents first met that somehow combined in such a way that in the end, she had no choice but to be a doll collector?" Mulder and Bruckman are contemplating the reasons we make the choices we do. If we peer carefully enough into Bruckman's dialogue, we can find two basic ideas about this.

On the one hand, people make decisions that don't seem to be compelled or determined by anything outside of the agents themselves. These decisions, from another's perspective, may sometimes seem completely spontaneous, as captured in Bruckman's, "I know . . . dolls!" However, they might be, and often are, the result of careful deliberation on the part of the agent. Such choices are believed to be genuinely free, exactly because they only occur as the result of processes of which the agent is in direct control. This isn't to say that she is in direct control of all the processes relevant to her decision, but it is to say that the choice is "up to her" in the sense that two viable choices were open to the agent at the time and the fact that she chose to begin collecting dolls (or whatever) is essentially explained by her activity and not anything external to her. Choices meeting these criteria are those that are freely made; we typically believe that some, if not most, of our choices meet these criteria.

On the other hand, we also tend to believe that the world around us operates through cause and effect. In fact, with just a bit of thought, it seems plausible to hold that everything that happens in the world around us was caused to happen. This intuition is supported by the fact that it is very difficult to conceive of an uncaused event. Everything that we experience happening, simply didn't pop into existence out of nowhere. The fact that my car didn't start this morning had a cause—perhaps the battery died during the night because I left the lights on again. Thus, the car did not fail to start for absolutely no reason. Sometimes we may not presently know why something—cancer, say—occurs, but everybody assumes that there is a cause; this is why we spend countless dollars on cancer research. But if *everything* has a cause, C, then whatever caused event E itself was caused. That is, if C caused E, then C itself was also caused. Of course, whatever caused C also was caused to happen. But because causes are sufficient for their effects in that, necessarily, if C obtains, then E obtains, it follows that for anything that happens, it couldn't have happened any other way, at least given what has happened in the past. This is known as the philosophical theory of *determinism.* Determinism is conveyed in Bruckman's alternative account of why the woman became a doll collector. It can be traced back through a long causal chain that reaches back before her birth. Because that chain was in place, she seemingly had no choice but to become a doll collector. Of course, if we were to ask why her parents got together, that, too, has a causal explanation that precedes their births, assuming the truth of determinism. So, the alternative account of our choices is to note that if determinism is true, then any choice a person makes is merely one more link in a causal chain that stretches back to a time before his birth. We still decide and we still choose, but, given the truth of determinism, we couldn't have decided any differently than we did, given what has happened in the past.[2] And this is why many philosophers hold that the truth of determinism is inconsistent with our being genuinely free. If being genuinely free requires that there be two viable options before us and which we select is up to us in the relevant sense, then the truth of determinism is inconsistent with our being genuinely free.

The goal of this chapter is not to explore the freedom and determinism problem in any great depth. However, that problem does serve as a conceptual model for the problem we will explore—namely, whether having knowledge of how a person will choose in the future is in some way inconsistent with that person's choosing freely. Even if it is true that determinism is inconsistent with our choosing with genuine freedom, it seems to be an open question whether the antecedent truth of future contingents (a necessary feature of foreknowledge) is inconsistent with our choosing with genuine freedom. Hopefully, the answer (or, at least, an answer) to that question will become clearer as this chapter develops.

The "Seen Future"

A dismayed Bruckman looks up at Mulder from his chair and rhetorically asks, "How can I see the future if it didn't already exist?" At first blush, Bruckman's statement seems a bit odd. How should we understand his alleged ability to see the future? This question might be answered in one of two ways. First, we might focus on the specifics of his being able to see the future. That is, by what distinguishable means is Bruckman able to see the future? Second, we might focus on the necessary conditions for this happening at all, more or less leaving aside the specific processes involved. That is, generally speaking, what must the world be like for Bruckman to have this ability in the first place, regardless of whether he actually possesses it? The second version of the question is much more philosophically interesting; thus, we will focus on it, although we will not completely ignore the first.

We might interpret Bruckman's claim quite literally. Perhaps he peers into the future analogously to the way an astronomer gazes at a distant star. Astronomers have access to powerful telescopes; this accounts for their ability to see celestial bodies in great detail. But Bruckman doesn't rely on any such apparatus—not even some sort of fanciful "Jules Verne–o-scope," whatever that might be. Rather, he apparently relies on some sort of unique mental process—something akin to a "mind's eye"—to see future events like those that are allegedly to happen to Mr. Gordon (David MacKay). Consider the way Peter Boyle acts out his dialogue in the scene involving the Gordon newlyweds: His eyes roll back into his head, his eyelids are almost shut, and he begins speaking in a trancelike state, almost channeling what he apparently sees. In this eerie fashion, Bruckman states: "Two years from now, while driving down Route 91 . . . coming home to your wife and baby daughter . . . you're going to be hit head-on by a drunk . . . driving a blue 1987 Mustang. You'll end up looking worse than sixty feet of bad road your body slides across . . . after flying out your front windshield." This strongly suggests that Bruckman is indeed "looking within" himself to better *see* the young father's (proposed) gruesome death.

Episode director David Nutter seems to substantiate this interpretation of Bruckman's ability. The best piece of evidence of this is Bruckman's foretelling of Mulder's unfortunate demise in the hotel kitchen. Bruckman closes his eyes, and we the viewers experience Bruckman's *visualizing* Mulder's unfortunate demise. Actually, Bruckman claims that he is visualizing what the killer (Puppet) is visualizing. Presumably, this is why the vision is "so hazy." In a way only Morgan could devise, Mulder's throat is to be slit while he is standing in a banana cream pie. That Nutter provides a visual representation of Bruckman's visions is additional evidence that Bruckman actually sees, even if in a dreamlike fashion, what will happen regarding Mulder's death. Thus, the way the episode is constructed provides some credence to the claim that Bruckman literally sees the future.

However, interpreting Bruckman's unique perspective as akin to literal sight harbors some philosophically interesting implications. This gets us squarely back to exploring the philosophical import of Bruckman's claim. In order for him to literally see future events, they must already exist, now, in the present. For example, for Bruckman to actually see Mulder's death, Mulder must be dead (or dying); however, as Bruckman describes these events, Mulder is very much alive and standing in front of him. This leads us to conclude that Bruckman's previsions entail that events exist before they exist. But this is self-contradictory. Nothing can exist before it comes into existence. Therefore, it seems prudent to interpret Peter Boyle's acting methods and David Nutter's choice to share Bruckman's alleged visions with the episode viewer as *merely* dramatic effects and not evidence that Bruckman has the ability to literally see future events. Furthermore, Morgan's screenplay provides additional evidence that we need not interpret Bruckman's foreknowledge as literal sight. When Mulder inquires into how Bruckman receives his prophetic information, he asks, "I mean, are you seeing it in a vision or is it a sensation? How do you know where to go?" Bruckman responds, "I just know." When Mulder presses, "But how do you know?" Bruckman retorts, "I don't know!" Bruckman's responses are tantamount to his denying that he sees (literal) visions. Although this makes

Boyle's choice of acting methods a bit mysterious, it seems that we are on firm ground in reinterpreting Bruckman's statement "How can I see the future if it didn't already exist?" Bruckman's visions of the future seemingly require a less-than-literal interpretation.

The "Written Future"

We come to know the world around us primarily through the five senses. In doing so, we come to know propositions about our environment. A *proposition* is the exact meaning of a declarative sentence; philosophers tend to mark them by using single quotation marks. For example, 'Snow is white' and 'The earth has one moon' are both true propositions. Thus, propositional knowledge can be described as knowing what the facts are or being aware that such and such is the case. The suggestion proposed in this section will be that Bruckman might be able to know the future insofar as he now knows true descriptions of what will obtain; that is, Bruckman might know true propositions about how people will die.

Admittedly, the difference between the "seen future" and the "written future" may not be readily apparent. At the risk of oversimplification, the idea is something like this. On the "seen future" model, it is as if Bruckman is watching a play like any other member of the audience. The twist, however, is that Bruckman has the unique and paradoxical ability to see the play before the (actual) first-night performance. On the "written future" model, it is as if Bruckman is experiencing a play in that he has an advance copy of a very detailed script. The script contains descriptions, and thus propositions, of what will be said and done during the play. If the script is detailed enough, then Bruckman could have very explicit knowledge of how the play will proceed and, presumably, could be able to visualize these proceedings before they actually happen. Analogously, if Bruckman somehow had epistemological access to detailed descriptions of what will happen (leaving aside the practical issue of how he gained access to the "script"), then he could have propositional knowledge of the future. Thus, the difference between the two models could be explained this way: On the "seen future," Bruckman has immediate epistemic access to sensory input of future events and then translates those experiences into descriptions of future events; on the "written future," Bruckman has immediate epistemic access to the descriptions of the future and then translates these descriptions into mental pictures corresponding to events in the future.

Understanding Bruckman's unique perspective on the future in this way does not commit us to the view that Bruckman can literally see events before they happen. On the written future model, descriptions of events are conceptually distinct from the events they describe. An analogy with the past might be helpful here. Even though past events are no longer happening because time has "passed them by," their corresponding descriptions remain unaffected. So, propositions like 'The first episode of *The X-Files* episode airs on September 10, 1993' and 'Peter Boyle wins a 1996 Emmy for his portrayal of Clyde Bruckman' remain true, even though the events they describe have receded into the distant past. In a sense, then, the truth-value of the propositions remains forever unchanged, but the corresponding events in history are not. Analogously, the truth of future contingent propositions might always remain fixed even if the events they describe have yet to be. Therefore, if the truth-value of propositions never changes, it is possible (however unlikely) that someone could know future contingents before the events they describe obtain. Therefore, on the written future model, Bruckman possibly knows the descriptions of future events because he knows which propositions about the future are true.

Future Contingents and Fatalism

However, more than two millennia ago, Aristotle (384–322 B.C.E.) considered what it would mean to say that someone could know the written future. He believed that the written future model leads us straight into very familiar concerns about foreknowledge and fatalism—that is, the idea that the future is somehow unavoidable. If Aristotle is correct in this, then while we might obtain a defensible account that Bruckman possibly sees the future, it also seems to follow that Bruckman's knowledge of the future discounts our acting freely in it.[3]

Contemporary philosopher Theodore Schick encapsulates Aristotle's position like this:

> If someone knows that something is going to happen, then it's true that it is going to happen because you can't know something that is false. You can't know that 1 + 1 equals 3, for example, because 1 + 1 does not equal 3. But if it's true that something is going to happen, then it cannot possibly not happen. If it's true that the sun will rise tomorrow, for example, then the sun has to rise tomorrow, for

otherwise the statement wouldn't be true. So, if someone knows that something is going to happen, it must happen. But if it must happen—if it's unavoidable—then no one is free to prevent it from happening.[4]

If someone possesses foreknowledge, then there are now truths about how the future will unfold. If there are now truths that accurately describe future events, then the future must obtain in just that way. This leads Schick—and many others—to starkly conclude that the price of having foreknowledge is our freedom.

If no one is free to prevent future events from happening, then any deliberation about the future is meaningless. No matter what we decide, it was fated that we make just that decision. Mulder seems to agree with Schick on this score. Recall his response to Bruckman, "Then if the future is written, why bother to do anything?" Puppet echoes this sentiment in his anonymous letter to Bruckman, the one Bruckman allows Mulder to read aloud: "To whom it may concern. Like our lives, this is a mere formality to let you know I know that you know. Can't wait till our first meeting when I kill you. Not before you explain some things to me. First on the list, why in the world did I send you this letter? Sincerely, you know who. P.S.: Say 'hi' to the FBI agents." To avoid the meaninglessness of the future, Schick would no doubt hold (as Aristotle did) that the future cannot be foreknown because there aren't now any truths about it. Truths about our future choices become true only at the time of our decision and not before.

Recall that propositions are statements that make claims about how things are. If the proposition matches up with how things are (the facts of the matter), then it is true. If it doesn't match up with them—if it gets the facts wrong—then it is false. The statement 'I Want to Believe was released in July 2008' is true because it accurately describes the facts. 'Rob Bowman was the director of I Want to Believe' is false because Chris Carter directed the second X-Files motion picture. So, there indeed seems to be a necessary relationship between truth and how things are. If a statement about some set of events is true, it seems that the world must be that way. This leads Schick to claim that if there are now truths about the future, then the events it describes must happen. His example is: If it is now true that the sun will rise tomorrow, then it is impossible for the sun not to rise tomorrow. Sunrise tomorrow cannot possible not happen if it is now true that it rises. So, according to Shick, if Bruckman knows that Puppet will kill again, then it is impossible for Puppet to not commit murder (in the near future). Since this leads to fatalism, we are forced to deny the antecedent truth of future contingents so the freedom and foreknowledge problem never arises.

But there is another approach to the problem. The alternate way to understand the alleged freedom and foreknowledge problem involves rethinking the conceptual relationship between true statements and the events they accurately describe. In order for Schick's argument to work, the events described by a true proposition must obtain such that the events *themselves* become necessary or logically unavoidable. But the relationship between truth and facts need not be understood like this. Rather, any necessity involved only applies to the relationship *between* true propositions and the events they accurately describe; it need not apply to the propositions themselves or the events themselves. Consider: If there are three editors of *The Lone Gunman,* then the number of its editors is not equally divisible by two. This statement expresses a relationship between a number and its being odd or even. This relationship holds necessarily. However, we have no reason to believe that it is necessary that there are just three editors of *The Lone Gunman;* the "The Thinker" (played by Bernie Coulson in "Anasazi") could have become a full-fledged member. And it's not necessary that the magazine has an odd number of editors. Both are contingent matters. The relationship between true propositions and the events they describe works like this, too. Clarifying Schick's ambiguous use of the word "must," the relationship could be put this way: Necessarily, if a proposition is (now) true, then the event it describes happens. This interpretation, avoiding the ambiguous term "must," merely expresses a necessary relationship between true propositions and the events to which they accurately correspond. But this entails neither that true statements are necessarily so nor that the relevant states of affairs obtain necessarily. Because the alternative interpretation retains all that is crucial to the correspondence between truth and reality without sacrificing contingency, it is preferable to Schick's interpretation.

It is now easier to see how Schick's argument turns dubious. He holds that to foreknow a future event, it must (now) be true that it happens. If Bruckman knows that Puppet will kill again, it must be true that he does. Schick's specific example is that if it is now true that the sun rises tomorrow, then it has to so rise—the sun must rise tomorrow. His sense of the term "must" entails that it is impossible for the sun not to rise tomorrow if it is now true that it does. By now it is clear that we should avoid the usage of "must" and express this truth as: Necessarily, if it is now true that the sun rises tomorrow, then it does (or will do) so. This interpretation keeps the necessary relationship between true propositions and the events they describe, but it does not pertain to the propositions or events in themselves. In this way, even if it is true that the sun will rise tomorrow, this doesn't mean that the sun rises necessarily. And if Bruckman knows that Puppet will kill again, he will, but this doesn't entail that Puppet necessarily or unavoidably murders in a way that renders his terrible acts unfree.

Therefore, concerns like Schick's about the incompatibility of freedom and foreknowledge are invariably grounded in misconception. It is true that foreknowledge requires that there are now true statements about the future. But we fall into error if we interpret this to mean that the *determinate* antecedent truth of such statements *determines* how events unfold. This misconstrues the conceptual dependency. Because true propositions are merely descriptions of how things are, how future events unfold thus explains why some statements about the future are (determinately) true rather than others. So, if it is a contingent matter, as it seems, that the sun rises tomorrow, then the determinate antecedent truth of the corresponding statement cannot make its so rising necessary or unavoidable. If it is a contingent matter, which this debate must initially assume, that Puppet will kill another fortuneteller, then the antecedent truth of this cannot make his act necessary or unavoidable in a way that renders it unfree (even if there is a necessary relationship between true propositions and what they describe). Thus, how events unfold explains which statements are true, and not vice versa. Once this is realized, worries about freedom and foreknowledge begin to subside.

They continue to subside once we likewise grasp that, as knowledge requires truth, what is foreknown about the future is also explained by what will happen. The obtaining of future events as they do explains why there are (or can be) now true propositions about the future, and the current (determinate) truth of those propositions explains (in part) why they can be known. Therefore, assuming the purported knower is in a position to know the antecedently true statement about the future, knowing it does not impact how the corresponding events unfold. This knowledge cannot make a contingent fact necessary; knowing the facts cannot make them true or impact how they are true. Rather, how the corresponding events unfold determines what can be known about them. If Puppet does not choose to kill Detective Havez (Dwight McFee) in the hotel room, then Bruckman would never have known that he so kills him (or at the very least it would never be true that he would). Thus, what anyone foreknows about us depends on what we will do, and not vice versa.[5] Once these dependency relationships are kept straight, it is easier to see how the determinate antecedent truth of statements about the future—or having knowledge of them—does not determine our choices in anyway that poses a logical threat to human freedom.

Fatalism and Powerlessness

We have therefore discovered that Schick's (and Aristotle's) reasons for believing that the written future model entails fatalism are mistaken. But still, the intuition that the antecedent truth of future contingents leads to fatalism dies hard. Some may state: But if it has always been true that Chris Carter would move the show to Los Angeles for season 6, then this was true long before Chris Carter's birth. But if it this was true long before his birth, then how could he have done anything different? After all, if he were to do something different, like keep the show in Vancouver or move it to New York, doesn't that mean that he has the ability to change the past, namely, to make a true proposition about him false? But no one, not even Carter himself, has the ability to change what takes place before his birth. So, even if Schick's argument fails, it seems that the problem about the written future remains.

This last objection is understandable. Its spirit harkens back to the problem that determinism poses for human freedom. In fact, it seems to be another attempt to equate "determinate truth" with "determined truth." The idea is to somehow link the intuition that the antecedent truth of future contingents somehow determines, or otherwise makes inevitable, our future choices. To see how this might be attempted, let's go back the screenplay or script analogy. Before, we had suggested that what might explain Bruckman's knowledge of the future is that he has (less-than-perfect) cognitive access to an incredibly detailed script of what will be. But it is tempting to believe that if future contingents are always determinately true, then the script has always been in existence. If it has always existed, then you, I, Chris Carter, and everyone else must act in the future just as it is written in the script. Furthermore, acting differently than the script has it seems to entail that we have the ability to alter past events that were true long before our birth. But because no one has the ability to alter events that happened prior to birth, it seemingly follows that we don't have the ability to act differently than it is written in the script. And if we don't have the ability to act differently, then there are not two viable options open to us when we make our choices. True, there *appear* to be two viable options. However, just as it is with the case where determinism is true, it *merely* appears this way. The fact of the matter is that we must act as the script has it and we lack the ability to do otherwise. Therefore, the antecedent truth of future contingents remains inconsistent with our making future free choices, even if Schick's argument is not completely convincing.

This last argument for fatalism from the antecedent truth of future contingents can be resisted. Resisting it requires that we keep fully in mind that what we (will) do explains why the proposition is true at all. The truth of the proposition does not explain your action. Therefore, the only reason that the script says what it does is because of how we (will) act. The script, being what it is, reflects *whatever* we freely choose to do in the future. As such, determinate truths about how we will freely act do not entail that our choices are determined in a way that is inconsistent with our acting freely. Thus, had you, I, Chris Carter, or anyone decided to choose differently than he or she in fact does, then the script would have always reflected that choice instead of the one that we, in fact, will make. Understood in this way, our acting otherwise than written in the script does not entail that we have the ability to alter the past in terms of making a proposition that was (determinately) true for a time into one that then becomes false as a result of exercising our genuine freedom. Because the script will reflect *whatever* we freely decide to do, it is never changed (or falsified) in this way. All that is required is that we have the power, were we to use it, to make a *different* script actual. That is, had we exercised free will and chosen differently in some situation, then the script would have *always* been different from what it actually is.

In this way, our freedom is protected—and fatalism is avoided—by the realization that we are all coauthors of the script. Admittedly, it is a bit difficult to accept the possibility that a script about our lives, one that we co-author, can be written before our births. Many find this just as paradoxical as the suggestion that Bruckman can literally see events before they happen. However, we are not considering a regular script, typed on paper. The so-called script considered here is more abstract than substantial. There is no actual script containing typeset pages. Rather, it is "filled" with descriptions—what philosophers tend to call propositions, which are abstract objects—and because these abstract objects, like numbers, always exist if they ever do, then a script can be forever in existence. We might now wonder whether Bruckman could have cognitive access to such a script, but that question does not detract from the possibility that there might be the kind of script described here. Therefore, future contingents can be antecedently true—and determinately so—without this entailing that their being so is in any way inconsistent with our genuine freedom. Therefore, while it may be that determinism is inconsistent with our genuine freedom, the mere fact that future contingents possess determinate, antecedent truth-value does not entail that future contingents are determined in a way inconsistent with our acting freely. In fact, what explains their being determinately true at all is how we (will) freely act. Consequently, even if someone foreknows our future choices, our choices explain what is foreknown about them; their being foreknown doesn't explain why we choose as we do.

"Hey, It's Not Supposed to Happen that Way"

As we all know, Mulder doesn't get his throat slashed while standing in a banana cream pie. Scully mistakenly uses the service elevator, sees the struggle between Mulder and Puppet, and then fires two rounds into the serial killer's chest. Puppet's prevision of Mulder's murder was faulty. Should we interpret this scene as Morgan's affirmation of contingency and happenstance? And if so, is the episode not really about fatalism, but actually the opposite? Perhaps, but the point of the last two sections cannot be overlooked. Sometimes Bruckman's (and Puppet's) previsions turn out to be true. What should we say about *those* correctly foreseen events? Were *they* fated to happen because they were forseen? The answer seems to be "no." If the arguments (contra Schick) in the previous sections are correct, then the fact that a future event is foreknown is explained in part by what will happen and not vice versa. How the future unfolds shapes or determines what can be known about it; it's not the case that what is foreknown shapes or determines the future.

Why does Puppet incorrectly believe that he will murder Mulder in the hotel kitchen? The answer must be the fact that Bruckman somehow tapped into Puppet's prevision and told Mulder about it. Armed with this information, Mulder threw up his hand when he stepped in the cream pie, keeping Puppet's knife from his throat. So, we might say that Puppet didn't foresee Bruckman sharing his prevision and, because of this, things turned out in a way that he didn't expect. Had Bruckman not told Mulder about Puppet's prevision, we might have met John Doggett (Robert Patrick) much sooner than season 8! (Of course, Mulder still needs to be careful about "autoerotic asphyxiation," leading us to wonder whether Scully shouldn't dispose of his desk drawer "movie collection" after all.)

When psychics or soothsayers make false predictions, it might be wondered whether the future can be known at all. Morgan's belief is clear: Fortunetellers are invariably frauds, and people who spend huge sums of money seeking their advice are fools. This is expressed in the episode's teaser when Puppet tells Madame Zelma, "You're a fortuneteller. You should have seen this coming." But the mere fact that some prognosticator's predictions turn out to be true doesn't mean that they know the future. The Stupendous Yappi is an excellent example of this. After Yappi's performance at the crime scene, Mulder comments, "His leads are so vague as to be practically useless yet easily interpreted to be correct after the fact." When Detective Cline (Frank Cassini) reminds Mulder that Yappi made many predictions, Mulder replies, "Yeah, and some are bound by percentages to be right, but most will turn out wrong. Now, which is which?" Ignoring Mulder's reservations, Cline utters one of the funniest pieces of *X-Files* dialogue ever: "Look, all I know is that so far, Yappi has provided more solid, concrete leads on this case than you have. Now, if you don't mind, I have to get an APB out on a white male, age seventeen to thirty-four, with or without a beard, maybe a tattoo . . . who's impotent. . . . Let's roll."

This leads to a discussion of what it means to know anything. Philosophers tend to discuss knowing propositions (because these allegedly describe the facts). A proposition is known only if it is true. Asserting false propositions is a sign of being ignorant of the facts, and ignorance is opposed to knowledge. Furthermore, a proposition is known only if it is believed. Knowledge thus requires true belief. But it also requires justification—we must be justified in holding a true belief. This is where the difficulty about having foreknowledge arises. Yappi can have beliefs about the future that turn out to be true, but if these are merely lucky guesses—if he's "just playing the odds," as Bruckman would say—then Yappi's true belief doesn't count as knowledge. If you're just guessing about something, you don't know it; if you did know it, then you wouldn't have to guess. But what could justify a soothsayer's (true) belief? Bruckman's terse "explanation" doesn't satisfy (although Morgan should be credited for addressing it). It's difficult to see how obsession about the Big Bopper's plane crash could lead to having justified belief about a person's future death. However, Bruckman's morbid previsions might be justified simply because they invariably turn out to be true. After repeated and constant predictive success, it couldn't be that Bruckman is merely guessing. And if his prognostications are specific enough (unlike Yappi's, but as his were with Mulder and the Gordon newlyweds), requiring no strained interpretation, it seems that his morbid previsions count as knowledge. Whether anyone could actually have this kind of foreknowledge (without somehow causing the murders to happen, as Mulder initially suspected of Luther Lee Boggs [Brad Dourif] and Scully initially suspected of Father Joe Crissman [Billy Connolly]) is another matter, which is one of the reasons the freedom and foreknowledge debate invariably involves God.

Bruckman's Sense of Powerlessness

We have seen how the antecedent truth of future contingents—even if they are known to be true—need not lead to fatalism. However, it admittedly may be *psychologically* difficult for a possessor of foreknowledge not to develop a fatalistic *outlook* on life. This was certainly true of Bruckman. Consider Scully's estimation of Bruckman's general demeanor. Although not quite yet convinced of his psychic abilities, she nevertheless confides to Mulder, "By thinking he [Bruckman] can see the future, he's taken all the joy out of his life." Upon becoming convinced that Bruckman possesses psychic abilities, Mulder confronts him, "But you admit to having this gift." Bruckman replies, "Oh, I got it, all right. The only problem is, it's non-returnable." To say the least, Bruckman doesn't cherish his unique ability. When Mulder presses Bruckman for his help in catching the serial killer (Puppet), a dejected Bruckman replies, "And he'll commit more [murders] whether I help you or not." When Mulder inquires why Bruckman is so sure of this, Bruckman answers with the now familiar, "How can I see the future if it didn't already exist?" Mulder retorts, "If the future is written, then why bother to do anything?" And, finally, Bruckman adds, "Now you're catching on." This exchange clearly expresses Bruckman's fatalistic psychological approach to life. It's clear that Bruckman's outlook is grounded in his ability to divine the future.

We quickly learn the depths of Bruckman's resignation. Still in Bruckman's apartment, Mulder regroups and tells him, "Mister Bruckman, I believe in your ability but not your attitude. I can't stand by and watch people die without doing everything in my, albeit unsupernatural, power to interfere with that fate." Rather than making another attempt to convince Mulder that the future is unavoidable, Bruckman takes a different tack. He explains, "I can't help you catch this guy. I might adversely affect the fate of the future." But, then, after posing to Mulder some fantastic events that might happen if he helps him, Bruckman finally comes to the conclusion that if he does help Mulder, something might result "in the fact that my father never meets my mother and consequently, I'm never born." Only this potential result motivates Bruckman to aid Mulder and Scully. Clearly, Bruckman believes that he would be better off if he had never been born. Ironically, or perhaps in the last gasps of irrationality, Bruckman strives to change things so that he never exists, even though he also believes that the future cannot be changed. Bruckman's psychological outlook is dark indeed.

Let's assume that, Bruckman's previsions (unlike Puppet's) always turn out to be true. If so, then Bruckman foresees his own pending suicide. Perhaps he would have taken his own life regardless of whether he has the "gift" to foresee the future. But it seems more plausible to contend that the reliability of his previsions led to his darkened demeanor, which ultimately led him to take his own life. I acknowledge that this raises the specter of a causal loop: Did Bruckman's foreknowledge cause his suicide, or did his pending suicide cause him to foresee it? The thesis of this chapter is that, strictly speaking, the fact that he foresaw his suicide is explained by his choosing to kill himself. His previsions may influence his dour demeanor and eventual suicide. However, it still seems defensible to hold that Bruckman's resignation is ultimately due to his choice (assuming, of course, that it was a matter of choice at all).

Therefore, how Bruckman reacts to the discovery in 1959 that he has the ability to foretell someone's death is up to him. Furthermore, his reaction to any prevision after 1959 is also up to him. Thus, it can be concluded that the reason Bruckman commits suicide is that he regularly chooses to deal with his "gift" in an unhealthy way. Further, it seems plausible to maintain that Bruckman's foreknowledge of his death is explained by what he chooses; his choice is not caused by his foreknowledge, at least not in any way that impedes his freedom. That is, Bruckman's coming to know about his "gift" might have influenced his decision to eventually commit suicide and was a contributing factor in his choice. However, if Bruckman is free, none of this rendered his choice necessary or unavoidable.

"All Right, So How Do I Die?"—"You Don't"

By the end of the episode, Scully becomes open to the possibility that Bruckman knows how people will die. Despite herself, but after some gentle goading from Bruckman, she asks him how she will die. Smiling, Bruckman looks up at her and claims that she doesn't. This very brief dialogue exchange has become mythic among X-Philes. (It plays a central role in the mythos of the Internet Order of the Blessed Saint Scully the Enigmatic [OBSSE], for instance.) Can Scully really be immortal?

There seem to be three leading X-Phile theories about Bruckman's response. The first is that he is merely being considerate, subtly suggesting to Scully that she is far too young to worry about such things. The other two theories evolved as the series progressed. In "En Ami" (season 7), CSM drives Scully to a remote location where they meet Marjorie Butters (Louise Latham). CSM tells Scully that he is "Marjorie's angel," in that the woman is now 118 years old even though she doesn't look a day over 60. As Scully tries to ignore his words, she sees a scar at the base of Marjorie's neck—one that is very similar to Scully's. Could Scully also live as long as Marjorie with CSM's help? What would she have to do to garner his aid? The third theory is solidified with "Tithonus" (season 6). Tithonus is a character from Greek mythology whom was granted immortality; he is also the immortal narrator of a Tennyson poem by the same name.[6] In the episode, Scully meets photographer Alfred Fellig (Geoffrey Lewis). We learn that Fellig is roughly 150 years old, incessantly attempting to photograph Death. He claims to be immortal because he cowardly looked away from Death, in effect hiding behind the nurse who was caring for him as he suffered from yellow fever. Death took the nurse rather than Fellig; it seems he missed his turn to die. But at the end of the episode, Fellig makes amends. Scully has been mortally wounded (by her temporary partner). Fellig grasps her hand (as the nurse was grasping his all those years ago) and tells her not to look at Death. Fellig, also wounded, faces his fate this time and dies. But Scully lives. Many X-Philes thus interpret Bruckman's words as the prognostication that Scully missed *her* turn to die, leaving her immortal.

It seems incredibly unlikely that Morgan intended to provide the spark for this titillating piece of *X-Files* lore. It seems that something closer to the first theory explains Bruckman's response. Morgan's episodes don't neatly follow *The X-Files'* driving imperative to find the "truth out there" at all costs. In his first episode, "Humbug," Morgan writes, "Some mysteries are never meant to be solved." In his second, "Clyde Bruckman's Final Repose," he in effect tells us a story of an ordinary man who learns (in part) the mysteries of death. Is he better off for knowing this? In anti-Socratic fashion, Morgan implicitly answers, "no." It would be better if he had remained ignorant. Knowledge of when people will die has led him to become bitter and lonely. It has driven him to lead a solitary life; after all, once he sufficiently knows a person, he begins to see how his new friend will die. His bitterness drives him to selling life insurance. But this only immerses him completely in death. It is no wonder that Bruckman agrees to help Mulder only after he entertains the idea that he might accomplish his own nonexistence. Bruckman wishes only to spare Scully the pains of worrying about death. It is a mystery that was never meant to be solved.

When we meet Mulder and Scully in *I Want to Believe* (2008), after a six-year hiatus, Mulder strikingly resembles Bruckman. He shares a roof with Scully, a woman he deeply loves, but he doesn't seem to share his life with her. Rather, he spends his days—alone—in a spare bedroom-turned-office combing the Internet and clipping newspapers. Searching out the paranormal has become a full-blown obsession for ex-Agent Mulder. He keeps a picture of his sister, Samantha, clearly displayed among clippings on the back of his door. It directly faces his "I Want to Believe" poster on the opposing wall. He has accepted her death but still searches for her from his desk chair. Scully has reentered the world as a medical doctor, but Mulder remains isolated. Anxious to engage Mulder in the world, Scully suggests that he consult on an X-Files-type case, even though the X-Files is the ultimate source of his dour demeanor. Her suggestion is desperate (and she later regrets it). Like Bruckman, Mulder has become embittered and resigned as a result of learning some of life's mysteries, not about death, but concerning earthly biogenesis, "star children," and the nature of evil itself. Morgan's summation of Mulder's character—via novelist Jose Chung in season 3—prophetically rings true: Mulder's "quest into the unknown has so warped his psyche, one shudders to think how he receives pleasures from life." So, is Mulder better off for chasing monsters in the dark, searching for that elusive thing he calls "the truth"?

But crafting episodes that require *The X-Files* to examine itself has always been the beauty of Morgan's work. His artistry was making us (the X-Phile viewer) laugh while he (subtly) poked fun at our favorite show. (Does anyone else remember the pose Mulder strikes at the end of "Humbug"?) But his poignant commentary was neither merely inflammatory nor spiteful. Are we always better off knowing the truth? Is ignorance always bad? Socrates (especially in Plato's *Apology*) is famous for his affirmative answers to these questions. Morgan, for his part, implicitly invites us to reconsider Socrates' answers by providing us rather rogue *X-Files* episodes that question Mulder's and Scully's heroism. Are they heroes, or merely two obsessed people (Mulder especially) flirting with psychological disaster? This isn't to say that Morgan's implicit philosophical views are always correct, but he did raise important questions. These led many to reevaluate *The X-Files* and profound issues beyond television. In this way, he (implicitly) played an important role in the crafting of this book.

Notes

I am grateful for helpful commentary by Al White and Patricia Kowalski on earlier drafts of the 2007 version of this chapter. I am grateful to Internet X-Phile "Who-ToTrust?" especially, and other contributors to the NewSpace XPhile Forum (http://anewspace.20.forumer.com/index.php) for the suggestion to recraft this essay for the 2009 edition. (Website last accessed August 26, 2008.)

1. Other fans of this episode have recognized this long ago. In her 1995 online review, noted X-Phile Sarah Stegall (coauthor on the first three official guides to *The X-Files*) writes: "If Clyde Bruckman or any other visionary can accurately foretell the future, then it is immutable, and the concept of free will vanishes. We cannot 'choose' to do that which is already set in concrete; it distorts the meaning of the word to insist that we do. On the other hand, if we have true existential freedom, there can be no future set in concrete (for a prophet to discover) because we have not yet made the choices that will create it." See http://www.munchkyn.com/xf-rvws/bruckman.html (accessed October 12, 2006).

2. If determinism is true, it doesn't follow that we choose against our will. In "Pusher," *The X-Files* vividly conveys people making choices they don't want to. Through an extreme power of suggestion, Robert Modell (Robert Wisden) has the ability to force people to choose against their will merely by talking with them, as he did in compelling the SWAT officer to set himself on fire. Clearly, with tears streaming down his face and begging Mulder to stop him, the SWAT officer is not acting freely. But determinism doesn't entail anything like this. It very well may be that we choose what we want. However, if determinism is true, then our wants and desires are also the result of a very long causal chain stretching back before birth. Thus, the philosophical problem remains, even if we choose to do what we want.

3. The 2007 version of this essay, "'Clyde Bruckman's Final Repose' Reprised," appearing in *The Philosophy of* The X-Files (189–208), contains a much more extensive treatment of Aristotle's views of future contingents and fatalism. This section contains similar arguments as its 2007 predecessor, but it does not offer such careful exposition of Aristotle's *De Interpretatione* 9.

4. Theodore Schick Jr., "Fate, Freedom, and Foreknowledge," in *The Matrix and Philosophy,* ed. William Irwin (Chicago: Open Court Press, 2002), 93. Given the overall tenor of Schick's article, he clearly is not merely espousing this argument; he embraces the conclusion that freedom and foreknowledge are incompatible.

5. This does not necessarily lead to the counterintuitive position of the effect (what Bruckman knows) existing prior to the cause (what Puppet will do), as some have

claimed; see, for example, Schick, "Fate, Freedom, and Foreknowledge," 94–95. The relationship is not causal in the straightforward sense; thus, the claim that freedom and foreknowledge are compatible does not commit one to the position that effects predate their causes. Philosophers tend to characterize the relationship as counterfactual dependence. This complex notion is addressed a bit more fully in the "Fatalism and Powerlessness" section.

6. For an in-depth study of Tithonus and his relationship to the *X-Files* episode that bears his name, see Matthew VanWinkle, "Tennyson's 'Tithonus' and the Exhaustion of Survival in *The X-Files*," in The X-Files *and Literature,* ed. Sharon Yang (Newcastle, UK: Cambridge Scholars Publishing, 2007).

The Many Tales of "Jose Chung"

Dean A. Kowalski and S. Evan Kreider

In his last known piece of writing for *The X-Files,* an uncredited rewrite of "Quagmire," Darin Morgan again questions Mulder's incessant pursuit of "the truth out there." Chapter 10 (per episode DVD) bears his distinctive clever exchanges between Mulder and Scully. While they are marooned on a rock in Heuvelman's Lake, Scully compares Mulder's quest for an "intangible" truth "out there" to Ahab's search for the white whale. She laments to her partner, "It's the truth or a white whale. What difference does it make? I mean, both obsessions are impossible to capture, and trying to do so will only leave you dead along with everyone else you bring with you." Here, as he did in "Clyde Bruckman's Final Repose," Morgan questions whether pursuing the truth at all costs is worthwhile. If chasing "monsters in the dark" brings with it the death of your own father (among other casualties, like Scully's sister), perhaps your quest is misguided? Morgan, not content with leaving us with that (to him) rhetorical question, takes his modus operandi of adroit *X-Files* critiques a step further. He claims (through Scully) that the truth cannot be captured. So, not only is Mulder's quest a matter of inverted priorities, it is simply impossible, though he doesn't tell us here why it is impossible—this might be because he believes that he already expressed this in "Jose Chung's *From Outer Space.*" In fact, it seems that in "Jose Chung's *From Outer Space,*" Morgan attempts to topple the *X-Files'* main credo: "The truth is out there." But if Morgan is correct and the truth is not "out there" to be found, then what is "the truth," and where can we find it? Exploring these questions serves as the cornerstone for this essay.

In this celebrated episode, Morgan crafts a tale about two Klass County teenagers, Harold Lamb (Jason Gaffney) and Chrissy Giorgio (Sarah Sawatsky). During their first date, they are allegedly abducted by aliens. However, the now familiar account of their car systemically shutting down in the middle of the highway and their passing out, leading to "missing time," receives a new wrinkle. The gray alien abductors are themselves abducted by what appears to be a rocklike creature bathed in a red light. Enter flamboyant novelist Jose Chung (Charles Nelson Reilly). In the months following the abduction, he has been interviewing Klass County residents in the faint hope of discovering what really happened that night. He quickly gives up that goal and begins pursuing another, one his publisher had originally suggested: writing the first nonfiction science fiction novel. Mulder and Scully were also called to Klass County to investigate the alleged "double abduction." Chung visits Washington, D.C., to interview our heroes to get their professional opinion about what happened that night. Mulder refuses to speak with Chung, but Scully agrees only because she greatly admires his work (Chung's *The Lonely Buddha* and *The Caligarian Candidate* are among her favorite novels).

The episode is shot in flashback sequences with Scully narrating and Chung occasionally interjecting in her narration. An early exchange between Scully and Chung is especially pertinent. After Chung admits that the ultimate driving factor in writing the book is money, Scully admonishes Chung: "Well, just as long as you're attempting to record the truth." He quickly replies, "Oh, God, no. How can I possibly do that? I spent three months in Klass County, and everybody there has a different version of what truly happened. Truth is as subjective as reality. That will help explain why when people talk about their 'UFO experiences,' they always start off with, 'Well, now, I know how crazy this is going to sound . . . but.'"

It seems to us that this exchange between Scully and Chung sets the tone for the episode to follow. In fact, it seems that this episode is plausibly interpreted as Morgan conveying some classic philosophical ideas regarding truth and knowledge. The inherent uncertainty about truth and knowledge leads Morgan (we believe) to two implicit conclusions: (1) that disagreement about the alleged facts casts doubt on the existence of a truth "out there" independent of our experiences of it; and (2) the lack of truth independent of our experiences leads him to an existentialist-type position captured by his concluding line, "For although we may not be alone in the universe, in our own separate ways on this planet, we are all . . . alone," which has rightfully taken its proper place in *X-Files* lore.

Appearance, Reality, and Values

The teaser opens with a camera shot that appears to be a close-up of an Empire Cruiser (from *Star Wars*). The episode's soundtrack reinforces this judgment. But as director Rob Bowman's camera pans back, we (the X-Phile viewers) quickly realize that we are deceived. The shot is actually the bottom of a power company utility bucket, lifted high off the ground. Roky Crickenson, a power company engineer, is checking some power lines. This opening sequence foreshadows the dominant theme of the episode: things may not be as they appear.

This theme continues as Scully shares with Chung her version of the alleged double abduction. Scully tells him about her first meeting with Detective Manners, the lead investigator of the case. Bowman provides us a flashback; we see Manners complaining to Mulder and Scully, "You really bleeped up this case." Bowman's camera quickly cuts back to Scully and Chung in the basement office; she explains to the novelist, "Manners didn't actually say 'bleeped.'" Scully censored Manner's "colorful phraseology." What the X-Phile viewer can surmise from this exchange is that all of Scully's narration is filtered through her experiences. This leaves us to wonder whether the Klass County events actually transpired *exactly* as she describes. Furthermore, X-Phile viewers also soon learn that our vantage point of the alleged double abduction was actually that of Roky Crickenson. Note that our perspective of the teenagers' car is from the back, as Roky's truck approaches it. We see what Roky sees—or so it seems. Through Roky's eyes, we see the rocklike creature, a lava monster from the earth's molten core named Lord Kinbote, lumber to Roky's truck. Kinbote announces, "Roky! Roky! Be not afraid! No harm will come onto thee. Your efforts are needed for the survival of all earthlings. Come, I shall showeth thee." Roky (as we see later in the episode) takes this charge very seriously. Nevertheless, the point remains: the viewer is again left to wonder what, if any, of Roky's experiences actually happened? Has he embellished anything? He swears that he hasn't, as he admits to Mulder and Scully later, "I know how crazy this sounds, but . . ."[1]

Additional worries about discovering the truth of that night soon emerge. There are discrepancies among the personal reports. Harold's and Chrissy's accounts of what happened that night in Klass County are far from identical, at least at first. Harold believes that they were abducted along with the grey alien abductors, but Chrissy claims date rape. Blaine Faulkner's (the jobless, living-at-home, twenty-something UFO fanatic played by Allan Zinyk) recollections of that night include Mulder acting like an emotionless mandroid at times and a menacing "man in black" at others. But this is never substantiated. Faulkner also claims that Scully threatened his life, but Scully emphatically denies it. Mulder evidently has a meeting with Air Force lieutenant Jack Shaefer (Daniel Quinn) at a local diner. Shaefer confides to Mulder that the government orchestrates many "alien abductions" for scientific and psychological research, and that he is one of the government's "UFO" pilots. The cook at the diner denies that Shaefer was there. Rather, the cook informs Chung, Mulder sat alone at the counter and order piece after piece of sweet potato pie. For each new piece, Mulder asked the cook a question, including, "You ever had the suspicion that you've been abducted by aliens?" and "Have you ever found a metal implant in your body?" and "Have you checked everywhere?" Which of these reports is true? Are any of them true? It is no wonder that "How the hell should I know?" was a mantra echoed throughout the episode.

It is tempting to argue that because each of us is a distinct individual, all of our respective experiences describe each of us (the "experiencer") more than they describe how things are in themselves. Which experience is privileged enough to discern reality as it *truly* is, independent of our experiences of it? If no one's experiences are so privileged, then how can we know anything at all about how things actually are? And if this is correct, then it must be wondered whether Mulder could ever capture the truth. If the truth represents reality (in itself), but no one's experiences—not even Mulder's—are privileged in terms of discerning the truth about how things actually are, then Mulder has no hope of accomplishing what he seeks. Furthermore, it is tempting to press these considerations to argue that the widely divergent experiences of reality lead to the conclusion that there isn't any objective truth ("out there") to know apart from our experiences of it. After all, if there were an objective truth apart from our experiences, then we wouldn't expect our experiences to differ as much as they do. But, as "Jose Chung's *From Outer Space*" reminds us, our experiences do widely diverge. Therefore, it seems unlikely that there is any objective truth or reality to know apart from our experiences. All that exists are our experiences, which, by their very nature, are subjective.

Morgan isn't the first to broach this sort of reasoning; it is rather common. However, it is most prevalent when it comes to the interrelated issues of ethics (matters of right or wrong) and values (what is good or bad). The default view is that, although there are many judgments about right, wrong, good, or bad, there isn't any (objective) truth to the matter apart from those beliefs. Many are inclined to believe that, when it comes to right and wrong or good and bad, such judgments are little more than personal preference. The value judgments made by Harold, Chrissy, and Roky about their experiences that night all seem equally valid, at least for each individual. Harold wasn't affected all that much by it, after all. Thus, he wished to resume his relationship with Chrissy, in the hope of rekindling their blossoming romance. Chrissy sees more value in leading her life to make the world a better place. She has left Harold behind and now lives for such organizations as Greenpeace. Roky took Lord Kinbote at his word; he left for California in the hope of enlightening other human beings about the spiritual journey that awaits us—to the center of the earth ("assuming, of course, that your soul is able to avoid . . . the lava men"). Blaine, Scully, and Mulder have also made choices about what makes their lives meaningful, but in a more pervasive way. Blaine, already convinced of the existence of extraterrestrials, now looks toward the sky more frequently in his new post as Roky's successor at the power company. Scully continues to view her current assignment as merely a nine-to-five job (according to Chung at least), despite Mulder's best efforts to convince her otherwise. Mulder's passionate quest for "the truth" (again, according to Chung) has warped him to the point that "he receives no pleasure from this life." So, Harold longs for love, but Chrissy now shuns it. Blaine searches the skies for a better form of existence, but Roky looks toward the center of the earth. Mulder's life is his work—he sleeps on the couch and can't bear to take a vacation (except for a raucous trip or two to Graceland)—but Scully does her best to leave her work at work, despite Mulder's constant interference.

Here art imitates life. There is the debate between the so-called pro-life and pro-choice positions regarding abortion. Pro-life advocates believe that the value associated with human life is more or less absolute, while the latter believe that this value must be balanced with a woman's right to have autonomy over her own body. There is the debate between utilitarian conceptions of the greater good and issues pertaining to the rights of individuals. Utilitarians believe that a person's rights can be superseded when more good will come of it, but supporters of individual rights believe that it is always impermissible to practice injustice. In the debate about protecting the environment, some environmentalists believe that active but reasonable measures must be employed to safeguard our natural resources, while "environmental activists" sometimes find it necessary to use extreme tactics to preserve resources. Which value judgment is correct, or even "truer" than another? There doesn't seem to be any plausible way to tell. Furthermore, if there was something like an objective fact of the matter about ethics or values, then we wouldn't expect such divergent opinions about right or wrong and good or bad. But opinions about these matters are especially divergent. Thus, it is unlikely that there is some sort of objective fact of the matter about ethics or values.

Freedom and Responsibility: The Existentialism of Jean-Paul Sartre

French philosopher and novelist Jean-Paul Sartre would no doubt concur with much of the previous section. He believed that we couldn't make any meaningful claims about reality apart from our experiences of it. Thus, reality (in itself) is either unknowable or an incoherent notion. Sartre was also concerned about intractable moral disagreement. His famous example involved a young Frenchman during World War II. On the one hand, the young man seems obligated to help his fellow countrymen fight against Nazi occupation. On the other hand, he seems obligated to care for his ailing mother, as she has no one else. What should he do? Sartre believed that there wasn't an objectively true answer to this question, at least not one that pertained to everyone in relevantly similar circumstances. There are no truths about right or wrong and good or bad until the person chooses as she does. In this sense, we create truths about ethics and values by our personal choices. Furthermore, Sartre wondered, for the sake of argument, how objective moral standards might be grounded. He saw two possibilities. The first was God; the nature of right or wrong and good or bad could be grounded in features of the omnipotent, omniscient, and omnibenevolent Creator. However, Sartre believed that God did not—in fact could not—exist. The divine concept, thought Sartre, was self-contradictory because (as we shall see) there are no fully actualized or perfect persons. The second possibility was human nature; what is universally right or wrong and good or bad for us might be grounded in the distinctive kind of thing we, as humans, are. But persons possess no defining characteristics; we continually define ourselves via the choices we make (which begins to explain why there are no fully actualized persons). Sartre claimed, "Man is nothing else but that which he makes of himself."[2] The failure of these possibilities led Sartre to construct a different conception of right, wrong, good, and bad. This is known as existentialism.

Defining—much less explaining—existentialism is no easy task, since particular existentialists differed so greatly from one another. However, in the minds of many, Sartre is the definitive existentialist. Thus, for our purposes here, we will confine ourselves to a brief elucidation of some of Sartre's basic tenets, which themselves will then shed light on the episode's various characters and the ways in which they choose to live after their various encounters with entities described in Chung's *From Outer Space.*

We can profitably understand Sartre's existentialism as a rejection of the philosophical notion of *essence* and a committal to the philosophical notion of *existence*—thus the term "existentialism." The existence/essence distinction is not an obvious one, especially considering they both connote "being" of some sort. Roughly, the existence of something is *that* it is, while the essence of something is *what* it is. In other words, when we say that something exists, we are merely saying that it *is,* that it is a real thing. However, when talking about the essence of something, we are talking about whatever it is that makes something the kind of thing that it is, whatever it is that defines it. Sartre's existentialism is a rather radical philosophical position in that it rejects the notion of essence altogether. According to Sartre, when we strip away all of the nonessential properties of something, we are left with nothing—or rather, Nothingness. That is, there is something—it does exist, after all—but it is something stripped of *all* of its properties. All that remains is a brute, undifferentiated, propertyless "Isness," a something which is nothing in particular—thus, Being in its barest form is Nothingness. There are no essences. There is only existence.[3]

This might not seem like much on paper—"Nothingness" is rather abstract, after all. However, Sartre believed that an actual encounter with this Nothingness would be a horrifying, nauseating experience, like being suspended in a nightmarish void or peering into Nietzsche's famed abyss: the world as we know it disappears and coalesces into a single, indescribable, primordial Nothingness. Worse yet is the realization that it is not only the world which is this way, but ourselves as well. There are no essences; thus, there is no human essence, no human nature on which we can base our lives or in which we can ground our choices. Take a moment to grasp the seriousness of this conclusion. One of the major motivations for philosophers to discover the human essence is to provide some sort of ethical guidance; the idea is that if we can know *what* we are, then we can figure out what we *should* be—that is, how we ought to live. For example, if we were to determine that the essence of a human being is an immortal soul created by God, then we might reasonably conclude that we ought to live in a way that pleases God. Alternatively, if we were to determine that the essence of a human being is reason, then we might conclude that we ought to spend our lives developing and exercising our powers of reason to their fullest. However, if Sartre is correct, and there simply is no such thing as human nature, then we seem to have nothing on which to base our lives.

Still, one might say: "Whether or not there is some abstract metaphysical human essence, I am still guided by my own personal identity. That is, I am a particular kind of person—a person with a particular character, personality, memory, experience, et cetera—and I base my life, my choices, and my actions in that individual personhood. For example, there are some things I simply would not, even *could* not do (say, commit murder), because I am simply not that kind of person (that is, a murderer)." However, this too is an illusion, according to Sartre: personal identity has no more reality than essence and is nothing more than a convenient myth. At its core, the ego is Nothing, but a Nothing that can be anything, a kind of pure potentiality. Thus, we are not our pasts, our memories, our previous actions, all of which we tend to lump together and call a "personality" or "moral character," as though it were something essential to us. Instead, we create ourselves anew from moment to moment through our choices and actions, on which there are no literally limits. For example, it is tempting to utter such sentences as "I am not a murderer," implying that one has a certain essential moral character and, further, that one could not ever commit murder because that action simply could not follow from one's character. According to Sartre, this is a self-deception. One cannot say that one is or is not a murderer. One simply chooses to murder or not to murder at any given moment. One might go one's whole life without murdering, but then commit murder the very next second.

This is roughly Sartre's notion of human freedom. Everything that we are and everything that we do is freely chosen. Of course, the obvious implication of this complete freedom is that we are also completely responsible for our choices, our actions, our lives, and our whole world. It is simply never true that we are forced to do anything against our will or to live in a world not of our choosing. This truth, and the burden of responsibility it embodies, is invariably forced on us by our experiences of anxiety, anguish, and despair—what is often called existential "angst." We might be tempted here to think of counterexamples to this kind of radical freedom and responsibility. "What if I were mugged at gunpoint? Couldn't I say that I had no choice but to hand over my wallet?" "Certainly not," Sartre would say. "You had a choice: you could have chosen not to hand over your wallet. You probably would have been killed, of course, but don't say that you didn't have a choice. That you exist in a world in which you were mugged is a result of your choice, and nothing and no one else could literally force you to make that choice." Thus, we cannot blame others for our choices and actions—no "Society is to blame" or "I accuse my parents!" The world that each of us has is the product of our own choices, over which we always have control.[4]

Of course, most people can't live with the crushing angst that is total responsibility. As a result, they live "inauthentically" or "in bad faith," as Sartre alternately characterizes it. That is, they live in denial of their freedom and responsibility and blame circumstance and other people for their lives. They create myths—such as religion or human nature or theories of morality—so they can pretend there is something else that determines what they are and what they ought to be. According to Sartre, we are to live "authentically" or "in good faith." We do this by accepting our freedom and responsibility and choosing for ourselves what we want to be, how we want to live, and what projects we want to create and commit ourselves to. There are no external standards—no absolute morality, no divine commands from God—that make a project "good" or "bad"; all that matters is that it be authentic. Certainly, this has an empowering and optimistic tone to it. However, there is a dark side to it as well, which creates a fundamental kind of ambivalence in the human condition. Total freedom from everything and everyone else is also a kind of radical alienation from the world and others in it. (Note Jose Chung's opening comment: "I had never thought much about it before. I guess that's because I always felt like such an alien myself. That to be concerned with aliens from . . . other planets, that just seemed so, uh . . . redundant.") We cannot look to anything or anyone other than ourselves for guidance, advice, or validation. Thus, in a very real sense it is just as Jose Chung says in his closing comment: "For although we may not be alone in the universe, in our own separate ways on this planet, we are all . . . alone."[5] Jose Chung makes this remark just after having given us his take on the various characters in it. But is it true? How well do each of Morgan's characters stack up against Sartre's call to authenticity, and is the result that they are in fact each alone?

A Sartrean Assessment of Morgan's Characters

Regarding Blaine, Chung says: "Evidence of extraterrestrial existence remains as elusive as ever, but the skies will continue to be searched by the likes of Blaine Faulkner, hoping to someday find not only proof of alien life, but also contentment on a new world. Until then, he must be content with his new job." This evaluation of Blaine is fairly optimistic, and as such, we might be tempted to characterize him as authentic. However, perhaps the main reason we feel good about how things turned out for Blaine is simply that he's finally gotten out of the house and landed a job. (Recall Blaine's admission to Chung: "I know how crazy this is going to sound, but . . . I want to be abducted by aliens. . . . I hate this town. I hate . . . people. I just want to be taken away to someplace where I . . . I don't have to worry about finding a job.") Once we see past that, it's hard to assess whether or not his project to find proof of alien life is authentic. On the one hand, the series certainly suggests that there are aliens, so Blaine's project isn't without merit, and it could be seen as the result of a free and responsible choice. On the other hand, as the episode repeatedly shows us, Blaine has a way of disingenuously describing everything that happens to him. He's living in a fantasy world he has created for escapist purposes. This kind of escapism rings of inauthenticity. Ultimately, Blaine is a mixed case, with elements of both authenticity and inauthenticity.

Regarding Roky Crickenson, Chung tells us, "Others search for answers from within. Roky relocated to El Cajon, California, preaching to the lost and desperate." What to make of this? It's possible that Roky is simply delusional; Scully believes he has a fantasy-prone personality. If so, then an evaluation of his choices in terms of good faith or bad faith is probably moot. Still, assume for a moment that he is not delusional. If Sartre requires of us that we create and commit to our own projects, and that there are no particular criteria for choosing one or the other, why couldn't Roky choose to found a new religion? We might be tempted to say that Sartre would reject this on the grounds that there is no God. However, Roky doesn't seem to have traditional God in mind, so Sartre's arguments against the existence of God simply don't apply. Furthermore, it's perfectly possible that Roky is correct; after all, for all we know, everything he is saying about Lord Kinbote and his inner realm is true. Unfortunately, there might simply be no single, definitive way to evaluate Roky. Without knowing more, we might reasonably argue both a bad- and a good-faith interpretation of Roky's decision: on the former, Roky is inauthentic because he has allowed Lord Kinbote to determine his projects for him; on the latter, Roky is authentic because he has freely and with full responsibility chosen to follow Lord Kinbote. Ultimately, Roky's case is probably indeterminate—he may or may not be authentic, based on what the episode shows us.

Finally, what of the teens of the episode, Harold Lamb and Chrissy Giorgio? Regarding Harold, Chung says: "Then there are those who care not about extraterrestrials, searching for meaning in other human beings. Rare or lucky are those who find it." Harold is still looking for validation from others. He wants to be the object of the projects of others rather than create his own project—the worst kind of Sartrean inauthenticity. However, Chung says that Chrissy "has come to believe her alien visitation was a message to improve her own world, and she has devoted herself to this goal wholeheartedly." Of all the characters in this episode, Chrissy fares the best in Sartrean terms. Rather than worry about what "really" happened, Chrissy expressed her freedom and responsibility by making her experiences into what she wants them to be. Furthermore, she has used her experiences as the basis for the creation of her own project: a commitment to humanistic political activity. This is ultimately what Sartre himself advocated and lived, as evidenced by his commitment to Marxist-inspired activism. If there is anyone in the episode who is authentic, it is most certainly Chrissy.

After considering the authenticity (or lack thereof) of each of the characters unique to this episode, we are finally left with a question: Are they all, in fact, alone, as Jose Chung claims? Certainly Sartre's philosophy entails an "aloneness" in that each of us has to choose our own projects. However, not every one of the characters is alone in the same way and to the same degree. In fact, it appears that the more authentic the character, the less alone he or she is. Leaving Chung's assessment of Mulder and Scully aside for now, Harold was the most inauthentic character of the lot and the most alone. The authenticity of Roky and Blaine was unclear, but they are less alone than Harold—Roky has his followers, and Blaine, at least, is out of his room and in a new job. The only truly authentic character is Chrissy, and she is the least alone of any of them. True, she is still alone to the degree that she must choose her projects without the external validation of knowing what really happened to her. However, it is precisely her authenticity that leads her to connect with others and actively engage with the world with full freedom and responsibility. So in Sartrean terms, we can see though we are all alone in having to choose our own projects, the authenticity of our choices can mitigate that aloneness.

So much for the characters unique to the "Jose Chung's *From Outer Space*" episode. But what about Jose Chung himself? Is he authentic? In many ways, Chung is the most Sartrean person of the episode. Chung explicitly denies the possibility of a single, objectively correct way of looking at the world or living one's life. Recall that when asked by Scully to record the truth about the events in Klass County, Chung flatly asserts that this would be impossible.

Furthermore, Chung deliberately refuses to engage in any sort of bad-faith self-deception. He is blunt with Scully about his motives for writing: "At first I was reluctant, until I realized that I had an opportunity here to create an entirely new literary genre: a non-fiction science fiction. Now, see, that gimmick alone will guarantee its landing on the best-seller list. In short, to answer your question? Money!" At the same time, he has no illusions about his literary importance, despite the fact that he clearly enjoys the adoration of his fans. In "Jose Chung's *Doomsday Defense*" (an episode of the *X-Files* spin-off *Millennium*), Chung asks Frank Black (*Millennium's* protagonist, played by Lance Henrickson) to guess which two authors will still be read in a thousand years time. Frank guesses "Shakespeare and Chung?" In spite of the great pleasure that this answer clearly gives Chung, he disagrees, answering instead "Shakespeare and Goopta" (the latter being the fictional author around whom the events of the episode turn). In addition, Chung recognizes the equal value of all good-faith projects, even to the point of comparing his work as an author—despite its apparent lack of lasting value—to Frank's criminal profiling: "I realized how similar our jobs are. You see, based on some vague details and notions, you try to sketch out a person's past, in order to imagine their future actions. Detection, dramaturgy: it's all the same."

Finally, Chung's own characterization of his life has a distinctly existentialist ring to it (as long as we take his reference to God as tongue-in-cheek). When confronted by a member of the Selfosophist religion (which Chung had recently ridiculed in a short story) about why Chung would make fun of their beliefs, Chung replies: "It's not just your beliefs: I ridicule a whole bunch of other beliefs. . . . If I used your therapies to wipe away my pains, I'd disappear! And if my right to choose amusement wherever I want, if that were wiped away too, I'd die! . . . But I've developed a few therapies of my own. I've learned to appreciate the preposterousness of any profundity, and in my distress, I am able to find the smallest, most absurd details, as if God were looking down, winking at me, and letting me in on the joke."

Mulder and Scully in Sartrean Terms

Morgan, through Chung, offers his interpretation of Mulder and Scully as he sees them at near the end of season 3. Chung calls Scully's character in *From Outer Space* "Agent Diana Lesky" and Mulder's literary pseudonym is "Agent Reynard Muldrake." Regarding Agent Lesky, Chung says "Seeking the truth about aliens means a perfunctory nine-to-five job to some. For although Agent Diana Lesky is noble spirit and pure of heart, she remains, nevertheless, a federal employee." This is clearly a description of a character that lives in bad faith. Rather than committing herself to a project of her own choosing, she allows the FBI to choose her projects for her. Worse, she pursues those projects only perfunctorily, without passion, or even any real interest in whether or not the cases are solved, so long as she can clock out at five and draw her paycheck. Of Muldrake, Chung says "As for her [Lesky's] partner, Reynard Muldrake—that ticking time bomb of insanity—his quest into the unknown has so warped his psyche, one shudders to think how he receives pleasures from life." This is a description of a person who may have been authentic at one point but has lost his way. Certainly, his project—to discover proof of alien life—is one of his own choosing, and one that he has pursued even in the absence of external validation. However, as Chung sees it, Muldrake's commitment has turned to obsession. He now feels compelled to pursue this project because he allows it to define him as a person and thus determine his choices and actions.

However, we may wonder whether Chung—that is, Morgan—fairly interprets Scully and Mulder. Is Chung's terse assessment too quick? The series continued for six more seasons, and six years after that we meet Scully and Mulder again in *I Want to Believe* (2008). If we include these data, what should we say about whether our heroes—as we (the X-Phile viewers) know them—live in good or bad faith?

The first time we see Scully showing signs of existential angst is perhaps in "Beyond the Sea." Luther Lee Boggs, a convicted serial killer, claims to have psychic abilities after his first (stayed) brush with the gas chamber. Mulder is uncharacteristically skeptical, but Scully begins to believe in Boggs's abilities. With Mulder in the hospital from a gunshot wound, Scully cracks the case, following Boggs's psychic leads. But when she files her field report, she doesn't admit to the veracity of Boggs's abilities. By the end of the episode, she strains to develop one of her Scully-type scientific/naturalistic explanations for Boggs's leads. Mulder subsequently asks, "Dana, after all you've seen, after all the evidence, why can't you believe?" She confesses that she is afraid to believe. Believing in the paranormal would mean giving up her training as a scientist and FBI agent. This seems to be an example of Scully living in bad faith. However, in "Empedocles" (season 8) she has overcome her fear. Agent Doggett (Robert Patrick) abruptly seeks Scully's counsel: "You never believed in any of this stuff. This paranormal or whatever you call it. So, what changed your mind?" She informs him:

"I realized it was me, that I was afraid. Afraid to believe." Scully has given up the fetters of her scientific and FBI training. She doesn't completely disregard them (which itself might be a sign of leading an authentic life), but she no longer fears living her life without them. At the end of the episode, she thanks Mulder for providing her the courage to believe as the evidence—paranormal or naturalistic—presents itself. She no longer allows people to define her as (merely) a medical doctor, FBI agent, or "time-card puncher," and her life is freer for it. She is no longer the character Morgan knew in season 3; she has transcended her former self.

Even so, it must be admitted that along the way she sometimes acted like Mulder simply because she was the senior X-Files agent. When Doggett, a skeptical New York police officer turned FBI agent, is assigned to the X-Files (to find Mulder), he asserts (in "Invocation" from season 8) that words like "'anomalous,' 'supernatural,' 'paranormal'—they purport to explain something by not explaining it. It's lazy." Scully finds herself working very hard to acclimate Doggett to his new post. Sometimes she works too hard. In "Patience" (season 8) we find her taking leaps of logic and making opaque connections that only Mulder (on his bravest of days) would dare. However, it seems that she does so only because this is what Mulder would do and not as a result of making an authentic choice. Arguably, Scully's early interactions with Doggett are in bad faith. But by season 8, acting in bad faith was the exception for Scully and not the rule—we might explain these instances away with the angst she feels due to Mulder's disappearance. In "Without" (season 8) she declares to Doggett's incredulity that a scientist like Scully could ever believe in the paranormal: "I will go on record to say this; that I have seen things that I cannot explain. I have observed phenomena that I cannot deny. And that as a scientist and a serious person it is a badge of honor not to dismiss these things because someone thinks they're BS." This might be the epitome of Sartrean authenticity (although her looking for Mulder in "Without"—alone at night in the desert with only a flashlight—perhaps is a close second).[6]

For the most part, then, Scully lives in good faith, at least as the series progresses. An important turning point might be Scully's cancer (diagnosed in season 4). She refused to let it define her. But when we (the X-Phile viewers) meet Scully again in *I Want to Believe*, the assessment of Scully in Sartrean terms seems a bit clouded. She has left the bureau. This was her choice, and it seems that she could choose to return; at least this is what the *I Want to Believe* novelization implies.[7] She now practices pediatric medicine full time at Our Lady of Sorrows hospital. She consults specialists at more prestigious institutions but doesn't blindly follow their advice. She chooses to contravene the authority of Chief of Staff Father Ybara (Adam Godley) about stopping treatment on one of her patients. He believes that the boy should receive palliative care, but Scully is not ready to accept that course. She lives with Mulder and continually strives, presumably, to be a good partner even though Mulder refuses to leave the house. All of these data point to Scully leading an authentic life. In this way, her character continues to develop from its humble beginnings of a young woman labeled at a scientist, doctor, and FBI agent.

Another source of angst for Scully was her religious (Roman Catholic) upbringing. Clashes between Scully's faith and (scientific) reason occurred more than once in the series—"Revelations" and "All Souls" are two notable examples. This clash arises again in *I Want to Believe.* Her disagreement with Father Ybara seems to be over not the facts of the case but whether Scully can let go of the boy. It is hinted in the movie that he reminds Scully of her son, William, primarily because they are about the same age. If the image of the son she placed for adoption is impeding her judgment, it might be argued that her dispute with Father Ybara is in bad faith. However, near the end of the film, it seems that, with Mulder's help, Scully begins to believe in her own abilities to cure the boy with a radical stem-cell treatment. This might be evidence that she treats the boy in Sartrean good faith, especially given Catholicism's official stance against most stem cell therapies.

Scully has different difficulties with another priest, Father Joseph Crissman (Billy Connolly). "Father Joe," now defrocked, is a convicted pedophile. But he begins to have psychic visions of kidnapped women. The FBI calls on Mulder and Scully to consult in the case, and they hesitantly agree. Scully is revolted by Crissman. Her revulsion leads her to not believe in his alleged psychic abilities. In perhaps the most controversial aspect of Sartre's position, it might be argued that Scully's preconceived notions about ethics, grounded as they are in her religious upbringing, are leading her to choose in bad faith. Sartre seems committed to the position that no act in itself—even pedophilia—is impermissible. Consequently, it could be argued that Scully's choice to deny Father's Joe's abilities is grounded in her fear of giving up her religious background. But in the end, as she did with Boggs, she gets herself to believe that Father Joe's eerie command, "Don't give up," was meant for her. It becomes a source of strength for her as she decides to proceed with the radical stem-cell treatments.

A Sartrean assessment of Mulder is perhaps murkier than of Scully. The immediate source of existential concern is that his character has not grown very much. The microcosm for this is his sister, Samantha. At first, Mulder's decision to reopen the X-Files unit—at the risk of a comfortable and decorated career in the violent crimes division—is a prime example of leading an authentic life. In Sartre's terms, the value Mulder places on Samantha's disappearance and her rescue is Mulder's own choice. It's a choice that he continues to make, even though it earns him a basement office and the nickname "Spooky." This embodies his assertion to Scully in "Memento Mori": "The truth will set you free. It will set us both free." His choice to pursue the truth at all costs can only be an example of good faith. However, Morgan is correct in that this choice has arguably consumed Mulder. The problem isn't that "he receives no pleasure from life," because that, too, could be an existential choice Mulder makes for the sake of finding Samantha and ultimately "the truth." The problem seems to be his obsession with pursuing the truth. Consider that in "Closure" (season 7) Mulder manages to find Samantha's teenage journal. He seems to accept that it is written in her hand. In it he reads about all the times she was abducted (presumably in ways similar to Cassandra Spender) and all the experiments that she suffered through. The last person to see Samantha alive was Arbutus Ray (Patience Cleveland), a registered nurse. She tells Scully that Samantha somehow disappeared from a locked hospital room, never to be seen again. Later in the episode, he has something of a paranormal encounter with Samantha, which leads him to believe that she is deceased. At the end of the episode, he murmurs, "I'm free." It seems that Mulder has found the truth about his sister, but it has *not* set him free. He continues to search for her, even though he seems to know she is dead. She died long before he reopened the X-Files.

When we meet Mulder in *I Want to Believe,* he has shut himself in a makeshift office. Much like in his basement FBI office, he throws pencils at the ceiling as he combs newspapers and the Internet for evidence of paranormal activity. A picture of Samantha is clearly displayed on the back of his door. It appears that his obsession with Samantha and the elusive "truth out there" prevents him from being a good partner for Scully. We (the X-Phile viewers) believe that Mulder loves Scully (from "Existence" in season 8). But it seems that he cannot fully commit to that love. When he finally decides to leave the house to consult for the FBI, it looks pretty clear that it only fuels his obsession (which is why Scully quickly regrets her decision to involve him). However, if there is evidence of Mulder choosing in Sartrean good faith, it might be at the very end of the film. With the case solved, rather than lament the fact that Father Joe's involvement wasn't truly conveyed to the public, he promises Scully that after her operation they will—together—get as far away from the darkness as they can (at least for a while). In a surprise scene at the end of the closing credits, we see Mulder and Scully on a small boat—alone in the bright sun—sailing on tropical waters. What exactly this scene represents is unclear, but it might be evidence that Mulder has finally grown, headed for a more authentic life.

"You Seem Non-Nonplussed by These Contradictions?"

Darin Morgan's episodes are invariably rich with philosophical content. But philosophy, by its very nature, is also invariably controversial. We believe that the arguments about knowledge and truth implicit in "Jose Chung's *From Outer Space*" can be resisted.

Morgan's first implicit argument, that knowledge of reality as it is in itself is impossible because of the subjective nature of experience, seems to assume that knowledge requires certainty. If it is possible that our belief is false, then it cannot count as knowledge, even if the belief turns out to be true. So, because no vantage point is privileged, it is always possible that it doesn't accurately represent how things actually are. It thus allegedly follows that knowledge of reality is impossible. Immediately, whether *no* epistemic vantage point is privileged must be questioned. Doesn't it seem plain that some—due to poor health or psychological disorders—are clearly diminished? Nevertheless, this argument faces two additional damaging objections.

First, it isn't clear that all judgments are prone to the possibility of error. Ironically, Morgan brings this issue to the foreground in the diner scene via Lieutenant Shaefer, who tells Mulder: "Don't you get it? I'm absolutely positive me, my copilot, and those two kids were abducted but I can't be absolutely sure it happened. I can't be sure of anything anymore! . . . I'm not sure we're even having this conversation. . . . I don't know if you even exist." Mulder responds: "I can only assure you that I do," to which Shaefer replies, "Well, thanks, buddy. Unfortunately, I can't give you the same assurance about me." René Descartes would disagree. He argued that you can have knowledge of your own existence, at least whenever you think about it, indeed, whenever you doubt it. This is so because doubting (or thinking generally) requires a doubter (or thinker). Because a thinker has immediate and self-certifying cognitive access to her thoughts, it follows that she can never be wrong in her belief that she exists, at least whenever she thinks about it. This is Descartes' celebrated "cogito ergo sum," or "I think, therefore I am" argument. It shows that there are pieces of knowledge we cannot believe falsely.[8] Thus, some knowledge of reality—that you are included in it—is obtainable.

Second, it is not clear that knowledge requires the impossibility of error in the first place. Think of all the beliefs you might be incorrect about: who your parents are, your birthday, your phone number, whether you have two hands, whether you're reading this book. It seems more likely that you know these things than it is that knowledge requires the impossibility of error. Moreover, if knowledge did require the impossibility of error, how could that requirement itself be known? Isn't it possible that knowledge doesn't require this stringent standard? Note the difference with Descartes' "cogito." It is impossible to believe falsely that you exist, even when you doubt your existence, because thought requires a thinker. Since you cannot mistakenly believe that you are thinking, you cannot mistakenly believe you exist. But the assumption that knowledge requires the impossibility of error isn't self-certifying in this way. Thus, it cannot be known, and relying on it for a condition of knowledge seems self-defeating.

Morgan's second argument is that the fact of disagreement about reality entails that there are no objective truths about reality to be known. If there are no objective truths, then everything is subjective. This is a very common argument, heard most often from those who are brand new to philosophy. It also has two flaws. First, there have been many cases of disagreement that don't lead to subjectivism. Cultures disagreed about the shape of the Earth: some held it was perfectly round like a marble; others that it was flat with four corners; others that it is spherical, but not perfectly so. But from this disagreement, it cannot be concluded that it there is no objective truth to the matter about the shape of the earth. This conclusion does apply generally, however. Theists disagree with atheists about God's existence, but whether God, in fact, exists is immune to this debate. Either God exists or he doesn't, just as the Earth has this determinate shape or not. Belief is one thing, but truth (and existence) is another. If so, then disagreements about ethical beliefs and value judgments don't necessarily lead to ethical subjectivism either. Secondly, and ironically, the claim that everything is subjective is itself supposed to be objectively true. But by its own meaning, there cannot be any objectively true claims, as these would describe reality as it is in itself. Thus, the very idea of subjectivism about truth is self-contradictory. But if it cannot be true, then its logical opposite must be, which entails that there are some objective truths about reality.

Therefore, perhaps Mulder is correct: the truth is out there, even about philosophical topics like God, ethics, and values. We are to discover it; we don't merely invent it. If so, then perhaps we are not forced to conclude that we are all alone—in a moral world of our own making—as Morgan suggests at the end of the episode. Perhaps Mulder and Scully should be our guides: if we all put new batteries in our flashlights and help each other find the truth about ethics and values, we could live in the same moral universe together, or at least live more peacefully in more reward-ing ways.

But we suspect that the spirit of Morgan's trenchant criticisms of *The X-Files* remains. In fact, *The X-Files* would be incomplete without them. How can a show that obstinately refuses you closure on any thematic topic—whether Krychek is lying this time, if CSM is really dead, why the black oil behaves differently in various situations, if William was a miracle of God or technology, or what *really* happened to Samantha—not allow someone to question its own ideals. Week after week we (the X-Phile viewers) are told "the truth is out there." Morgan asks (in "Jose Chung's *From Outer Space*"), "Is it?" Mulder is canonized for his relentless search for the truth regardless of personal sacrifice. Morgan asks (in "Clyde Bruckman's Final Repose"), "Wouldn't he be happier [and less lonely] if he relented?" Mul-der drags Scully across the globe in the hopes that she, Skinner, Doggett, and everyone else will believe. Morgan asks, "Isn't this megalomaniacal?" Mulder appears as a modern day Arthurian knight on a Grail quest for the truth.[9] Morgan asks (in "War of the Coprophages"), "Isn't he more like Don Quixote jousting windmills [especially when traveling without Scully]?" Mulder and Scully will find the truth and set us free, even the circus folk. In "Humbug," Morgan asks, "But, then, why do *they* seem like the freaks?" By raising these questions—by encouraging us think about them for ourselves—he ironically wrote the most genuine *X-Files* episodes of the series. He didn't advance the mythology. He didn't create frightening monsters or creepy villains. He got us to ponder what we should believe about *The X-Files.* Many of us wanted to believe that Mulder and Scully were heroes. Morgan asked whether we should believe this of them. For this we (and, perhaps, even Chris Carter) owe him our gratitude. Only a writer of Morgan's caliber could get us to ponder what we believe about show that requires us to think about our beliefs (and also make us laugh in the process).

Notes

I again express my gratitude to "WhoToTrust?" and my other new NewSpace XPhile Forum friends ("SecretAgentGirl," "kamish42," site administrator "Marita Covarrubias") at NewSpace XPhile Forum (http://anewspace.20.forumer.com/index.php) for the inspiration to recraft this essay for the 2009 edition. There isn't a more cordial bunch of X-Philes on the Internet. (Website last accessed August 26, 2008.)

1. Margaret Kaner has also recognized the significance of perspective in this episode. See "Believing the Lie: Interpretive Strategies and Epistemic Choices in *The X-Files*," in *The X-Files and Literature,* ed. Sharon R. Yang (Newcastle, UK: Cambridge Scholars Publishing, 2007), 234–36.

2. Jean-Paul Sartre, "Existentialism Is a Humanism," trans. Philip Mairet, in *Existentialism from Dostoevsky to Sartre,* ed. Walter Kaufman (New York: Meridian Books, 1956), 290–91.

3. The preceding is very freely summarized from Sartre's *Being and Nothingness,* trans. Hazel E. Barnes (New York: Washington Square Press, 1984)—see especially the introduction and part 1, chapter 1.

4. See *Being and Nothingness* part 4, chapter 1 for more on freedom.

5. See *Being and Nothingness* part 1, chapter 2 for more on bad faith.

6. In the desert scene, Scully doesn't (quite) find Mulder, but Doggett finds Scully. An enlightening exchange ensues between the new X-File partners:

> SCULLY: For someone who claims he's not following me, you sure have a knack.
> DOGGETT: Hey, you're where the action is.
> SCULLY: What does that tell you? That I'm crazy or that I'm right?
> DOGGETT: Wandering around in the desert in the dead of night, you call it.
> SCULLY: You say you want to find Mulder, but you won't do what it takes. You're afraid that I'm right.
> DOGGETT: I'm not afraid of anything. Except that maybe Mulder's got even you believing in this crap now.
> SCULLY: You've seen this crap for yourself now. How do you explain what took place today?
> DOGGETT: Let me ask you something hypothetically. Now, if you were to find him out here or this ship or this alien bounty hunter, what would you do then?
> SCULLY: I know what Agent Mulder would do. He'd do whatever it took.

Because Scully refuses to kowtow (or revert back) to Doggett's entrenched skepticism and disdain for all things paranormal, she is leading an authentic life. Moreover, here she relies on Mulder's example in good faith, unlike in "Patience." She fully realizes the important and pervasive role that Mulder has in her life, and she authentically chooses to act accordingly—as he would authentically choose to do "whatever it took" to rescue Scully.

7. Max Allan Collins (based on the screenplay by Chris Carter and Frank Spotnitz), *The X-Files: I Want to Believe* (New York: HarperCollins, 2008), 23–25.

8. René Descartes, *Meditations on First Philosophy,* trans. John Cottingham (Cambridge: Cambridge University Press, 1996). See especially Meditations 1 and 2 for Descartes' argument that the thinker has knowledge of her existence.

9. For more on the analogy between *The X-Files* and the Arthurian knights, please see Joan R. Vredenburgh, "The Grail of Truth: *The X-Files* as a Modern-Day Arthurian Quest," in The X-Files *and Literature,* ed. Sharon R. Yang (Newcastle, UK: Cambridge Scholars Press, 2007), 43–65.

Feelings and Fictions

Exploring Emotion and Belief in *Fight the Future*

Christopher R. Trogan

Film has enormous power to affect our emotions. Sometimes, as in documentary, our emotions are targeted via the intellect. More often than not, however, our emotions are provoked directly through the fictional presentation of characters and events. *The X-Files* movie *Fight the Future* demonstrates the ways in which film as an aesthetic medium can induce a plethora of feelings and emotions — from skepticism to belief and anxiety to relief — in order to put forth a series of propositions for intellectual consideration. While any single episode in *The X-Files* also induces emotions in order to carry out such ends, the feature-length film gives viewers the chance to experience a longer, sustained, and wide-ranging emotional experience. The nearly two hours of continuous narrative gives viewers an extended opportunity to enter into the lives of the characters and to suspend disbelief through emotional identification. We are moved by Fox Mulder, Dana Scully, and the challenges they face. And we experience emotions — fear, relief, anger, excitement — due to their experience of events that are, like the characters themselves, fictional.

Real Responses, Fictional Characters

When we stop to think about it, films like *Fight the Future,* which depict these fictional characters and events, make our emotional responses puzzling. Of course, it may be that some part of us does not quite "know" that the film is fictional — after all, some of us are fans of *The X-Files* series because it "could be" real. However, this would only partially explain our emotional reactions to it. In fact, we know that Special Agents Fox Mulder and Dana Scully and the events they encounter in the film are the deliberate creation of screenwriters. Yet we experience some of the same emotions we would if they were real people and events. The film raises interesting aesthetic issues about the connection between beliefs, judgments, and emotional responses. The nature of this connection forms the core of an intense aesthetic debate. Regarding this debate, it will be argued here that although our beliefs, judgments, and emotional responses to *Fight the Future* (and to other fictional works) may *seem* unjustified because the events are not "real" events, a proper appreciation of the imagination will allow for a rationally justified and even ethically advantageous response. In short, it will be argued that our appreciation of *Fight the Future* is more than an enjoyable pastime: it allows us to enhance our capacity for empathy and understanding of other people in general — in effect, to become more "human."

The film begins in 37,000 BC when a deadly secret was buried in a Texas cave; two cavemen hunt down what is recognizable as an extraterrestrial in an ice cavern. A mood of suspense and loneliness arises immediately as these primitive humans trudge through the snow and ice. Within minutes, we are shuttled to the present (1997), when the secret has been unleashed. A young boy, Stevie, falls through the ground while playing with his friends and lands in the same cavern. As his friends peer down from above, young Stevie is attacked by the black cancer, which also infects two firemen who attempt to rescue him and two additional firemen who go in after the first two. It is worth noting here that Stevie is infected in a unique way. For the first five seasons of the show, if a character was infected by the black cancer, the cancer entered through the facial orifices. Here, however, the black cancer attacks Stevie through his skin (presumably his feet).

Watching a child being infected in this mysterious way is alarming enough. However, for fans of the show — the so-called X-Philes — the situation was even more emotionally charged. It is learned that there are *two* strains of the alien virus. X-Philes were familiar with the pooling, swarming version that infected Krycek in "Apocrypha." This alien life form then used Krycek's body to return to an alien craft buried in the missile silo. Stevie is infected with the wormlike version that was first witnessed infecting the scientist in "Tunguska." In that episode it was left ambiguous exactly how (besides how the "oil" moved and entered the body) this second version was different. The Syndicate originally believed that colonization would take place via the pooling/swarming version, which leaves its human subjects physically intact but takes away control of their bodies.

However, in *Fight the Future,* it is made clear that a human infected with the second strain becomes merely a source of nutrition for the alien as it gestates. The victim's body literally turns to a bag of jelly before the alien bursts out of the torso. Furthermore, the gestated alien is large, clawed, and vicious, evoking even greater fear and dread among the X-Philes.[1] All this information is strategically placed at the very beginning of *Fight the Future* to evoke suspense, excitement, anxiety, horror, dismay, and — if one is a truly sensitive fan — perhaps even grief.

But what role do our beliefs and judgments play in these emotional responses? Does the experience of these emotions indicate that we believe that these events are "true"? Moreover, these questions are significant in relation to our emotional reactions as the film continues: we experience anxiety (and perhaps confusion) as we watch the FBI agent sitting in front of the bomb waiting to explode in his face, dread when the bees are unleashed on Mulder and Scully in the strange metallic half globes, frustration (or relief!) during Mulder and Scully's first aborted kiss, regret that Mulder can no longer believe what the Well Manicured Man (or anyone like him) has to say about the alien conspiracy or his sister.

In everyday circumstances, beliefs and judgments clearly play a crucial role in our emotional responses. If I am afraid of someone chasing me, I must first judge and believe that someone is chasing me. If I feel sorry for my friend Jones because he is experiencing hardship, I must believe that Jones exists and that he is, in fact, having difficulty. Is it any different in film? If we feel sorrow at the loss of young Stevie through an attack of the black cancer, do we believe that Stevie and the black cancer exist and that this event has actually occurred?

On the one hand, it seems that in many circumstances an emotional response is in one way or another dependent on belief in the existence of what we are responding to: I cannot feel sorry for Jones unless Jones and the reasons for feeling sorry for him exist. On the other hand, it seems that — as in the case of Stevie, the firemen, and the black cancer — we are moved by what happens to fictional characters and events, even though we know full well that they do not and never did exist. So, it seems that we must choose between the conclusion that our emotional responses to fiction are unjustified because they are irrational and the opinion that our justified emotional responses, at least sometimes, need not be grounded in truth.

Aestheticians (philosophers who debate issues in the arts) are divided in their approach to resolving this apparent dilemma. One approach is to analyze the rationality of our responses to film in which fictional characters and events are portrayed. These philosophers argue that our emotional experiences are inconsistent and irrational since we *know* that these characters and events do not exist. A second, and quite different, approach is to argue that certain emotions depend on the adoption of a certain sort of perspective — that is, on "seeing things from another point of view" by focusing on the power of the imagination. Perhaps films even demand such a response from viewers.

The Paradox of Being Moved and "Being Moved"

Before we undertake an analysis of what it means to be "moved" by this, or any, film, we would do well to consider emotions and how they differ from other affective states, such as feelings, moods, and desires. Many philosophers subscribe to a "cognitive" theory of emotion in which emotions are defined by having cognitive components. A "cognitive component" is a mental proposition — what one contemporary philosopher calls an "unasserted thought" — a thought tentatively considered but not believed (i.e., not thought *actually* to correspond to facts in the world).[2] The cognitive theory of emotion, then, maintains that to experience an emotion like fear or anger requires that (1) I have a certain kind of belief, for example, that I am in danger or that I have been wronged (and that there is sufficient cause in the external world to warrant this belief); and that (2) I have certain corresponding values or desires (i.e., that I want to stay out of danger so that I can survive, or that I should not be held responsible for something I have not done).

If we think about "feelings" in light of the cognitive theory of emotion, we might conclude that they are unlike emotions in that they have no cognitive import and are not linked to a particular external object (we may "feel" one way or another regardless of what we believe to be the case externally). Desires, unlike feelings, *are* cognitive because they require a belief that what we desire is (for lack of a better term) somehow to our advantage (whether physically, psychologically, etc.). In fact, it may be only because of that belief that we have the desire to do something in the first place (e.g., I desire to go swimming because I know that exercising is beneficial to me). But we must not forget that some desires are desires to do things whether or not we believe they are good for us (e.g., my desire to take a walk in Central Park). We might even have the belief that something is good simply because we want to do it, rather than the other way around. Finally, we cannot neglect to mention that some desires are completely irrational. These are the kinds of desires we have even though we know full well that fulfilling them will be bad for us (e.g., deliberately becoming intoxicated). As we can see, arriving at clear definitions of emotion, feeling, and desire is no easy feat, and the relationship between these is even more complicated, yet thinking about these issues is crucial for understanding the relationship between our affective responses to film and our responses to real-life situations.

If my friend Jones sits me down to tell me a story about how his mother and brother were killed in a horrific automobile accident the day before, and if I react to that story with sadness—perhaps even with tears—only to find out that the story is false, that Jones has no sister and that his mother passed away in her sleep years ago, I would feel quite embarrassed at myself for behaving the way I did and probably angry (and somewhat perplexed) at him for lying to me about something so serious. Yet, when I sit down to watch *Fight the Future* and watch Scully become infected with a virus and get taken to a secret installation in Antarctica, I might also have emotions of frustration, sadness, and anger even though the events depicted are clearly fictional ("It's just a movie"). In the first case, my reaction to Jones's deception is justified, even expected, once I find out the truth. In the second case, the same reaction would be ridiculous since the success of the film hinges upon its ability to deceive us even though we are never *unaware* that we are, in fact, being deceived. In other words, my reaction to learning of Jones's deception (embarrassment, outrage) is expected, while this same reaction to the "deception" of what happens to Scully would be considered lunacy. How do we reconcile these two scenarios?

Some philosophers argue that we simply cannot. Jerome Shaffer has argued that emotions are irrational and indefensible. Here and there an emotion might be beneficial because it is pleasant or has some practical advantage, but as a whole there is no good reason to have emotions and we would be better off without them.[3] But the argument can be made that, under the right circumstances, emotions need not be irrational: perhaps they are arational. Although less extreme, but still skeptical, Colin Radford challenges philosophers to explain how it is possible and desirable for us to have emotional reactions to fictional works.[4] Radford offers several "solutions" to this dilemma. Although Radford's analysis is focused on fiction and drama, it would be useful to apply some of his proposals to our cinematic case study.

First, Radford proposes that when we read a book or watch a play, we get "caught up" in it so that we "forget" we are being deceived. Analogously, as we watch *Fight the Future,* we are "taken in" to such an extent that, among other things, we "believe" in the shadowy Syndicate set up to aid aliens in their colonization plans. We forget that "it's just a movie" and that there is no Syndicate, there are no aliens, and so on. Our emotional reactions are excused because the intensity of the film cajoles us into losing ourselves in the narrative. In fact, one way to interpret what people mean when they say a film or television series is "good" is just that it is powerful enough to get us caught up. But Radford argues that this is not a real solution to the problem because it "turns adults into children." After all, we are adults and we know that what is *really* happening on the screen is fictional, that the characters are actors, and that the events are not real. Radford, therefore, dismisses this as a viable solution to the problem.

Perhaps, Radford continues, we can explain our emotional reactions to fictional events by saying that we "suspend our disbelief" in their reality. After all, millions of dollars are spent to create a world that makes it easier for us to do this. Directors, writers, cinematographers, and producers dedicate their lives to enabling the suspension of disbelief. When we went to the theater to watch our favorite characters Mulder and Scully, we would have been quite upset if there were a baby crying in the seat behind us, or if the picture were out of focus. That is, we would have been annoyed if we had paid admission to the illusion of the film and not gotten what we paid for. We consciously and voluntarily went in to be deceived, to enter into the minds and worlds of Mulder and Scully. So, Radford maintains, since we are fully aware of the deception, we cannot be fully justified in our emotional reactions since these reactions are, again, predicated upon fictional characters and events.

Could it be that when we see Scully encased in a cryotube in the antarctic installation and feel pain and sorrow for her, we are actually experiencing the pain and sorrow we would feel for a real person in a similar *situation?* Radford agrees that there is something to this explanation, but that it is not enough. He maintains that we feel for Scully the *character,* not for someone like her in a similar situation. Even though Radford's comments are here focused on the fictional character of Anna Karenina, they apply just as well to Agent Scully: "We are moved by what happens to her, by the situation she gets into, and which is a pitiful one, but we do not feel pity for her state or fate, or her history or her situation, or even for others, i.e. for real persons who might have or even have had such a history.[5]

In other words, Radford discounts the possibility that our emotional reaction is directed toward someone else in a similar situation. Instead, he argues that we are emotionally invested in *this* character and *this* situation. So we are sad for Scully because of the situation *she* faces. But because Scully isn't an actual person, feeling sorry for her is analogous to feeling sorry for my daughter's imaginary friend, Molly. The only problem, for Radford, would be that since Scully does not actually exist, our emotional reaction would be based on a false belief. Since our emotions in everyday situations are based on true beliefs (I feel angry at Jones because Jones stole my wallet; in order for Jones to steal my wallet, there must "really" be a Jones and a wallet), Radford holds that it is "inconsistent and so incoherent" that we would apply one standard to life and another standard to art. Radford proposes that our emotional reactions to any fictional character or event mirror the kind of fear one might have of death. To be sad for a fictional character like Scully is similar to fearing death in that, according to Radford, there is no true *belief.* Just as it is inconsistent and incoherent to base our emotional reaction to Scully's situation on a belief in her existence (since she doesn't exist), it is equally as inconsistent and incoherent to be fearful of death since, in Radford's estimation, fearing death is, literally, fearing nothing. To fear death is to experience an emotion not based on true belief: "There is, literally, nothing to fear."[6]

Accordingly, Radford does not accept that one could justifiably experience an emotion based on a *fictional* belief. But others would argue that entertaining this possibility would explain away the apparent experiential, epistemological, and — by extension — aesthetic paradox that so confounds him. Perhaps the kinds of beliefs we have when watching *Fight the Future* or reading a novel are fundamentally different from those we have when experiencing real people and events. If so, then it might not be incoherent to have two different standards for beliefs regarding fictional and actual scenarios.

The Ethical Significance of Imagination

To resolve this seeming paradox we might adopt a less narrow view of "belief" than Radford does. Perhaps the beliefs involved are of a more general sort than he lets on. Perhaps I (justifiably) believe that the events of the sort presented in *Fight the Future* have occurred, or that they are likely to occur, or even that they might possibly occur, even if I do not believe in the existence of the particular people, situations, and events described in the film. Perhaps I may respond to the film as a result of my more general beliefs about what the world is like.

We might also question Radford's assumption that belief in the truth of what one reads or sees is necessary for having an emotional response. It could be that the "cognitive component" of an emotion could be an unasserted thought, rather than an actual belief; we would then avoid the charge of irrationality (i.e., that the emotion is irrational because the belief is irrational). To generate an emotional response, it might be enough simply to think of Mulder and Scully and the events of the film and *imagine* that they are real. However, the question remains as to whether an unasserted thought is potent enough to get us as emotionally worked up as a belief can. If I believed that Jones's mother and brother were on the plane that crashed, I would feel intense despair for him. Once Jones admits that he was lying and that his family members were not on this plane, I would no longer feel intense despair for him (although I probably would be angry at his deception).

It is also the case that many unasserted thoughts pass through our heads. Some unasserted thoughts are emotionally affecting while many others are not. How could this be? Something else besides simply having the thought and the relevant desires and values is necessary to explain why watching a film that generates such thoughts can be emotionally affecting. Perhaps it is a mark of a "good" film that it can present characters and events in such a way that they are emotionally affecting (that they "stick"). A film that affects us emotionally must have convincing actors, an engrossing plot line, perhaps even some special effects.

In truth, the problem Radford poses is broader than even he lets on. We respond to fictional works—including film—not only with emotions but also with feelings, moods, and desires. Feelings and moods are not generally held to have cognitive components in the form of beliefs or unasserted thoughts (the jury is still out about desires). So, it is unclear how beliefs or unasserted thoughts could help to explain non-emotion affective responses, such as feelings and moods, which do not have cognitive components. How does one explain such responses?

Any explanation of the emotional effectiveness of a film, assuming that the film in question presents fictional events, needs to develop some account of how imagination is involved. Kendall Walton responds to this by developing a systematic account of imagination.[7] He argues that responding to fiction is an extension of ordinary games of make-believe similar to, but more sophisticated than, those that children play. In responding to fictional events we are using a book (or in our case, the film) as a prop in a game of make-believe, and within the game I believe what happens to

Mulder and Scully and the world they inhabit. It becomes provisionally "true" in this game of make-believe that they are faced with great challenges to save the world, they suffer unjustly, and so on. On this view, just as it may be true in the game of make-believe that I feel sorry for Scully or admire Mulder, it is not true of me (qua *me*) that I "really" have these emotions. Contrary to Radford's view that a response like this would transform an adult into a child, it is important to note that Walton argues for an *extension* of the game of make-believe that children play. Far from suffering a change from adults into children who are "victims" of a game's logic and emotional effect, we adults willingly and self-consciously enter into the "game" of the film and are aware — on some level — that we are playing the game. Unlike children who are often (but not always) unable to detach themselves from make-believe, we can make this conceptual separation. It may take some effort to make the transition, but it can be done. Radford's view does not take this into consideration.

But if emotional responses to film are not mere child's play, then how we respond may importantly matter. It certainly seems that anyone who cheers on the Syndicate's colonization plans and laughs when Scully is kidnapped and encased in a cryotube in the Antarctic is responding inappropriately to the film. What makes these cheers and laughter inappropriate? Little work has been done on explaining how to make any such assessments of our responses, but clearly they are of the greatest import. If I laugh when the FBI agent allows himself to be blown up, when Scully is kidnapped, or when the scientist is locked in the cave with the gestated alien, I seem to have missed a very important part of the point of the film. Those events are created to move us to sorrow and outrage. If we don't experience these feelings, it seems fair to conclude that we've failed to get some of the most important value from the film.

Assessments of responses as appropriate or inappropriate are intimately connected with questions about why it is important to respond to fiction of any kind at all. So what if the events in the film don't have the intended emotional effect upon us? Is anything lost? Why bother watching the film at all? It seems that the value and importance of film, literature, or any other kind of fiction is wrapped up with our responses to it, and a failure to respond is (to that extent) a failure to appreciate the work. And this helps to understand why it is so important to have not just any old response to a work but to have appropriate responses (conceding that several responses may be equally appropriate, revealing different qualities or aspects of a work). Rather than settling the issue, however, this solution merely raises another question.

Having appropriate affective responses to a film are part of what it means to appreciate it, but why is it important to appreciate a film in the first place? To put this another way, why is it good to have things around like films that are supposed to (and presumably do) move us in all sorts of ways? A very old idea is that the function of the arts is to delight and instruct. Suppose we say that the function of a film is solely to please or delight us. It would then appear that we should respond with emotions and feelings that provide the most delight or pleasure; this would remove the need for an exclusively objective standard for the responses (i.e., a standard that resides in the properties of the object, the film, to which we respond) and accept the preferences of each viewer. But some ways of responding to film may be more likely to produce richer and more fulfilling pleasures than simply reacting or responding in any way one wishes. If so, the approach with the richest overall potential in the long run could provide a basis for judgment of the appropriateness of the responses.

Furthermore, delight might not be separate from instruction. Aristotle pointed out that learning can be pleasurable. How can emotions and other affective responses instruct? Martha Nussbaum has argued persuasively that literature teaches us to "see," where seeing involves not merely a cognitive or sensory dimension but is broadly experiential and affective as well.[8] Perhaps something like this kind of "seeing" connects to Walton's notion of experiencing something like sophisticated "make-believe." Far from turning us into children, as Radford claims, temporarily allowing ourselves to accept propositional content and the resulting emotional states may hone our ethical sensitivities. This is no small change: these sensitivities are affective as well as cognitive and influence how we experience the world and how we relate to other people. We can learn in a very straightforward way what it is like to be another sort of person, or to be in a situation other than our own. We can certainly imagine how this would apply to empathizing with Mulder and Scully. By watching this film and seeing it in the way Nussbaum suggests, we might enhance our capacity for empathy and understanding of other people in general. And contrary to Radford's notion that responding emotionally to film turns adults into children, an emotional response to film may help us as adults better deal with other adults. Perhaps by developing the cognitive and affective skills required to appreciate *Fight the Future,* by expanding the capacities of the human mind, by genuinely experiencing what this film — or any "good" film — can do *to* us, we are put on the road toward awareness of our own choices and what leads to them in order that we can begin to understand the choices of others. We can then appreciate what film can do *for* us.

Notes

1. [In *Fight the Future*, the Well-Manicured Man (John Neville) claims that the original virus has mutated unexpectedly into what was found in the cave in Texas. However, given other finer points of the storyline surrounding the black oil, it may make more sense to interpret this as the Well-Manicured Man merely giving us his limited perspective on the alarming, recent development. It's conceivable that there have been two different strains on Earth for thousands of years and not only the one given to the Syndicate. — ed.]

2. Roger Scruton, *The Aesthetic Understanding: Essays in the Philosophy of Art and Culture* (London: St. Augustine's Press, 1983).

3. Jerome A. Shaffer, *Philosophy of Mind* (Englewood Cliffs, NJ: Prentice-Hall, 1968).

4. Colin Radford, "How Can We Be Moved by the Fate of Anna Karenina?" *Proceedings of the Aristotelian Society,* supplementary vol. 49 (1975): 67–80.

5. Radford, "How Can We Be Moved?" 72.

6. Radford, "How Can We Be Moved?" 78.

7. Kendall L. Walton, *Mimesis as Make-Believe: On the Foundations of the Representational Arts* (Cambridge, MA: Harvard University Press, 1990).

8. Martha Nussbaum, "'Finely Aware and Richly Responsible': Moral Attention and the Moral Task of Literature," *Journal of Philosophy* 82, no. 10 (October 1985): 516–29.

I Want to Believe . . . But Now What?

Dean A. Kowalski and S. Evan Kreider

> You've always said that you want to believe. But believe in what, Mulder? If this is the truth that you've been looking for, then what is left to believe in?
>
> —Dana Scully in "The Truth"

Most X-Philes remember the final scene of the series finale. Mulder and Scully, pursued by the FBI (or at least shadowy factions within it), take refuge in a motel room. The scene is blocked similarly to the motel scene in "Pilot," in which Mulder first tells Scully about Samantha. In a way, then, their circle is complete, but Chris Carter, once again, has left us hanging. Yes, Mulder and Scully are together. Yes, they speak of hope, however ephemeral, for the future. But we simply don't know what the future holds, except that December 22, 2012, looms ominously on its horizon.

X-Philes waited more than six years to reconnect with their intrepid heroes Mulder and Scully. Where have they gone? What have they done? Are they still together? Some of those questions are answered in *I Want to Believe* (2008). They are no longer on the lam. For the past five years, they have lived together in a modest home outside of Richmond, Virginia.[1] Scully practices pediatric medicine at Our Lady of Sorrows hospital in urban Richmond. Mulder remains interested in the paranormal, albeit from his makeshift home office. Rather than gallivanting across the continental United States chasing leads about unexplained phenomena, he now incessantly cruises the Internet and combs through newspapers and magazines for glimpses of his former life's work. But perhaps it has remained his work; he never leaves the house, except for covert missions to his post office box in Richmond. In some ways, our intrepid heroes—for good or for ill—have become more like us.

What, then, is the point of our being reacquainted with Dr. Scully and her reclusive partner Fox Mulder? Many X-Philes have asked themselves that question after seeing *I Want to Believe*. We were promised a stand-alone, "monster of the week" episode, having little or nothing to do with the series mythology (which immediately disappointed a number of X-Philes). But some of the "monster of the week" episodes were memorable: "Squeeze/Tooms," "The Host," and "Home" are X-Phile favorites. The online trailers suggested that it might contain a psychic element; this was also reassuring, as "Beyond the Sea" and "Clyde Bruckman's Final Repose" appear regularly on X-Phile "top ten episodes" lists across the Internet. But even those who preferred the stand-alone episodes left the theaters scratching their heads (at least many of them). The villains weren't nearly as frightening as Eugene Victor Tooms (Doug Hutchison) or the incestuous Peacock family; they weren't nearly as creepy as the Flukeman (played by famed episode writer Darin Morgan).[2] The psychic was neither insidious, like Luther Lee Boggs (Brad Dourif), nor sadly familiar, like Clyde Bruckman (Peter Boyle), at least not exactly (and more on this below). There were no gunshots and very little CGI. Mulder and Scully spent most of their time apart, which prevented X-Philes from reminiscing about their completely complementary investigative styles. Many X-Philes thus left the theater confused *and* disappointed; in a matter of mere weeks, our heroes were gone again. For some, all hope was lost, the last nail in the *X-Files* coffin; others awaited the DVD release, hoping for copious "bonus features" to soothe their pain.[3]

But we believe that if you look past the familiar archetypes of mythology or "monster of the week" episodes, and focus on the characters themselves, the value of the film is easier to discern. Carter and Spotnitz took advantage of the fact that our heroes have become more like us. What they provided us gets to the core of *The X-Files:* a meditation on what to believe. After years of credit tag lines like "Trust no one," "Deny everything," "Deceive inveigle obfuscate," and "Believe the lie," Carter and Spotnitz, themselves six years older, have realized that each of us must believe in something. It's simply human nature. But in what should we believe? Can we believe whatever we want, or are there standards we should follow in forming our beliefs? What would such standards be, and why are they so important anyway? *I Want to Believe* is infused with these sorts of questions. Upon careful inspection, it also begins to answer some of them, thereby manifesting a philosophy of *The X-Files*. Understood in this way, we argue, *I Want to Believe* is not the disappointment that many X-Philes and movie critics believe.

Connections to the Series

An often heard complaint about *I Want to Believe* is that it had nothing to do with *The X-Files,* but this seems brash. To see why, consider how the movie relates to the series corpus. The movie probably most resembles "Beyond the Sea," with perhaps a dash of "Clyde Bruckman's Final Repose." The connection to "Beyond the Sea" is obvious. In that classic episode, we meet Luther Lee Boggs, a convicted serial killer—guilty of murdering his entire family on Thanksgiving Day. Boggs announces that he has a psychic connection to a recent kidnapping case. He will divulge what he knows only if he is spared the gas chamber. Mulder (uncharacteristically) immediately doubts Boggs. Mulder's profile (when he worked the violent crimes division) helped apprehend Boggs; he believes that this is another of Boggs's stunts to avoid execution. Although Scully (uncharacteristically) begins to believe in Boggs's psychic abilities, our heroes soon learn that Lucas Henry (Lawrence King), a known Boggs accomplice, is the kidnapper. So, the evidence suggests that Boggs is indeed orchestrating this charade as a way to avoid the gas chamber. Similarly, the Mulder and Scully of fifteen years later meet Father Joseph Crissman (Billy Connolly), who also claims to have a psychic connection to a kidnapping. But doubts about his psychic abilities swirl; that Father Joe is a convicted pedophile—having molested thirty-seven altar boys—provides reason to doubt his story. Moreover, Agent Dakota Whitney (Amanda Peet), who calls on Mulder to consult in the case, hypothesizes that he might be staging this stunt for reconciliation with the Church. But when it is later discovered that one of the kidnappers is a boy Father Joe molested years ago, even Mulder doubts his psychic connection. The one difference from Boggs is that Father Joe seems remorseful, almost penitent, for his crimes. He castrated himself at twenty-six. He now lives voluntarily with other sex offenders in a dormitory-type compound where the residents police each other. Father Joe says of his neighbors, "We hate each other as we hate ourselves for our sickening appetites." It's tempting to feel sympathy for him, at least decades removed from his crimes. This is where the dash of Clyde Bruckman applies: we feel sad for lonely Bruckman and wish that he could overcome his resignation. In fact, one of the challenges for the viewer is that Father Joe seems to be more like Bruckman than Boggs. Father Joe has done monstrous things, but he is far from the monster that Boggs is.[4]

There is another episode that seems relevant, namely, "Empedocles" from season 8. This episode also contains psychic visions, but the connection to *I Want to Believe* lies elsewhere. First, recall how "Empedocles" portrays John Doggett's (Robert Patrick) memory of his son's tragic death. The following dialogue exchange between Doggett and Agent Monica Reyes (Annabeth Gish), the FBI agent who participated in the case involving Doggett's son, is particularly telling. After Reyes comforts him by saying that he did everything he could to save his son, Doggett reiterates: "I got to believe that I did everything I could to save him, to get him back safe, to not let him down. I got to believe that I did everything humanly possible 'cause if I can't believe that then these other possibilities that you talk about, that Mulder talks about, that Agent Scully talks about . . . if they're real . . . if they're real, then . . . that's something else I could have done to save my son." Doggett, a skeptic, expresses his fear about giving into the possibility of "extreme possibilities" as Scully has. If the paranormal is a possible avenue to explore, then Doggett believes he has failed his son. In effect, he gave up the fight when there was something more—no matter how unlikely or unorthodox—that could have been done.[5]

This connection helps to clear up some concern about the plot of *I Want to Believe*. Some X-Philes complained that Scully's interactions with her patient Christian Fearon (Marco Niccoli) had little to do with the theme of the movie. This complaint is probably grounded in the fact that Dr. Scully and her patient didn't seem to have any substantial link to Father Joe's visions, nor, in fact, was there any paranormal element to it at all. However, there is a parallel between Scully's commitment to saving Christian and the Russians' dire attempt at saving Franz Tomczeszyn (Fagin Woodcock). Going back to Doggett and the memory of his son, we can imagine that both Scully and Janke Dacyshyn (Tomczeszyn's partner, played by Keith Rennie) might believe that if there was something else that they could have done to save the life of those they care about—no matter how unlikely or unorthodox—then they have failed. Now we can better see the force of Father Joe's eerie command of "Don't give up." What if someone like Father Joe had uttered this to Doggett? Would he have taken additional, unorthodox steps to save his son? Interesting ethical questions soon arise with this interpretation, but these will be discussed later.

The second connection to "Empedocles" involves its treatment of the nature of evil. We are given at least four distinct interpretations. We have Agent Reyes's and Mulder's more-or-less straightforward psychological view. Reyes's speaks of "stressors" that tend to cause psychological trauma; Mulder notes how one's environment and upbringing are factors. The second is more philosophical. Catha Dukes (Wendy Gazelle), the sister of the man whom the FBI seeks for murder, voices the idea that human beings are born good, but society—life itself, perhaps—somehow corrupts us. The third view isn't voiced so much as dramatized. It is a supernatural one, such that evil is a demonic entity that possesses the people it encounters, jumping to the nearest body when its last host-body dies. The fourth view is provided by Mulder near the end of the episode. After informing Doggett that none of the straightforward psychological explanations satisfied him, given what he saw working in the violent crimes division, he now thinks of evil as a disease that we become susceptible to in some circumstances. But by the end of the episode, we aren't quite sure which explanation we are to believe. In fact, Mulder admits to Doggett, "The pisser is you may never know."[6] In true *X-Files* form, the exact nature of evil is left up to us to ponder and determine for ourselves. Similarly, in *I Want to Believe,* we must determine which things are we to believe and which things we should never give up on. Thus, the connection to "Empedocles" is not about what to believe about evil but what to believe at all and what to do about those beliefs.

Blaine Faulkner, Fox Mulder, and "Don't Give Up"

If you look closely, you can see an "I Want to Believe" poster on Blaine Faulkner's (Allan Zinyk) bedroom wall in "Jose Chung's *From Outer Space.*" However, it is unlike Mulder's poster in one important way: Blaine has blotted out the words "Want" and "to." His poster simply reads "I Believe." By doctoring his poster, Blaine provides the impression that he believes in extraterrestrial visitors regardless of what anyone else believes. Moreover, it seems that he would believe regardless of any evidence or new findings to the contrary. Many (like Richard Dawkins, perhaps) ascribe this view to Mulder; however, this is unfair. Mulder is much more careful about the evidence. He invariably looks for scientific explanations and uses sound principles of reasoning in developing his hypotheses. Thus, we could interpret Mulder's poster as omitting words, rather than crossing out those that appear. It might read: "I Want to Believe, So Long as the Evidence Allows." Presumably, then, Mulder displays his poster as a statement, but not the one you might think. He is reminding others to keep an open mind about what the evidence shows—or doesn't show—and how one might profitably proceed depending on what one discovers. Thus it is an explicit affirmation of neither extraterrestrial visitors nor of his credulity.

This interpretation of Mulder's favorite tag line is solidified as the series progresses. It is personified in Scully's character development (and probably Skinner's, too). It is voiced in the season 9 episode "Daemonicus," written and directed by Frank Spotnitz. Scully, having been reassigned to an FBI academy teaching post, announces to her forensic pathology class: "An X-File is a case that has been deemed unsolvable by the bureau, because such a case cannot be solved it may beg other explanations. . . . Science, however, tells us that evil comes not from monsters but from men. It offers us the methodology to catch these men, and only after we have exhausted these methods should we leave science behind to consider more . . . extreme possibilities." This statement echoes Mulder's admonishment from "Pilot": "When convention and science offer us no answers, might we not finally turn to the fantastic as a plausibility?" Fifteen years ago, Scully would have none of this; her response was: "What I find fantastic is any notion that there are answers beyond the realm of science. The answers are there. You just have to know where to look." Fifteen years of chasing after the likes of Eugene Victor Tooms, Jeremiah Smith (Roy Thinnes), and Donnie Pfaster (Nick Chinlund) has led her to look beyond the realm of current science. It has also led her to the position she shares with her students in "Daemonicus" and brings her much closer to the spirit of Mulder's famed poster.

The question *The X-Files* often raises is whether the evidence is always sufficient to adjudicate our beliefs. Some philosophers, like W. K. Clifford (and perhaps Richard Dawkins), answer this question affirmatively. Belief should be determined by the evidence, and the evidence alone, and if the evidence isn't sufficiently decisive, one should suspend judgment (presumably until additional evidence can be garnered). This philosophical position is often called "evidentialism"; contemporary philosophers Theodore Schick and Lewis Vaughn express it powerfully: "It is wrong for belief to outstrip the evidence because our actions are guided by our beliefs, and if our beliefs are mistaken, our actions may be misguided."[8] But as Scully notes at the end of "Daemonicus," another thoughtful episode (like "Empedocles" and "Grotesque") that forces the X-Phile viewer to determine "the truth" herself, rarely is the evidence completely decisive. She lectures: "Just as juries seek to convict beyond reasonable doubt, the forensic investigator will seek conclusions supported by a preponderance of evidence. Rarely will you encounter a case where all of the variables, all of the open questions, are fully answered." Evidentialists would no doubt agree but remind us to believe in probabilities, especially when they are strong. Regularly ignoring the evidence and the probabilities it establishes and instead choosing to believe in bare possibilities is being a bad investigator and (according to the likes of Clifford) a bad person. But what if all the scientific evidence has been marshaled, but no hypothesis is more probable than another? Is it always prudent to withhold belief and thus deny personal commitments and corresponding action? What kind of life would this entail?[9]

These difficult questions are most pressing in situations where disagreement among competing beliefs is intractable. In such cases, the evidence, which is supposed to provide us signposts for what to believe, is often ambiguous. In fact, what counts as evidence in the first place comes into dispute. This often happens with fundamental issues—philosophical explorations—about how the world is. Can science explain all of life's mysteries, or must we include a religious or supernatural element to provide a satisfying account of the universe and our experiences of it?[10] Contemporary theologian and philosopher John Hick has investigated this issue, calling it the "religious ambiguity of the universe."[11] Naturalists or atheists argue that the universe, including our experiences of it, is sufficiently explained via science. Theists (among others) disagree. Both have provided a rather sophisticated battery of arguments for their respective positions. What does the evidentialist advise in these cases? Should we believe neither, having no personal commitments or activities (except perhaps to keep searching for new evidence or arguments) with respect to the debate? Wouldn't this necessarily preclude religious commitments?

The idea of "religiously ambiguous" is nothing new to *The X-Files*. Recall Mulder's voice-over at the beginning of "Essence" (season 8) about the miracle of life, especially given the fact that Scully was left barren. (In fact, Carter's treatment of William's birth in this episode has obvious religious overtones, complete with the three Lone Gunmen arriving, each bearing gifts.) In "Improbable" (season 9), another episode written by Chris Carter, we are left to wonder whether the numerical patterns we find in nature are merely coincidental or whether there is a supernatural intelligence behind them (who surprisingly looks a lot like Burt Reynolds). Reyes agrees with Einstein that God does not play dice with the universe; however, she wonders whether it is more like playing checkers, leaving room for analysis of the numbers and, thus, free will.

Questions involving religious ambiguity are continued in *I Want to Believe.* Interestingly, however, they are more pressing exactly because Mulder and Scully have become more like us. Each of us, we suspect, has pondered

God's existence and whether he is the Creator. On the one hand, it seems reasonable to conclude that the universe, like all dependent things, must be explained by something apart from it. However, the explanation cannot involve another dependent thing, for the existence of dependent things is exactly what you are trying to explain. Thus, the explanation must reside with something that is not a dependent thing. But what? When you remember that the independent thing in question must have causal powers sufficient to explain the existence of the universe, the list of candidates seems short (cue Burt Reynolds). On the other hand, many of us, like Scully, have wondered why God would place a child on this Earth only to have it suffer terribly and then die so young. That this happens makes many of us, like Scully, lie in bed, "cursing God for all of His cruelties." But, of course, God isn't cruel; God is supposed to be perfectly good. Furthermore, God, being omnipotent and omniscient, has the ability and knowledge to prevent cruelty, especially those involving innocent children. Thus, it seems that God does not exist and cannot be the Creator. Should we believe that God exists or not? Might other pieces of evidence (scientific data or philosophical arguments) be relevant? If none are decisive, what should we believe? On what personal commitments should we act? Should Scully give up on her religious convictions? Should any of us?

There are other examples of religious ambiguity in *I Want to Believe*. First, Father Joe, as a convicted pedophile, has committed the gravest kind of sexual immorality. In the book of Corinthians, it clearly states, "Do you not know that the wicked will not inherit the kingdom of God? Do not be deceived: Neither the sexually immoral nor idolaters nor adulterers nor male prostitutes nor homosexual offenders nor thieves nor the greedy nor drunkards nor slanderers nor swindlers will inherit the kingdom of God" (1 Cor. 6:9–10). Corinthians goes on to state that Christians should "flee sexual immorality" (1 Cor. 6:18). All other sins are committed outside the body, but this one is committed against the sinner's own body. It is thus no wonder that Father Joe, now penitent, continually prays "for the salvation of his immortal soul." And the movie suggests that his prayers have been answered. He cold-calls the FBI, informing them of his alleged visions of a missing woman—who bears some resemblance to missing FBI agent Monica Bannan (Xantha Radley). In crying tears of blood, he exhibits stigmatic marks. He presses on in aiding Mulder and the FBI, even though Scully despises him. His visions, while at times a bit hazy, turn out to be helpful in cracking the case. And don't forget the thief on the cross next to Jesus. He was redeemed. Furthermore, Augustine of Hippo, once a regular visitor of prostitutes and, thus, a fornicator, was later canonized by the Catholic Church. So, what are we to believe about Father Joe? Was he granted the chance to redeem himself? Moreover, what should Father Joe believe about his own situation? Should he give up on himself—his immortal soul—like everyone else has? Mulder believes (at the end of *I Want to Believe*) that Father Joe's redemption is grounded in the very fact that the disgraced priest *didn't give up*—even though any evidence of his being redeemed was insufficient to warrant this belief. Was his personal commitment to the salvation of his immortal soul improper, as the evidentialist would have us believe?[12]

The issue of what to believe and corresponding personal commitment is just as pressing in this life, especially end of life situations. Scully and Father Ybara (Adam Godley) disagree about the proper care for Christian, given his brain illness. Ybara believes that it is time for palliative care and claims that he has it on "the highest authority" that this is so. Scully believes that there are treatments for the boy's condition yet to be explored. If these cutting-edge (and largely untested) treatments prove successful, the boy could be cured. In these sorts of circumstances, weighing the evidence can be difficult. The scientific community is agreed that there is no known cure for Christian's illness. Scully believes that a new stem-cell treatment is potentially successful. Would the evidentialist hold that we should side with Ybara and prepare the Fearons for palliative care? May the Fearons permissibly side with Scully and attempt the radical new treatment even though it is unlikely that it will succeed? Reconsider Doggett's memory of his son. He is willing to admit that if *paranormal* avenues were possibly successful, then he would be willing to explore them. Stem-cell treatments are not paranormal; they are cutting-edge science. Do Doggett, the Fearons, Scully, or any parent act impermissibly for exploring the possibility of success, even if the evidence is against them? At this point, Father Joe's "Don't give up" echoes.

But an objection is brewing. The Russian same-sex couple, Dacyshyn and Tomczeszyn, presumably could also appeal to Crissman's imperative in exploring the Dr. Frankenstein–like experiments. Tomczeszyn, suffering from terminal cancer, apparently has run out of treatment options. In a desperate move, his partner somehow arranges for a Russian scientist and medical doctor—a researcher who has had success in transplanting the heads of dogs onto new canine bodies—to conduct his research on human mammals. The idea is that if this scientist has had success with dogs, it is possible that a human head could be transplanted onto a torso that wasn't infected with cancer. Thus, there is a possible cure to explore. Presumably, Dacyshyn would feel exactly the same way as Doggett: if there was another avenue—no matter how unlikely or unorthodox—to be explored, not pursuing it would be tantamount to failing the person he cares for most.[13] But the obvious objection is that the Russians act impermissibly in exploring this possibility. Does Scully also act impermissibly is exploring her cutting-edge treatment? If not, what is the difference between the two cases? Why do the Russians go too far in following the "Don't give up" imperative, but Scully does not?

It's tempting to argue that the Russians act impermissibly because their actions are unnatural. On this account, acting unnaturally is (more or less) equated with acting in morally objectionable ways. Because it is unnatural to sever a human head and attach it to another body (not to mention a body of a different sex), it follows that the Russians act impermissibly. This kind of reasoning is common. However, it is also very difficult to defend. First, note that Scully's injection of stem cells from one body into another seems eerily close to what the Russians are attempting. Regardless of how close the analogy is, Scully's treatment still smacks of being unnatural. Extracting cells from one person and injecting them into another simply doesn't occur naturally. So, it's not clear that this response will sufficiently distinguish Scully's treatment from the Russians.

A deeper problem with the unnatural response remains. As the example about stem-cell therapy begins to suggest, it is not entirely clear what counts as being unnatural. Two definitions are regularly proposed. First, something is unnatural if it corresponds to behavior that is statistically infrequent. What happens regularly—as a matter of course—is natural and what doesn't happen regularly is unnatural. Second, something is unnatural if it contravenes a thing's primary function. The eye's primary function is to see, and the primary function of teeth is to chew food. But both definitions lead to counterintuitive results. The first makes doing theoretical physics or speaking Sanskrit unnatural and, thus, morally wrong. The second, even if it is granted that things have primary purposes, makes winking and opening packages with your teeth unnatural and, thus, morally wrong. Because doing theoretical physics, speaking Sanskrit, winking, or opening packages with your teeth is not morally wrong, it follows that neither of the proposed definitions for being unnatural is successful.[14]

We believe that a different response is more defensible. Quite simply, the Russians conduct their treatments by failing to respect the rights of innocent persons. It is universally believed that knowingly taking the life of an innocent person (especially that of a healthy person against her will) is a hallmark of impermissible behavior. Scully, it seems, does no such thing in treating Christian.[15] There is a lingering philosophical concern that Scully causes unnecessary harm (pain and suffering) to Christian by conducting these treatments. This is, perhaps, where concerns about evidentialism again emerge. If there is evidence neither that the treatments will work nor that they won't, then (the argument goes) Scully impermissibly causes Christian harm. However, it is important that Scully gets consent from the patient or his surrogates, in this case, his parents. Again, Doggett's memory of his son is relevant, and Mrs. Fearon clearly concurs, as she asks Scully, "You're saying that you can save my son?" Even Scully's colleagues who disagree with her decision to proceed with the radical stem-cell therapy demur when Scully asks, "What if it were your son?" Can a parent's personal commitment to the life of his or her child necessarily be improper if it is chosen on insufficient evidence?[16]

Mulder, Scully, Aristotle, and Friendship

Although all of us are concerned about the end of our earthly lives, there are, obviously, concerns to face along the way. We want our lives to go as well as possible. Many believe that a full life includes genuine and meaningful relationships. But even here, there are elements of uncertainty. How well do we know anyone? Do we know anyone well enough to determine whether our friendship with him or her is genuine? Many of us want to believe that our close relationships are genuine and, thus, able to withstand hardship or even temporary separation. Some of us pledge ourselves exclusively to another, pinning our hopes on true friendship. What evidence is there to justify the belief that a friendship is genuine? If there is evidence supporting genuineness but also evidence to the contrary, what should we believe? Do we simply weigh the evidence and let it determine the fate of the friendship? But is genuine and meaningful friendship possible if you are incessantly weighing the evidence to see whether the other person is being a friend?

The nature of friendship has long been a topic of philosophical discussion. At first this seems odd. Why would philosophers worry about something that is so obvious? We assume we know what friendship is, how to identify it, and how to judge its worthiness. For example, in *I Want to Believe,* it seems rather obvious that Walter Skinner (Mitch Pileggi) acts as a worthy friend when he comes to Mulder's rescue at Scully's request, despite the risks to his personal safety and possibly even his professional well-being. But once we remind ourselves that we have different kinds of friends, and that our friendships come in varying degrees, we soon see that understanding the nature of friendship can get a bit tricky. Moreover, some people claim to be "the best of friends." But what does this actually mean? What kind of friendship is best, anyway? Aristotle tried to answer questions like these in his *Nicomachean Ethics*. Indeed, he devotes two full books to the nature of friendship, and in doing so distinguishing its true form from two lower forms.[17]

The first of the lower forms of friendship is that based on pleasure. Friendships of this type are made and sustained because they "feel good" or are fun in some way—for example, a drinking buddy or tennis partner. Aristotle is certainly not claiming that true friendships shouldn't give us pleasure or that we shouldn't engage in fun activities with true friends. He is only claiming that friendships that are based primarily on pleasure are of a lower form. One reason for this is rather obvious: pleasure friendships tend not to last once the fun is gone or something better comes along. We can rather easily rule out pleasure friendship as the type that best describes the relationship between Scully and Mulder. Neither one of them seems to have much fun alone, much less together, and, in any event, there is clearly something deeper between them.

The second of the lower forms of friendship is that based on utility. Friendships of this type are made and sustained because they are useful or profitable to us in some way—for example, a business partnership. Again, even true friendships can be useful to us, but here Aristotle has in mind those friendships based primarily on utility. As with pleasure friendships, utility friendships are easily dissolved once the other is no longer useful to us and, as such, constitute a lower form of friendship. Some friendships in *The X-Files* are arguably like this. Perhaps Deep Throat (Jerry Hardin) and Mulder are friends of this sort—assuming that they are friends at all. Perhaps Alex Krycek (Nicholas Lea) and Marita Covarrubias (Laurie Holden) have this kind of friendship, even though it also became physical (and, thus, perhaps also qualifies as friendship for pleasure). We might conceivably place Scully and Mulder in this category of friendship based on a few early episodes—say, if Mulder merely relied on Scully's expertise in doing autopsies or Scully merely saw her partnership with Mulder as a stepping-stone in her career. However, their relationship clearly develops into something much more—even by the end of the first season, we can see that they are more than mere partners in the FBI.

According to Aristotle, the best friendships are not based merely on pleasure or utility. True friendship is a relationship between good people, each of whom recognizes the good character of the other, and each of whom desires to preserve and promote the other's virtue simply because it is good to do so. True friendship occurs between equals—a relationship in which one person is vastly superior to the other in moral virtue is more likely a paternalistic relationship than a true friendship. Unlike pleasure and utility friendships, true friendships must involve a genuine caring for the well-being of the other person, not merely egoistic motives. Of course, that doesn't mean that one may not consider how the friendship affects one's own interests—Aristotle is not advocating slavishness or radical self-sacrifice. It just means that one cares about the other person for his or her own sake and wants to see the other person flourish, regardless of any benefit that one might also receive as a result. Nevertheless, Aristotle does believe as a matter of fact that true friendships are beneficial to those involved. In that way, true friendship involves a happy convergence of self-interest and altruism and, as such, results in an ideal kind of moral motivation.

So, for Aristotle, the highest form of friendship occurs between persons of roughly equally good moral character (virtue) that is enhanced in various ways due to their interactions. They spend a great deal of time together, participate in joint ventures, and engage in activities that exercise their own virtues for the betterment of the other and the friendship. All of this is done primarily for the sake of the other person (and not for selfish purposes), even though their interests have grown so close together that it is difficult to separate one's good from that of the other.[18] That is true friendship. Sound like anyone we (X-Philes) know?

That the relationship between Mulder and Scully satisfies Aristotle's conditions for true friendship arguably begins with "Memento Mori." The episode opens with Scully's voice-over; we are privileged to hear some of Scully's innermost thoughts and feelings as she faces the very real prospect of losing her battle with cancer. Much of her soliloquy concerns the issue we'd expect—fear of death—but it's also revealing how her thoughts turn to Mulder. Scully thinks of Mulder as an equal partner on an important journey of shared values and trusts him as one can only trust the closest of confidantes, someone with shared values and a mutual concern for the other's well-being. Also note Mulder's resounding refusal to accept that Scully's cancer is terminal. Mulder goes to great lengths to find a cure and considers making a deal with CSM (William Davis). He expresses his passion and determination for Scully, not because he is merely fond of her phone voice or fears that no one else will perform all the autopsies he requests, but simply for her own sake. Scully reciprocates in "Sixth Extinction" (season 7). Mulder has been beset by a mysterious and mentally-debilitating illness after encountering an alien artifact. Scully continues the investigation without him, in part for the hope of curing him and in part to continue his work, despite her own doubts. She perseveres for Mulder and utilizes her unique traits for their joint pursuit of "the truth." She does so on her own terms—as a scientist—because she believes that "in the source of every illness lies its cure." But she does this for Mulder's sake—not for any glory of discovering a cure to his fantastic illness. Indeed Mulder and Scully regularly act on the behalf of the other, thereby satisfying one of the conditions Aristotle requires for true friendship.

Our intrepid heroes have also strengthened each other, shoring up their virtuous character traits. Recall that in *Fight the Future*, Scully visits Mulder's apartment to tell him she has resigned from the FBI. In pleading for her not to quit, Mulder replies: "But you saved me! As difficult and as frustrating as it's been sometimes, your goddamned strict rationalism and science have saved me a thousand times over! You've kept me honest . . . you've made me a whole person." Mulder recognizes that he has gained a kind of temperance through his relationship with Scully and is a better investigator—and person—for it. But Mulder has also strengthened Scully. In "Empedocles," Scully confides in Mulder that the greatest gift he has given her is courage—courage to accept the possibility of unexplained phenomena. Before she met Mulder, she was afraid to reexamine her worldview and, thus, simply rejected any experience that didn't fit it. She now wishes to impart this gift to her new X-Files partner, John Doggett. As a result of her relationship with Mulder, Scully is a better investigator—and person. Thus, another of Aristotle's conditions is met.

Mulder and Scully's joint venture of seeking the truth "out there" has also led to the intertwining of their individual goods into one, unified good. Going back to *Fight the Future*, after Mulder suggests (near the end of the film) that she was right to quit, Scully replies, "I can't. I won't. Mulder, I'll be a doctor, but my work is here with you now. That virus that I was exposed to, whatever it is, it has a cure. You held it in your hand. How many other lives can we save? Look . . . If I quit now, they win." Mulder's quest has become her work, too. Their work requires, and deserves, complete solidarity. This solidarity reaches its pinnacle in "Sixth Extinction: Amor Fati" (season 7), and the penultimate scene is especially telling. Mulder is trapped in his own mind. Either as a result of the illness from which he suffers, or an insidious plan hatched by the CSM (or both), Mulder is tempted to give up his search for the truth in exchange for the (false) comforts of a "normal" suburban life, complete with Samantha, a wife (Diana Fowley!), and children. Scully arrives and somehow taps into Mulder's psyche. She calls him a "traitor, deserter, and coward." She tells him to get up and continue his "true mission." He must "fight the fight." She soon becomes desperate and pleads with him: "No one can do it but you, Mulder. Mulder, help me." He finally regains consciousness, only to see Scully standing over him in a Department of Defense medical room, and hoarsely rasps, "You . . . help . . . me." The episode concludes with a shaken Scully visiting a mending Mulder. She is confused and uncertain of what exactly happened. She is no longer sure who to trust or, even, what the truth is. Mulder confides in her: "Scully, I was like you once. I didn't know who to trust. Then I . . . I chose another path . . . another life, another fate, where I found my sister. The end of my world was unrecognizable and upside down. There was one thing that remained the same. You were my friend, and you told me the truth. Even when the world was falling apart, you were my constant . . . my touchstone." She replies, "And you are mine." Thus it seems clear that the interests of these virtuous persons have become intricately linked, and their bond strengthens them.

By season 9, Mulder and Scully can only be separated by distance. For their own good and that of their son, William, they decide to temporarily part, but even this becomes a source of strength. That this is so is poetically embodied in Scully's voice-over from "TrustNo1":

> Know there is an answer, my child, a sacred imperishable truth, but one you may never hope to find alone. Chance meeting your perfect other, your perfect opposite—your protector and endangerer. Chance embarking with this other on the greatest of journeys—a search for truths fugitive and imponderable. If one day this chance may befall you, my son, do not fail or falter to seize it. . . . You will learn the truth is not found in science, or on some unseen plane, but by looking into your own heart. And in that moment you will be blessed—and stricken. For the truest truths are what hold us together, or keep us painfully, desperately apart.

In words meant for her infant son, Scully tells of knowing truths that can only be discovered through the perfect other. And even though embarking on and sustaining this sort of friendship inherently involves risk and personal commitment that doesn't fit neatly into the evidentialist program, Scully reaffirms what Aristotle knew long ago: a life fulfilled with true friendship is worth the risk.

Having established this sort of idyllic relationship, the early scenes of *I Want to Believe* come as a bit of a shock. Mulder and Scully's relationship here seems far from idyllic. Strain on it is evident from their first scene together. In attempting to convince Mulder to help with the Monica Bannan case, Scully says, "Wouldn't you like to step out into the sunshine again, Mulder? Wouldn't it be nice if we *both* could? Together?" Mulder eventually responds, "I'm fine, Scully. Happy as a clam here."[19] It seems that their interests are no longer closely intertwined. Mulder doesn't seem to grasp the force of her question: togetherness. Furthermore, Scully approaches Mulder about the Bannan case apprehensively. She believes that it is the right thing to do. She also believes that getting Mulder out of the house will be good for him. Being involved with a paranormal case may even reenergize him, bringing back some of the passion, courage, and determination that once defined him. But she also fears that it isn't right for him to be out chasing monsters in the dark again. It may reignite his obsessive tendencies, especially with respect to the misguided notion of saving Samantha. Thus, Scully's choice is risky. Are there any relevant evidentiary considerations to guide her here? This is difficult to say. She is already deeply committed to Mulder. What of her new personal commitment to keep the darkness away from the home that they now share?

As it turned out, Mulder's obsessive tendencies became problematic as a result of his consulting on the Bannan case. It seemed as if he couldn't help but keep searching in the dark wherever Father Joe's visions led. But this time, Scully didn't impart temperance to Mulder. Rather, she starkly tells him to leave the case; it is no longer his job to search out monsters in the dark. Maybe he could write a book about it? When Mulder gently scoffs at these suggestions—reminding Scully that seeking the truth wherever it might lead is part of who he is—she not-so-subtly threatens that she won't be coming home. The Scully of old would never react this way. This is more evidence that living under the same roof has actually caused them to grow further apart. Because this is reminiscent of so many relationships, we again can see how Mulder and Scully have become more like us. All of us have faced a difficult fork in the road after traveling so long with the same companion. What should they do? Should they give up? What evidentiary considerations are relevant to this choice?[20]

Throughout the movie, it is never quite clear whether Father Joe's "Don't give up" refers to Scully's attempt to cure Christian or Mulder and Scully's involvement in the Bannan case. But it seems to equally apply to Mulder and Scully and their relationship. But perhaps all three threads weave together. Should Mulder decide to remain involved in the Bannan case—seeking the truth out there—he must be mindful of Scully's protests to the contrary. In being reinvigorated by Mulder's passion, courage, and determination, Scully more effectively proceeds with Christian's treatments. As a result, their relationship is renewed, as intimated by the first signs of spring at the end of the movie. Mulder and Scully have made it past one of the darkest, coldest winters of their relationship and have found each other again. Their passing from the dark of winter to the renewal of spring is dramatized by Carter's decision to include the rowboat scene after the credits. Because they didn't give up on each other, we see Mulder and Scully in the warm tropical sun, literally basking in their being away from the darkness (at least for a while).

Mulder's choice to escape the darkness with Scully is actually quite significant because it now seems that he can either "fight the fight" and continue his "true mission" of seeking the truth out there, or he can nurture his relationship with Scully, but no longer can he do both. Presumably, the truths he pursues now—those of his "own heart"—are in competition with seeking the truths "out there." Which personal commitment should he pursue? How could evidentialism decide this for him? Note that his choice is not unlike Scully's hesitation to inform Mulder of the missing FBI agent in the first place. She misses her "perfect other"; Mulder has become someone else holed up in his makeshift office. But to find him again, she must risk reawakening her "endangerer" and face all the psychological and physical perils of searching for monsters in the dark. It is interesting that both characters decided to pursue the truths of the heart—to nurture their Aristotelian friendship. Paradoxically, might the most elusive but important truths—the "truest truths"—only be found by looking within oneself? Is this the truth "out there" that Mulder has finally found?[21]

Of Rowboats and *X-Files* Philosophy

But what should X-Philes make of the now famous (or infamous) rowboat scene? Let's quickly consider the evidence. It certainly looked as if Scully was waving goodbye to the X-Phile viewers. Perhaps our intrepid heroes were literally sailing off into the sunset? This conjecture is strengthened in retrospect by the fact that the film didn't do very well at the box office. But that scene was oddly filmed. The X-Phile viewer could see a helicopter shadow on the water in the shots leading up to it. If Scully was waving to some sort of omniscient perceiver above (us in the theater), why allow the helicopter shadow into the shot? Perhaps this is explained by shoddy or rushed camera work? But why not edit it out later? Furthermore, many X-Philes claimed to see a submerged "X," noticeable to the careful eye beneath the rowboat. Why include this imagery? Might we thus contend that the X-Files has found Mulder and Scully again, as signified by the submerged "X," and Scully is waiving to (perhaps) Skinner in a helicopter just before he lands and again asks for their assistance? If the evidence does not sufficiently warrant believing one hypothesis over the other, how should we (the X-Phile viewers) proceed? Perhaps our personal commitment to *The X-Files* allows us to take action? Perhaps being committed to the possibility of a third movie—not giving up on seeing our heroes again—is not only permissible in this case, but also beneficial? Once again, Chris Carter has left us hanging.

'Ihis essay admittedly provides as many questions as it answers.[22] Certainly, evidentialists like Schick and Vaughn would welcome the opportunity to respond to it. But ending the book in this way follows the modus operandi of *The X-Files* itself: you, the reader, are invited to ponder questions about evidence, belief, and commitment, thereby beginning to determine "the truth" yourself. Nevertheless, this essay achieves (we think) one goal: it articulates what *the* philosophy of *The X-Files* might be. It seems that there are or might be times when evidentiary considerations don't sufficiently justify one competing hypothesis over another. In such cases, we aren't sure which to believe. But we may want to believe one of them over another. How should we proceed? The answer we seem to get from *The X-Files* is this: so long as we have honestly and carefully weighed the available evidence and remain open to new evidentiary findings, we may choose to follow our personal commitments, knowing our own hearts so long as we do not violate any obvious, "common-sense" ethical constraints in doing so. Our personal commitments should not run contrary to insurmountable evidence, and we should not choose to harm innocent people. And, short of these two qualifiers, we should not give up on our personal commitments.[23]

Notes

Thanks go to X-Phile Natalie Floeh and (especially) Frank Spotnitz for sharing their respective ideas and insights about *The X-Files* and *I Want to Believe*. Natalie read and commented on a draft of the essay, and Frank took time out of his busy schedule to aptly field my various *X-Files* and philosophy–related questions.

1. This is per the novelization; see Max Allan Collins (based on the screenplay by Chris Carter and Frank Spotnitz), *The X-Files: I Want to Believe* (New York: HarperCollins, 2008), 24.

2. In conversation, Frank Spotnitz confirmed that he and Chris Carter intended to leave the villains of *I Want to Believe* with underdeveloped characters. They thought that too much time spent developing the Russians' backstories and motivations would take away from the main storyline, which was the relationship between Mulder and Scully. *I Want to Believe* is thus similar to the season 8 episode "Alone," which Spotnitz wrote and directed. The reptilian monster in "Alone" (as Spotnitz fully intended) took a backseat to the dramatic interactions among Mulder, Scully, and Doggett. As a monster of the week episode, "Alone" is far from extraordinary. However, it is a rather moving character study of the evolution of the X-Files team. We argue that *I Want to Believe* is best interpreted as an episode like "Alone" rather than more archetypical "monster of the week" episodes like "Squeeze," "The Host," or "Home."

3. Natalie Floeh is concerned that I have overstated this point. She argues that the predominantly negative reviews and commentary found on Internet Movie Database (http://www.imdb.com/title/tt0443701/board, last accessed on October 8, 2008) are counterbalanced by the positive reviews found on http://www.xfilesultimate.com and http://www.biglight.com/blog (both last accessed October 8, 2008). She wonders whether a majority of the negative response to the movie cannot be explained away by fans of the show who became disillusioned with it in the latter seasons.

4. The novelization contains a scene deleted from the movie. The scene involves Scully finding Father Joe in her young patient's hospital room. Scully is horrified. But when she barges into the room, Father Joe is merely attempting to comfort the boy in his suffering. The patient looks up at Scully and says, "It's okay, Dr. Scully. He didn't do anything bad. He's nice. Sad . . . but nice" (188).

5. This sentiment was arguably first raised in "Memento Mori," as Scully (in a voice-over) reassures Mulder: "If the darkness should have swallowed me as you read this, you must never think there was the possibility of some secret intervention, something you might have done." Undoubtedly, if Mulder believes that there was something more he could have done to spare Scully's life, he surely would believe himself to be a failure. This is why Scully preventively assures him of the contrary.

6. In the end, it's not immediately clear how Mulder's view—the idea that evil is some sort of supernatural or non-natural disease that we become susceptible to in times of stress or loss—is all that different from the more straightforward or conventional psychological explanation involving "stressors" voiced by Reyes. Perhaps the difference is the level of depravity Mulder has witnessed working violent crimes. Perhaps Mulder wonders whether any human being, without being "infected" with something that isn't human, could do the sorts of monstrous things that he's seen. In this way,

Mulder hypothesizes that the scientific explanation can only take us so far. At some point, we must begin looking elsewhere for an adequate explanation. Without commenting on the plausibility of Mulder's theory in this case, suffice it to say that that the theme of science only taking us so far (obviously) pervades the entire series, beginning with "Pilot."

7. Interestingly, on the rare occasion that Mulder is not sufficiently mindful of the evidence (regarding Samantha or the infamous ectoplasm hypothesis in "all things" [season 7]), he clearly seems to be misguided in ways analogous to Blaine Faulkner (which is probably the connection Darin Morgan wanted us to make in the first place). This is either a case of obsession clouding his judgment (Samantha), or simple investigative laziness (ectoplasm). What is more interesting, we think, is that these instances are clearly the exception to the rule (contra Darin Morgan), which make Mulder's character so intriguing.

8. Theodore Schick and Lewis Vaughn, *How to Think about Weird Things: Critical Thinking for a New Age,* 4th ed. (New York: McGraw-Hill, 2005), 123. (See pages 12–13 for another affirmation of believing with the evidence and pages 72–73 for commentary that sounds strikingly similar to Scully's view of the paranormal in "Pilot.") Interestingly, on page 38, Schick and Vaughn seemingly describe Mulder in his more Blaine Faulkner–like moments: "Part of the task of critically evaluating an unusual claim is to control our tendency to believe or disbelieve without good reason. For some people, the need to believe in paranormal phenomena is very strong—so strong that in some cases people have refused to accept the confessions of others, who admit (and sometimes demonstrate) that their paranormal feats are fraudulent."

9. For more on questions like these, see "'I Want to Believe': William James and *The X-Files,*" by Keith Dromm in this volume.

10. For an argument that we must add at least a non-natural element, see "Science and the Mystery of Consciousness: A Dialogue between Mulder and Scully," by Gordon Barnes in this volume.

11. John Hick, *An Interpretation of Religion: Human Responses to the Transcendent* (New Haven: Yale University Press, 1989), esp. 73–125.

12. In an incredibly thoughtful review, blog critic John Kenneth Muir has also seen the importance of redemption in *I Want to Believe.* See his "Reflections on Film/ TV" at http://reflectionsonfilmandtelevision.blogspot.com/2008_07_27_archive.html (site last accessed August 24, 2008). My thanks go to Natalie Floeh for sending me the link to Muir's site.

13. Some have wondered why Carter and Spotnitz decided to write this couple as Russian. It's tempting to argue that this is just a cold war holdover, but another answer is available. The kind of Dr. Frankenstein research conveyed in the movie was, in fact, seemingly pursued in Russia circa 1940. (See http://www.archive.org/details/ Experime1940, last accessed September 1, 2008.) So, it is plausible to assume that Russians would explore this kind of treatment.

14. The quick analysis of being unnatural expressed in this paragraph is indebted to Burton M. Leisure, *Liberty, Justice, and Morals: Contemporary Value Conflicts,* 3rd ed. (Upper Saddle River, N.J.: Prentice Hall, 1986), 51–57.

15. We assume that the stem cells Scully uses are obtained via umbilical cord blood and are not embryonic. In fact, as Scully works at a Catholic hospital, it seems certain that they could not be embryonic. Consequently, any relevant philosophical qualms about abortion are circumvented.

16. We admit that, at some level, ethical disputes appear to be intractable. However, there are many issues about which there is very little (or no) disagreement. Consequently, "commonsense" morality seems equipped to provide a sort of constraint on the personal commitments we make when the evidence among competing hypotheses isn't decisive.

17. See books 8 and 9 of Aristotle's *Nicomachean Ethics,* trans. David Ross (Oxford: Oxford University Press, 1998).

18. This paragraph (but not the three preceding it) is indebted to Richard Kraut's discussion of Aristotle's ethics (section 9), which can be found online at the Stanford Encyclopedia of Philosophy. See http://plato.stanford.edu/entries/aristotle-ethics/#Fri (site accessed September 1, 2008). (We thought that we would provide you an example of sound scholarship that is done via the Internet—even Google—rather than simply admit that we also use the Internet in our research; the trick is figuring out which sites are trustworthy and which aren't—sound familiar?)

19. This is per the novelization, page 24.

20. Evidentiary considerations do play a role in assessing friendships. If your partner routinely ignores your interests, then it's clear that he (or she) is not a true friend. However, there are elements of friendship that, given the level of personal commitment involved, don't fit neatly into the evidentialist program. The trick is to determine how much of friendship fits it and how much is left over to adjudicate in other ways.

21. Thanks go to Natalie Floeh for the suggestion to develop Mulder's character transformation in this way.

22. In this way, it is more like William Schneider's "Ancient X-Files" essay than it is Gordon Barnes's "Science and the Mystery of Consciousness" or Dean Kowalski's "'Clyde Bruckman's Final Repose' Reprised 2009."

23. This imperative has been a philosophical staple (even if not the only staple) of the *X-Files* corpus. Scully tells Mulder not to give up in the parking garage scene of "Little Green Men" in season 2, and the Lone Gunmen say the same to their associates at the end of "Jump the Shark" in season 9. But it is one thing to correctly articulate what someone's philosophical doctrines are; it is another thing to ask whether those doctrines can plausibly withstand the assessment of others. Each philosophical doctrine should be properly evaluated for plausibility. Whether the imperative here would require revision after a proper evidentialist critique remains to be seen.

Appendix A
The X-Files Mythology

In July 1947, at a site in Roswell, New Mexico, it is reported that the U.S. military engaged in a salvage mission of a crashed alien vessel. Although contradictory stories emerge as to whether this incident was real or merely a dodge concocted to divert attention from other covert operations, it is around this time that members of a clandestine order known as the Syndicate, operating on behalf of government and economic interests around the world, made contact with extraterrestrials. It was through this contact that the Syndicate was informed of an extraterrestrial plot to colonize Earth, and it was revealed that alien colonists were Earth's original inhabitants. The origin of all life on the planet, it was discovered, was extraterrestrial, stemming from microorganisms on a meteor that struck Earth millions of years earlier. Subsequently, also before human history, aliens traveled to Earth to study it for potential colonization. However, the coming of the Ice Age forced the aliens to depart, leaving a command ship and its crew hidden and dormant in Antarctica. The aliens were now returning to put into motion a full-scale colonization of the planet, which would result in the complete extermination of all human life.

The Syndicate agreed to collaborate with the alien colonists in exchange for safe haven during colonization. The aliens would use the Syndicate as their operatives on Earth, so as to continue to hide knowledge of their colonization plans. Additionally, the Syndicate would help the aliens develop a population of alien-human hybrids that would constitute a new race of slaves to serve the colonists upon their arrival. The rest of humanity would be used as a host for a virus known as the "black oil," a virus that infects the human body, turning the host into a gelatinous substance and killing it so that it might be used to feed the gestating alien life form until it matured.

The collaboration between the Syndicate and alien colonists was implemented under the working title of "The Method," which drew upon the horrific eugenics experiments performed in World War II concentration camps by Nazi doctors who were granted immunity for war crimes by the allied powers to continue their experiments. In exchange for alien biomaterial needed to carry out experimentation on human ova, Syndicate members allowed the aliens to abduct members of their families, who would be released back to them upon the successful creation of an alien-human fetus that would provide the genetic materials necessary for the creation of the slave race.

While working on the development of the hybrid, the Syndicate began conducting its own secret experiments under the code name Purity Control to develop a vaccine that would make its members immune to the effects of the black oil. Such experiments made the secrecy of their existence and operations all the more vital, as they had to keep the alien colonization plot hidden from humanity, and the effort to develop the vaccine hidden from the alien colonists. Soon, although maintaining their ties and access to the governments of Earth they once served, members of this shadow agency began to operate independently, with no accountability to any single government or organization.

In December 1991, Agent Fox Mulder of the Federal Bureau of Investigation was assigned to work on a series of unsolved, unexplained cases known as the X-Files. His work, which includes an investigation into the abduction of his sister, Samantha, leads him on to the path of discovering the truth about extraterrestrials and the covert work of the Syndicate. The danger Agent Mulder poses to their secret operations prompts members of the Syndicate to assign Agent Dana Scully, a medical officer, to use established scientific knowledge to debunk Agent Mulder's investigations into the paranormal. Although the two agents are initially skeptical of each other, in time they begin to develop a deep mutual trust, which only serves to increase their effectiveness as investigators.

In the course of their work on the X-Files, Mulder and Scully begin to peel back the layers of secrecy insulating the Syndicate. This magnifies the threat of exposure of the organization, which must maintain control over its covert operations. The tensions within the Syndicate begin to mount as a power struggle among its members threatens their cohesion and singular purpose in furthering their work. Agent Mulder is even contacted by members of the Syndicate and given information to assist him with his quest for the truth about the existence of extraterrestrials.

Soon Mulder and Scully find how deep the conspiracy to withhold the truth from the world truly runs; they discover that the abductions of thousands of humans can be linked to the eugenics tests overseen by the Syndicate. They also discover a complex catalog of human DNA compiled during the administration of smallpox vaccinations that could be used to identify and track individuals and test subjects. The Syndicate employs a program a disinformation to conceal its work. The Syndicate's members even twist the truth about the existence of extraterrestrials into a story so fantastical as not to be believed, making it easier for them to continue testing abductees without fear of exposure.

Work on the X-Files reveals to Mulder and Scully the truth not only about alien life but also about humanity itself. They discover that humankind — its physiology, religious beliefs, and social and political institutions and arrangements — can be traced to extraterrestrial origins. In their pursuit of the reality behind our reality, the agents are pulled into a multifarious plot that runs beyond borders and outside the scope of any recognized governmental agency. It is then that they discover that the Syndicate is working with the alien colonists to bring about a total genocide of humankind and that the timetable for colonization is set. When the date arrives, the Syndicate will seize control of the entire social order by declaring a state of emergency and using the power of established agencies like the Federal Emergency Management Agency in the United States. By then, Agents Mulder and Scully would be powerless to prevent the holocaust of humankind.

The date of colonization was foretold in the last entry on the traditional Mayan calendar: December 22, 2012 . . .

Joseph J. Foy

The X-Files Debriefed

(September 10, 1993–June 19, 1998)

SEASON 1

Pilot (1X79)

Story: Chris Carter
Director: Robert Mandel

Dana Scully is assigned to her new partner, "Spooky" Fox Mulder, to debunk his work on the so-called X-Files.

This episode implicitly raises philosophical issues associated with abductive inference. (See the first chapter, "Truth Is Out There.")

Deep Throat (1X01)

Story: Chris Carter
Director: Daniel Sackheim

A mysterious informant approaches Mulder to caution him against investigating a U.S. military base.

(This episode is featured in "Postdemocratic Society and the Truth Out There" and elsewhere.)

Squeeze (1X02)

Story: Glen Morgan and James Wong
Director: Harry Longstreet

Genetic mutant Eugene Victor Tooms is the prime suspect in a series of gruesome murders; Scully faces ridicule about her new post from a former colleague.

(This episode is featured in "Science and the Mystery of Consciousness" and elsewhere.)

Conduit (1X03)

Story: Alex Gansa and Howard Gordon
Director: Daniel Sackheim

While investigating the alleged abduction of a teenage girl, Mulder relives the pain of losing his sister.

The Jersey Devil (1X04)

Story: Chris Carter
Director: Joe Napolitano

Mulder and Scully investigate Bigfoot-type sightings in the Atlantic City area.

Shadows (1X05)

Story: Glen Morgan and James Wong
Director: Michael Katleman

Someone is protecting a young office worker; Mulder suspects that it is her deceased boss.

This episode raises the philosophical issues of disembodied existence and interactionism between physical and nonphysical entities.

Ghost in the Machine (1X06)

Story: Alex Gansa and Howard Gordon
Director: Jerrold Freedman

In a seeming homage to Kubrick's *2001*, Mulder and Scully investigate a strange murder at a research development company.

This episode raises issues in the philosophy of mind, including artificial intelligence, machine consciousness, and personhood. (See "Science and the Mystery of Consciousness" for other issues relevant to the philosophy of mind.)

Ice (1X07)

Story: Glen Morgan and James Wong
Director: David Nutter

Mulder and Scully clash over what ought to be done with a parasite found deep in the ice north of the Arctic Circle.

This episode raises philosophical issues pertaining to axiological and normative issues in scientific research. (This episode is featured in "Science and the Mystery of Consciousness.")

Space (1X08)

Story: Chris Carter
Director: William Graham

A NASA official relives the horrors he once faced as an astronaut.

This episode broaches the philosophical debate over whether it is ever permissible to be dishonest and, if so, when.

Fallen Angel (1X09)

Story: Howard Gordon and Alex Gansa
Director: Larry Shaw

Deep Throat informs Mulder of a UFO that has allegedly crashed near Townsend, Wisconsin.

Eve (1X10)

Story: Kenneth Biller and Chris Brancato
Director: Fred Gerber

Deep Throat informs Mulder of the Lynchfield Experiments—an attempt to clone and genetically engineer human beings during the cold war.

This episode raises philosophical issues germane to biomedical ethics: are cloning and genetic engineering ever permissible and, if so, when?

Fire (1X11)

Story: Chris Carter
Director: Larry Shaw

When British Parliament members begin spontaneously combusting, Mulder receives a visit from his old flame during his Oxford days.

This episode raises philosophical issues pertinent to mental causation and interactionism.

Beyond the Sea (1X12)

Story: Glen Morgan and James Wong
Director: David Nutter

As Scully mourns her father, incarcerated serial killer Luther Lee Boggs contacts Mulder claiming to have psychic knowledge of new homicides.

This episode raises issues pertaining to life after bodily death and disembodied existence. (This episode is featured in "Scully as Pragmatist Feminist.")

Gender Bender (1X13)

Story: Larry Barber and Paul Barber
Director: Rob Bowman

Strange events surrounding a metropolitan murder lead Mulder and Scully to a secretive, rural religious community.

Lazarus (1X14)

Story: Alex Gansa and Howard
    Gordon
Director: David Nutter

Scully aids a fellow FBI agent—who is also her former lover—in tracking down two bank robbers; the agent then undergoes a radical personality shift.

This episode raises the philosophical issues of reincarnation and the alleged possibility of "body switches." (This episode is featured in "Freedom and Worldviews in The X-Files.*")*

Young at Heart (1X15)

Story: Scott Kaufer and Chris Carter
Director: Michael Lange

Mulder's past catches up with him when a criminal seemingly returns from the grave to exact his revenge.

This episode raises philosophical issues pertaining to axiological and normative issues in scientific research.

E.B.E. (1X16)

Story: Glen Morgan and James Wong
Director: William Graham

Deep Throat purposely sends Mulder and Scully on a wild-goose chase regarding a downed UFO; the Lone Gunmen make their first appearance.

Miracle Man (1X17)

Story: Howard Gordon and Chris
    Carter
Director: Michael Lange

Mulder and Scully are led to Tennessee to investigate a young religious man with the power to heal by laying on of hands.

Shapes (1X18)

Story: Marilyn Osborn
Director: David Nutter

Strange events at an Indian reservation in Montana prompt Muller to reopen the very first X-File.

Darkness Falls (1X19)

Story: Chris Carter
Director: Joe Napolitano

Mulder and Scully are trapped in a forest with light as their only protection from unknown insects.

This episode raises philosophical issues germane to environmental ethics: What reasons are there for protecting our environment, and to what lengths ought we to go in order to protect it?

Tooms (1X20)

Story: Glen Morgan and James Wong
Director: David Nutter

Victor Eugene Tooms is released from the psychiatric ward and plots his revenge against Mulder and Scully.

(This episode is featured in "Science and the Mystery of Consciousness.")

Born Again (1X21)

Story: Howard Gordon and Alex
   Gansa
Director: Jerrold Freedman

Mulder and Scully are called to Buffalo when a young girl manages to hurl a police officer out a window to his death.

This episode raises philosophical issues regarding reincarnation and personal identity.

Roland (1X22)

Story: Chris Ruppenthal
Director: David Nutter

Tragedy befalls a team of scientists attempting to develop a cutting-edge supersonic jet engine.

The Erlenmeyer Flask (1X23)

Story: Chris Carter
Director: R. W. Goodwin

When a scientist mysteriously disappears, Deep Throat tells Mulder that he has never been closer to the truth about the alien conspiracy.

This episode implicitly raises philosophical issues associated with pragmatism. (See "'I Want to Believe.'") It also raises philosophical issues related to ethics of trust and egoism. (See "Some Philosophical Reflections on 'Trust No One,'" which features this episode.)

SEASON 2

Little Green Men (2X01)

Story: Glen Morgan and James Wong
Director: David Nutter

Although the X-Files Unit has been officially dissolved and Mulder and Scully reassigned, Senator Matheson sends Mulder to a SETI listening post in Puerto Rico.

When explored in conjunction with "The Erlenmeyer Flask," this episode furthers the philosophical connection to pragmatism and the ethics of belief. (See "'I Want to Believe.'")

The Host (2X02)

Story: Chris Carter
Director: Daniel Sackheim

Mulder and Scully investigate a mutant humanoid fluke worm (played by Darin Morgan) trapped in a sewer system.

Blood (2X03)

Story: Darin Morgan, Glen Morgan,
   and James Wong
Director: David Nutter

Mulder suspects secret government tests when several inhabitants of a small New England town become violent.

This episode implicitly raises issues in political philosophy, including the government's proper role and relationship with society. (See "Postdemocratic Society and the Truth Out There.")

Sleepless (2X04)

Story: Howard Gordon
Director: Rob Bowman

Alex Krycek teams with Mulder when a sleep-disorder specialist dies, leading them to a sleepless Vietnam veteran with unique abilities.

Duane Barry (2X05)

Story: Chris Carter
Director: Chris Carter

Former FBI agent and alleged alien abductee Duane Barry escapes from a psychiatric ward, leading to Mulder's first hostage negotiation.

Ascension (2X06)

Story: Paul Brown
Director: Michael Lange

Duane Barry survives a bullet wound, escapes from the hospital, and takes Scully to the place he was first abducted; Skinner reopens the X-Files Unit.

(This episode is featured in "Walter Skinner" and elsewhere.)

3 (2X07)

Story: Chris Ruppenthal, Glen
   Morgan, and James Wong
Director: David Nutter

While Scully has mysteriously disappeared, Mulder investigates a case that presumably involves vampires.

One Breath (2X08)

Story: Glen Morgan and James Wong
Director: R. W. Goodwin

Scully is found at a hospital near death, and Mulder resorts to unofficial channels to discover what happened to her.

(This episode is featured in "Walter Skinner" and elsewhere.)

Firewalker (2X09)

Story: Howard Gordon
Director: David Nutter

A scientist enlists the help of Mulder and Scully to determine what happened to his colleagues inside a volcano.

Red Museum (2X10)

Story: Chris Carter
Director: Win Phelps

Mulder and Scully once again leave for Wisconsin, this time to investigate teenagers who mysteriously disappear only to be returned changed people.

This episode raises philosophical issues associated with animal rights and the ethics of vegetarianism. (This episode is featured in "Postdemocratic Society and the Truth Out There.")

Excelsis Dei (2X11)

Story: Paul Brown
Director: Stephen Surjik

At a convalescent home, Scully convinces Mulder to investigate a nurse's claim that she was raped by a ghost.

This episode raises several philosophical issues, including the ethics of death and dying, moral relativism, and interactionism.

Aubrey (2X12)

Story: Sara B. Charno
Director: Rob Bowman

When a young police officer unknowingly digs up the skeleton of a pioneering FBI agent from the 1950s, Mulder and Scully are led to reopen a forty-year-old serial murder case.

This episode raises the philosophical issue of human freedom and biological determinism. (See "Freedom and Worldviews in The X-Files.*")*

Irresistible (2X13)

Story: Chris Carter
Director: David Nutter

Scully is caught up in a psychopath's extreme fetishes of collecting the hair and fingernails of his female victims.

This episode raises (at least implicitly) philosophical issues relating to moral responsibility and the nature-versus-nurture debate.

Die Hand Die Verletzt (2X14)

Story: Glen Morgan and James Wong
Director: Kim Manners

After a boy is murdered in demonic, ritualistic fashion, Mulder and Scully are called to a town that seems entrenched in the occult.

Fresh Bones (2X15)

Story: Howard Gordan
Director: Rob Bowman

Suicidal tendencies among the soldiers housing Haitian immigrants put Mulder and Scully in the middle of a voodoo war.

This episode implicitly raises issues pertaining to moral relativism. (This episode is featured in "'I Want to Believe.'")

Colony (2X16)

Story: Chris Carter and David
    Duchovny
Director: Nick Marck

As Samantha seemingly appears at William Mulder's house, a shape-shifting alien bounty hunter is sent to quash a colony of renegade alien-hybrids.

This episode raises philosophical issues associated with biomedical ethics, most notably cloning and genetic engineering. (This episode is featured in "'I Want to Believe.'")

End Game (2X17)

Story: Frank Spotnitz
Director: Rob Bowman

In hopes of discovering the true whereabouts of his sister, Mulder tracks the alien bounty hunter to the Arctic Circle.

This episode raises philosophical issues pertaining to personal identity and psychological continuity.

Fearful Symmetry (2X18)

Story: Steven DeJarnatt
Director: James Whitmore Jr.

A rampaging invisible elephant leads Mulder and Scully to investigate a zoo that has never had one successful mating attempt among its animals.

This episode raises philosophical issues associated with animal rights and endangered species.

Død Kalm (2X19)

Story: Alex Gansa and Howard
Gordon
Director: Rob Bowman

When a twenty-eight-year-old naval officer dies of old age, Mulder convinces Scully to investigate an area of the North Atlantic that presumably contains a wrinkle in time.

This episode raises philosophical issues associated with ethical dilemmas involving limited resources, sometimes called "lifeboat" ethics. (This episode is featured in "Freedom and Worldviews in The X-Files."

Humbug (2X20)

Story: Darin Morgan
Director: Kim Manners

Mulder and Scully investigate an unusual string of murders involving carnival sideshow folk.

(This episode is featured in "Clyde Bruckman's Final Repose.")

The Calusari (2X21)

Story: Sara B. Charno
Director: Michael Vejar

Four Romanian holy men aid Mulder in removing a family from an evil influence.

F. Emasculata (2X22)

Story: Chris Carter and Howard
Gordon
Director: Rob Bowman

Mulder and Scully are sent to investigate a biological contagion mistakenly sent to a prison.

Soft Light (2X23)

Story: Vince Gilligan
Director: James Contner

A physicist experimenting with "dark matter" is cursed by his own success.

This episode raises philosophical questions pertaining to axiological and normative issues in scientific research.

Our Town (2X24)

Story: Frank Spotnitz
Director: Rob Bowman

An extremely rare brain disease afflicts workers at a chicken-processing plant.

Anasazi (2X25)

Story: Chris Carter and David
Duchovny
Director: R. W. Goodwin

A computer hacker provides Mulder a tape of top-secret data encrypted in

Navajo, leading him to a buried train car (and perhaps an untimely, fiery end) in the New Mexico desert.

SEASON 3

The Blessing Way (3X01)

Story: Chris Carter
Director: R. W. Goodwin

Mulder is rescued and healed according to ancient Navajo tradition by Albert Hosteen, as the Syndicate strives to retrieve the lost data tape.

(This episode is featured in "Post-democratic Society and the Truth Out There" and elsewhere.)

Paper Clip (3X02)

Story: Chris Carter
Director: Rob Bowman

With the help of a mysterious, well-manicured man, Mulder and Scully learn about operation "paper clip," an early attempt to develop alien-hybrid technology; Scully discovers that she was an unwitting participant in the current stages of the operation.

D.P.O. (3X03)

Story: Howard Gordon
Director: Kim Manners

A troubled teen acquires the ability to control lightning.

Clyde Bruckman's Final Repose (3X04)

Story: Darin Morgan
Director: David Nutter

A Minnesota insurance salesman's ability to foresee future deaths proves helpful to Mulder and Scully in their attempt to catch a serial killer.

This episode raises a variety of philosophical issues: freedom, fate, and foreknowledge and questions in epistemology generally. (See "Clyde Bruckman's Final Repose," which features this episode.)

The List (3X05)

Story: Chris Carter
Director: Chris Carter

A well-read death-row inmate vows vengeance from beyond the grave upon five people who mistreated him in this life.

This episode raises philosophical issues related to transmigration of the soul, reincarnation, and personal identity.

2SHY (3X06)

Story: Jeffrey Vlaming
Director: David Nutter

A genetic mutant who is also a translator of medieval Italian texts uses the Internet to meet women to ingest their fatty tissues.

The Walk (3X07)

Story: John Shiban
Director: Rob Bowman

A bitter quadriplegic Desert Storm veteran is somehow involved in a string of murders at the medical hospital where he resides.

This episode raises philosophical issues related to mind-body dualism.

Oubliette (3X08)

Story: Charles Grant Craig
Director: Kim Manners

A woman becomes psychically linked to a teenage girl when her abductor strikes again thirteen years later.

Nisei (3X09)

Story: Chris Carter, Howard Gordon, and Frank Spotnitz
Director: David Nutter

Mulder is warned by Skinner and X not to pursue a lead he discovers by ordering an alien autopsy video; Scully meets women who, like her, have had microchips extracted from their necks.

731 (3X10)

Story: Frank Spotnitz
Director: Rob Bowman

As Mulder pursues a Japanese scientist and the purported alien-hybrid the scientist created, the Syndicate assassin pursues all three of them.

Revelations (3X11)

Story: Kim Newton
Director: David Nutter

While Scully is investigating alleged stigmatics, her religious convictions lead her to believe in the veracity of the case even though Mulder is skeptical.

This episode raises philosophical issues associated with faith and reason and divine command theory ethics.

War of the Coprophages (3X12)

Story: Darin Morgan
Director: Kim Manners

Mulder stumbles on a small town dealing with a string of strange deaths all involving cockroaches; Mulder suspects extraterrestrial involvement even though Scully's scientific and psychological explanations seem persuasive.

(This episode is discussed in "The Many Tales of 'Jose Chung.'")

Syzygy (3X13)

Story: Chris Carter
Director: Kim Manners

After quickly debunking the local authority's demonic-cult theory, a perturbed Scully and a vexed Mulder attempt to solve murders involving two teenage girls who have the same birthday.

This episode implicitly raises philosophical issues associated with freedom and compatibilism. (See "Freedom and Worldviews in The X-Files.*")*

Grotesque (3X14)

Story: Howard Gordon
Director: Kim Manners

One of Mulder's mentors from the academy enlists Mulder's help to solve a string of murders involving gargoyles.

Piper Maru (3X15)

Story: Chris Carter and Frank Spotnitz
Director: Rob Bowman

A French salvage ship (sharing the same name as Gillian Anderson's daughter) uncovers a forty-year-old secret, and Mulder's nemesis, Alex Krycek, is responsible.

(This episode is featured in "The Truth Is Out There.")

Apocrypha (3X16)

Story: Frank Spotnitz and Chris Carter
Director: Kim Manners

The shapeless, "black oil" alien force inhabits Krycek's body, presenting problems for the Syndicate and the Cigarette Smoking Man; Scully finds the man who killed her sister.

This episode raises philosophical issues associated with personal identity and virtue ethics. (This episode is featured in "Moral Musings on a Cigarette Smoking Man.")

Pusher (3X17)

Story: Vince Gilligan
Director: Rob Bowman

Mulder matches wits with a man who has the power to control people merely by talking with them.

(This episode is featured in the introduction and "Clyde Bruckman's Final Repose.")

Teso Dos Bichos (3X18)

Story: John Shiban
Director: Kim Manners

When the bones of a South American shaman are excavated and sent to the United States, all those involved begin to die.

This episode raises philosophical issues associated with moral relativism.

Hell Money (3X19)

Story: Jeff Vlaming
Director: Tucker Gates

Mulder and Scully investigate a ghostly lottery with grave consequences in San Francisco's Chinatown.

This episode raises philosophical issues associated with autonomy, paternalism, and moral relativism.

Jose Chung's *From Outer Space* (3X20)

Story: Darin Morgan
Director: Rob Bowman

In an homage to *Rashomon*, an eccentric fiction writer interviews Scully about an alleged double alien abduction; Mulder fears that the writer's story trivializes his work.

This episode raises philosophical issues associated with truth, knowledge, objectivity, and existentialism and how these are interrelated. (See "The Many Tales of 'Jose Chung,'" which features this episode.)

Avatar (3X21)

Story: Howard Gordon and David Duchovny
Director: James Charleston

Skinner can't fully explain his involvement in events that may ruin his career; he is aided by a mysterious elderly woman.

This episode implicitly raises philosophical issues associated with virtue ethics. (See "Walter Skinner," which features this episode.)

Quagmire (3X22)

Story: Howard Gordon and Kim Newton (and Darin Morgan)
Director: Kim Manners

Mulder drags Scully out to lake country in the hope of finding definitive proof of "Big Blue."

This episode implicitly raises philosophical issues associated with environmental ethics.

Wetwired (3X23)

Story: Mat Beck
Director: Rob Bowman

Scully is influenced by subliminal messages from watching hours of videotape; Mulder, not affected, is aided by Scully's mother in rescuing her.

This episode implicitly raises philosophical issues associated with compatibilism and moral responsibility. (See "Freedom and Worldviews in The X-Files.*")*

Talitha Cumi (3X24)

Story: Chris Carter and David
    Duchovny
Director: R. W. Goodwin

In an homage to Dostoyevsky's "Grand Inquisitor," Jeremiah Smith miraculously heals gunshot victims, which threatens to expose the CSM and the Syndicate.

This episode raises philosophical issues related to human nature, freedom, happiness, and existentialism. (See "Moral Musings on a Cigarette Smoking Man," which also features this episode.)

SEASON 4

Herrenvolk (4X01)

Story: Chris Carter
Director: R. W. Goodwin

Jeremiah Smith leads Mulder to a Canadian agricultural site where genetically altered bees pollinate strange flowers; there he finds his cloned sister as she was when she was abducted in 1973.

This episode implicitly raises philosophical issues associated with personal identity and psychological continuity.

Home (4X03)

Story: Glen Morgan and James Wong
Director: Kim Manners

Mulder and Scully investigate an isolated, incestuous family.

This episode raises philosophical issues associated with ethical subjectivism and Kantian ethics.

Teliko (4X04)

Story: Howard Gordon
Director: James Charleston

A genetic mutant with no pituitary gland arrives from Africa.

This episode implicitly raises philosophical issues relevant to folk theories and scientific explanations: Will mature science explode all of our "folk theories"?

Unruhe (4X02)

Story: Vince Gilligan
Director: Rob Bowman

A dentist's disturbed son with the ability to produce "thought-o-graphs" stalks young women, including Scully.

The Field Where I Died (4X05)

Story: Glen Morgan and James Wong
Director: Rob Bowman

Mulder and Scully become part of an FBI team sent to subdue a religious cult accused of child abuse and stockpiling weapons; Mulder undergoes regression hypnosis, which seemingly reveals that his previous lives have invariably included Scully.

This episode raises philosophical issues associated with reincarnation, personal identity, and psychological continuity.

Sanguinarium (4X06)

Story: Valerie Mayhew and Vivian Mayhew
Director: Kim Manners

A plastic surgeon who is also a powerful witch preys on the vanity of his patients and colleagues to change his identity every ten years.

Musings of a Cigarette Smoking Man (4X07)

Story: Glen Morgan and James Wong
Director: James Wong

As Frohike tells his cohorts (and Mulder) what he seemingly discovered about the mysterious "smoking man," we are taken back in time to witness some of the CSM's *alleged* "achievements."

This episode implicitly raises philosophical issues associated with epistemology: How can we determine which conflicting reports are true? (Compare with "Apocrypha.") There also seems to be a connection with Alasdair MacIntyre's views on narrative, self, and character. (See "Moral Musings on a Cigarette Smoking Man" generally for more on the CSM.)

Tunguska (4X09)

Story: Chris Carter and Frank Spotnitz
Director: Kim Manners

Mulder makes an uneasy alliance with Krycek (recently rescued from the abandoned missile silo) as both leave for Russia to discover the contents of a diplomatic pouch destined for Siberia; the CSM and the Well-Manicured Man move to intercept them.

("Walter Skinner" features this episode.)

Terma (4X10)

Story: Chris Carter and Frank Spotnitz
Director: Rob Bowman

Mulder survives being infected by the "black cancer," escapes the Tunguska gulag, and follows the evidence to an oil refinery near the Canadian border; Krycek's true diplomatic colors are revealed.

Paper Hearts (4X08)

Story: Vince Gilligan
Director: Rob Bowman

When convicted serial killer John Lee Roach, in prison for kidnapping and killing young girls, crosses Mulder's path again, Mulder starts to question whether his memories of Samantha's disappearance are accurate.

El Mundo Gira (4X11)

Story: John Shiban
Director: Tucker Gates

Mulder and Scully run up against the mythical Chupacabra (a small, gray carnivorous creature with a big head and a small body and big, black, bulging eyes) near a migrant workers' camp.

Leonard Betts (4X14)

Story: Vince Gilligan, John Shiban, and
    Frank Spotnitz
Director: Kim Manners

In the next step of evolutionary adaptation, EMT Leonard Betts ingests cancerous tissues to survive; at the end of the episode he approaches Scully, saying, "I'm sorry, but you have something I need."

Never Again (4X13)

Story: Glen Morgan and James Wong
Director: Rob Bowman

When Mulder is forced to take vacation time, Scully travels to Philadelphia and meets a newly divorced man with a fantastic tattoo.

Memento Mori (4X15)

Story: Chris Carter, Vince Gilligan,
    John Shiban, and Frank Spotnitz
Director: Rob Bowman

Scully is diagnosed with inoperable cancer; as Mulder races to discover a cure, Scully keeps a journal for him to read later if no cure is found.

Kaddish (4X12)

Story: Howard Gordon
Director: Kim Manners

When a Brooklyn Jewish man is murdered in his own store, Mulder and Scully suspect that it is a racially charged hate crime; when his murderers begin turning up dead, Mulder con-

sults a local Jewish scholar about the Golem myth.

This episode raises philosophical issues associated with moral relativism.

Unrequited (4X16)

Story: Howard Gordon and Chris
    Carter
Director: Michael Lange

Mulder and Scully are assigned to protect two American generals from an assassin who can hide in plain sight.

Tempus Fugit (4X17)

Story: Chris Carter and Frank Spotnitz
Director: Rob Bowman

When Max Fenig's sister contacts Mulder and Scully about a plane crash, the two agents travel to Albany, and Mulder soon suspects UFO involvement.

Max (4X18)

Story: Chris Carter and Frank Spotnitz
Director: Kim Manners

Mulder's suspicions are confirmed when he determines that Max was carrying a piece of alien technology he stole from the government; the aliens again appear to reobtain the technology.

Synchrony (4X19)

Story: Howard Gordon and David
    Greenwalt
Director: James Charleston

A scientist uses futuristic technology to travel back in time to prevent a mistake he made years before.

This episode raises the philosophical issues of freedom, fate, and time travel. (See "Clyde Bruckman's Final Repose.")

Small Potatoes (4X20)

Story: Vince Gilligan
Director: Cliff Bole

Only two things about Eddie van Blundt (played by Darin Morgan) make him unique: the scar near his tailbone, and musculature that allows him to take the form of other men. When five babies, all with four-inch tails, are born in Eddie's hometown, Mulder and Scully investigate.

This episode raises philosophical issues related to Kantian ethics, specifically the impermissibility of not respecting another's autonomy.

Zero-Sum (4X21)

Story: Howard Gordon and Frank
    Spotnitz
Director: Kim Manners

Not heeding his own advice, Skinner agrees to do the CSM's dirty work in hopes of obtaining a cure for Scully's cancer; Skinner soon realizes just how ill advised his choice was.

This episode implicitly raises philosophical issues associated with virtue ethics and the ethics of tragic situations: What measures may someone permissibly take to save the life of another? (See "Walter Skinner" for connections to Skinner's character.)

Elegy (4X22)

Story: John Shiban
Director: James Charleston

After investigating strange occurrences at a bowling alley, Mulder hypothesizes that ghosts of the recently deceased appear to those who are themselves dying; one such ghost appears to Scully.

This episode raises philosophical issues associated with disembodied existence.

Demons (4X23)

Story: R. W. Goodwin
Director: Kim Manners

Mulder's desperate attempt to recapture his fleeting memories of his sister's disappearance embroils him as the primary suspect in a murder investigation.

This episode raises philosophical issues involving the ethics of scientific research (Do researchers have an obligation not to conduct dangerous research even if their patients consent to it?) and epistemology (Are drug-induced experiences evidence of anything?).

Gethsemane (4X24)

Story: Chris Carter
Director: R. W. Goodwin

After searching for an alien preserved in solid ice, Mulder is visited by Department of Defense employee Michael Kritschgau; Kritschgau presents Mulder with information that he has been duped by governmental forces, and Scully reports to her superiors that Mulder has died from a self-inflicted gunshot wound.

SEASON 5

Redux (5X02)

Story: Chris Carter
Director: R. W. Goodwin

Upon faking his death, Mulder gains access to highly restricted areas of the Department of Defense; while inside, he finds a potential cure for Scully's cancer.

Redux II (5X03)

Story: Chris Carter
Director: Kim Manners

The CSM provides Mulder the two things he wants most: the missing piece of the puzzle for Scully's cure, and a meeting with Samantha; in return, the CSM asks Mulder to leave the bureau to work for him, which draws the ire of the Syndicate.

Unusual Suspects (5X01)

Story: Vince Gilligan
Director: Kim Manners

We learn the backstory between Mulder and the Lone Gunmen: in 1989, their paths cross over a case involving biologist Suzanne Modeski.

Detour (5X04)

Story: Frank Spotnitz
Director: Brent Dowler

While driving to an FBI "creative team" seminar, Mulder and Scully are sidetracked by reports of forest creatures that are invisible except for their glowing red eyes.

The Post-Modern Prometheus (5X06)

Story: Chris Carter
Director: Chris Carter

In this black-and-white episode, Mulder and Scully investigate a Frankenstein-type character called the Great Mutato; the creature possesses an unusual attraction to peanut butter sandwiches and Cher.

This episode implicitly conveys philosophical issues associated with postmodernism, including the deconstruction of truth. (See "Postdemocratic Society and the Truth Out There" and "Some Philosophical Reflections on 'Trust No One'" for interesting applications of postmodernism.)

Christmas Carol (5X05)

Story: Vince Gilligan, John Shiban, and
   Frank Spotnitz
Director: Peter Markle

Scully meets Emily Sim and through a strange twist of events comes to believe that Emily is the daughter of her deceased sister Melissa; after Emily's (adoptive?) parents die, only Scully is left to protect the girl.

Emily (5X07)

Story: Vince Gilligan, John Shiban, and
   Frank Spotnitz
Director: Kim Manners

Scully discovers that she—and not Melissa—is Emily's biological mother; as Scully attempts to become Emily's legal guardian, and while Emily's health fails, Mulder uncovers disturbing facts about mother and daughter.

This episode raises philosophical issues associated with parental rights involving surrogate mothers and genetic donors.

Kitsunegari (5X08)

Story: Vince Gilligan and Tim Minear
Director: Dan Sackheim

Robert "Pusher" Modell returns to continue his cat-and-mouse game with Mulder; however, Mulder is led to believe, seemingly by Modell, that a new player has joined the "fox hunt" game.

Schizogeny (5X09)

Story: Jessica Scott and Mike Wollager
Director: Ralph Hemecker

In an orchard community, the parents of children being treated by the same psychologist begin to die mysteriously.

Chinga (5X10)

Story: Stephen King and Chris Carter
Director: Kim Manners

On her vacation, Scully is drawn into a New England town's obsession with a woman and her daughter, who are suspected to be witches.

Kill Switch (5X11)

Story: William Gibson and Tom Maddox
Director: Rob Bowman

Mulder and Scully are led to a female computer hacker who wishes to achieve immortality by being uploaded onto the Internet.

This episode raises issues associated with the philosophy of mind, including
artificial intelligence, functionalism, and personal identity. (See "Science and the Mystery of Consciousness" for other philosophy of mind issues.)*

Bad Blood (5X12)

Story: Vince Gilligan
Director: Cliff Bole

Mulder drags Scully to Texas to investigate exsanguinations; after Scully's autopsy reveals that the latest victim ingested a powerful sedative, Scully hypothesizes that a local has seen too many vampire movies.

This episode raises philosophical issues associated with epistemology and critical thinking: When reports, memories, and biases conflict, how can we determine what actually happened?

Patient X (5X13)

Story: Chris Carter and Frank Spotnitz
Director: Kim Manners

Mulder and Scully meet Cassandra Spender, an alleged alien abductee and the mother of their new colleague Jeffrey; Mulder is now skeptical of Cassandra's reports, but Scully sympathizes.

The Red and the Black (5X14)

Story: Chris Carter and Frank Spotnitz
Director: Chris Carter

While Mulder remains skeptical, despite Krycek's best efforts the Syndicate learns that its alien colonization plan has become even more complicated by a race of rebel aliens who resist the plan.

Travelers (5X15)

Story: John Shiban and Frank Spotnitz
Director: Billy Graham

In 1990, violent crimes specialist Fox Mulder visits a former FBI agent who knew Mulder's father, Bill, as a result of working on an early X-File.

Mind's Eye (5X16)

Story: Tim Minear
Director: Kim Manners

A young woman blind from birth is suddenly able to see events surrounding a string of murders; Mulder discovers that the woman and the murderer share a special bond.

All Souls (5X17)

Story: Frank Spotnitz, John Shiban,
    Billy Brown, and Dan Angel
Director: Allen Coulter

Mulder and Scully investigate a religiously charged case involving quadruplet sisters, all of whom have severe biological abnormalities.

This episode raises philosophical issues associated with faith and reason and, implicitly, the nature of religion itself.

The Pine Bluff Variant (5X18)

Story: John Shiban
Director: Rob Bowman

Mulder goes under deep cover to investigate a troublesome militia group bent on anarchy through the use of a dangerous bioweapon.

This episode implicitly raises philosophical issues relevant to political philosophy, including the government's proper role and relationship with society. (See "Postdemocratic Society and the Truth Out There," which features this episode.)

Folie à Deux (5X19)

Story: Vince Gilligan
Director: Kim Manners

After Mulder becomes unexpectedly involved in a hostage situation, he begins to suspect that the perpetrator sees what no one else does; Scully suspects that Mulder is suffering from a well-documented psychological disorder as a result of being held hostage.

The End (5X20)

Story: Chris Carter
Director: R. W. Goodwin

A twelve-year-old boy becomes the linchpin to the Syndicate's alien conspiracies and attempts to subdue Mulder and Scully.

Fight the Future (feature-length film)

Story: Chris Carter and Frank Spotnitz
Director: Rob Bowman

With the X-Files Unit again shut down, Mulder and Scully are reassigned to a new division. They stumble on to the Syndicate's attempt to cover up an unexpected appearance of the black oil, which leads them back into investigating the alien conspiracy. The Well-Manicured Man, instructed to kill Mulder, instead shares with him all of the Syndicate's grim secrets about colonization. Scully is once again captured, but this time she is infected with the black cancer and taken to an alien craft buried in Antarctica. Mulder must rescue her before it is too late.

This movie, like most, can be mined for philosophically significant issues related to aesthetics. (See "Feelings and Fictions," which features this episode. It is also featured in the introduction.)

Contributors

GORDON BARNES is an associate professor of philosophy at SUNY Brockport. He is the author of several articles in epistemology and the philosophy of mind, including "Conceivability, Explanation, and Defeat" (*Philosophical Studies,* 2001) and "Belief, Control, and Conclusive Reasons" (*Southern Journal of Philosophy,* 2002).

KEITH DROMM is an associate professor of philosophy at the Louisiana Scholars' College in Natchitoches. His publications include "'Based on True Events': Filmmakers' Obligations to History" (*International Journal of Applied Philosophy,* 2006), "Wittgenstein on Language Learning" (*History of Philosophy Quarterly,* 2006), and "Imaginary Naturalism: The Natural and Primitive in Wittgenstein's Later Thought" (*British Journal for the History of Philosophy,* 2003). He tends to trust no one, except his mother, who always tells him that he can believe whatever he wants, no matter how ridiculous.

TIMOTHY DUNN is an assistant professor of philosophy at the University of Wisconsin–Waukesha. He is the author of "The Value of Solidarity" (*Southwestern Journal of Philosophy,* 2005). He earned his PhD from Rice University; his research interests include ethics, egoism, and social/political philosophy. His favorite *X-Files* episode is the one in which the government does something bad and tries to cover it up — you know, the one with aliens.

RICH EDWARDS is currently a visiting assistant professor of philosophy at the University of Wisconsin–West Bend and an adjunct professor of humanities for the Milwaukee School of Engineering. He is the author of *Scriptural Perspicuity in the Early English Reformation in Historical Theology* and over 150 encyclopedia articles in *The Handbook of Business Ethics: A Guide for Employees, Managers, and Corporate Officers; The Encyclopedia of the Age of Political Revolutions and New Ideologies, 1760–1815; The Historical Encyclopedia of the First, Second, and Third Industrial Revolutions; The Encyclopedia of the Arab-Israeli Wars: A Political, Social and Military History: American Espionage: A Historical Encyclopedia;* and *The Encyclopedia of American Science.*

JOSEPH J. FOY is an assistant professor of political science at the University of Wisconsin–Waukesha. He earned his PhD at the University of Notre Dame, having also served as a Manatt Fellow for Democracy Studies at the International Foundation for Election Systems. He is a contributing author to *The Executive Branch of State Government* (2006), and current research interests include executive power, democracy studies, and issues of ethnic peace and conflict. Although terrified of the potential abuses of governmental power and secrecy that he studies as a political scientist, he didn't spend all those years playing Dungeons and Dragons without learning a little something about courage.

DEAN A. KOWALSKI is an associate professor of philosophy at the University of Wisconsin–Waukesha. He is the author of *Classic Questions and Contemporary Film: An Introduction to Philosophy* (2004) and coauthor of *Moral Theory and Motion Pictures: An Introduction to Ethics* (forthcoming). He has published a handful of articles on the freedom and foreknowledge problem, including "Some Friendly Molinist Amendments" (*Philosophy and Theology,* 2003) and "On Behalf of a Suarezian Middle Knowledge" (*Philosophia Christi,* 2003); most recently his "Hobbes and Locke on Social Contracts and Scarlet Carsons" appears in Joseph Foy's anthology *Homer Simpson Goes to Washington* (University Press of Kentucky, 2008). He, too, often tapes an X on his window in hopes that someone — even a grizzled man in a trench coat — will appear with answers to all his questions.

S. EVAN KREIDER is an assistant professor of philosophy at the University of Wisconsin–Fox Valley. He received his PhD from the University of Kansas. His primary research interest is ethics, including virtue ethics (e.g., "Justice as a Character Virtue" [*Auslegung,* 2005]). He rarely smokes, but when he does — like all men of real conviction — he prefers Morleys.

DAVID LOUZECKY, professor of philosophy, and RICHARD FLANNERY, professor of political science, are frequent collaborators. Currently, they are team teaching a course on political science and political philosophy, and a while back they coauthored *The Good Life: Personal and Public Choices* (1989). Although they both took their doctorates from the University of Wisconsin–Madison, they didn't meet until they became members of the University of Wisconsin–Sheboygan faculty.

ERIN MCKENNA is a professor of philosophy at Pacific Lutheran University in Tacoma, Washington. She has published *The Task of Utopia: Pragmatist and Feminist Perspectives* (2001) and coedited *Animal Pragmatism: Rethinking Human-Nonhuman Relationships* (2004). Her current work focuses on animals and ethics, using both pragmatism and feminism to rethink old debates and develop new positions. Her family includes four Australian shepherds and two Morgan horses, but her research interests include all life forms, terrestrial and extraterrestrial. She has never been accused of having hair "that was just a little too red."

MARK C. E. PETERSON is a professor of philosophy at the University of Wisconsin–Washington County. He has contributed articles on Hegel's natural philosophy to *The Owl of Minerva* and on philosophical authorship to the latest volume of *The International Kierkegaard Commentary*. He speaks and writes on environmental philosophy and ethics, most recently at the inaugural conference of the International Society for the Study of Religion, Nature, and Culture. He is just returning from a sabbatical year spent studying (a) John Cassian's concepts of sin and spiritual practice and (b) Taoist and Confucian models for the relation between humans and nature. With interests as eclectic as these, he hopes that William B. Davis (the Cigarette Smoking Man) will play him in the screen adaptation of the University of Wisconsin Colleges' Department of Philosophy.

WILLIAM SCHNEIDER teaches philosophy at the University of Wisconsin–Waukesha. He completed his graduate work at the University of Rochester. His current interests include work on epistemic rationality, environmental ethics, and the model of Socratic education in Plato's dialogues.

CHRISTOPHER TROGAN is currently an assistant professor of English and humanities at the U.S. Merchant Marine Academy in Kings Point, New York. He has published articles on the relationship between ethics, epistemology, and aesthetics and teaches literature, philosophy, and ethics. When he is not teaching, researching, or writing, he is either at the gym or sleeping, or both (but never in red Speedos).

V. ALAN WHITE is a professor of philosophy at the University of Wisconsin–Manitowoc. His interests include free will, the philosophy of time, and pedagogy, and his papers have appeared in *Analysis, Philosophy,* the *Review of Metaphysics, Teaching Philosophy,* and the *Southern Journal of Philosophy* among others. A former Carnegie/CASE Professor of the Year for the state of Wisconsin, he manages his Internet page, Philosophy Songs, which is known internationally for its parody and middling tenor vocals. A fan of γνῶπι σεαυτόν, which is Socrates' version of "The truth is in here" — literally, "Know yourself" — he describes himself as a truly excellent second-class philosopher.

Index

abductive inference, 17, 21, 23–32, 35n22
abstract object, 127, 135, 200, 237
aesthetics, 19, 230–33, 236–39, 282
Ahrenhoerster, Greg, 13n10
alien: abduction, 2, 6, 17, 34n11, 42, 50, 57, 96, 124, 146, 209, 263–64, 265, 274; colonists, 75n18, 89–90, 144, 145, 147, 149, 154, 262–64; rebels, 89–90, 280. *See also* extraterrestrials
alienation, 17–18, 20–23, 29–30, 217
Allen, Reginald E., 112
"All Souls," 223, 281
All the President's Men, 58, 72n2
"all things," 12n4, 42, 107n24, 126–28, 130, 136–38, 260n7
"Alone," 259n2
Al-Qaeda, 70, 156
altruism, 150, 152–53, 253
analogy, argument by, 6
Anderson, Gillian, 1, 126, 197, 273
angst (existential), 221, 223
anomalies, 81–82, 84–85
Anytus, 112, 113, 118, 121, 123, 124
"Apocrypha," 157n2, 166, 231, 274, 276
Apology (Plato), 112, 114–15, 117, 120, 121–22
Aristotle, 1, 2–5, 11n3, 158n9, 159–62,

164, 165, 166–67, 170, 172, 173n5, 190, 195–96, 199, 207n3, 252–53, 256
"Ascension," 31, 146, 148, 151–52, 163, 169, 269
Athens, 18, 33n4, 112, 114, 115, 117–18, 121, 122–23
Augustine of Hippo, 43, 248–49
"Avatar," 105, 164, 168–69, 171, 274
axiological worldviews, 44
axiology, 212–14, 266, 267, 281

bad faith (inauthenticity), 217–20
"Beginning, The," 146
Bentham, Jeremy, 59, 63–66
Bernstein, Carl, 58, 72n2
"Beyond the Sea," 4–5, 8, 46, 130–31, 132, 221, 243, 267
Bin Laden, Osama, 68
black oil (black cancer), 1, 43, 63, 147, 158n8, 227, 231–32, 240n1, 262–63, 274, 276, 281–82
"Blessing Way, The," 34n10, 53n12, 59, 103–4, 105, 146, 272
Boggs, Luther Lee, 203, 221, 223, 242
"Born Again," 5, 268
Bowman, Rob, 196, 211
Boyle, Peter, 189, 192–94, 195, 242
Broeker, Jaap, 189

Brothers Karamazov, The (Dostoyevsky), 148, 275
Bruckman, Clyde, 189–90, 192–98, 203–4, 206, 242, 243

Carter, Chris, 3, 56, 57–59, 70, 73n6, 143, 196, 199, 200, 227, 241, 247, 258, 259n2, 260n13, 265–82
categorical imperative, 66, 144, 145–46
Charno, Stu, 1, 189
Chung, Jose, 206, 210–11, 219–20
Cigarette Smoking Man (CSM), 22, 34n10, 37, 47, 59, 60, 63, 71, 77, 79, 80, 85–89, 90, 92n9, 105, 111, 117, 142–58, 163, 164, 171–72, 205, 227, 253, 274, 275, 276, 278, 279
citizenship, 56, 60–64, 66, 68, 69, 71, 74n8, 112–15, 117, 121–24
Cleisthenes, 113
Clifford, William Kingdon, 7, 93–97, 98, 100, 103, 246, 247
"Closure," 224
"Clyde Bruckman's Final Repose," 107n30, 189–208, 227, 242, 271, 272, 274, 278
Code, Lorraine, 134–36
cogito ergo sum, 225–26
cognitive component, 233, 237
Collins, Max Allan, 229n7, 259n1
colonization, 87, 147, 231, 235, 238, 262–64, 280, 281
"Colony," 99–100, 270
Colquitt, Jack, 152
compatibilism, 40–43, 51, 52n8, 273, 275
conceptual framework, 20, 28, 80, 82
conceptual relativist, 77, 83
"Conduit," 61, 265
Connolly, Billy, 203, 223, 243
consciousness, 3–4, 33–34n8, 38–39, 173n11, 174–85, 216, 265, 266, 268, 280
conspiracy, 8, 19, 22, 41, 47, 64, 70, 87,

89–90, 98, 117, 153, 166, 232, 264, 268, 281
Corinthians 1, 248
courage, 143, 159, 160–64, 165, 167, 169, 170, 172n3, 222, 254
Covarrubias, Marita, 144, 252
Crissman, Joseph ("Father Joe"), 203, 223, 225, 243, 244, 248–49, 256–57

"Daemonicus," 246
Davis, William B., 77, 143, 147
Dawkins, Richard, 5–11, 13nn9–10, 245, 246
deduction, 17, 23–26, 32, 35n21
Deep Throat, 22, 58, 60, 71, 77–79, 85, 89, 92n7, 117, 144, 153, 163, 252, 266, 267, 268
"Deep Throat," 71, 85, 265
Delphi, 112, 114
democracy, 55–76, 113–18, 122–23
deontology, 65
Descartes, René, 69, 225
determinism, 39–41, 48–49, 52n4, 52n6, 52n8, 190–92, 199–200, 252
Dewey, John, 136, 138–39, 141n27
Diakun, Alex, 1
Diogenes Laertius, 113
"Død Kalm," 10, 42, 253
Doggett, John, 201, 221–22, 227, 244, 245, 249–50, 251, 254, 259n2
Dostoyevsky, Fyodor, 148, 278
Doyle, Arthur Conan, 19
dualism, 126, 133, 183, 266, 272, 280
Duchovny, David, 1, 198, 199, 229, 270, 271, 274, 275
Dunn, Timothy, 13n10

"E.B.E.," 8, 97–98, 267
ectoplasm, 12n4, 42, 107n24, 137, 260n7
Einstein, Albert, 35n20, 247
Ellsberg, Daniel, 60

emotion, 97, 126, 133–35, 160–62, 164–65, 230–39

empathy, 139n1, 231, 239

"Empedocles," 221, 244, 246, 254

empiricism, 2, 130, 133, 139

"En Ami," 150, 153, 205

"End Game," 10, 35n22, 91n2, 163, 169, 270

epistemology, 21, 37–36, 66–68, 126–40, 194, 198, 202–3, 212, 225–26, 272, 274, 276, 278, 280. *See also* knowledge

"Erlenmeyer Flask, The," 10, 47, 77, 78–79, 80, 83, 140n11, 268

essence, 215

"Essence," 247

ethics. *See* morality

Ethics of Belief, The (Clifford), xiv, 7, 93–95, 103

eudaimonia, 158n9

Euthyphro, 115–16, 118, 124

Euthyphro (Plato), 115, 117, 118

evidence, 2, 5, 7–8, 9, 13n9, 24, 26–28, 30, 41–45, 48, 55, 59–60, 66–67, 70, 73n6, 74n8, 75n19, 79, 88, 93–101, 105, 108n34, 116, 131–34, 139n1, 140n2, 147, 151, 156, 178, 278

evidentialism, 246–47, 249, 251, 256–57

evil, 7, 44, 54n17, 64, 143, 145, 147, 149–50, 154–57, 206, 244–45, 259n6

"Existence," 224

existentialism, 17–19, 29, 33n8, 214–25, 274, 275

extraterrestrials, 1, 4, 17–19, 21, 22–23, 28–29, 31, 32, 33n1, 42, 44, 56, 57, 61, 63, 64, 66, 79, 83, 87, 99, 140n11, 144, 147, 209–10, 243–45, 255, 259. *See also* alien

"extreme possibilities," 1, 4–5, 46, 131, 189, 246

extrinsic good, 150–51

"Fallen Angel," 107n31, 266

fatalism, 10, 48, 52n4, 235, 272, 278

Faulkner, Blaine, 211, 213, 217–18, 245, 260n7

FBI (Federal Bureau of Investigation), 1, 5, 17, 19, 21–23, 27, 29–30, 34n10, 56–57, 59, 69–71, 72n2, 73n8, 75n19, 79, 86, 87, 93, 102, 111, 114, 123, 128, 135, 162–64, 165, 168, 169, 170, 181, 238, 263, 267, 269, 270, 276, 279, 281

Fearon, Christian, 249, 251, 257, 259n4

feelings, 98, 162, 169, 176, 216, 217, 230–40, 282

"F. Emasculata," 168–69, 271

feminism, 126–27, 133–39, 267

"Field Where I Died, The," 53n12, 163, 276

Fight the Future, 5, 48, 66–7, 87, 100–101, 147, 153, 230–32, 234–36, 239, 240n1, 254, 281–82

"Firewalker," 10, 229

fishbowl (conceptual scheme), 29–32

Floeh, Natalie, 259n3, 260n12, 261n21

foreknowledge, 189–90, 192–203, 272

Fowley, Diana, 255

Foy, Joseph, 13n11, 264

freedom of the will, 37–54, 190–92, 215–17, 267, 270, 271, 272, 273, 275, 278

"Fresh Bones," 96, 270

friendship, 251–57

Frohike, Melvin, 143, 152, 276

"Gethsemane," 68, 278

God, 20, 21, 41, 43–45, 47, 50, 61, 130, 203, 214, 215, 218, 220, 226, 227, 247–48

good faith (authenticity), 217–20

good temper, 159, 164–66, 169–70

Gorgias, 119

Gorgias (Plato), 116, 121

Great Mutato, The, 8, 279

Grote, George, 112

"Grotesque," 9, 246, 273

Hamilton, Alexander, 69

happiness, 35n23, 88, 146, 150–54, 156, 158n9, 159, 169–72, 173n11, 275
"Herrenvolk," 146, 275
Hick, John, 247
Hitler, Adolf, 151, 156
Hobbes, Thomas, 85
"Home," 242
"Host, The," 10, 19, 242, 268
hubris, 171–72
"Humbug," 205, 206, 227, 271
hypothesis, 2, 5, 8–9, 17, 21, 23–31, 34n16, 35n21, 46, 66–67, 79, 103, 107n31, 108n34, 127, 129–33, 136, 174

"Ice," 10, 175, 266
identity theory (of mind and brain), 178–79, 183
Ignatieff, Michael, 64
imagination, 63, 97, 231–37
"Improbable," 247
incompatibilism, 40–44, 48, 51, 190–92
indeterminism, 39, 48–49, 51
induction, 17, 23–32, 35nn21–22
Internet, 7, 254, 280
intrinsic good, 150, 151, 156, 158n9
"Invocation," 222
Iraq, 59, 61, 68, 72n6, 75n18
"I Want to Believe," 2, 41, 42, 43, 70, 93–108, 131, 140n2, 206, 245–46, 268, 270
I Want to Believe, 206, 241–61, 221, 222, 224

Jackson, Frank, 179, 185n1
James, William, 93–108, 129, 131, 132–33, 136–37
Jefferson, Thomas, 59
Jones, W. T., 11n3
"Jose Chung's *Doomsday Defense*," 220
"Jose Chung's *From Outer Space*," 13n9, 274, 209–28
"Jump the Shark," 261n23

justice, 57, 63, 67, 69, 112–13, 116, 161, 214

Kant, Immanuel, 59, 63–66, 144–46, 149
Kantian ethics, 144–46, 148–49, 150, 153, 275, 278
Kennedy, John F., 58, 73n7, 142, 157n2
King, Martin Luther, Jr., 142
knowledge, 2–3, 20, 30–31, 80, 81–85, 91n1, 93, 106n1, 112, 115, 121, 123–24, 126–40, 170, 183–85, 192–95, 201–3, 210, 274
Kowalski, Patricia, 207n
Kreider, S. Evan, 13n10
Krycek, Alex, 146, 151–52, 158n8, 166, 227, 231, 252, 269, 273, 274, 276, 280
Kuhn, Thomas Samuel, xiv, 45, 77, 81–85, 91n4
Kurtzweil, Alvin, 153

"Lazarus," 9, 45–46, 267
Levinas, Emmanuel, 19
linear regression, 19, 26, 32
"Little Green Men," 9, 43, 50, 97, 165, 261n23, 268
logic, 21, 24, 106n4, 127, 129, 206n5
Lone Gunmen, 19, 59, 77, 88, 89, 98, 197, 247, 261n23, 267, 279

media, 6, 13n10, 58, 59, 60, 62, 67, 69, 73n7
Melchert, Norman, 3, 9
Meletus, 112–13, 115, 121, 124
"Memento Mori," 157n2, 171–72, 224, 253, 259n5, 277
Meno, 118–20, 124
Meno (Plato), 117–20, 123
metaphysics, 1, 4, 11, 17, 20–21, 27, 39, 44–45, 47, 50, 54n17, 66–67, 68, 101, 126–27, 129–30, 214–16. *See also* reality
Mill, John Stuart, 59
Millennium, 220

Modell, Robert ("Pusher"), 5, 12n5, 207n2, 274, 280

morality, 6–7, 11, 20, 44, 47, 62, 64, 67, 69, 80, 85, 89, 94, 118, 120, 123–24, 134, 143–58, 164–65, 170–72, 182, 212–14, 231, 236, 239, 266, 267, 268, 269, 270, 271, 273, 274, 275, 276, 277, 278

Morgan, Darin, 13n9, 189, 193, 201, 202, 205–6, 209, 210, 212, 221, 222, 224, 225–28, 242, 260n7, 268, 278

Mulder, Bill, 145, 153, 155

Mulder, Fox: abductive inferences of, 28–32; authentic life of, 220–21, 223–25; episode dialogue, 9, 12n4, 12n5, 13n6, 28, 53n12, 54n17, 73–74n8, 87, 99, 255; James comparison, 97–100, 140n2; and Plato, 2–4; religiosity of, 53n12; Socratic parallels, 111–25; Scully friendship, 253–57

Mulder, Samantha, 2, 33n1, 42, 50, 75n1, 87, 91n1, 99, 100, 111, 117, 124, 146, 205, 224, 227, 232, 256, 263, 265, 270, 276, 278, 279

Mulder, Teena, 47, 145

"Musings of a Cigarette Smoking Man," 143–44, 152–53, 157n2, 276

myth of the metals (Plato), 62

naturalism, 2–4, 80

necessity, 23–25, 40

NewSpace XPhile Forum, 207n, 228n

Nicomachean Ethics (Aristotle), 172n1, 252

9/11 Commission Report, The, 70, 71

1984 (Orwell), 20, 151

Nixon, Richard, 60, 72n2

noble lie, 59–63, 64–65, 69, 72n5

Nothingness, 215–17

Nutter, David, 193–94

objectivity, 80, 129, 135–36, 274

"One Breath," 85–86, 146, 148, 151, 163, 269

O'Neill, Onora, 145

"One Son," 89, 145–46

Order of the Blessed Saint Scully, 205

Orwell, George, 20, 90, 151, 154

Oswald, Lee Harvey, 157n2

Oxford University, 1, 22, 97, 112, 113, 266

"Paper Clip," 146, 152, 163–64, 272

paradigm, 20–22, 29, 31–32, 34n11, 80–86, 90, 91n4, 174. *See also* worldview

paranormal, 6–11, 37, 43, 44, 53n12, 91n1, 93–94, 96, 97, 99, 103, 105–6, 107n30, 262

"Patience," 222

"Patient X," 158n2, 280

Peet, Amanda, 243

Peirce, Charles Sanders, 17, 21, 23–26, 28, 31, 34n12, 34n16, 101

Pentagon Papers, 60, 72n6

Peterson, Mark C. E., 13n10

Pileggi, Mitch, 74n9, 77, 152

"Pilot," 8, 83, 94, 107n30, 142, 246, 265

"Pine Bluff Variant, The," 73–74n8, 281

"Piper Maru," 9, 28, 169, 273

Plato, 2–4, 9, 11n3, 59–60, 62, 65, 68–69, 72n5, 112–25, 160–68, 173n5

pluralism (truth and knowledge) 129–30, 132, 136, 138–39

Poetics, The (Aristotle), 172

political freedom, 63, 68, 69

political philosophy, 55–76, 85, 89–91, 121–22, 139n1, 269, 281

postdemocratic society, 55–76, 265, 269, 272, 279, 281

"Post-Modern Prometheus, The," 279

postmodernism, 66–69, 261

pragmatism, 101, 107n23, 108n34, 127–29, 132–33, 136

Pragmatism (James), xv, 101, 129

pride, 159–60, 171

privacy, 63, 75n15

property dualism, 183

proposition (statement), 24, 102–3, 107n19, 194–95, 198, 200, 202, 230, 233, 239

psychological egoism, 77–78, 85–89, 92nn8–9

publicity, 56, 61, 63–66, 68–69, 71, 72n7, 73n8

Puppet, 189, 193, 196, 197–98, 201

"Pusher," 207n2, 274

Pythagoras, 2–3

"Quagmire," 9, 96, 209, 274–75

qualia, 176

Quine, Willard Van Orman, 107n27

Raphael, 2, 4

rationality, 33n6, 46–47, 50, 63, 66, 68, 105, 232–33

Rawls, John, 62, 69

reality, 22–23, 48, 80, 82, 91n1, 98, 105–6, 108n34, 174, 235, 263. *See also* metaphysics

"Red and the Black, The," 69, 158n8, 280–81

"Red Museum, The," 72n6, 269

"Redux I," 10–11, 47–48, 68, 86–87, 279

"Redux II," 47–48, 68, 86–87, 146, 279

Reilly, Charles Nelson, 210

Republic (Plato), 20, 68–69, 72n5, 161, 172–73n4

Respect for Persons Formula (Kantian ethics), 145

"Revelations," 223, 273

Reyes, Monica, 244, 247

Reynolds, Burt, 247, 248

Russia (USSR), 8, 57, 89, 90, 142, 158, 276

Sartre, Jean-Paul, 214–17

Schick, Theodore, 195–97, 246

School of Athens, The, 2–4, 5, 11

science, 4–5, 10–11, 24, 26, 37, 42, 44–46, 51, 79–85, 91n2, 91n4, 94–95, 100, 103, 127, 129–30, 135–36, 140n11, 174–79, 184, 265, 266, 268, 275, 280

Scully, Dana: authentic life of, 220–21, 221–23, 228n6; in "all things," 126–28, 12n4; and Aristotle, 2–4; comparison to Clifford, 94–97; episode dialogue, 9, 10, 12n5, 13n6, 28, 53n12, 54n17, 73–4n8, 83, 97–98, 142, 221–22, 228n6, 241, 246, 255; feminist interpretation of, 126–40; inductive inferences of, 28–32; Mulder friendship, 253–57; reliance on science, 9–11, 174–75; trusting Mulder, 90–91, 85–89; worldview of, 79–81

Scully, Melissa, 146, 166, 279

Scully, William, 223, 227, 255

secrecy, 55–56, 61, 63–65, 68–71, 72n6, 74n8, 147, 263

self-knowledge, 112, 121, 123–24

September 11 (9/11), 63, 64, 75n19

Serling, Rod, 19

Seventh Letter (Plato), 121

Shelley, Mary, 19

"Sixth Extinction, The," 254

"Sixth Extinction II: Amor Fati, The," 150, 254–55

Skinner, Walter, 71, 74n8, 77, 88–89, 94, 100–6, 111, 152, 157n2, 159–73, 251–52, 269, 273, 274, 276, 278

Smith, Jeremiah, 148, 149, 246, 275

social contract theory, 85, 89–91, 133–34

social stability, 60–61, 65, 69

Socrates, 18, 32, 111–25, 205, 206

Sokrates. *See* Socrates

soul, 96, 116, 121, 162, 166, 171, 172–73n4, 215, 272

Sparta, 113

Spender, Jeffrey, 86, 145, 157n6

Spinoza, Baruch, 61

spirit, 146, 147, 162, 164–65, 173n4

Spotnitz, Frank, 246, 259n2, 260n13, 270–71, 273–74, 276–82

"Squeeze," 22, 68, 242, 259n2, 265

"S.R. 819," 104

Stalin, Joseph, 151, 156

Stegall, Sarah, 207n1

Stupendous Yappi, 189, 202

subjectivism, 135–36, 138, 275

suspension of disbelief, 235

Syndicate, the, 22, 34n10, 43, 61, 63, 66, 70, 80, 86, 90, 144, 147, 149, 153, 155, 158n8, 231, 235, 238, 240n1, 262–64, 272, 273, 274, 275, 279, 280, 281

"Talitha Cumi," 37, 148, 149, 275

tanha, 32, 35n23

teleological, 65

temperance, 159, 161–62, 166–70, 254

"Terma," 158n8, 165, 258

terrorists, 64, 68, 156

"The truth is out there," 1, 2, 3, 17–36, 37, 42, 43, 46, 55–76, 77, 79–80, 83–85, 98, 105, 126–41, 209, 211, 227, 265, 269, 272, 273, 279, 281

Thirty Tyrants, 113, 118

"Tithonus," 205

To Perpetual Peace (Kant), 66

"Tooms," 163, 242, 268

Tooms, Eugene, 180–84, 242, 246, 265, 268

tragic flaw, 171–72, 173n11

transvaluation of power, 150–56

"Trust no one," 77–85, 89–91, 145, 268, 279

"TrustNo1," 255

"Truth, The," 53n12, 142, 153–54, 241

"Tunguska," 158n8, 164, 166, 231, 276

"2Shy," 29, 272

unexplained phenomena, 1, 4, 46, 53n12

unhappy consciousness, 29, 33n8

Universal Law Formula (Kantian ethics), 144–45

unnatural acts, 250

utilitarianism, 146, 147–48, 149, 150, 155, 158n9, 213

value judgment, 143, 213–17, 231–32

van Inwagen, Peter, 48–50

Vietnam, 58, 60, 61, 68, 72n6, 73n7, 163, 168, 269

virtue (ethics), 89, 118, 119, 123–24, 151, 153, 156, 159–73, 253, 274, 278

voodoo, 96, 270

"War of the Coprophages," 9, 131–32, 227, 273

Watergate, 58, 60, 72n2

weapons of mass destruction, 59, 73n7

Well-Manicured Man, 59, 153, 232, 240n1, 276, 281

whammy, 5, 12n5

White, V. Alan, 13n10, 207n

Whitehead, Alfred North, 59

Whitney, Dakota, 243

"William," 157n6

"Without," 222

Wittgenstein, Ludwig, 102–3

Woodward, Bob, 58, 72n2

worldview, 19–20, 23, 29–31, 37–39, 40–48, 50–51, 79–81, 267, 270, 271, 275

X (character), 22, 85

X-Files, mythology of, 144, 147, 262–64

X-Phile(s), 8, 13n10, 142, 143, 144, 145, 147, 157n6, 231, 232, 241–42, 257–58

"Zero Sum," 144, 166